Guaranteed Solutions!

(HOW to Solve our Local and Global Problems in the Most Rational Manner Possible!)

By

The Worldwide People's Revolution!®

Book 080 ◆

(Cover Photo from CreateSpace of the Earth)

Copyright, Dedication and Introduction

By our Chief Editor,
Dr. Samuel Walker Edison, Ph.D., MA, BS, and QC!

| ISBN | — | 13: | 978-1974-3599-43 |
| ISBN | — | 10: | 1974-3599-48 |

00-01 [_] This Inspired Book is COPYRIGHTED 2017—40018 AD, by **The Worldwide People's Revolution!®** All Rights are Reserved for the Truth's Sake. However, anyone in the World has the Right to Reproduce Exact Copies of this Unique Book, and Sell those Copies for a Reasonable Profit, and KEEP 90% of the Net Profits for their own Prosperity: beCause our Selected King only wants 10 percent of the Net Profits for his own Prosperity, which seems to be Reasonable enough to us Members of **The Worldwide People's Revolution,** who are Heaven-bent on bringing Down the Evil Empire, along with all of its False Doctrines — such as that Nonsense about all People being Created EQUAL, when it is most Obvious that no one was ever Born Equal with anyone else in any Way. For Example, were you Born Equal with Moses, Elijah, Jesus Christ, Judas Iscariot, Joseph Stalin, Osama ben Laden, Saddam Hussein, Adolf Hitler, Buzzeldick the Great, or the Devil, himself? Chances are that you were not Born Equal with any of those People, nor with any Fictitious Characters as Buzzeldick the Great. So, why Believe any such Superstitious Nonsense about the Non-existent Equalities of People?

00-02 [_] Awe, but, someone says: "We were all Born with EQUAL RIGHTS! For Example, I and Adolf Hitler should have the Right to Govern the World with Jesus Christ!" §§ {Please Check the Boxes [_] with Xes, if you Agree with such Foolish Statements.}

00-03 [_] This Inspired Book is now DEDICATED to the Billions of People, who Sincerely Believe that they have Equal Rights to Govern the World with Jesus Christ, who Failed to Present even ONE Reasonable Solution for anything that everyone in the World can Agree with, even though almost everyone would Agree that this would be a Far Better World to Live in, if everyone were as Good, Honest, Compassionate, Helpful, Trustworthy, Reliable, and Righteous as Jesus Christ — assuming, of course, that he was and still is a Real Person. Yes, even President Donald Trumpeter would Play a Different Tune on his Mouthpiece, if he were Converted to the Teachings of Jesus Christ — that is, unless he is Actually INSANE, which, of course, he could be, whereby certain Parts of his Brains are Malfunctioning, being Perverted by his Lusts for Material Wealth, which is the Case to some Degree for most of us Earthlings. Nevertheless, our Selected King has *Guaranteed Solutions* for the following Massive Problems: Pollution of Air, Water, Land, Plants, Animals and People; Climate Changes, Melting Glaciers, Melting Icebergs, Rising Sea Levels, Climate Refugees, and Related Problems; Hurricanes, Floods, Typhoons, Tornadoes, Droughts, Forrest Fires, House Fires, Frozen Water Pipes, Heating Bills, Cooling Bills, Termites, Rat-infested Cities, Trash Disposal, Unemployment, Underemployment, Low Wages, Poverty, Crimes, Hunger, Riots, Police Brutalities, Prisons, Election Deceptions, Civil Wars, Education Slavery, Work Slavery, Tax Slavery, Insurance Slavery, Interest Slavery, Drug Slavery, Sex Slavery, Rent Slavery, ElecTrickery Bills Slavery, Food Bills Slavery, Water Bills Slavery, Gas Bills Slavery, Traffic Tickets, Traffic Accidents and the Multitude of Related Problems that come with those Accidents; Sicknesses, Diseases, High Medical Costs, Drug Abuses, Drug Trafficking, Drug Overdosing, Gluttony, Drunkenness, Obesity, Starvation, Alcoholism, Bad Addictions, Eating Disorders, Child Abuses, Old People Abuses, Battered Wives and Abused Husbands; Stinking Sewage Systems, Lead-contaminated Water Pipes, Smoking Chimneys, Chemical

Spills, Chemical Fires, Chemical Explosions and Related Problems; Terrorists, Gang Wars, Gun Violence, Murders, Robberies, Muggings, Stealing, Lying, and Related Problems; and, best of all, he has the Best Solution for Stopping all Wars, Worldwide, while taking Proper Care of all Refugees, and without making anyone into a Tax Slave to Cover the Costs! Yes, it Sounds too Good to be True, huh?

00-04 [_] O Doctor Samuel Walker Edison, are you Certain that all Parts of your own Brains are Functioning Correctly with a Capital C? After all, many of those Natural Disasters are beyond our Control — such as those Tornadoes and Hurricanes. Indeed, it is Impossible for us to Build Fireproof, Mouse-proof, Termite-proof, Hail-proof, Tornado-proof, Insurance-proof, Self-air-conditioned Houses like those of your Selected KING, who must be a Real NUT, just to Think that we could Solve all of those Problems and hundreds that are not even Listed! For Example, HOW is your Selected King going to STOP People from Committing Suicide? {Please Check this Box [_] with an X, if you are in any Doubt about your own Brains Functioning Correctly, whereby you can Visualize what is Needed for Solving all such Problems — that is, unless you Judge yourself to be a Perfect Person, who has no such Problems, in which Case you may be Excused from Studying this Inspired Book: beCause you have already Learned all of your Lessons, and are no Doubt QUALIFIED for some Position in the Holy Kingdom of All that is GOOD, which is otherwise known as the Kingdom of GOD, who is ALL that is GOOD, who would most Certainly Check the above Box with an X: beCause he Knows for a Fact that my Brains are NOT Functioning Correctly, or else I would not be Supporting a Man who Claims to have Guaranteed Solutions for ALL of our Massive Problems, including Insanity!}

00-05 [_] O Doctor Sam, it is Humble of you to Confess that certain Parts of your own Brains are not Functioning Correctly; but, apparently you Sincerely Believe that all Parts of your Selected King's Brains are Functioning 100% Correctly: beCause you find no Faults with his Guaranteed Solutions, and neither do I: beCause I have Carefully Studied them for myself, and cannot Present any Reasonable Arguments against his Guaranteed Solutions. In Fact, I Wish to God that everyone in the World had to Study his Master Plan, and then Present any Reasonable Arguments against it; but, that is only Wishful Thinking, which has nothing to do with the Realities of Life. In Fact, it is Doubtful that your Selected King can even Obtain the Attention of the Masses of People, whose Minds are Totally Distracted by their own Ambitions, Lusts, Fears, and Wishful thinking without a Capital T, as well as being Distracted by the Pure Nonsense on TVs — such as those Talk Shows that Deal with the Political POOP and PISS in Washington, District of Chief Criminals, who Squat on one or the other of those 2 Stinking Holes in **"The BIG White OUTHOUSE on the Not-so-Biblical Capitol DUNGHILL!"** (see Book 023), which is by Far the most Corrupted Government in the Whole World! For Example, that False Government has Legalized the Selling of Addictive and Harmful Tobacco Products, just to Collect X-amount of Revenue for the Treasury DEPARTment, even after Knowing for a Fact with a Capital K and F that all such Poisonous Weeds CAUSE Cancers when Smoked and/or Chewed: beCause they are EVIL Things, which should be Avoided at all Costs. Therefore, those Politicians are First Class HYPOCRITES of the Lowest Order of Demon-possessed People! Moreover, they also Know for a Fact that the Burning of so-called "Fossil Fuels" is very Harmful to our Environment, and the Pollution that is Produced by it Causes Various Kinds of Sicknesses and Diseases, even among the Trees, which are Weakened by Acid Rains, which have also Weakened the Shells on Shellfishes and Marine Life. Therefore, in Order to Solve that Massive Problem, all of those Wicked Politicians should be Summoned for Court Hearings, whereby they can be Proven to be WRong with a Capital WR, which should be speld "R-o-n-g," even as Right should be spelled "R-I-I-T": beCause it is not Right to Force little Children to Memorize the Spellings of Millions of Misspelled "Werdz," which should be spelled in "Funetik" English, just to Avoid 8 Years of Nonsense in **"The Public School of IGNERUNT FQLZ!" (HOW we have been GRAATLEE DISEEVD by Capitalism!)** Book 024. Indeed, Knowledge should be spelled N-o-l-i-j: beCause those Silent Letters are not Needed. However, if they are Needed, then Truths should be spelled K-t-r-o-w-t-h-o-u-g-h-s. Yes, we could make it even more Confusing by adding some more Silent Letters — such as an L in could, would and should, which should be "koud, woud, and shoud," if all Parts of our Brains were Functioning Correctly: beCause that would be somewhat Consistent, and not nearly so Confusing within the Minds of Little Children, who could possibly "Lern HOW TQ REED and RIIT dering u Week oor 2!" — that is, IF they had Computers to Write with, which they would all have, if we Tax Slaves should Establish **"The New RIGHTEOUS One-World Government!"** (HOW to Establish a Righteous One-World Government without Going to WAR!) By The Worldwide People's Revolution!®, Book 056, and then DEMAND it of our Good GovernMINT, which would simply Mint and Print the Necessary New Money for HIRING **"Seven Great Armies of Working Soldiers!"** (HOW to Provide a Way for Everyone to WORK: so as to Eliminate Poverty, Crimes, Drug Abuses, Prisons and Unnecessary Taxes!), Book 015, to Build those **"GLORIOUS Swanky Hotels Castles and Fortresses!"** (Beautiful Planned City States for WISE Intelligent Well-Educated People with Common Sense and Good Understanding!), Book 019, which would Represent that New Money, which would make it the very Best Money in all of the World, which would have to be Earned by Honest Labor, without any Loans, without any Interest, without any Taxes, and without any Rent, whereby X-amount of Problems would just Automatically be SOLVED! {FOOTNOTE: Please Check the above Box, if you Agree with such a Statement. Otherwise, it will be Assumed that you Disagree with it. Moreover, you are Welcome to ~~Cross Out~~ any Words that you Disagree with, in order to make the Statement Read Correctly with a Capital C within your own Mind, which we Trust is a Good Honest Healthy Mind.}

00-06 [_] Well, my Friend, all of that Important Information will not likely Appear in the Book Preview on www.Amazon.com: beCause of Skipping page 3, which will Test the Faith of the Readers, who will then be Forced to Buy the Book, just to Learn whatever Information is Found on page 3 — except that People just HATE to be *Forced* to Do anything, and especially to Spend Money that they do not presently have! However, when someone goes Online to do some Shopping, it is Assumed that such a Person does have some Money to Spend, or else he or she would not be Shopping. However, that Assumption is not always True: because some People go Online Looking for FREE Information, which they can often Discover in those Free Book Previews, whereby they can somewhat Satisfy their Appetites for Inspiration. Indeed, if they were to just read nothing but those Free Book Previews within our Literature, they would Learn a LOT of Important Truths — such as you Mentioned above, which would Naturally Inspire them to THINK; and, the more that they would Think with a Capital T, the more they would become Involved in a Good Thing, which is **The Worldwide People's Revolution!®** Yes, it is a Necessary GOOD Thing to get Involved in: beCause our Selected KING has *Guaranteed Solutions* for our Massive Problems, or else we would not have Voted for him to be our Selected King, who is the Gifted King of the Inspired Authors in this World of Wonders, who Holds the World Record Number of Inspired Books with *Guaranteed Solutions!* Indeed, if his Solutions were not Foolproof, WHY would we Want to Support him in all Ways, or even in any Way?

00-07 [_] O Doctor Sam, if your Selected King's Solutions are Foolproof, why have the Masses of People not Discovered them and thus Promoted them, Worldwide? Indeed, they Discovered Cokes, Beers, Pizzas, Hamburgers, and many other Products for Sale, which Cost much more than a Book — such as those Stinking Noisy Polluting Automobiles — which Books can be Shared with thousands of People, just by Placing them within Public LIE-braries, which are Visited by less than one-tenth of one-hundredth of one percent of the Population; but, that is a Sufficient Number of People to Spread the Message far and wide, if it is a GOOD Message. Indeed, you must be Aware that Jesus Christ is the single most Popular Person who ever Lived, who never Wrote so much as a single Book, nor did he Preach a single Sermon, as far as we Know; but, according to the *Holy Bible,* he did Miracles to get Attention, which is what your Selected King will have to Do, if he Intends to get any Attention at all:

beCause it is Extremely Unlikely that the Masses of Ignorant People are going to Pay any Serious Attention to another BOOK, seeing that there are already BILLIONS of uninspired books for Sale, and the Vast Majority of those books do not present any Reasonable Solutions for anything! Therefore, if this Book presents just ONE Workable Solution for some Multiple Trillion-dollar Problem — such as the Climate Changing Problems, or even the Problems that are Involved with Car Accidents — then this Book will Certainly be Well Worth the Cost of it, in spite of all of those Capitalized Words. {See www.Amazon.com for: **"Justifications for Capitalizations!" (WHY our Elected King Defies the School of Fools by Capitalizing LOVE and HATE!)** Book 049.}

00-08 [_] Well, my Friend, NONE of those other books, which are written by Well-Intentioned People, Offer any *Guaranteed Solutions* that I know of, including the *Holy Bible,* which is Regarded as *"the Word of God,"* who only spoke just ONE Word: beCause the Translators were far too Stupid, or too Lazy, to put an S on WordS. However, it can Rightfully be Argued that the *Holy Bible* does NOT Contain nothing but the Words of some God: beCause it is mostly an Unproven Jewish History Book with about one-third of it being so-called *"Prophecies,"* which never Mention anything that is Happening Today — such as a Multitude of Vehicles running all about, which are Polluting the Air, Waters, Lands, Plants, Animals, and Peoples. In Fact, I Challenge you to Discover anything in the *Holy Bible* about Telephones, Radios, Televisions, Computers, Airplanes, Cars, Motorcycles, Chainsaws, Weed-eaters, Viruses, Drugs, Medical Operations, Microscopes, Telescopes, nor any of a Million Vain Inventions that were never Needed for True Prosperity. Indeed, I Challenge you to Discover anything within the *Holy Bible* about HOW a Good Government would even Obtain and Maintain a Good Economy; or even Money, itself, which is the Source of all Economic Life in a Capitalist System, which the *Bible* never Mentions, even once: beCause it is Obvious that none of those so-called *"Holy Prophets"* had any Idea concerning what is Happening in our World, nowadays, much less the Extreme Complications of our Money Systems, Medical Systems, Communication Systems, Legal Systems, and Tax Systems. Indeed, they could have at least Mentioned the American Tax Code, which fills several large Volumes of Books! But, behold, nothing in the *Holy Bible* is Crystal Clear about any given Subject, including Marriages and Divorces, which seem to be Total Failures for the most part, which only Complicate our Problems, rather than Solve them. In Fact, after the Fifth Divorce, a certain Hollywood Actor proclaimed: "I do not believe that I will try it again, seeing that I am unsuccessful at it, and cannot win this game." Yes, it was just a Game to him: beCause he had no Idea HOW to Discover a GOOD Life Mate! {See: **"The Complete SURVEYS of our VALUES!" (SURVEYS of Religious Spiritual Political Governmental Sexual Social Moral Economic Business Labor Habitual and Miscellaneous VALUES!) By The Worldwide People's Revolution!®** Book 059.}

00-09 [_] O Doctor Sam, are you Suggesting that it might be Possible for us to Prosper with a Capital P, and even Live within those **"Beautiful Swanky PALACES!" (A New Concept in Living Habits — Swanky Palaces for Poor People!) By The Worldwide People's Revolution!®,** Book 066? If so, WHY do the Poor People of Venezuela not Accept that Good Idea, and thus Provide a Way for almost all of them to become Moderately RICH, and without Telling any Lies, nor Selling any Capitalist TRASH? After all, they are Intelligent People.

00-10 [_] Well, my Friend, that is what this Inspired Book is all about, which Explains HOW that you and everyone else can become Moderately RICH, and Live within one of those **"Beautiful Swanky PALACES,"** without Telling any Lies, nor Selling any Trash, which will Solve X-amount of Problems, including the Temporary Insanity of People like Donald Trumpeter, Sir Winston Cigar-chomping Alcoholic Churchill, Saint Joseph Mass-Murderer Stalin, Adolf Hitler, and Related Zealots, who could have all been Liberated by **"The Swanky Sword of Divine Truths!" (The Most Powerful Weapon in the Whole Universe!) By The Worldwide People's Revolution!®** Book 067.

The Menu for a Feast of Provable Solutions

‡ This Symbol is called the Double-edged Sword of Controversy, which follows Statements that should be Proven at: **"The Great Worldwide TELEVISED Court HEARING!"** Book 041.

§ This Section Symbol is used after Sarcastic Statements. 2 such Symbols (§§) Represent a Double Sarcasm, which is so Sarcastic that the Statement Proves itself to be WRong. For Example, there are no Mistaaks in this Inspired Book. §§

This Book contains about 117,470 Words, and 2 Drawings, without any Pictures: because both of my Mac Computers CRASHED — Thanks to Capitalism. Moreover, it remains to be seen whether or not I will be Able to Publish this Book, seeing that my Chief Enemies do not really Want it to be Published, and they Control the System from Wall Street and from London's Square Mile. Nevertheless, we must keep Trying to VENT the Boilers, as Mark Twain might say, lest they should EXPLODE with Frustrations! After all, there are so many HOT Issues to Address, and this Inspired Book Touches on many of them, and Manhandles most of them Properly — at least to the Best of my Intellectual Abilities, which you will no doubt Discover are far BELOW Average: beCause I just Happen to be a Grade School DROPOUT! Nevertheless, that is not to say that I am as STUPID as some of those Greedy Things over there in the District of Criminals, in Washington, who are Obviously Suffering with Chronic Constipation of their Minds, who Desperately Need High Enemas with the Water of Life! § {See www.Amazon.com for: **"The BIG White OUTHOUSE on the Not-so-Biblical Capitol DUNGHILL!" (The Chief Sins of the Divided States of United LIES!) By The Worldwide People's Revolution!®** Book 023.}

— Chapter 01 —

A Guaranteed Solution for no more Car Accidents

01-01 [_] O Selected King of **The Worldwide People's Revolution!**®, you must be INSANE to Think that we could Solve those Billions of Problems that are brought about by using Automobiles — such as Cars Slipping on Icy Streets, Drivers Speeding through Intersections with Red Lights, Drunk Drivers, Terrorists with Car Bombs, Terrorists on Suicide Missions in Speeding Vehicles on Crowded Streets, and all such Evil Things! Have you Lost your Riit Miind, or what? {Please Check the Box with an X, if you are inclined to Agree with such a Rational Statement. Thank you.}

01-02 [_] Well, first of all, I must Confess that it is Impossible to Lose something that I have never had — such as a "Right Mind," which would Naturally be a WRong mind within the Minds of many Miseducated People, who just Assume that our TRADITIONS are Correct, even if those Traditions are Totally INSANE! For Example, if I told you and all of the other Readers of my Inspired Books that you stand a Good Chance of getting KILLED, just by Reading this Book, would any of you bother to Read any more of it? Probably not! However, when it comes to Driving Vehicles at Horrendous Speeds on Interstate Highways, most People are Willing to Gamble their Lives on it. Yes, I have done it many Times, myself, while Trusting the Machines to Work Correctly, which they always did for me; but, I must Confess that it was an Unnecessary and DANGEROUS GAMBLE, which could have easily Killed me and other Ignorant People! Remember that all such Dangerous Vehicles KILL an Average of 40,000+ Americans, each Year, while Wounding upwards of a Million other People, at a Cost of Billions of Dollars, which is the Equivalent of another World War 2, every 10 Years, in Terms of American Lives Lost, not to Mention the Multitude of other Deceived Nations that use such Vehicles! But, when it comes to Selling and Buying Cars, Vans, Pickups, Trucks, Buses, and Especially Motorcycles, most People simply Disregard any of the Dangers that might be Involved in it, even after Learning that there is a Good Chance for them to get Wounded, or even Killed by it, and a 4000% Greater Chance of being Killed on a Motorcycle, than in a Car! In Fact, many Thoughtless Teenagers are the Victims of all such Vehicle Accidents, who are never told that it is Possible and most Practical for them to become Moderately RICH, without the Use of any Dangerous Motorized Vehicles on Highways, and without making themselves into Education Slaves, Work Slaves, Tax Slaves, Insurance Slaves, Interest Slaves, Endless Bills Slaves, Rent Slaves, Sex Slaves, nor any other Kinds of Slaves, whereby they are Free to Live within those **"Beautiful Swanky PALACES"** with the Polished Marble-faced Walls, Granite-faced Floors, and SPACIOUS Comfortable Self-air-conditioned Houses, which are also Fireproof, Mouse-proof, Termite-proof, Rot-proof, Paint-proof, Hail-proof, Tornado-proof, Flood-damage-proof, Earthquake-proof, Mudslide-proof, Insurance-proof, Loan-proof, Interest-proof, and Tax-proof! Yes, it Sounds UNBELIEVABLE, huh? But, I will Prove it to you — that is, if you still have a RIIT Miind, which can Think and Remember!

01-03 [_] O Crazy King of the Ignorant Fools, if God is out to Kill you, that can easily be Arranged by a Tiny GERM or Contagious Virus. For Example, there are more People Killed each Year by Malaria, than there are with Vehicle Accidents. Therefore, why do you not Solve that Problem, first, and stop Worrying yourself over the million or so Fools who get Killed by Vehicles, each Year? In Fact, a Pedestrian is more apt to be Killed by a Vehicle, than a Person Riding in a Vehicle. Therefore, should we all Stop Walking, just beCause of that Fact of Life? Indeed, a Pedestrian has a 3000% greater chance of being Killed by a Vehicle, than someone in a Car. Therefore, should we Ban all Pedestrians; or, should we Ban all Cars from Cities of Confusion? ‡

01-04 [_] Well, my Potential Friend, my Solutions will Solve ALL such Problems for the Vast Majority of the People who Believe; but, for the Unbelievers, there is NO Solution for anything: beCause they are not even Willing to Experiment with the New and Wonderful Lifestyle that I Propose. Therefore, they will just have to go on Suffering: beCause, "we cannot Help them to See the Light," as Hank Williams would Sing, over and over, like a Chant of a certain Hindu, whose Mind is so Constipated that he cannot Remember that he just said it. Indeed, the Greatest Obstacle to Overcome in this World of Woes is that Unbelief, which is more Deadly than Cancers. Nevertheless, there is also a Remedy for Unbelief, which Requires **"The Great Worldwide TELEVISED Court HEARING,"** whereby the Leaders of all Nations are Invited to Attend that Great Meeting of the Most Intelligent and Well-Educated Minds, whereby the Whole Truth can be Discovered about each Important Subject, which will Help People to Change their Minds about those Subjects, if they have been WRong. For Example, most People used to Believe that the Earth is FLAT, being somewhat Like a Dinner Plate that is turned Upside Down, which is a bit Rounded on the Top; but, not Like a Globe, nor Ball, as we now Believe, which still has yet to be Proven in a Courtroom with a Righteous Juj in Charge of it: beCause the Evidences are still in the Favor of the Flat Earth Society! For Example, if Scientists are Correct — that the Earth is about 8,000 Miles in Diameter, being a Round Globe — then the Curve of the Horizon on the Earth should Drop by about 1 Mile every 20 Miles, for a Total of about 1,256 similar "Drops," going around the Earth. In other Words, those Mountains that are Protruding into the Sky by 2 Miles should Disappear behind the Curvature of the Earth within just 40 Miles; but, behold, the Tops of the Rocky Mountains can be seen as far away as North Dakota, which is hundreds of Miles away from those Mountains! Likewise, Islands in the Oceans can still be seen at Long Distances from them, which should have Disappeared behind the Curvature of the Earth — that is, IF there is any such Curvature? Chances are that some Ignorant Person with a College Degree in Philosophies PRESUMED what the Facts are, rather than Investigate the Subject for himself. For Example, a Person could get a Perfectly Straight and Level Red String, or Red Rope, which is Tied TIGHT and Perfectly LEVEL between 2 Posts, and then stand back at a certain Distance from that String, and take a Good Look at the Horizon on the Pacific Ocean, and Discover that the Ocean has NO Curve on the String: beCause the Ocean is Obviously FLAT! Moreover, Water just Naturally Seeks to Level itself out, which is why it makes a Good Level when it is put inside of a Water Hose, which can be used to Accurately Level the Foundation for any large or small Buildings. In Fact, you could use the Horizon on the Ocean to Level your Red Rope, Accurately. Chances are that the Great Pyramid of Egypt was Leveled by Water, which is still used in Carpenter's Levels: beCause it is Reliable. Moreover, if you look through a Good Telescope from a High Point in North Dakota toward those Rocky Mountains in Montana, you can see much more than just the Tops of the Mountains: beCause there is no Curvature of the Earth between you and the Mountains, which will make you Wonder just WHO has been Lying to you, and WHY?

01-05 [_] O Unelected King, it could be that the Great Plains between North Dakota and the Rocky Mountains are DISHED OUT, whereby the Curvature of the Earth is not Visible: beCause of being like a Dinner Plate that is Right Side Up. Therefore, that is no Proof that the Earth is NOT a Globe, seeing that we are speaking of a Space that is only a few hundred miles long. Indeed, if your Calculations are at all Correct, the Curvature of the Earth would Drop by 5 Miles every 100 Miles, or about 15 Miles between the Rocky Mountains and North Dakota, whereby the Mountains would Disappear from our Eyesight: because they are only 1 to 3 Miles Tall for the most part, the Tallest one being 14,431 feet.

01-06 [_] Well, Personally, I must Confess that I will be Happy to Accept whatever can be Proven in a Proper Courtroom with a Righteous Juj in Charge of it; but, only AFTER ALL of the Evidences have been Presented to me, whereby I might Judge such Subjects with a Rational Mind, as Opposed to Assuming that certain so-called "Scientists" are Correct about all such Things: beCause it would not be the First nor the Last Time that all such "Scientists" have Changed and will Continue to Change their

Minds: beCause other Scientists have Proven their Theories to be WRong. Indeed, this is a very Complicated World that we Live in, which is not so Simple as some People might Imagine. Nevertheless, in the Meantime, I will Continue to Believe that the Earth is a Rough Globe; and, that there is not a big Dish-shaped Plains between the Rocky Mountains and North Dakota: beCause Water in Rivers seldom run Uphill — at least they did not used to run Uphill; but, "The Times are Changing," you might say, and the Old Ways are about to come to an END. {See: **"The END of CONFUSION!" (The Great CELEBRATION of the Magnificent Wedding of the Most Humble Honest Nations, and the Grand Year of JUBILEE!) By The Worldwide People's Revolution!®** Book 050.}

01-07 [_] O Elected King, it is for Certain that there could not be any Vehicular Accidents, if no one in the Whole World should Use any such Vehicles, nor even Horses, Mules, Asses, Camels, nor Bovines: because of Transporting ourselves on our own 2 Feets — that is, 2 Feet for you, 2 Feet for me, and 2 Feet for everyone else, which Adds up to FEETS, and not just Feet, if you want to get Technical about it, even as 12 Sheeps of one Speeshee is more Grammatically Correct than 12 Sheep and 10 Goats of one Species. Indeed, it is Possible, Safest, most Economical, and most Practical to use Elevators, Escalators, and Electric Subway Trains for Transportation within Beautiful Planned City States, which are Designed to Eliminate all such Vehicular Accidents, including those on Bicycles, which have been known to Kill People at Dangerous Speeds, going down Steep Hills and Mountains. Nevertheless, that is not to say that Bicycles cannot be Rode / Ridden at Safe Speeds on Level Highways, or in Proper Underground Tunnels, where there is no Ice to Slip on, nor any Wet Floors. Personally, I much Prefer to use a Pedal-powered Quadruped, which can also Carry a considerable Load of Groceries, Tools, People, or whatever, which is very easy to Pedal on Level Pavement, as well as Quiet, Peaceful and Environmentally Friendly. Therefore, there could be One-way-only Streets and Tunnels for them to Travel on or in, and thus be quite Safe, even at the Hair-raising Speed of 20 Miles per Hour (MpH), which some People might Imagine is entirely too Slow; but, that is the Speed Limit of a Person in a Race, on his or her Feet, which is quite Fast for going Shopping, and far too Fast for Observing all of the Wonderful Flower Gardens in those **"GLORIOUS Swanky Hotels Castles and Fortresses!" (Beautiful Planned City States for WISE Intelligent Well-Educated People with Common Sense and Good Understanding!) By The Worldwide People's Revolution!®** Book 019. Yes, a Moderate 10 MpH Speed is plenty Fast enough in any Swanky Fortress, and is very unlikely to Kill anyone.

01-08 [_] Well, my Friend, for the Lack of Proper Spellings and Usages of Words in the Barbaric English Language, we Earthlings have all Kinds of Misunderstandings among us, which will be Difficult to Correct without a LOT of Cooperation among the Nations, some of whom are Determined to NOT Cooperate, even as they have not Agreed about what to Do for Climate Changes. However, at **"The Great Worldwide TELEVISED Court HEARING,"** they will have to Humble themselves and Accept the Proven Truths about it. For Example, those **"GLORIOUS Swanky Hotels Castles and Fortresses"** will use Electric Subway Trains, Elevators, and Escalators for Transportation, rather than Dangerous Motorized Vehicles — that is, the WISE People in the World will be Using their FEETS, as you say, and will therefore Eliminate those Needless Traffic Accidents, whereby Millions of Lives will be Saved from Deaths and Serious Injuries, which should make them much Richer in all Ways. For Example, one Family got into a Wreck, about 32 Years Ago, and he was Paralyzed from the Neck on down to his Toes on his Feet, whereby he has had to Wear Diapers ever since then, and be Spoon-fed like a Baby at Government Expenses, which has Added Up to MILLIONS of Wasted Dollars! However, if someone Vainly Imagines that it is a Tiny Problem, that Person should have to Attend to such a Big Baby for a Month or 2, just to Discover what a HUGE Problem it is. Amazingly enough, his Mind is still Working, and his Mouth is still Talking, which Freely Confesses that he would have been a million Times more Blest to have been WALKING with Jesus Christ and the Apostle Paul, rather than Driving a Dangerous Car. Yes, after 32 Years of Thinking about it, he Cheerfully Agrees with

ME, and has Willingly Checked the above Box with an X, you might say, even though his Hands are not Able to make the simple Mark on the Paper, which has to be Marked for him: beCause he is Totally Helpless. Moreover, he can also Remember the Good Old Days when he could Run and Play, which makes him Cry, just to Think about it: beCause he has Lost his True Riches, which Begin with Good Health. Furthermore, I Seriously Doubt that anyone could Persuade him to Give Up his FIRM Belief in those **"GLORIOUS Swanky Hotels Castles and Fortresses!" (Beautiful Planned City States for WISE Intelligent Well-Educated People with Common Sense and Good Understanding!) By The Worldwide People's Revolution!®** Book 019.

01-09 [_] O Elected King, I certainly Hope to God that I do not have to lie around in some Hospital Bed for 32 Years, just to make such a Confession of Truths; but, if that is what God Requires, just to Straighten Out my Thinking, then so be it.

01-10 [_] Well, my Potential Friend, God does not Require any such Self-inflicted Punishments: beCause all such Punishments are only Self-inflicted, which can easily be Avoided by DEMANDING **"The Great Worldwide TELEVISED Court HEARING!" (That Great Meeting of the Most Intelligent and Well-Educated Minds!)**, Book 041, whereby we can easily Discover any Ignorant FOOLS who Disagree with my Master Plan, which calls for the Construction of Millions of those **"GLORIOUS Swanky Hotels Castles and Fortresses,"** which will Solve no less than 5,000 Problems, just by their Designs, alone! However, if someone Objects to Solving those Problems, including Poverty, Crimes, Drug Abuses, Prisons and Unnecessary Taxes, they are Welcome to Continue to Live in their Wooden / Plastic Firetrap Mouse-infested Cockroach Dens, along with any other Ignorant Fools in those Stinking Noisy FILTHY Polluted Cities of Confusion! Yes, they should be Free to Do that; but, not at the Expense of any Unwilling TAX SLAVES, who should be Liberated! {See www.Amazon.com for: **"The Right Design for Living!" (A List of Great Advantages for Building Beautiful Planned City States!)**, Book 012, which is a Companion Book of: **"The Low Court of Supreme Injustices is Brought to Trial!" (Our Elected King Butts Heads with the United States Supreme Court, with or without their Black Robes of Hypocrisies and Lies!) By The Worldwide People's Revolution!®** Book 011.}

— Chapter 02 —

A Guaranteed Solution for HOW to Liberate the SLAVES!

02-01 [ ] O Unelected King, I Strenuously Object to the Construction of MILLIONS of Swanky Fortresses: beCause there is not Sufficient SPACE in the Great State of Flexible Texas to Build even ONE such Beautiful Planned City State: beCause all of the Land from El Paso to Dallas-Fort Worthless is OWNED by some Possession Worshiper, who would Naturally Refuse to Sell his or her Land, and would rather DIE, than to Give Up Smoking, and would go to War to Save his Pickup Truck. §§

02-02 [ ] So, are you saying that there is not so much as 16 Square Miles of Unoccupied Land in a State that has no less than 268,000 Square Miles, or 696,000 Square Kilometers of Land? If so, it seems like it would be a Good Idea to Declare Independence from **"The Divided States of United Lies!"** **(The so-called "United States of North America" in Disguise!)** Book 058. Indeed, I would Think that Texas / Mexico might have Space for at least a thousand Swanky Fortresses, and even several large ones a hundred Miles or more in Diameter on both Sides of the Rio Grande! After all, most of that Land is nothing but a Useless Desert, which could hardly Feed a Jackrabbit, which we could make very Productive by Mining Out Topsoil from the Louisiana Delta, and putting that Precious Topsoil behind Terraced Stone Walls, whereby Texas could Feed most of the People in the Whole World! — that is, IF we Planted it to Fig Trees, Pecans, Dates, Coconuts, Pistachios, Walnuts, Persimmons, Grapes, Bananas, Papayas, Apples, Pears, Peaches, Plums, Apricots, Cherries, and all Kinds of Berries. But, if none of those Fruits can be Grown there, perhaps we should Plant them in Venezuela, after Mining Out the Topsoil at some other Deltas, which might not be so Polluted as the Louisiana Delta. ‡

02-03 [ ] O Unelected King, I am saying that there is no Space within the entire United States of America for even ONE Swanky Fortress: beCause we do not Believe in Fortresses of any Kind, even if they will Solve ALL of our Massive Problems: beCause we do not Sincerely Believe in Freedom of Speech, much less in the Law of Liberty, whereby an Independent State might be Established within any given State: beCause that is Unconstitutional. Therefore, your whole Swanky Fortress Plan will not WORK in **"The Divided States of United Lies!"**

02-04 [ ] Well, it Sounds to me as if Liberty and Freedom were Hanged on the same Cross with Jesus Christ, and without a Fair Hearing. Indeed, the Tax Collectors would Naturally Object to anyone being Liberated from Tax Slavery, whereby they put it in their Phony Constitution, which also Permits the Selling of all Kinds of Drugs, Abominable Automobiles, Stinking Noisy Chainsaws, Lawnmowers, and you Name it: beCause the Great False Economy is Built on the Assumption that Capitalism is a HOLY Thing, which must not be Interfered with, nor Interrupted in any Way: beCause it is what has made it Possible for 1% of the People to get Excessively RICH, while the 99% Support them. Yes, I am now Wondering if it might have been that 1% who made up all such so-called "Laws," which seem to Favor them by a thousand Times, while the Education Slaves, Work Slaves, Tax Slaves, Interest Slaves, Credit Card Debt Slaves, Mortgage Slaves, Rent Slaves, Insurance Slaves, Drug Slaves, ElecTrickery Bills Slaves, Gas Bills Slaves, Water Bills Slaves, Food Bills Slaves, Mortuary Slaves, Graveyard Slaves, and all of the other Multitudes of SLAVES have to Cover the Costs, who could all be Living in those **"Beautiful Swanky PALACES!"** **(A New Concept in Living Habits — Swanky Palaces for Poor People!) By The Worldwide People's Revolution!®** Book 066.

02-05 [_] O Elected King, are you saying that WE, the PEOPLE, could Elect to OWN all of our own Mountains of Rocks, Rivers of Water, Sand, Gravel, Minerals, and all Natural Resources, Collectively? Is that not called Communism, in a Nutshell?

02-06 [_] Well, you may Call it whatever you Like; but, neither Capitalism, Communism, Socialism, nor Fascism did anything similar to what I have Proposed, which is to make almost everyone Moderately RICH, and without Selling anything except the IDEA, which can easily be Proven in a Courtroom to be the Best Idea since Adam and Eve, who could have been the First Capitalists, if they had Wanted to, and thus Claimed ALL of the Lands for themselves, including those Lands that already Belonged to the Natives — such as the Aborigines of Australia, and the Negro Tribes of Africa, who were here on the Earth long before Adam and Eve, who were the Parents of the First White People, who were Supposed to Govern this World, Properly; but, they Goofed Up, and got Cast Out of the Paradise of Peace and Happiness in the Blest Land of Perfect Oneness; and thus their Children got into Wars with those Natives, and made them into their SLAVES, with the Permission of their Imaginary God, you might say, who Supposedly Inspired them to Write a Holy Book of many Holy Books, beginning with *Genesis,* which tells about Noah and his Imaginary Ark, which Supposedly Contained enough Fresh Water to Water 28,000+ Bovines, each Day, or roughly 1,000,000 Gallons of Water per Day! Indeed, the Myth Makers forgot to Calculate just how MUCH Water would be Required, whereby they made Fools of themselves. For Example, a single Cow can easily Drink Up 50 Gallons of Water per Day, and there were 7 Males and 7 Females of each Clean Animal, including a thousand Species of Deers, Antelopes, Goats, Sheeps, Mooses, Elks, Yaks, Giraffes, and you Name them — all of whom had to Eat and DRINK! Therefore, if just 14 American Bisons Required 50 Gallons of Fresh Water, each, per Day, that would Add up to no less than 252,000 Gallons of Water for one Year! However, let us say that those Bisons or Buffaloes were rather Conservative, and only Drank 100,000 Gallons of Fresh Water during that Year — what about the Giraffes, Water Buffaloes, Yaks, Wildebeests, Musk Oxens, Camels, Elephants, Sheeps, Goats, Deers, Caribous, Elks, Mooses, Lions, Bears, Tigers, Wolves, Coyotes, Foxes, Dogs, Jackals, Hyenas, Anteaters, Sloths, Skunks, Wolverines, Badgers, Opossums, Raccoons, Squirrels, Chipmunks, Monkeys, Apes, Kangaroos, Rats, Mice, and a Host of a Million or more Birds — all of which like to DRINK? Yes, there are no less than 2 Million Species of all such Creatures — all of whom must have been in Noah's Ark, if the *Holy Bible* is True, including the Dinosaurs. Moreover, all of them were Locked Up in Cages, according to that Jewish Myth; and therefore, each Set of Animals would have Required someone to Feed and Water them, and also Clean Up after them: because the Methane Gases would have Killed all of them, if their Poop and Piss were not Cleaned Up! Just Imagine how many Tons of Flesh would have been Required to Feed 2,000+ Species of Skunks, Badgers, Wolves, Wolverines, Dogs, Coyotes, Foxes, and Cats, alone, during just one Day? But, not to Worry: beCause the Magic Pitcher never Stopped Pouring Out Fresh Living Water, which was Naturally Flushed Down the million or so Toilets, except that Noah was Smarter than most of us, and figured out how to get all of that Poop and Piss Out of the Ark by simply Praying to his Imaginary God for it to be Done — much the same as any Magician might do, if he had a Magic Wand — except that the Bible has no Explanations for HOW it was Done. (And yes, I am being very Sarcastic: because it is Truly one of the Greater Fairy Tales in the World, and People Believe it.) ‡§§

02-07 [_] O Unelected King, have you already Lost Faith in the *Holy Bible,* which was Inspired by Jehovah God, who made Murderers of his Chosen People, by Commanding them to Kill Babies? (See *First Samuel 15:3, King James Version.*)

02-08 [_] Well, I have Certainly Lost Faith in any Outlandish LIES, and would Hope to God that you have also Lost Faith in any such Lies: beCause you could be Damned for Believing any Lies, if your *Bible* is Correct; and it probably is — at least concerning that Subject. (See *Second Thessalonians 2:12,*

KJV.) After all, why would God Want any Stupid People in his Holy Kingdom? Would YOU Want any such Ignorant People in your Righteous Kingdom, if you were a Selected King? Of course not! Therefore, it is the Best Way to Sift Out all such Deceived People from among the Righteous Honest People, who might be Disappointed with their *Unholy Mutilated Bibles;* but, after Discovering the Whole Truth, it would be most Reasonable for them to Think of it as a very Good Plan for getting RID of Unbelievers, Doubters, Mockers and Scoffers. ‡

02-09 [_] O Elected King, your Reasoning seems to be most Reasonable to me: beCause I have already Studied all of your Previous Books, and I must Confess that the so-called *"Holy Bible"* is in Fact a Mutilated Book, which is Missing many Inspired Books, which should be in it — such as *the Book of Jasher, the Book of Iddo, the Book of the Sayings of the Seers, the Book of Shemaiah, the Book of the Acts of King Solomon, the Book of Nathan the Prophet, the Book of Gad, the Book of Jehu, the First Epistle of the Apostle Paul to the Laodiceans, the Gospel According to Saint Thomas, the Gospel According to Saint Bartholomew, the Gospel According to Saint Philip, the Gospel According to Saint James, the Gospel According to Saint Matthias,* and many other Letters and Important Documents that the *Bible* Mentions, or Quotes, which one cannot Find within its Covers: beCause there is no doubt some Conspiracy to keep us Tax Slaves in a State of Extreme Ignorance!

02-10 [_] Well, my Friend, there is only One Way to Liberate the Slaves, and that is by Exercising **"The Swanky Sword of Divine Truths!" (The Most Powerful Weapon in the Whole Universe!)**, Book 067: beCause, it is Exactly as Jesus said, *"You shall Learn the Whole Truth about all Important Subjects, and those Great Truths will make you Free in all Ways when you Practice them."* — *The Gospel According to Saint Judas, the Brother of James, 2:29.* Therefore, the Objective that is now most Important, is to Learn the WHOLE Truth about each Important Subject, even if those Truths should Prove all of us to be WRong! And the One and Only Way for everyone to Discover all such Truths is for us Tax Slaves to DEMAND **"The Great Worldwide TELEVISED Court HEARING!" (That Great Meeting of the Most Intelligent and Wel-Ejukaatid Miindz!)** Book 041. Yes, that will also Require some Faith, Hope, Trust, Love, Patience, Persistence, and OBEDIENCE, which are **"The Seven Basic Spiritual Building Blocks of LIFE!"** Book 036.

— Chapter 03 —

A Guaranteed Solution for
10,000 Contradictory Religions!

03-01 [_] It is as Elijah said, *"Let the God who Answers by Devouring Fire be the Supreme Ruler."* In other Words, let each Religious Body of People Pray to their Gods, and the God who Responds with Devouring Fire will be the God that we all Respect and Worship as the Supreme Ruler: beCause he has the Powers that Demand it, while the other so-called "Gods" do not have any Powers at all. ‡

03-02 [_] O Selected King, what do we Need with any such Supreme Ruler? Can we not Manage our own Lives as we see fit to do, and leave all Gods and Goddesses out of the Equation?

03-03 [_] Well, that would be like the Chair, who says to the Table: "Have you Seen any Gods or Goddesses? What makes you Imagine that we were Constructed by some God?"

03-04 [_] And the Table might Respond, "There is very little Chance that we Constructed ourselves, seeing that we do not have Hands to Work with, nor any Tools to Work with."

03-05 [_] And the Chair might Respond, "I do not Believe that any Carpenter made us, do you?"

03-06 [_] And the Table might Respond, "Well, it is for Certain that we did not Make ourselves, nor do we have Minds whereby we might Comprehend such a Carpenter, who is much more Complex than we are, whom we should Worship for his Abilities and Skills, lest he should Decide to Cast us into his Fireplace, just for Refusing to Honor and Worship him."

03-07 [_] And the Chair might Respond, "Well, if that is your Belief, go ahead and Worship some Imaginary Carpenter; but, I do not Believe in him: beCause he did not Identify himself to me."

03-08 [_] And the Table might say, "Well, I cannot Prove to you that any such Carpenter Exists: beCause you do not have Eyes that See anything, and neither do I; but, it is only Reasonable to Think that it Required some Professional Carpenter to Make us, or else we would not be Able to Stand on our own Legs. Therefore, if he gives to me a Tongue and Mouth to Praise him, I will be Happy to do so, and also Love and Obey his Commandments: beCause it is for Certain that I did not Create anything, including the Legs that I Stand on. Moreover, there is only One God who did Identify himself as the Creator God, and he called himself Yohoovu God, who is the God of the Hebrews, who may be the Supreme Ruler of this World, even though I have no Real Proof of it."

03-09 [_] And the Chair might Respond, saying: "I will use my Mouth and Tongue to Praise myself for my own Goodness, if you do not Object. Moreover, if Yohoovu God is Offended by that, he can Cut Out my Tongue and Sew my Lips Together; but, the Last Thing that I will Do is to Praise some Imaginary Carpenter for Creating me. Therefore, if Yohoovu God is my Creator, he should come down here and Identify himself to me. Otherwise, I will not Believe in him."

03-10 [_] And the Table might Respond, saying: "Why would you be so Foolish, seeing that it does not

15

Cost you anything to Give Credit to whom Credit is Due? Moreover, Credit must be Given to the Great Creator God or Gods, whomever he or they might be: beCause none of us can Rightfully Accept any Credit for having Created anything in this World, in spite of Countless Inventions of Men, none of which have LIFE, whereby they can Reproduce more Life. Indeed, what if you should make the Master Carpenter very Angry with you for Speaking Evil of him? Are you not Aware that he has all Power over you? Therefore, if he should Break you into Pieces, and Cast you into the Fire, do not Blame me for   it."

03-11 [_] And the Chair might Respond, "Well, sooner or later, we will all be Cast into the Fire: because of being Worn Out. Therefore, what Difference does it make if I Speak Evil of some Imaginary God — such as that Contradictory Hebrew God, who Commanded the Children of Israel to Murder all of the Children in the Land of Canaan, just to Steal their Lands, when there were Plenty of Lands   to   be   Inherited   without   Stealing   nor   Robbing   them   from   other   Peoples?"

03-12 [_] And the Table might Respond, "I would Think that you should Respect and Love your Creator, seeing that you would be a Useless Thing without his Skills and Abilities and Gifts to you."

03-13 [_] And the Chair might Respond, "I Think that it is Presumptuous of you to Assume that any such   Carpenter   even   Exists."

03-14 [_] And the Table might Respond, saying: "I Instinctively Know that he must Exist, or else we would not Exist: beCause we have no Abilities to Create ourselves, nor Give Life to any Kind of a Creature, not even to a New Kind of Tree, nor a little Flower. However, even if we could Create another Kind of Creature, it would only be Proof that it Requires Great Nolij to Do so, which would be Proof that all Created Things Require a Creator, without whom no such Creation could Exist: because nothing   in   the   World   has   the   Power   to   Create   itself."

03-15 [_] And the Chair might Respond, "Well, after Thinking about it, I will have to Confess that you are Correct about that. However, I still Refuse to Honor a Murderous God, who would Ask his so-called 'Chosen People' to Murder Innocent Babies in his Name, whereby all such Murderers would be Guilty of the Worst Kind of Murder, which is the Shedding of Innocent Blood. Therefore, I cannot even   Respect   such   a   God,   much   less   Praise   him   for   his   Goodness."

03-16 [_] And the Table might Respond, "Well, suppose it was the Intentions of that God to Recycle those Murdered Souls into Israelite Families? Indeed, you Look at it as a very BAD Thing; but, God Looked at it as a very Good Thing: beCause it Liberated those Souls from Eternal Damnation. Indeed, they had to Escape from their Vain and Foolish Traditions by Means of DEATH, and then be Born into Israelite Families, where they could be Taught GOOD Traditions — such as Remembering the Sabbath Day, to Keep it HOLY, which is the Seventh Day of the Week, which God did not Change: beCause his Laws are Eternally the SAME, both Yesterday, Today, and Forever! Indeed, if it were not so, he could not be Trusted: beCause he would be a Changeable God. But, behold, he is an Unchangeable God from all of Eternity to all of Eternity, whose Disobedient Servants made the Grave Mistake of DELETING very Important Information from the *Scriptures,* which cannot be Rightly Understood without that Information. For Example, few People would Know that Yohoovu God is in the Business of Reproducing more Gods to Govern more and more Worlds, which are Multiplying, even as the Fishes in the Seas and the Birds of the Air are Multiplying: beCause it is the Glory of the Gods to MULTIPLY, whereby there are Countless Worlds with Countless Inhabitants, each of which Needs some Sane Person to Govern it, who is otherwise known as the Supreme Ruler, which the *Holy Bible* calls GOD. Therefore, Jesus Christ will be the Supreme Ruler of this World: beCause he Qualified by

Reason of the Fact that he Passed all of his Tests, while the other Children of Israel did NOT Pass their Tests — one of which was to Murder all of those Canaanites, Hittites, Hivites, Gergushiits, Jebuuziits, and whatever other Ites Inhabited that Land called Palestine, which was a Mean Thing to Do, you might say; but, it was a Test of their Obedience, which would have Proven to be a Good Thing, if they had only OBEYED Yohoovu God, and gotten RID of those Heathen Nations, whereby there would now be Peace in the World. But, behold, they Disobeyed Yohoovu God, and thus brought onto themselves the Curses of these Times, whereby there are Eternal Wars in the Middle East. ‡

03-17 [_] "Yes, Yohoovu God Wanted to Establish **'The New RIGHTEOUS One-World Government'** over all of the Nations, under the Administration of his Chosen People, who are Identified as ISRAELITES in the *Holy Bible,* which does have some Credibility; but, his so-called 'Chosen People' did not OBEY his Commandments, and thus they brought onto themselves Various Curses for Humiliations, in Order for God to Teach certain Good Lessons to them, which they could have Learned by simply Studying Good Books. But, behold, they are very Stubborn People, who are Extremely Slow to Learn any such Lessons, who have also Rebelled Against such a Good Government Plan, and have taken up their own Great False Economy, called Capitalism, which is a Mixture of Communism, Socialism, Fascism, and other Isms, which are Based on the Production and Sales of Goods and Services, rather than being Based on *the Garden of Eden* Lifestyle, which is much more Simple and Easy to Control: beCause almost everyone in that Economic System is a Gardener, who also has some Special Craft — such as Shoemaking, Furniture Making, Tile Setting, or whatever is Needed; but, the Basic Foundation of that Lifestyle is GARDENING, according to: **'The LUSCIOUS All-Mineral Organic Method of Gardening!' (HOW to Grow DELICIOUS Satisfying Foods for Potential Kingz and Kweenz in Swanky PALACES!) By The Worldwide People's Revolution!®** Book 021. In other Words, each Family must be Set Up Properly for Living on the Land that Feeds and Clothes them, which can be done in many Different Ways, whereby everyone is Happy with the Plan that   they   Adopt.

03-18 [_] "For Example, if someone Hates Gardening, he may Want to Join **'The Swanky Association of Professional Tile Setters,'** since there is lots of Work to be Done Setting Tiles within those **'GLORIOUS Swanky Hotels Castles and Fortresses!' (Beautiful Planned City States for WISE Intelligent Well-Educated People with Common Sense and Good Understanding!) By The Worldwide People's Revolution!®** Book 019. Yes, there will be a Great Multitude of Enjoyable Occupations to Choose from. However, beCause of Establishing **'The New RIGHTEOUS One-World Government,'** everyone in the World will have to be Taught HOW to Grow their own Foods in their own Gardens, whereby they will Learn to Love and Respect their Great Creator God, without whom there would be nothing to EAT nor DRINK! Therefore, all School Children will have to Learn HOW to Do their own Gardening, which will be the Foundation of a Good Dependable Life, which will Eliminate Poverty, Hunger, Riots, Strikes, Brutalities, Election Deceptions and Civil Wars!" {See www.Amazon.com for: **"Poverty Hunger Riots Strikes Brutalities Election Deceptions and Civil Wars!" (The High Price that we Earthlings have Paid for Leaving the Good Land!) By The Worldwide People's Revolution!®,** Book 014, which is a Companion Book of: **"The Right Design for Living!" (A List of Great Advantages for Building Beautiful Planned City States!),** Book 012, which is a Companion Book of: **"The Low Court of Supreme Injustices is Brought to Trial!" (Our Elected King Butts Heads with the United States Supreme Court, with or without their Black Robes of Hypocrisies and Lies!) By The Worldwide People's Revolution!®,** Book 011.}

03-19 [_] O Elected King, are you saying that each Beautiful Planned City State may Worship whatever God or Goddess that it Chooses, and even Invent New Gods to Worship, and it will not be of any Concern to Yohoovu God, whose Chosen People will also Build their own Beautiful Planned City

States, whereby they might Prove their Way of Living to be the Best Way for Mankind, and a Good Example for other Peoples to Follow? In other Words, if the Muslims want to Worship Buzzeldick the Great, they will be Free to Do so, just to have some Peace among them; while Jehovah's Witnesses will be Free to Build their own Beautiful Planned City States, and Worship as they Please; while the Mormons will be Free to Build their own Beautiful Planned City States, and Worship as they Please; while the Catholics, Hindus, Buddhists, and all other Groups of People will be Free to Build their own Beautiful Planned City States, and to Worship as they Please.

03-20 [_] Well, can you Think of any other Way to make all of them Happy with themselves, while at the same Time they can Prove whose Way of Living is the Best: because of having Total Freedom to Choose HOW they Want to Live? For Example, if they have Zero Crimes among them, Zero Divorces, Zero Poverty, Zero Debts, Zero Slavery, Zero Sicknesses, Zero Diseases, and so on, we will Know that they are on the Riit Path of Life. For Example, when Demon-ocracy came to Russia, along with Capitalism, during the 1990's, the Crime Rate INCREASED by 7000%! Therefore, it seems that Communism was a much Better Plan for them, in spite of its Shortcomings. Indeed, there were many Unhappy Poor People among those Communists: beCAUSE they Failed to Build Properly Planned City States for them to Live in, which Naturally Require Home Gardens for each Family, which Moses Understood, more than 4,500 Years Ago, and thus Wrote about the Great Year of JUBILEE in *Leviticus 25,* which you should take the Time to Study for yourself: beCause it is now Time for **"The END of CONFUSION!" (The Great CELEBRATION of the Magnificent Wedding of the Most Humble Honest Nations, and the Grand Year of JUBILEE!) By The Worldwide People's Revolution!®** Book 050.

— Chapter 04 —

A Guaranteed Solution for the Great False Economy!

04-01 [_] If you have Listened to and Watched the Evening Snooze Reports on TV, you have no doubt Noticed that the American Economy is Based on the Stock Market, which Rises and Falls on a Daily Basis, which can also CRASH, even as it did during the 1929—1942 Great Depression Days; but, only in America, France, Great Britain, Germany, Italy, Spain, other Capitalist Nations, which were Dependent on the Production and Sales of TRASH, Junkyard Cars, and all such VAIN Things, which are not Needed for True Prosperity, nor for True Riches, which Begin with Fresh Clean Air, Pure Living Water, Wholesome Natural Foods, Natural Clothing, Secure Water Supplies, Secure Bomb-proof Terrorist-proof Fireproof Mouse-proof Termite-proof Rot-proof Paint-proof Hail-proof Tornado-proof Flood-proof Hurricane-proof Earthquake-proof Insurance-proof Rent-proof Loan-proof Interest-proof Tax-proof Houses, Home-craft Workshops, and Beautiful Sales Shops! Yes, a Good Economy is Based on those Basic Necessities of Life, including Well-made TOOLS to Work with, which can now be Produced in Factories that are already Set Up for Producing those Tools, which can make Special Tools for Harvesting the Mountains of Rocks that will be Necessary for Constructing those **"GLORIOUS Swanky Hotels Castles and Fortresses!" (Beautiful Planned City States for WISE Intelligent Well-Educated People with Common Sense and Good Understanding!) By The Worldwide People's Revolution!®** Book 019.

04-02 [_] O Unelected King, will that not Cause an Environmental DISASTER? Would you Tear Down all of the Mountains of Rocks in this World of Wonders, just to Build those **"Beautiful Swanky PALACES!" (A New Concept in Living Habits — Swanky Palaces for Poor People!)**, Book 066? Do you not know that a Swanky Stone Dome Home Complex would Require no less than 1,000 Cubic Meters of Concrete, just to Cover the 20+ Rooms in each Complex with THICK Concrete Domes, like the Pantheon in Rome? Therefore, the Production of so much CEMENT would Prove to be an Environmental DISASTER!

04-03 [_] Well, my Friend, that all Depends on HOW that Cement is Made and Used, which should be Made FRESH on a Daily Basis: beCause Fresh Cement is 7 Times as Strong as Old Cement. Therefore, it should be Made and Used during the same Day, even as the Ancient Romans did when they Constructed the Pantheon, which has Endured for no less than 1,800 Years, and is still Looking Good! Therefore, it is up to us to figure out HOW to Make that Cement Properly, and to Use it Wisely to Cover those Solid Stone Walls on those BILLIONS of Stone Domes, which Walls could also be made with Concrete, except that it Requires a LOT of Energy to Produce Gravel from Crushed Rocks, which also makes Stronger Concrete: beCause of the Sharp Edges on the Pieces of Gravel. Nevertheless, for most Concrete Walls, any Natural Gravel could be used with Rough Clean Rocks: beCause those Walls must be at least 10 feet THICK within all Houses, just to Stabilize the Temperatures within the Houses, whereby no Energy will be Wasted on Heating nor Cooling any such Houses, which will also Require ICE Houses, Walk-in Coolers, Freezers, Pantries, Spacious Kitchen Domes, and Living Room Domes that are at least 24 feet in Diameter, being Connected with Spacious Bedroom Domes by Tunnels, which are at least 4 feet Wide and 12 feet High, having Double Doors that are at least 3 feet Wide and 8 feet Tall, just to Accommodate Wheelchairs and very Tall FAT People, even though it is Hoped that most People will be Satisfied to be Free of all such Ugly Fat and Unnecessary Blubber, whereby they might Feel like Running with the Innocent Deers and Wild Mountain Goats.

04-04 [_] O Elected King, would such a Stone Dome Home Complex not Cost a BILLION Dollars?

04-05 [_] Well, if you had to Personally Buy the Materials and Labor, it might Cost a Million Dollars; but, I Propose that we, the People, simply Claim our own Mountains of Rocks, Sand, Gravel, Water, Tools, Forms, Heavy Equipment, and whatever we Need for Constructing those Fortresses, and thus Bypass those Greedy Edomite Bankers, which will Greatly LOWER the Costs, whereby a Cubic Meter of Concrete might Cost all of 10$, instead of 140$, or more, as it now does. After all, the Rocks, Sand, Gravel and Cement will be Managed by **"The Swanky Associations of Working Soldiers!" (A Fascinating Collection of Various Kinds of Voluntary Working Soldiers!) By The Worldwide People's Revolution!®** Book 018. Indeed, they will Manage the Production of whatever is Needed for True Prosperity for EVERYONE, Worldwide — that is, if most People are Interested in becoming Moderately RICH, and without Telling any Lies, nor Selling any Trash! But, as of now, Unbelief is the Main Obstacle in the Way of True Progress. In Fact, as long as most People are Contented to be SLAVES of Various Kinds, there is not much that can be Said nor Done to Help them: beCause they are like the Ignorant People during the Great Depression of the 1930's, who were never told that the Germans soon got Out of the Great Depression by 1933: beCause of Electing a True Leader, whereby the German Economy became the Best Economy in the whole World, and in all of History, which had Zero Unemployment, and was even Importing Workers by 1936: because they had too much Work to do, and for the Best Wages in the World, which would be the Exact same Case for us, if we were to get to Work on the Construction of those **"GLORIOUS Swanky Hotels Castles and Fortresses!"**

04-06 [_] O Elected King, are you saying that we could keep ourselves Busy for the next thousand Years, just by Building Swanky Fortresses? Would a lot of People not become Unemployed, just for not Driving any Cars? Would that not Upset the entire Economy? §§‡

04-07 [_] Well, when you are Living in a Beautiful Swanky PALACE, and have lots of Good Foods and Drinks at the Royal Swanky Buffet, what do you Care about Unemployment? Indeed, you can Play your Violin, and Laugh at the Great False Economy: because your Belly is Full, and your Palace is Finished. Therefore, with just 3 to 4 Hours of Work per Day — Growing, Harvesting, Preparing and Preserving Foods and Drinks — you can Live like a King or Queen in one of those **"Beautiful Swanky PALACES!" (A New Concept in Living Habits — Swanky Palaces for Poor People!) By The Worldwide People's Revolution!®** Book 066. Therefore, having a Boring Job will be the least of your Worries: beCause you can always Live and Work at Home: beCause the System is Set Up for Doing that, whereas now we are Dependent on those Limited JOBS, or Minimum Wage Jobs, or even BAD Jobs! For Example, how would you like to be the Unhealthy and Unhappy Son of Capitalism, whose Wonderful All-American Job is Gathering Live Chickens inside of a HUGE Stinking Chicken House with some 30,000 Chickens fluttering about, stirring up the Dust, making a thick Cloud of Unbearable DUST, whereby you could get Asthma within a Month or so? Moreover, you would have to Bend Over for 8 Hours, every Day, just to do that Hateful Job with Poor Jobe and Nigger Jim, who would soon have Boils all over their Bodies from the Bad Foods that they would be Forced to Eat: beCause they could never Afford Good Foods nor Natural Drinks — such as Fresh Coconut Water with some Lime Juice, as Opposed to Cokes and Imitation Fruit-flavored Drinks made of Highly-Sugared Recycled Sewage Water with a List of Forbidden Chemicals, Preservatives, and Poisons. ‡

04-08 [_] So, O Elected King, are you saying that no one would have to Gather Up those Frightened Chickens in any Stinking Dusty Chicken Houses, if you were in Charge of Things around here?

04-09 [_] Well, when People have an *Unlimited* Amount of Money to Work with, they can Afford to Build Proper Chicken Houses for Chickens that spend most of the Day Scratching around for Bugs and

Worms in Open Fields, whereby their Flesh is much Tastier than those Capitalist Factory Chickens. Moreover, when it comes Time to Gather them up, they can be Coaxed into a Clean House that is Designed for Catching them and Caging them without much Assistance at all, whereby that normally Hateful Job is Eliminated — that is, if anyone is still Interested in Eating any Chickens during those Days, after Discovering what a Holy Man Looks like, who has been Living on mostly Sweet Juicy Fruits, who can Run all Day and not be Weary, who can Walk all Night and not Faint. {See: **"HOW to Become a HOLY Man!" (40 Good Reasons WHY People Should FAST and PRAY!) By The Worldwide People's Revolution!®**, Book 045, which is a Companion Book of: **"The Proper RULES for FASTING!" (The Complete Instruction Manual for True Repentance!)**, Book 046, which is a Requirement for Entering into the Holy Kingdom of All that is GOOD.}

04-10 [_] O Elected King, I Think that I am Beginning to Visualize what is Required for True Prosperity, and it is Certainly NOT more of those Stinking Noisy Polluting Vehicles on Endless Highways to Hell. Indeed, we can all use Elevators, Escalators and Electric Trains when we need to Travel. Otherwise, we can simply Walk to Work in our own All-Mineral Organic Gardens, Vineyards, Orchards, Home-craft Workshops and Sales Shops, which will Greatly Enhance our Standard of Living: beCause of Saving hundreds of Trillions of Dollars on those Stinking Noisy Polluting Vehicles during the next 1,000 Years. Moreover, many People will no doubt Choose to Ride Bicycles and Quadrupeds around those Fortresses, just to See some of the Luscious Gardens in those Great Terraces, which will be Stone Walls no less than 40 feet Tall, and as much as 200 feet Tall; and also Smell the Fragrant Flowers as they Ride by. At least that is what I would do. Indeed, I would Enjoy the Fantastic 5-dimentional Views of Looking Down, Out, Across, Around, and Up at the other Terraces on the other Side of my Swanky Palace, facing what some People might Rightly Call, "The House of the Gods!" {Please Check the above Box with an X, if you Agree. Otherwise, use the Space below to Explain why you Disagree; and be Ready to Defend yourself with Reason and Logic in a Courtroom, or else be put to Open Shame for your Unbelief, O Lady Doubtfulness!}

— Chapter 05 —

A Guaranteed Solution for Extreme Poverty

05-01 [_] Now, it may not be of any Great Interest to you that no less than 2 Billion People Suffer with Extreme Poverty in this World of Woes; but, if you were one of those Extremely Poor People, it might be of some Interest to you to Learn that there is no Good Reason for any Poverty at all, much less for any Extreme Poverty. For Example, how would you like to Live on the Street, without any House, without any Shower, without any Bed, without any Kitchen, without any Entertainment, without any Cold Water during a very Hot Day, and without anyone to Care for you at 70 Years of Age? Well, for many People in this World of Woes, that is the Case, except for the Age Factor: because very few of those Kind of People ever Live to be 70 Years Old. But, what can be Done about it? HOW can that Problem be Solved, seeing that most of those Extremely Poor People are all Scattered Out around the World, many of whom are Refugees in Foreign Countries. Yes, you could become the next Victim of Capitalism, and find yourself in a Homeless Jobless Situation on the Street, and perhaps Discover a Vacant Spot under a Freeway Bridge to make your Bed on a Used Piece of Dirty Carpet, which Smells like Dog Piss, or something Worse, without a Pillow to lay your Head on, whereby you might Decide that it is Time for a Regime Change in Washington, District of Criminals; but, behold, no one will Listen to your Complaints: beCause they will say that you should have taken Better Care of yourself when you were Young, and also Saved up some Money for Hard Times, without Realizing that it is Possible to go from Riches to Rags within a Week or less: beCause of Uncontrollable Circumstances, such as it was during the Great Depression of the 1930's, when those Friendly Bankers Collected millions of Houses, Cars, Furniture, and Properties: beCause their "Clients and Debtors" could not make their Payments. Yes, they Lost their JOBS. However, such would have been Impossible, if all of those People had been Living within those **"GLORIOUS Swanky Hotels Castles and Fortresses,"** which are Designed for Eternal Employment, whereby it is Impossible for anyone to Lose his Job at Home: beCause his Garden will always Require his Attention, just to Feed himself: beCause it is his SECURITY and Survival Plan in a Nutshell, you might say. Yes, his Pantry will also be Full of Canned Foods, just in Case the Garden might Fail for Unexpected Reasons — such as Freezing Weather in July in Wisconsin, or an Invasion of Locusts from North Dakota, which can Blacken the Sky with their Great Multitudes. Therefore, it is Wise to have a Backup Plan, just in Case Nature gets VIOLENT! ‡

05-02 [_] O Unelected King, would you be ORDERING People to Preserve their Foods, and have at least a 7-year Supply of Groceries in their Houses? Are you not Aware that People must have FRESH Foods to Eat: beCause Canned Foods are not Totally Satisfying for a Lack of Enzymes?

05-03 [_] Yes, I am most Aware of all such Things, including those 7-year Droughts that can come along, which is WHY that I Strongly Suggest that everyone should have at least a Million Gallons of Fresh Pure Living Water in their Ceramic-tiled Cisterns for each Family, even though it might Require 10,000,000 Gallons of Water to keep the Fruit Trees Alive and Growing: beCause it Requires at least one Gallon of Water to Produce just one Fruit, or one Nut — such as an Almond. Therefore, all Swanky Fortresses must be Built Up on a Foundation of Large CISTERNS, in Great TERRACES, whereby Water can be Pumped from Lower Cisterns to Higher Cisterns: beCause of taking Advantage of FREE WIND POWER, which I have already Explained in other Inspired and Fascinating Books. {See www.Amazon.com for: **"UNLIMITED ENERJEE 99 Percent Pollutions Free!" (HOW to Obtain FREE ElecTrickery, Worldwide!) By The Worldwide People's Revolution!®** Book 029.}

05-04 [_] O Elected King, it might be Better Explained in your other Inspired Book, called: **"The Gospel According to our Elected King!" (The Good News from the Most Modern Perspective!) By The Worldwide People's Revolution!®** Book 077.

05-05 [_] Well, as I said, I have Explained it in several Inspired Books: beCause some People are more Interested in one Subject, than in another Subject. For Example, one Person might be Greatly Interested in, **"Does a Good Soldier have to be a MURDERER?" (Seven Great Swanky Armies of Voluntary Working Soldiers!)**, Book 027, while another Person might be more Interested in **"Are you a Jobless Graduate of the SKQL uv FQLZ?" (HOW to Get a GOUD EJUKAASHUN without Robbing the Bank!) By The Worldwide People's Revolution!®** Book 020. Indeed, an Environmentalist would just Naturally be more Interested in **"The Environmentalists' Paradise!" (HOW almost Everyone could be Living in a Beautiful Manmade Paradise!)** Book 035; but, a Follower of the Political Rabbits, would likely be more Interested in **"Mark Twain Races for the PRESIDENCY!" (The 2020 Presidential Candidates Desperately Need Some STRONG Undefeatable COMPETITION!) By The Worldwide People's Revolution!®** Book 033. However, all of those People Need to Learn what I have to Say about many Important Subjects, which, if all put Together within one Big Bible, would be too Heavy for some of them to Pack to Church Services, which is WHY you can find those Inspired Books in Separate Volumes — such as: **"The New MAGNIFIED Version of The Book of MOORMUN!" (The Story of the White and Dark Indians in the Americas!) By The Worldwide People's Revolution!®** Book 040, Volumes 1 and 2, which contain about 1,000 Pages, together.

05-06 [_] O Elected King of the Birds, I am Wondering just WHY many of your Books are Listed on Amazon.com as being Authored by **Master Mark Revolutionary Twain, Junior,** instead of by **The Worldwide People's Revolution!®?**

05-07 [_] Well, that is beCause I wrote no less than 50 Books by that Pen Name, after which Amazon informed me that it was not an Acceptable Pen Name: beCause it was supposedly Misleading to their Customers, who might get Mark Twain JUNIOR confused with Mark Twain, who was America's Greatest Author during the late 1800's and early 1900's. Therefore, Amazon asked me to come up with a New Pen Name that was Acceptable to them, and also Change all of the Books to read appropriately; but, after I got almost all of the Books Updated to **The Worldwide People's Revolution,** within the next 8 Months, they Changed their Minds about it all, and Decided that I could not Update my Old Books; but, that I must come up with New Titles and New ISBN Numbers for New Books, whereby my 8+ Months of Work was Wasted. To be Fair about it, they should have Informed me with the very First Published Book, that the Pen Name of Master Mark Revolutionary Twain, Junior, was not Acceptable, rather than wait for me to Publish 50 Books, and then Inform me with several Apologies for my Inconveniences. So, as of this Date, the Original Pen Name is still Valid, even though I Prefer the New Pen Name of **The Worldwide People's Revolution!®**: beCause a Worldwide Revolution will be Required to Fix our Massive Problems — such as Radical Climate Changes. So, you might say that it is somewhat Like Dealing with the BureauRats in Washington, who cannot quite make up their Minds about those Pen Names, which I can Fully Understand: beCause **The Worldwide People's Revolution!®** is a Great Threat to the Evil Empires: beCause of **"The Swanky Sword of Divine Truths!" (The Most Powerful Weapon in the Whole Universe!)**, Book 067, which Threatens to put all Capitalists, Communists, and Socialists Totally OUT of Business! — that is, EXCEPT for www.Amazon.com, which stands to Gain several Billions of Dollars from the Sales of my Inspired Books! Indeed, they freely Confess that my Inspired Books are by Far the Best Books on the Market, and even much Better than those of Master Twain: beCause I am the Reincarnation of King Solomon, himself! Indeed, that is easy to Prove to yourself, if you just Study: **"Thu Nq MAGNUFIID Verzhun uv Thu PROVERBZ uv KING SOLUMUN in Plaan Ingglish!" (The Understandable Version of**

the Famous Proverbs of King Solomon in Plain English!) By Master Mark Revolutionary Twain, Junior! Book 028. In Fact, I am also the Reincarnation of Mark Twain, himself, which can be Proven by Carefully Reading those first 50 Books, which have a lot of Subtle Mark Twain-type Humor in them by Mean of Double Sarcasms, which are Identified by 2 Section Symbols (§§).

05-08 [ ] O Crazy King, if you are the Reincarnation of Mark Twain, that would Mean that Mark Twain was also the Reincarnation of King Solomon, if you were also King Solomon. However, I venture to say that you were neither Person, even though there is a Slight Chance that you are Possessed by Several Different SPIRITS, including that of King Solomon and Mark Twain, who had Strange Spirits within them, who were both Wise in their own Ways; but, not nearly as Wise as yourself, whereby you have Changed the Minds of even your Enemies, who are now Promoting you and your Crazy Ideas: beCause they are Flip-floppers, you might say, who are also just as likely to Turn Against you again, if you do not Play your Cards Correctly: beCause they are Possession Worshipers of the Worst Kind, at Heart. Therefore, if you Fail to make all of them Moderately RICH, they will Turn Against you, without even Considering the FACT that it will be their own Faults, if they Fail to make themselves Moderately Rich: beCause of their Unbelief and Disobedience. After all, the Swanky Fortress System will not Work Perfectly Correctly without the United Effort of ALL Intelligent Peoples in the Whole World, and Especially those of all Major Western Nations, including **"The Divided States of United Lies!" (The so-called "United States of North America" in Disguise!)**, Book 058, which has many Useful Tools that will be Required by **"The New RIGHTEOUS One-World Government!" (HOW to Establish a Righteous One-World Government without Going to WAR!) By The Worldwide People's Revolution!®** Book 056.

05-09 [ ] Well, my Friend, if the United States of America does not get Onto our Revolutionary Bandwagon, as the saying goes, they will Greatly Regret it: beCause they will Reap what they have Sown, which Means that the Remaining Nations of the World will put Economic Sanctions on them, and Refuse to Buy any of their TRASH, whereby they will go Out of Business, and thus become the Laughing Stock of the Whole World, which is a Just Punishment for such Hardhearted Rebels, who will be Calling me Dirty Names — such as a Communist: beCause I Propose having all Natural Resources in the World in COMMON among all Peoples, whereby the Mountains of Rocks can be Shared with whomever Needs some of them. For Example, there is an Extremely Poor Nation not very far from our Coast, called Haiti, which could use several Shiploads of Cut and Polished Stones, just to Build their own **"Beautiful Swanky PALACES!" (A New Concept in Living Habits — Swanky Palaces for Poor People!)**, Book 066, which will be a Small Sacrifice for Americans, who have tens of thousands of Mountains of Rocks, who should Love their Naaberz just as much as they Love themselves, and Do unto others as they would have other People Do for them, if they were so Poor and Miserable. In Fact, I Dare say that the Haitians would be Happy to Voluntarily Build their own **"GLORIOUS Swanky Hotels Castles and Fortresses,"** if they were given a Chance to Do so; but, now they are Totally Restricted by their Extreme Poverty, being Deprived of those Mountains of Rocks to Work with. Likewise, I Dare say that Africans would be Happy to Trade Shiploads of Sand for some Cut and Polished Stones for Building their own Swanky Fortresses, and would not even Miss those Shiploads of Sand: beCause the Sahara Desert has enough Sand to Supply the entire World with Sand for making Concrete and Glass. Likewise, I Dare say that the People of Brazil would not Object to Sharing the Water of the Amazon River with whomever Needs it: because they are not Greedy Selfish Capitalists, like Americans, who would Want to be Selling that Water for a Good Price, just to Help Pay Off their National Debts to those Edomite Bankers, who are already Excessively RICH, who should just FORGIVE all Debts, even as Moses Ordered them to, and thus Celebrate the Great Year of JUBILEE! But, of course, that would Require some Humiliation on their Part, along with some Honesty. After all, those Edomites have been Robbing the Nations for thousands of Years! Yes, they have Built Great Mansions for themselves, while Billions of Poor People have been Starving to Death! Yes, they are Like the Rich Man and Lazarus in the Parable of Jesus Christ, which you can read about in Chapter 16 of: **"The New MAGNIFIED Version of The GOOD NEWS According to Saint LUKE!" (The Magnified Gospel of Luke in Plain English!)**, Book 061. However, you might say that you could never Afford to Buy all such Books, and especially if they are Hand-carved Leather-bound Books. Well, it is only beCause of Capitalism that you could not Afford them: because, if I were the Elected King of **"The New RIGHTEOUS One-World Government,"** everyone in the World could Afford them: because they could Discover them within Swanky Truth-braries within Beautiful Swanky Castles, and in all of those **"Beautiful Swanky PALACES!" (A New Concept in Living Habits — Swanky Palaces for Poor People!) By The Worldwide People's Revolution!®** Book 066. In Fact, you could Discover all of those Books for FREE on the Internet, and thus Fill your Soul with the Satisfying Fruits of Spiritual Truths. However, Extremely Poor People cannot even Afford to Buy Computers, much less the Monthly Payments for being Connected to the Internet, which should be Free of all Charges, even as Air, Water and Land should be. But, the Edomites have figured out how to Capitalize on the Internet, and thus rake in Billions of Dollars for doing almost nothing! Meanwhile, Multitudes of Ignorant People are going on Suffering for no Good Reasons. After all, the Internet could be the Best Teaching Method in the World, instead of the Cesspool of Lusts, and Advertisements for TRASH   for   Sale.

05-10 [_] O Elected King, if you do Away with all Poor People, WHO will be our SLAVES? Indeed, WHO will Butcher our Livestock, Mop our Floors, Wash our Windows, Mow our Lawns, Gather our Tomatoes, Trim our Hedges, and Sew our Clothes Together for us? Do you not Realize that most Americans would be Extremely Poor People without that Slave Labor, which is mostly done by Poor Mexicans, Indians, Koreans, and other Colored People with Slanted Eyes? For Example, a Poor Mexican Slave might get a Penny a Pound for Picking Tomatoes, and thus Pick 4,000 Pounds of Tomatoes for only 40 Dollars per Day, when he should be getting at least 5 Cents per Pound, whereby he might Earn 200$ per Day for such Extremely Difficult Work during the Heat of the Day in some Hot Humid Sweaty Swamp like Florida, which would raise the Price of Tomatoes by just 4 Cents per Pound; but, those Richer Mexicans would have more Money to Spend on Newer Cars, Vans, and Buses, which would also raise the entire Economy, and give more Work to Automobile Manufacturers, Gas Companies, and all Kinds of Service People, who would in turn have more Money to Spend on the Vain Things that they might Want to Buy, which would just Naturally make the Rich People Richer, which should also make all of them Happier. However, their Goal is to Maintain the Slavery Status of Millions of Poor Mexicans, to whom they can Loan Money, and thus Collect Interest or Usury on those Pay-day Loans, whereby they can make Interest Slaves of them, and thus take Advantage of them, Forever! Yes, that is the Way of Capitalism, which Works very Well for the 1% of the Population, who already   have   far   too   much   Money.   ‡

— Chapter 06 —

A Guaranteed Solution for Getting Free Services!

06-01 [_] First of all, we must all Confess that we Need some "Free" Services — such as Cleaning Houses, Cleaning Clothes, making Natural Fruit Juice Drinks, providing Wholesome Natural Foods to Eat, providing Transportation, Communications, Weedless Gardens, Healthy Productive Fruit and Nut Trees, as well as Clean Swimming Pools, Clean Subway Tunnels, Clean Public Restrooms, and Free Medical Care; but, just HOW to make it all FAIR and Square is the Great Question? Is anyone in his or her Riit Miind going to Rely on someone else to Do his or her House Cleaning, Gardening, and whatever? After all, if you Want something Done Correctly, you have to Do it yourself! For Example, if you were about to Sneeze, and you were making a Salad at a Royal Swanky Buffet, would you Sneeze into your Hand, into your Shirt Sleeve, or Bend Over and Sneeze on the Floor, with the Hope that no Germs were Wafted about in the Air?

06-02 [_] O Elected King, I would Choose to Live in a Swanky Fortress that had all Healthy People, whereby no one would be Sneezing on anything, much less Sneezing onto the Salad Bar.

06-03 [_] O Elected King, I would Sneeze into my Handkerchief, and then put it back into my Pocket. After all, some Dust or Black Pepper might get into my Nose, and thus Cause me to Sneeze.

06-04 [_] O Elected King, if I were making my own Salads, I would not have to Worry about where I might be Sneezing: beCause I would be Eating my own Salads, and Cleaning my own House, and Doing my own Service Jobs, which would be the most Efficient Way to get it all Done Correctly, and without making anyone into my SLAVE.

06-05 [_] Well, suppose you had 5 Voluntary SERVANTS, who Agreed to Obey all of your Commands, and Do whatever you might Ask, would that Offend you? For Example, suppose **"The Swanky Association of House Cleaners"** came around once per Week to Clean your House, for Free — seeing that it would not Actually be YOUR House: beCause of it Belonging to **"The New RIGHTEOUS One-World Government"**: beCause of Costing a few Million Dollars for a Proper and Spacious House with Polished Marble Walls and Polished Granite Floors — would you Object to their Services, who would use nothing but Pure Water to Wash the Windows, seeing that there would be no Grease in the Air to Contaminate those Windows nor Polished Marble Walls?

06-06 [_] Well, O King, I suppose that I would not Object to that Plan, if they did not Steal my Precious Things — such as my Rolex Watch, Diamond Rings, or Laptop Computer. Indeed, if they did a Good Job of it, while Under my Snoopervision, I suppose that it would be Acceptable to me; but, if the House was full of LIE-sol Stink, I would not Like it at all.

06-07 [_] Well, my Friend, you will only have to Check the above Box with an X, in order to Get your Desires, whereby the Computers can Place your Adopted Nickname with other Like-minded People, who also Hate Chemical STINKS. And, as for those Germs that they are Supposedly Killing with LIE-sol, you might Remind them that a Filthy Human Being is a Walking Germ Factory, who could Pollute an entire City, if he or she did not Do some Personal House Cleaning of his or her own Body and Mind. Therefore, if you Want to Live with Holy People, you should Check the above Box with an X.

06-08 [_] O Elected King, I would not Object if **"The Swanky Association of Professional Gardeners"** did ALL of my Gardening, and all of the Gardening within our entire Planned City State: beCause that would make it much more Beautiful, than if each Resident did his or her own Gardening without any Overall Plans. Indeed, with someone in Charge of the Gardening, everyone might be Able to EAT, and also Eat GOOD Foods; but, with no one in Charge, they might all Starve to Death: beCause very few People would Know HOW to Do their Gardening by **"The LUSCIOUS All-Mineral Organic Method of Gardening!" (HOW to Grow DELICIOUS Satisfying Foods for Potential Kingz and Kweenz in Swanky PALACES!)**, Book 021. In Fact, before anyone does any Gardening, they should Study: **"Orgimmick Gardening at its Best!" (HOW to Grow Delicious Satisfying Foods without a 10-million-dollar Investment!) By The Worldwide People's Revolution!®**, Book 079, which contains many Photographs with Enlightening Explanations.

06-09 [_] Well, my Friend, you should be Wise and Join **"The Swanky Associations of Working Soldiers,"** who will get everything Well-Organized, and also do their Best to become Professional at whatever they Do, as if they were Doing it for GOD, and not for some Drunkards on MADison Avenue. In other Words, they will Need GOOD Nolijuboul Masters and Humble Obedient SERVANTS — all of whom will get to Live in those **"Beautiful Swanky PALACES!" (A New Concept in Living Habits — Swanky Palaces for Poor People!) By The Worldwide People's Revolution!®** Book 066. After all, no Master could Accomplish anything without Obedient Servants, nor could any Servants Accomplish any Good Things — such as the Building of those Swanky Palaces — without some Honest Obedient Masters, who are those Humble Men who Think and Act like Jesus Christ, who would be the First to Confess that **"A Sound Argument for Masters and Servants!" (WHY Everyone Needs a Good Master, and every Master Needs Good Obedient Servants!)**, Book 008, is an Eternal Classic Document that everyone should Study with an Open Mind: beCause X-amount of People were Born to be Masters, and X-amount were Born to be their Servants, who can all be Discovered when everyone Fills Out and Files on the Internet **"The Complete SURVEYS of our VALUES!" (SURVEYS of Religious Spiritual Political Governmental Sexual Social Moral Economic Business Labor Habitual and Miscellaneous VALUES!) By The Worldwide People's Revolution!®** Book 059.

06-10 [_] O Elected King, I must Confess that your Overall Vision of what is Required for True Prosperity is Miles ABOVE the Heads of most People, who cannot Visualize what is Required, who cannot Imagine Living like Royalties in those **"Beautiful Swanky PALACES,"** beCause of being Blinded by their PRIDE, Ignorance, Unbelief, Stupidity, and Lusts for Vain Things that no one Needs — such as those Stinking Noisy Polluting Vehicles, which Jesus Christ Lived Happily without. Indeed, if all such Vehicles were a Requirement for True Prosperity, it would be saying that no one Prospered until the Industrial Revolution, which is a Totally False Misconception: beCause almost all of the Palaces in the World were Built during Old Times, long before that Industrial Revolution. However, most of them were Built by Slave Labor, you might say, which can now be done by MACHINES, which will never Complain about the Low Wages. Therefore, it is now Possible and most Practical for everyone in the World to be Living in a Beautiful Swanky Palace.

— Chapter 07 —

A Guaranteed Solution for Insurance-proof Houses

07-01 [ ] You might have Heard about those Poor People who did not have Flood Insurance on their Houses, who got Flooded Out by Unexpected Rains, who had no Idea that the Water could get so HIGH: beCause of Climate Changes? Well, how about those Millions of Extremely Poor People in Wretched Places like Bangladesh, Pakistan, India, the Philippines, and many Low-lying Islands, who could never Afford any Kind of Insurance, who are at the Mercy of Mother Nature, who often has no Heart at all: beCause Satan is in Charge of the Wind and Rain, you might say? (See *the Book of Job.*)

07-02 [ ] O Selected King of the Mountains, it was their Choice to Live in all such Places, when they could have Chosen to Live in the Eastern Hills of Kentucky, in Stilt Houses, which are Designed for High Water Levels, which Houses are built on the Hillsides, and not in the Narrow Valleys, where their Gardens are, which often get Flooded with Water, which Washes their Gardens Away: beCause they are too Poor to Afford any Stone Terraced Walls on those Hillsides, which are mostly Shale Rocks, which are no Good for Building anything: beCause the Rocks are Crumbly. Otherwise, they could have Chosen to Live in the Low Lands of Netherlands, or on the Great Plains, along the Mississippi River, where People Suffer with Billions of Dollars-worth of Flood Damages each Year: beCause of Destroying the Tall Grasses on the Great Plains, which used to have Mats of Roots 2 feet deep, which Absorbed any sudden Rains, and then slowly Released the Water into Streams and Rivers, even as it was before the Capitalists arrived with their Hateful Plows, and also Murdered the Buffaloes, which Planted the Seeds of those Tall Grasses, which was a Perfect Ecosystem, until Capitalism Destroyed it. So, I would say that those People are getting the Unjust Rewards of the Ignorant Fools who Preceded them with their Greed — that is, if they are not Recycled Sinners, who were Reincarnated into the Bodies of the People who are now Living there, who are getting their Just Rewards for their Past Sins. Indeed, how else could God Teach to them all such Good Lessons, if they were not Born Again on the same Land that they Ruined in their Previous Lives? But, as for those Poor People in Bangladesh, that is a Case of Total Stupidity: beCause there are Huge Mountains of ROCKS right next-door to them in India, which could be used for Building TALL Stone Walls around their Swanky Fortresses, which would be Designed for Living, Surviving, and Thriving, even if it Rained 10 feet of Water during just one Day: beCause the Gardens would be Designed to Drain the Water into Huge Cisterns under them, which would be kept Empty, just for that Purpose, while the Excess Water would be Pumped through large Pipes into Large Cisterns in Desert Fortresses, where it would be Used Wisely to Water their Gardens, which would Require some United Effort by all of those People, as well as the Cooperation of **"The New RIGHTEOUS One-World Government!" (HOW to Establish a Righteous One-World Government without Going to WAR!) By The Worldwide People's Revolution!® Book 056. §§**

07-03 [ ] Well, my Friend, you seem to have some of your Wires Crossed, as the saying goes, whereby many People might get Confused by your Disorganized and Contradictory Words. However, you do make several Good Points to Remember, even though there is not much of a Connection with Insurance-proof Houses, which would also have to be Fireproof, Termite-proof, Rot-proof, Paint-proof, Hail-proof, Tornado-proof, Hurricane-proof, Flood-proof, Earthquake-proof, Volcano-proof, Mudslide-proof, Avalanche-proof, Mountain-slide-proof, Bomb-proof, Invasion-proof, Illegal-Immigration-proof, Criminal-proof, Virus-proof, Snake-proof, Rat-proof, Mouse-proof, Raccoon-proof, Opossum-proof, Armadillo-proof, Groundhog-proof, Rabbit-proof, Deer-proof, Bear-proof, Lion-proof, Tiger-proof, Squirrel-proof, Weasel-proof, Ferret-proof, Skunk-proof, Fox-proof, Coyote-proof, Wolf-proof, Jackal-proof, Wild-dog-proof, and so on: beCause all Houses must be SECURE, Safe Places to Live, which is Possible with the Correct DESIGNS, beginning with those TALL Stone Walls that Surround the Fortresses, which make it Possible to have FREE Electricity: beCause of Catching the Wind in Half-dome Stone Funnels, which Funnel the Wind into Wind Generators all around the Fortress Walls, which must be at the Correct Angles, like the following very Rough Drawings of an End View shows.

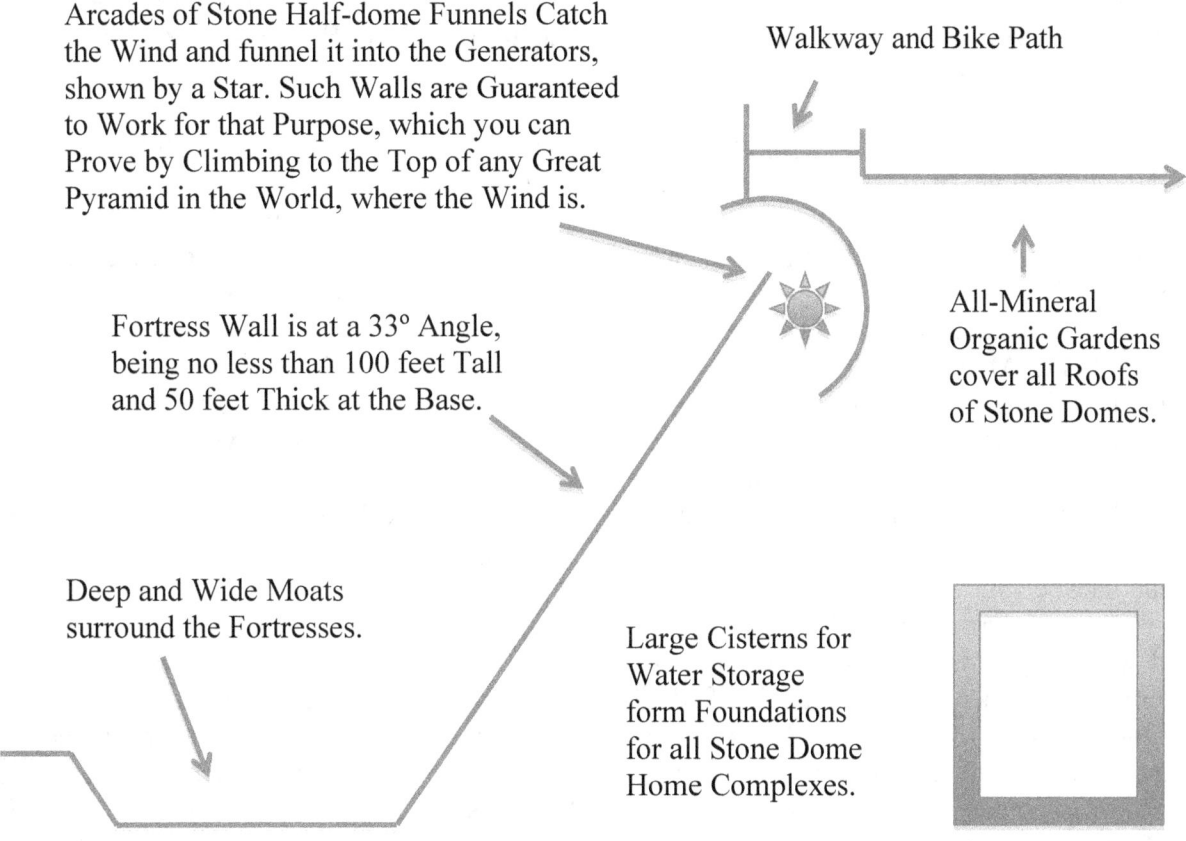

Arcades of Stone Half-dome Funnels Catch the Wind and funnel it into the Generators, shown by a Star. Such Walls are Guaranteed to Work for that Purpose, which you can Prove by Climbing to the Top of any Great Pyramid in the World, where the Wind is.

Walkway and Bike Path

Fortress Wall is at a 33° Angle, being no less than 100 feet Tall and 50 feet Thick at the Base.

All-Mineral Organic Gardens cover all Roofs of Stone Domes.

Deep and Wide Moats surround the Fortresses.

Large Cisterns for Water Storage form Foundations for all Stone Dome Home Complexes.

07-04 [_] O Elected King of the Master Architects, why did we not Think of that Great Idea some 200+ Years Ago? After all, I have never known the Wind to not be Blowing at the Tops of those Great Pyramids. Therefore, if the Half-dome Stone Funnels are Surrounding the Fortresses at the Tops of the Stone Walls on all Terraces, the Inhabitants are Guaranteed FREE Electricity: beCause the Wind is always Blowing from some Direction against such Walls. But, even if for some Strange Reason it is not Blowing, the Water in the Upper Cisterns can be used to Generate Electricity by Hydro-electric Generators: beCause there are Upper Cisterns and Lower Cisterns within all Great Terraces. Indeed, the Cisterns form the Foundations for all of those Terraces, which Cisterns have Tunnels between Rows of them, which are used for Elevators, Escalators, Water Pipes, Electric Conduit Pipes, Tombs, and Quiet Electric Subway Trains, which run at Various Speeds, and for Various Distances on One-Way Tracks, whereby there are no Accidents. Therefore, all Transportation, Wholesome Natural Foods, Natural Drinks, Clothing, Tools, and Communications are "FREE" to whomever Lives in such Beautiful Planned City States, in Exchange for only 4 Hours of Common Skilled Labor per Day, 6 Days per Week, or the Equivalent thereof. For Example, a Person may Work this Week for 8 Hours per Day, and have the next Week Off; or even Work for one whole Year, and have the next Year Off: beCause, if almost all People are Working in a Constructive and Positive Way, using the Correct Tools, the Work is Equally Distributed among the People, whereby only a few Hours of Work is Required per Workday.

Moreover, each Beautiful Planned City State will have the Right to Govern itself, according to its own Elected Laws and Flexible Rules; but, only after each Person has Filled Out and Filed his or her Complete SURVEYS of VALUES, whereby he or she can Discover other People of Like-mindedness, whereby they can all Live in PEACE with True Prosperity; or, otherwise, Prove themselves to be Crazy: beCause of having BAD Laws and Ridiculous Rules. However, it will not be long before some certain City State will Prove that their Laws and Rules are Correct, whereby they will have Great Prosperity, Perfect Peace, Cooperation, Harmony, LOVE, Trust, and all such Good Things. ‡ {See: **"The Complete SURVEYS of our VALUES!" (SURVEYS of Religious Spiritual Political Governmental Sexual Social Moral Economic Business Labor Habitual and Miscellaneous VALUES!) By The Worldwide People's Revolution!®** Book 059.}

07-05 [_] Well, my Friend, you are Beginning to See the Vision of it all. Indeed, each Beautiful Stone Dome Home Complex will be Designed for Good Comfortable Living, having Spacious Kitchens and Dining Rooms that are at least 20 feet in Diameter, being Connected by Barrel-vault Tunnels with Spacious Walk-in Coolers, Freezers, and Pantries, as well as Living Rooms that are at least 24 feet in Diameter, having Solid Stone Walls that are at least 10 feet THICK around all Rooms, whereby the Temperatures are Stabilized at 72° Fahrenheit, or 22.2° Celsius, except for the Workshops, which could be Cooler, being Attached to Ice Houses, which are also used Wisely for Sucking Out the Humidity from all such Stone Dome Home Complexes, which is made Possible by having the Houses in Great TERRACES, having an Ice House under each Stone Dome Home Complex, even if the Ice must be Imported from nearby Mountains in Special Stainless Steel Chutes. However, in most Northern and Southern Climates, which have Cold Seasons, the Ice can easily be Produced in the Upper Terraces, which will be Colder than the Lower Terraces, which will all be Designed for True Prosperity, whereby everyone can become Moderately RICH, and without Telling any Lies, nor Selling any Trash, Junk Foods, Addictive Drugs, Recycled Sewage Water that is Flavored with Imitation Fruit Juices, and Loaded with Sugar, which Causes Headaches and many other Physical Problems. Indeed, the Focus will be on the Production of Sweet Juicy FRUITS, which are the Life of Mankind, as Moses wrote in *Deuteronomy 20:19:* beCause the Perfect Foods for Mankind are the Sweet Juicy Fruits and Green Leaves on the Tree of Life, which we do not have Access to; but, the next Best Foods are found on TREES. For Example, who in this World does not LOVE those Sweet and Satisfying NUTS, which are now 20$ per Pound in their Shells!? Indeed, those Nuts should be FREE, being Provided by **"The Swanky Association of Professional Gardeners!"** — such as Pistachios, which can be made Extra Delicious by Treating them with Green Chili Peppers, even as the *Eagle Ranch* in New Mexico has Discovered, which used to Sell 5 Pounds for 100$, plus Postage and Handling, which will now be Produced FREE of all Charges by that Swanky Associations of Working Soldiers, who will also get to Live in their own **"Beautiful Swanky PALACES!" (A New Concept in Living Habits — Swanky Palaces for Poor People!) By The Worldwide People's Revolution!®** Book 066.

07-06 [_] O Elected King of the Whole World, are you saying that the Best of all Kinds of Foods will be Provided by **"The Swanky Associations of Working Soldiers!" (A Fascinating Collection of Various Kinds of Voluntary Working Soldiers!)**, Book 018, whereby everyone in the World will be Able to Eat all of the Green Chili Pistachios that they might Want at some Royal Buffet, FREE of any Charges, in Exchange for only 4 Hours of Common Skilled Labor per Day, or the Equivalent thereof?

07-07 [_] Yes, I am saying that the Days of Extreme Poverty are quickly coming to an END! After all, there are Machines that can do the Work of thousands or even Millions of People! For Example, an Electric Train can Haul a million Tons of Rocks down from the Mountains without Straining itself, while you would find it Extremely Difficult to Carry one Wheelbarrow full of such Rocks more than a Mile, downhill. Therefore, it is now Time to put those Mechanical Slaves to WORK for us, and STOP

Wasting Energy in those Gas-hog Vehicles: beCause they are not Needed for True Prosperity. But, those **"GLORIOUS Swanky Hotels Castles and Fortresses,"** are most Definitely Needed, just to Solve no less than 5,000 Problems, including the Lack of GOOD Wholesome Natural Foods to Eat, and Natural Fruit Juices to Drink, as well as Fresh Coconut Water, which some People would say is the Water of Life, itself: beCause of Feeling so GOOD after Drinking it with a little Fresh Lime Juice, which would now Cost no less than 40$ for a Proper Amount of it, each Day, which will be Free of all Charges during the Future — that is, IF I am Elected to be your RIGHTEOUS KING! {See www.Amazon.com for: **"Are Americans the Most STUPID People who ever Lived?" (HOW Working People can PROSPER and Live in PEACE Under the Rulership of a RIGHTEOUS KING!) By The Worldwide People's Revolution!® Book 047.**

07-08 [_] O Righteous King, if you are not Elected by the Vast Majority of the People in this World of Woes, it will only be beCAUSE they did not get to Hear your Inspiring Messages. Indeed, if your Provable Truths were Advertised on TVs and Radios every 10 Minutes, like Cigarettes used to be, it would not be long before those **"GLORIOUS Swanky Hotels Castles and Fortresses"** would be Springing Up like Beautiful Tulips, Irises, and other Bulbous Flowers in the Holy Gardens of the Angel Eden! Yes, just ONE such Swanky Fortress would Inspire the People of the Whole World to come to their Right Senses: beCause of those Millions of Blooming Fruit Trees, Nut Trees, Grape Vines, Berry Bushes, and Marvelous Flower Gardens in those Great Stone Terraces, some of which would Naturally be Covered with Grape Vines, just to Help Cool Off the Stone Walls, while Feeding the little Birds of Cheerfulness, which would be Singing with Sheer JOY! Yes, we could Build Special Bird Houses within those Walls, whereby all Swanky Fortresses would be Better than the Garden of Eden, itself, having Beautiful Waterfalls over Polished Colorful Rocks, which run into Streams of Living Water, which also have Polished Colorful Rocks for the Water to run over and around, which Streams are Bordered by Planned Flower Gardens and Vegetable Gardens, which are Attended to by **"The Swanky Association of Professional Gardeners,"** who Voluntarily do that Work, in Exchange for getting to Live in those **"Beautiful Swanky PALACES!" (A New Concept in Living Habits — Swanky Palaces for Poor People!) By The Worldwide People's Revolution!® Book 066!**

07-09 [_] Well, my Friend, if anyone Doubts the BEAUTY of any such Glorious Cities, they should Visit Mount ZION, which is the Holy City of the Great King, which you can read about in *Psalms 48, 50, and 87.* Yes, it is about 200 Miles Long and a hundred Miles Wide, being Built on Top of a Great Plateau, being Surrounded by Deep Gorges with Raging Rivers of Water on all Sides, being Surrounded by Mountains on all Sides, except for where the Mighty Jordan River runs Out of the Hollow Earth into the Arctic Sea, where it Deposits its Annual Icebergs, some of which are as much as 400 Miles Long! Yes, those Icebergs are Formed, each Year, while the Jordan River keeps Flowing toward the Hole in the North, which Builds Up with ICE, until it gives way each Summer: beCause of the Pressure behind the River Jordan! {See www.Amazon.com for: **"The Secret City of the Great King!" (HOW the True Church will Escape from the Great Tribulation!) By The Worldwide People's Revolution!® Book 042.**}

07-10 [_] So, O Elected King, if what you say is True, there is already a very Good Example of a Glorious Swanky Fortress in the Recesses of the Uttermost Parts of the Far North, just as King David wrote in *Psalm 48,* which God has Prepared and Preserved for his SAINTS. Therefore, why bother to Build any Swanky Fortresses for these Unbelieving IDIOTS, who do not even Believe in Reason nor Logic?

— Chapter 08 —

A Guaranteed Solution for Unbelief

08-01 [_] Most People in the World have never Visited the Pantheon in Rome, nor even Carlsbad Caverns in New Mexico; but, I can Assure you that they are Beautiful Places to Visit, as well as Educational Places. For Example, Carlsbad Caverns has a Year-around Consistent Temperature: beCause of its MASSIVE Stone Walls, which anyone can Imitate by Building THICK Stone Walls, or even DIRT Walls around THIN Concrete Domes, which are only 2 feet thick. For Example, you can make your own Underground Cave House on a Hillside, just by Digging Out a TRENCH with a Backhoe, which Mounds Up the Dirt in the Center, which Forms a DOME, which you can Cover with Plastic Sheeting, and then Pour Concrete and Rough Rocks into the Trench, and over the Dirt Dome, except for the Skylight Hole, which you should Build with Proper Stones before the Concrete is Poured into the Trench: so that the Roof puts Pressure against the Skylight Cylinder, which is also used as a VENT for the entire House, which Vents the "Winter House" into the "Summer House," on Top, as King Solomon would say, which is Formed by Building another Retainer Wall out around the entire Mound of Dirt, about 12 feet from it, which Forms a Water Barrier, and makes it Possible to fill in the Concrete Dome on the Mound of Dirt within just one Day, using a Concrete Pump Truck. {NOTE: You can see Pictures and Drawings in other Inspired Books that I have Posted on Amazon. *"Seek, and you shall Find,"* as Jesus said.}

08-02 [_] O Unelected King, most People in the World would not be at all Interested in Living in any such Dark Dank Cave House, even if they could Build one for less than 15,000 Dollars: beCause of using lots of large ROUGH Clean ROCKS, even as you did for your 100,000-gallon Cistern for Water Storage, which is Explained in: **"Orgimmick Gardening at its Best!" (HOW to Grow Delicious Satisfying Foods without a 10-million-dollar Investment!) By The Worldwide People's Revolution!®**, Book 079, which has about 60 Pictures with Explanations. Indeed, such a House might be DAMP and COLD without a Fireplace, or at least a Solar-powered Hot House to Warm it up. And WHERE would the Windows be Located in such a House? §§‡

08-03 [_] Well, my Potential Friend, there are many Ways and Means for doing all such Things; but, a Proper Stone Dome Home Complex would have to have an Ice House under it, just to Suck Out the Moisture, and to keep it Cool and Comfortable the Year around in Hot Climates. Nevertheless, there are People, even Today, who Live in Cave Houses around the World, in spite of not having any Windows. In Fact, many Department Stores are now Located in Underground Buildings, and no one has Died from a Lack of Windows. Nevertheless, it is Possible to have Beautiful Agate Windows at the Wide Barrel-vault Entrances to all Stone Dome Home Complexes: beCause of Building them in those TERRACES, which Vent into the above Gardens through the Skylight Cylinders, which also Prevent People from Looking into the Houses from the Skylight Holes: beCause of those Tall Cylinders, which Rest on Top of the Solid Stone Domes, which are made mostly of Hardened Concrete: beCause Concrete can be Shaped in a Million Different Ways — such as you can See in the Pantheon, in Rome, which has Endured for more than 1,800 Years, and is still Looking GOOD, which is the Widest Solid Concrete Dome in the World! Yes, it is 148 feet Wide, which is far too Wide for a Living Room Dome; but, it is Okay for a Church, Courtroom, Concert Hall, or Auditorium. The Solid Stone Walls of the Pantheon are 17 feet THICK, which is WHY that those Wise Romans have not had to Waste any Energy on Heating nor Cooling Bills during those hundreds of Years: beCause the Walls Stabilize the

Temperatures. Therefore, if People cannot Live in their Multi-million-dollar Stone Dome Home Complexes for the Lack of WINDOWS, they should do most of their Living OUTSIDE in the Fresh Clean Air and Sunlight, while Attending to their All-Mineral Organic Gardens, Vineyards, and Orchards: beCause no one must be Deprived of WINDOWS, nor of Glorious VIEWS, which would be Possible from the Bike Paths and Walkways along the Tops of the Arcades of Stone Funnels for the Wind Generators. (See the above Drawings.) Yes, if they Wanted a Photogenic Picturesque VIEW of the Terraced Gardens, they could take the Subway Train to the Swanky Castle, and then take an Elevator to the Roof of that Castle, whereby they could get a Grand View of the entire Swanky Fortress from one of the Corner Towers or Central Towers, which would be Designed for that Purpose: beCause the Castles would be Built Up extra High, and Surround the Swanky Hotels, which would also have Inside Terraces and Outside Terraces: beCause all of the Hotels, Castles and Fortresses would be made in Great TERRACES, except that the Inside Terraces would not have any Arcades of Stone Funnels in most Cases: beCause of not having much Wind, except around the Castles: beCause of their Heights. Therefore, the Terraces around the Hotels would not have any Obstructions of Views from the Gardens, which could have many Short Stone Terraces stepping down to the Great Terraces, which would Add to the Beauty when Looking at them from the Swanky Castles. In other Words, now that we have Unlimited Supplies of Money and Rocks to Work with: beCause of Establishing **"The New RIGHTEOUS One-World Government,"** there is no Good Reason why that we cannot make those **"GLORIOUS Swanky Hotels Castles and Fortresses"** like the Gods would Want them.

08-04 [_] O Potential Elected King, are you not Aware that there is only ONE God in this Vast Universe, whose Name is JEHOVAH, who told Isaiah that he did not know of any other God. Therefore, why do you use an S on God, as if there were more than one God?

08-05 [_] Well, my Potential Friend, you were Obviously not Taught the Whole Truth about the Gods, which I have already Explained in several Inspired Books, which I will now Explain to you, again: beCause it will not take up much Space in this Book. The Vast Universe that we know about contains Trillions of Stars, each of which has its own Worlds, even as this Solar System has many Planets, most of which are Inhabited on the Insides of them, except for this Earth, which is Inhabited on the Inside and Outside, which makes it very Special: beCause we get to See some of those Multitudes of Stars, each of which has a God to Govern it and the Worlds around it, even as Jehovah or Yohoovu God is the Governor of this Solar System, whose Headquarters is Located Inside of Jupiter, just in case that you did not Learn that in any Sunday School Classes. Likewise, each Solar System has a Father and Chosen Sons to Govern it, whereby Jesus Christ is the Chosen Son of this World, whose Holy Kingdom has not yet been Established over all of the Earth; but, it will be during the Future, after the Nations have Learned their Lessons, and have Decided to Establish **"The New RIGHTEOUS One-World Government,"** whereby they might Work Together to make Life Good for everyone on the Earth who BELIEVES, who will just Naturally Move themselves into those **"GLORIOUS Swanky Hotels Castles and Fortresses!" (Beautiful Planned City States for WISE Intelligent Well-Educated People with Common Sense and Good Understanding!) By The Worldwide People's Revolution!® Book 019.** Therefore, Goodness will Overcome Evilness, and only Evil People will Remain in those Cities of Confusion, who will Discover that it is more and more Difficult to Live within them: beCause of not having any Righteous People among them. Indeed, you can just Imagine how AWFUL it might be when all Policemen are BRUTAL, and all Judges are WICKED, and all Lawyers are Deceiving, and all Politicians and Preachers are nothing but LIARS: beCause all of the Righteous People have DEPARTED from them, in Order to Raise their Standards of Living by at least a hundred Times! Yes, just ONE such Swanky Fortress will Inspire them to Follow my Master Plan, which could be Built in Venezuela, or even in Mexico, which has far more Freedoms, where there are Great Plains to Build on, and lots of Mountains of Rocks. Otherwise, it could be Built in the Great State of Flexible Texas — except that it would be Unconstitutional: because the Constitution for **"The Divided States of United Lies"** forbids the Building of a State within a State: beCause of Tax Collectors, who want to make Tax Slaves of EVERYONE. Nevertheless, it is Possible for Texas to Secede from the Union, Legally: beCause that Provision was made for them.

08-06 [_] O Elected King, I would Think that any Religious Body of People could get Together and Build a Swanky Fortress, even if it is not so Glorious, whereby they could Prove that their Way of Living is Best. For Example, the Mennonites or Hutterites could Build a Beautiful Planned City State.

08-07 [_] Well, my Friend, only the Mormons would have the Money to get Started on such a Project, and not one-millionth enough Money to Finish it, unless they could Claim their own Mountains of Rocks, and also Muster up enough Volunteers to do the Work for FREE, which is a Possibility; but, it is also Impractical: beCause it would not be long before those Tax Masters would figure out a Way to TAX them to Death, even as they did to me, whereby I was Forced to Abandon the Farm and Move myself to Mexico, with the Hope that they would not Discover me: beCause of not being a Property Owner, whereby I am now Free with a Capital F — except that my Freedom does not Assure me of any Fresh Clean Air, Pure Living Water, Wholesome Natural Foods, Natural Drinks, Natural Clothing, Quiet Clean Transportation, Free Internet Services, nor any of the Wonderful Things that everyone could have within those **"GLORIOUS Swanky Hotels Castles and Fortresses!"** Nevertheless, I am still Surviving, even as most People are; but, I am Certainly NOT Thriving, even as most People should be, and would be, if they should GIVE UP their Possession Worshiping, and Do as I Teach. Yes, you might even FEAR that Idea, before giving any Thoughts to it; but, that was the Plan of the First Church of Jesus Christ, according to *the Book of the ACTS of the Apostles,* who had all Properties in Common among them, including their Money, which was Distributed among them as every Man had Need for it. However, in the System that I Propose, everyone would be Paid GOOD Swanky Wages for Building those Hotels Castles and Fortresses, according to: **"A List of FAIR Swanky Wages!"** Book 065. Therefore, no one could be taken Advantage of, if all Things were Set Up Properly. However, a Person could Lose his Temper, and do some Evil Thing, and thus be BANISHED from all Swanky Fortresses, which would be the Case for Convicted Murderers. Otherwise, they would be Sent to Cities of Refuge for Accused Murderers, where they could Live Normal Lives with other Refugees of the same Kind, who would not have the Protection nor Security of any Swanky Fortresses; but, at least they would be able to Prove themselves to be Worthy to Eat, who would have to Attend to their own Gardens, and Rely on themselves to Survive, who would no doubt eventually Discover that I have Proposed the Best Way for People to Live and Work Together by United Effort. ‡

08-08 [_] O Elected King, even an Independent Jackass could have a Good Life, if he should Submit to Reason and Logic: beCause you Propose the Construction of Wilderness Resorts for Mountain Hikers and Bikers, who can have Swanky Hotels for Lost Creatures to Rest themselves in, which will also be near National Parks, which will have Rooms to Rent for 50 Cents per Night, if they bring their own Bedding. Otherwise, they might Rent for 5$ per Night per Person, just to Cover the Costs of Washing their Bedding: beCause no one Wants to Sleep on the same Sheets that someone else has Slept on. Otherwise, they might Exchange some Work for a Place to Sleep and Eat, even without Joining **"The Swanky Associations of Working Soldiers!" (A Fascinating Collection of Various Kinds of Voluntary Working Soldiers!) By The Worldwide People's Revolution!® Book 018.**

08-09 [_] O Elected King, I am Wondering just HOW you will Persuade the Nations of Unbelievers to Accept your Master Plan, and thus Build those Swanky Fortresses for themselves, seeing that most People are Contented to Live in Swamps and in Slums and Ghettos, like Cockroaches in City Dumps?

08-10 [_] Well, my Friend, it should be fairly easy to Persuade the United Nations to go along with my Plan, seeing that they have Wasted Trillions of Dollars without Solving a single Problem, just to Exaggerate Things a bit for making a Good Point, which is also True for the Governments of most Nations, who have no Reasonable Solutions for anything. For Example, **"The Divided States of United Lies!" (The so-called "United States of North America" in Disguise!)**, Book 058, has Wasted Trillions of Dollars on Poverty, and still has as many or more Poor People as ever: beCause they apparently Forgot that People have to EAT, and the Best Way for them to Do that is to Grow their own Gardens, at Home, which would Require a little Education; but, not Trillions of Dollars in the Dumpsters. However, it would Require Millions of Trillions of Dollars to Build Properly Planned City States for everyone in the World, which is no Problem at all for **"The United States of the Whole World!" (A True Global Economy for the Masses of Working People!) By The Worldwide People's Revolution!®**, Book 055: because, **"The New RIGHTEOUS One-World Government"** would have an Unlimited Amount of New Money to Work with: beCause that would be its Main Function of Business — that is, if Moneys in the Forms of Coins and Papers were not TRASHED, which they could be: beCause no such Moneys are Needed for True Prosperity; but, only Numbers in Computers are Needed, which brings up the Subject of *the Mark of the BEAST!* Yes, that is otherwise known as an RFID Computer Chip, or a Radio Frequency Identification Computer Chip, which Identifies each Person, Dog and Cow, which is the Solution that the Babylonians and Edomites will Recommend; but, with the Swanky Fortress System, no such Chips are Needed: because there is no longer any Need for Buying nor Selling any Trash! For Example, I might Trade my Plums and Hickory Nuts for your Pears or Peaches, or even for a Pair of Shoes. But, **"The Swanky Association of Shoe Makers"** will have all Kinds of Free Shoes and Well-made Shoes to Choose from: beCause each Person will be allowed to have no less than 4 Pairs of those Free Shoes, as well as a Pair of Rubber Boots for whatever Reasons: beCause those are Necessities of Life, which will all be Covered by **"The Swanky Associations of Working Soldiers!"** Therefore, there will be no such a Thing as a Poor Person in that World of Wonders. {FOOTNOTE: Just the other Day, I went Looking for a Pair of Good Shoes, which would be Comfortable to Wear; and I Discovered some Converse Tennis Shoes for 900 Pesos, which were Constructed in Vietnam, which had some thin "uppers" made of light-weight Canvas, and about half as Strong as they used to be, some 60+ Years Ago, as if these Modern Converse Tennis Shoes were Designed to Wear Out, whereby Converse might Sell some more Cheap but Expensive Tennis Shoes. Indeed, I Thought to myself, "Why would Converse Attempt to Commit Economic Suicide by Producing such Trashy Capitalist Tennis Shoes, which should be Designed to Withstand the Abuses of Rough Tennis Players?" Therefore, I got a Pair of Mexican Sheep Skin Shoes for less Money, which will probably Endure for at least 5 Years, in spite of doing much Walking. In Fact, I have been Thinking about Walking 2,000+ Miles to the American Border, whereby I can Try to Persuade Poor Old Miserable Uncle Sam to give to me a Social Insecurity Check, now that Donald Trumpeter is Keeping his Promise to Assist the Vietnam Veterans with 430-dollar Monthly Checks, which might Buy a Bag of Peanuts and a few Avocadoes; but, not hardly Pay for any Rent, nor for any Shoes, seeing that the Tiniest Apartment in Dall-ass, Tex-ass is more than 500$ per Month, and 1,500$ per Month in Chicago! In other Words, for the Price of 12 Months of Rent in Chicago, a Person could Build one of those Cave Houses in Kentucky, except that it is probably Illegal to do so, by now. After all, those Governments are not Happy, unless everyone is a SLAVE of some Kind. Therefore, I Suggest that we Slaves put ALL of them OUT of Business. See: **"The UGLY Scarred Dishonest Face of Poor Old Miserable UNCLE SAM!" (A Memorial Day Legacy!) By The Worldwide People's Revolution!®** Book 054.}

— Chapter 09 —

A Guaranteed Solution for the Evils of Capitalism!

09-01 [_] The Chief Evil of Capitalism is the Stock Market, which makes it Possible for Rich People to Invest in Addictive Things — such as Tobacco Products, Cokes, Beers, and many other Alcoholic Beverages, as well as Fruit-flavored Sugar Water, Candies, Cookies, Cakes, and whatever has Sugar in it, which is almost Guaranteed to Rot Out People's Teeths, and Cause many other Unhealthy Ailments: beCause Refined Sugar is an Invention of Satan, the Devil, you might say, who is Hell-bent on Destroying Mankind by one Means or another: beCause he Hates the Godkind, who Created Mankind: beCause he Envies them for their Goodness, even as the Ancient Jews Envied Jesus Christ for his Goodness, and thus Arranged his Cruel Death, whose Descendants have now become the Primary Bankers, Chief Druggists, Top Chemists, Master Bomb-makers, Leading Book Publishers, Head Movie Makers, Grand Medical Scammers, Chief Weapons Manufacturers, Leading Insurance Agents, Primary Investors on Wall Street, and so on, whom I have Identified as Edomites, who are Descendants of Esau, whom Yohoovu God Hated for Various Reasons, who have now made the Masses of People into their SLAVES of Various Kinds and Colors, who Love that Evil Stock Market, whereby they can get Rich with very little Physical Work, while the Children of Israel do not Object to Difficult Physical Work, who would rather Shovel a Truckload of Sand, than to tell a Lie for Financial Gain, while the Edomites would much Prefer to tell the Lie for Gain. And thus we have what they call CAPITALISM, which is the Love of Money in Action, which Serves the Possession Worshipers very well. (See *Romans 6—9.*)

09-02 [_] O Unelected King of Outlandish Contradictions, it seems like I just finished reading something about ALL Peoples being able to Live in those **"Beautiful Swanky PALACES!" (A New Concept in Living Habits — Swanky Palaces for Poor People!)**, Book 066, which seems to be Promoting those POSSESSIONS that you Pretend to HATE. Indeed, if anyone is a Possession Worshiper, it is YOURSELF, O Contradictory King of Total Insanity! §

09-03 [_] Well, that is only your Misinterpretation of what I Teach, which is Based on the Assumption that People would be OWNING all such Swanky Palaces, when, in Fact, no one would be Owning any of those Palaces: beCause not even Bill Computer Software Gates, Incorporated, could Afford to Buy one: because of Costing a Trillion Dollars or more! Therefore, just Forget about Owning them, or even a Part of them: beCause that Ownership Nonsense is what has Messed Up your Mind, whereby you Vainly Imagine that you are Better than Poor People, who do not Own any such Expensive Things. Indeed, the Proof of it is found in the Fact that Car Owners, and especially the Owners of very Expensive Cars, are all PUFFED UP in PRIDE, as if they were more Important than Jesus Christ, himself! But, if you Doubt it, just go Hitchhiking on the Highway while Dressed in a White Robe with your Bible in your Hand, and Discover just how many Rides you get in Californicate, or any of the States that are Outside of the so-called "Bible Belt," which is mostly in South-Eastern United States, which is Famous for having Churches on most every Street Corner, whose Members may very easily Run Over you on the Highway, if not Proudly Drive by with their Noses Up in the Air, as if you were Lower than a Beggar, whom they Despise for your Poverty, and especially if you are Barefooted. Just Remember that Pedestrians are not Permitted to Walk on the Interstate Highways: beCause they are Reserved for Possession Worshipers. Likewise, the Best Seats at any Gathering of People are Reserved for the People with the Most Possessions, which was the Major Reason WHY George Washington was Elected to be America's First President: beCause he had the Most Wealth at that Time. And then

Donald Trumpeter came along to make America Great Again, like it was during its most Prosperous Time, during the 1950's, when Wages were Up and Crimes were Down, when there was very little Violence seen on TV Screens, except in the War Movies, which were Designed to make all such Wars seem to be RIGHTEOUS: beCause Americans were the "Good Guys," they told us, in spite of the Fact that the Germans had the Highest Standard of Living in the World, beginning in 1936, just 3 Years after Adolf Hitler was Elected, which Caused the Western Democracies to ENVY those Germans, and thus Seek Ways to Destroy them by Means of Propagandist LIES! Nevertheless, it Required the entire Capitalist and Communist Worlds to Defeat that one little Nation, including the Lives of 22 Million Russians, who Murdered some 2 Million Germans, and Raped tens of thousands of German Women, while Saint Joseph Stalin had some 50,000,000 Russians put to Death during his Reign of Terror, whom Americans and Brits Supported during World War 2: beCause he was "the Good Guy," and "the Lesser of 2 Evils," as other People Declared, in spite of the Fact that Stalin was the Worst of all of them by a hundred Times, who did not even Object to Sacrificing 22 Million Soldiers: beCause he was not about to Submit to **"The Swanky Sword of Divine Truths!" (The Most Powerful Weapon in the Whole Universe!)**, Book 067: beCause he was another Possession Worshiper. Yes, it is Granted that Adolf Hitler was also another Possession Worshiper. However, he at least Provided the Best Wages in the World at that Time, and had Zero Unemployment in Germany and Austria, who was so Well-Loved by those Germans that he could Ride around in an Open Car, until 1939: beCause no one was out to Assassinate him, which no American President would Dare to Do, even Today: beCause of being Afraid of being Assassinated! In Fact, Adolf Hitler was the Last Leader in the World to be so Loved by almost all of his People, who had a 99.98% Approval Rating before the War, while Donald has less than a 40% Approval Rating, and is a Well-known LIAR, Capitalist HOG, and Greedy Son of Satan, who Cheated Poor People out of their Wages, who has thousands of Lawsuits against him, while Adolf had NONE! Moreover, the Germans had a Just Cause for going to War, while Americans had none, and could only make up Propagandist Lies against them, which can be Proven in a Courtroom with a Righteous Judge in Charge of it. ‡

09-04 [ ] O Unelected King, if you are a Supporter of Nazi War Crimes, then you are on my Blacklist of Worst Enemies: beCause I have nothing Good to say in Favor of Adolf Hitler, who was the Worst of the Worst Criminals in High Places, who Murdered some 15 Million Jews, or roughly one-fifth of the German Population! {NOTE: If you Agree with that Statement, please Check the Box with an X.}

09-05 [ ] Well, my Poor Deceived Potential Enemy, I do not Seek to Justify any War Crimes, including those of Americans, which add up to far more than those of the Germans during World War 2, if you Study Howard Zinn's book, called: **A People's History of the United States**, which goes into some of the Details from the Founding of **"The Divided States of United Lies,"** which Exposes much History that was Covered Up by those Edomites, who would not want you to Learn that the United States Federal Government and the Edomite Bankers were Actually Supporters of Adolf Hitler, themselves: beCause they saw Profits in it. However, to make Hitler Look BAD, they Bombed the Railway Lines that led into the Nazi Concentration Camps, whereby their Food Supplies were Cut Off, whereby the Jews might Starve to Death, or near unto Death, whereby they might Blame the Nazis for it, instead of themselves, which was another Covered-up Scheme of the Capitalists, who held a Kangaroo Court after the War in Nuremberg, whereby the Nazis were found Guilty, while the Russians and Allies were found Innocent: beCause no one brought any of them to Trial for anything! Indeed, they were all just Assumed to be Innocent: beCause they Won the War! However, had the Germans Won the War, it would all be Turned Around the other Way, and the Germans would be found Innocent, even if there were some Trials: because they did NOT Exterminate even 600,000 Jews, much less 6 Million nor 11 Million, as the Edomites now Falsely Claim, who Totally Contradict the Accurate Records of the Red Cross, as well as Reason and Logic: beCause there is no Way that 4 nor 5 Bodies can be put into a Crematory Oven every 10 Minutes, as a Placard states in the Holocaust Museum in Washington, District of Chief Criminals: because it Requires at least one Hour just to Heat Up the Oven, and then another 2 to 6 Hours to Cremate a single Body, and then another Hour to Cool Off the Oven before the Door can be Safely Opened, which any Crematorium Manager will Testify under Oath in a Courtroom to be the TRUTH! Therefore, if those Edomites cannot Prove their False Statements to be Workable, they should be Cast Alive into Nebuchadnezzar's Fiery Furnace! Otherwise, they should be Boiled Naked in Extremely HOT Used Motor Oil, Toes first, until they make their Confessions. ‡

09-06 [_] O Elected King, I would say that you might be the Reincarnation of King Nebuchadnezzar, himself: beCause you do not Mince Words; but, you speak Candidly and Bluntly, like a True KING should. Indeed, if those Edomites have been Lying to us Tax Slaves, we should Learn all about it. Therefore, I am going to Secretly get some Pictures of that Placard in the HoloHOAX Museum in Washington, just for Incriminating Evidence against them.

09-07 [_] Well, my Friend, that is just ONE of the many Lies that those Edomites have in that Museum, which should all be Photographed — except that taking Pictures in there is Illegal: beCause it is such a Sacred Place, which Honors the Victims of the HoloCOST; but, it makes no Mention about any of the Goodness of Adolf Hitler, who was on the Side of the Working People in the World, who Helped to Form the *National Socialist German Workers' Party,* which did have some Anti-Christ Doctrines — such as the Superiority of White Peoples, and the Defamation of Jews; but, that is beCAUSE there are 2 Kinds of Jews, one of which is like the Judas Iscariot and Bernie Madoff Club, who cannot be Trusted, who brought about the Bursting Housing Bubble Financial Plan, which Caused Millions of People around to the World to LOSE, while they GAINED Trillions of Dollars! Yes, you might know of someone who is Seeking to Justify all such Edomite Scams, who should be brought to Trials, and Tried for TREASON! After all, a Bad Economy is most often something that People MAKE by Design, which might also Depend on the Weather in some Cases; but, for the most Part, a Bad Economy is something that those Edomites Produce, which was Proven by Adolf Hitler, whose Economy Flourished during the Great Depression, while Americans and other Capitalists Suffered! Indeed, it would be like a Present-day Financial "Miracle," whereby X-amount of Unemployed People would be Instantly Employed with Good Swanky Wages to Build those **"GLORIOUS Swanky Hotels Castles and Fortresses,"** which would soon begin to put the Edomite Bankers OUT of Business, which they would Naturally NOT LIKE, whereby they would Naturally Do as they have always Done, and Try their Best to Stir Up another World WAR, just to DEFEAT those **"Seven Great Armies of Working Soldiers!" (HOW to Provide a Way for Everyone to WORK: so as to Eliminate Poverty, Crimes, Drug Abuses, Prisons and Unnecessary Taxes!)**, Book 015, who would be the Envy of the World: beCause of Living in those **"Beautiful Swanky PALACES!" (A New Concept in Living Habits — Swanky Palaces for Poor People!) By The Worldwide People's Revolution!®** Book 066. Yes, the Edomites would become very Worried about their False Riches, and would thus use their Propaganda Machines to Badmouth those Swanky Fortresses and those Working Soldiers, in spite of the Fact that there are more than 5,000 Good Reasons and Great Advantages for Building those Beautiful Planned City States, which you can read about in: **"The Right Design for Living!" (A List of Great Advantages for Building Beautiful Planned City States!)**, Book 012, which is a Companion Book of: **"The Low Court of Supreme Injustices is Brought to Trial!" (Our Elected King Butts Heads with the United States Supreme Court, with or without their Black Robes of Hypocrisies and Lies!) By The Worldwide People's Revolution!®** Book 011.

09-08 [_] O Elected King, there are Good People and Bad People among all Races of People; but, the Worst of them are Known for their GREED and Selfishness, whereby they can Murder other People for Gain without it Bothering their Consciences, who are known as Psychopaths — such as George

Warmonger Bush and Little Dick Chicanery, Incorporated, who Caused the Deaths and Woundings and Displacements of Millions of People, and never even Apologized for it! Likewise, if any Nation Butts Heads with **"The Divided States of United Lies,"** that Nation will have Sanctions set up against it, even as was done to Cuba for many Decades, and is now being done to Venezuela, by which the People are Suffering, which the Edomites Blame on the Bad Government in Venezuela, instead of Blaming themselves for the Sanctions, which brought about the Sufferings. Moreover, you might Notice that the Biased News Reporters never give the Opinions of the Opposition Party, which now Governs in Venezuela: beCause it is always a One-sided News Report, even as it was for Cuba, North Korea, and Iran, which just Happen to Disagree with American Leaders, and for Justified Reasons, which are never Mentioned in **"The Divided States of United Lies!"** Indeed, when was the last Time that you Heard about those **"GLORIOUS Swanky Hotels Castles and Fortresses"** on the News Media? Chances are that if you ever do Hear anything from them about those Fortresses, it will be something NEGATIVE, instead of Positive: beCause the Last Thing that the Edomites Want is for Bankers to be put Out of Business, even though no Bankers are Necessary for True Prosperity, just as you have already Explained in a Previous Chapter. For Example, Moses did not say for the Israelites to Establish Banks in *Leviticus 25;* but, to Forgive all Debts, and Move BACK to the Land, which was to be Divided among all of the People, Fairly, even though Different Lands are not Equal by any Means; but, they can be made Equally as Productive with the Help of a Good Government, even if they are Deserts in Saudi Arabia: because the Amazon River has not yet Ran Out of Fresh Water, which can be Shipped over there by Solar Power, even though the Ship would move Faster by Diesel Power, which might be a Tolerable Excuse for using it to do Good. ‡

09-09 [_] Well, my Friend, Laura Knight has said that about 6% of all Societies are Psychopaths, which is likely True. Therefore, that 6% can be Sifted Out from among us, whereby the World will be a much Better Place to Live. Perhaps they are Descendants of some very Bad Aliens from other Worlds, who are without Consciences, who do not Recognize the Fact that some People were Born to be Masters, while the others were Born to be their Servants, which is not to say that all of the People who were Born to be Masters are GOOD People: beCause most Masters are Actually BAD People, who simply take Advantage of the People who were Born to be Servants. However, a Righteous King can get them Straightened Out, which is what will Happen when Jesus Christ Governs this World of Wonders, who will Separate the Sheeps and Goats from the Lions and Wolves; and thus Capitalism will be Buried, along with Communism, Fascism and Socialism: beCause they are all BAD Isms, which Keep Ignorant People in Extreme Poverty, who do not even have Fresh Clean Air to Breathe, Pure Living Water to Drink, Wholesome Natural Foods to Eat, Natural Clothing to Wear, nor Secure Houses to Live in: beCause they are nothing but Education Slaves, Work Slaves, Tax Slaves, Insurance Slaves, Interest Slaves, Rent Slaves, Credit Card Debt Slaves, Drug Slaves, ElecTrickery Bills Slaves, Gas Bills Slaves, Water Bills Slaves, Childcare Slaves, Mortgage Slaves, and you Name it — none of which are Needed for True Prosperity. Indeed, Education should be "Free," along with Water, Foods, Clothing, Telephones, Radios, Televisions, Computers, and Swanky PALACES, in Exchange for only 4 Hours of Common Skilled Labor per Day, or the Equivalent thereof: beCause, if all Hands are Busy, that is all that is Required for Living a GOOD Life, and without the Use of any Robbing Bankers, Credit Cards, Tooth-rotting Candies, nor other Trash — such as Endless Video Games, which never Enlightened anyone's Mind concerning any Subject. Therefore, why Produce any such Vain Things? Why not Attend to Spiritual Subjects, and Try to GROW UP, O Babies?

09-10 [_] O Elected King, what you are Proposing might have Worked a hundred Years Ago; but, this is a Lost Generation, which cannot Relate with Gardening, much less with *Bible Studies!* Therefore, you will have to become a TYRANT King, or Dictator, just to get their Attention!

— Chapter 10 —

A Guaranteed Solution for Uprooting the Thorny Tree of Death!

10-01 [ ] First of all, if People do not Humbly Submit to **"The Swanky Sword of Divine Truths,"** the World will be Cursed with a Great Drought, whereby it will not Rain for 3 Years and 6 Months, whereby most of the Spiritual Children will come to their Riit Senses, and Conclude that it is a Good Idea to Build those **"GLORIOUS Swanky Hotels Castles and Fortresses!" (Beautiful Planned City States for WISE Intelligent Well-Educated People with Common Sense and Good Understanding!) By The Worldwide People's Revolution!®** Book 019.

10-02 [ ] O King, I Hope to God that we have at least a few of those Fortresses Finished, before that Great Famine comes, or else most of the Human Species will DIE OFF! After all, without any Rain for 3.5 Years, nothing much will be Alive, except perhaps a few Cactus Plants. However, even they Require some Water.

10-03 [ ] Well, you have probably Heard about those Frogs in Australia, which can stay Buried for as much as 7 Years, and still come to Life after a Rainstorm. Indeed, the Roots of some Trees can also Survive Great Droughts; but, you are Correct — that most Creatures and Plants would simply DIE, which is Predicted in *the Book of Revelation,* which also tells about that Great Drought in Chapter 11. Therefore, if you Believe any of those Words, you would be Wise to tell your Friends, Relatives and Naaberz about this Inspired Book, whereby they might Work Up an Appetite for Doing something Constructive to SAVE themselves from the Disaster to Come! Yes, it will Require a HUGE Amount of Water, just to Flush the Toilets, which should also be Saved for Watering and Fertilizing the Trees in an Organized Way, just to have a little Shade: beCause it is also going to get very HOT, according to that *Book of Revelation,* and so Hot as to Burn Up all of the Grasses and one-third of all of the Trees in the Whole World, which would Mean that our Atmosphere would be Full of SMOKE. But, People also need to take Showers and Wash their Clothes, which will Require a Minimum Amount of at least 10 Gallons of Water per Day, per Person, even if they have Canned Foods to Eat, whereby they do not have to do any Cooking nor Washing Dishes. Therefore, if you Calculate the Amount of Water that you will Need to Survive, including the Water for your Unbelieving Friends, Relatives, and Naaberz, you will get a Rough Idea concerning how BIG to make your Cisterns for Water Storage, which will also Require a HUGE Amount of Water, just to make Proper Concrete, which might Cost as much as an Expensive Car, just for the Concrete Forms for making a Large Cistern. However, if you are Living from Paycheck to Paycheck, and have no Money Saved up for such Emergencies, you are at the Mercy of your Local Friendly Banker to Loan the Money to you, which he will not Do: beCause he will Naturally be another one of those Unbelievers, who will Suggest that you Drill a Well, if you want to Waste any Money on it, without Realizing that almost all Wells will go DRY! Moreover, if you are one of the Billions of People who Live in those Ugly Apartment Houses, having no Land to Work on, you will not even be Able to Build a Cistern of any Kind, even if your Friends and Relatives should Assist you, Financially: beCause it will be far too Late to Return to the Land: beCause it Requires TIME to Learn HOW to Construct Proper Buildings, and especially Proper Cisterns, which can LEAK, and thus Waste all of your Time, Materials, and Money! {See www.Amazon.com for: **"Orgimmick Gardening at its Best!" (HOW to Grow Delicious Satisfying Foods without a 10-million-dollar Investment!)**

By The Worldwide People's Revolution!®, Book 079, which has many Photographs with Explanations for HOW to Build a Proper Cistern for Survival, which Required 7 Years of my Labor, and was still not Finished! Indeed, such a Cistern should be Lined with Ceramic Tiles, which are not Cheap, just to keep the Water Clean — that is, IF you can Discover any Clean Water to put into it!}

10-04 [_] O Elected King, if *the Book of Revelation* is Correct, it would Require the Cooperation of those **"Seven Great Armies of Working Soldiers,"** just to get Prepared for such a Great Drought, which would have to have the Assistance of all Major Bankers, just to have enough Money for Doing what Needs to be Done. After all, a Family of only 4 People would Need no less than 50,000 Gallons of Water, just to Survive, without Flushing any Toilets more than twice per Day: beCause they could Drink at least 2 Gallons per Day, and would Need at least 2 Gallons per Person to take a Shower, which could be used afterwards to Flush a Toilet, if they did not Waste the Water by letting it run down a Drain. In other Words, they would have to Catch the Shower Water by Building a Special Shower Room with a Bucket under the Floor, whereby the Shower Water could Drain into the Bucket. Moreover, they would need a Shower Bucket, just to take a Shower, which is a Bucket with a Pipe coming out of it, which has a Valve on it, which can be Opened just enough to get WET, and then shut it Off while Soaping oneself down, and then Rinse Off with a Trickle of Water from the Shower Bucket, whereby just one Gallon of Water might do the Job, which would be Conservative. And then, after taking those Showers, the Dirty Water should be used for Washing some very Dirty Clothes, before it is used for Flushing the Toilet, which should also be Flushed into a Sewage Tank, which can be Hauled on a Wagon into the Woods, where it is Spread Out on the Topsoil that Feeds the Trees, which should then be Covered with some Sawdust. Otherwise, the Leaves should be Raked Away before it is Spread on the Topsoil, and then Replaced afterwards, just to keep the Flies Off of it, lest Diseases should be Spread around by them. Otherwise, it should be Buried under some Topsoil. However, such an Operation would be very Costly and Time-consuming, and thus Impractical for most Families, who should have their own Fruit and Nut Trees in their own Gardens, at Home, whereby they can Set Up Outhouses in their Gardens, and use the Dung and Piss around their own Trees, which might Help to keep them Alive during such a Great Drought. After all, a Fig Tree only Requires 2 to 3 Gallons of Water per Day to keep on Growing and Producing Figs — that is, if anyone can Tolerate the Thoughts of Eating Recycled Waste Products from their Piss and Dung, which is likely Loaded with Poisons from the Unnatural Foods that they have been Eating and Drinking. For Example, Refined Sugars are no Good for the Topsoil, which could make the Trees Diseased. Moreover, those Long Lists of Chemicals and Preservatives that can be found on the Labels of Packaged Foods are Forbidden in an All-Mineral Organic Garden: beCause they are not Natural, nor Wanted by any Plants. ‡

10-05 [_] Well, my Friend, those Swanky Fortresses would be Built Up on Foundations of HUGE Cisterns, whereby there would be an Abundance of Fresh Water to be Used Wisely, which should not be Wasted on Flushing Toilets, except that most of whatever is put into Toilets is not Healthy for a Good Garden: beCause it is not CLEAN, like Natural Cow Manure, Goat Manure, Sheep Manure, nor Horse Manure, which can be Composted with Tree Leaves, Grass Clippings, Straw, Sawdust, and other Organic Matter, and thus Greatly Improve the Flavors of Fruits, Nuts, and Vegetables. Yes, a Fruit Tree has a Way to Transform that Horse Manure into FRAGRANT Fruits, if it is used in Moderation; but, too much of it can Cause the Fruits to be Poisonous, and especially if it is Fresh Cow Manure, Hog Manure, Dog Dung, Cat Litter, or Chicken Manure, which should be Spread Out THINLY on the Topsoil, if it is used. Too much Manure can even "Kill" the Topsoil. However, 4 inches of Rabbit Manure can be Plowed Under and Tilled Into the Topsoil about a Foot Deep, at the End of Autumn, and be Planted with Kale Seeds and Green Onion Sets (or little Dried Onion Bulbs) in the Early Springtime, for the most Delicious Kale and Green Onions that you have ever Eaten! Such Kale will get 3 to 4 feet Tall, and Flourish beyond Belief. Likewise, the Green Onions will get 3 feet or more

Tall, and be as Sweet and Delicious as any Onions that you have ever Eaten, if the Soil has the Proper Minerals in it, which come from Powdered Rocks, which must be Digested by those Little Brown Earthworms, after going through the Gizzards of Chickens, Ducks, Peacocks, and other Pleasant Birds, which can be Fed Mashes of Grains with Powdered Rocks mixed in — such as Volcanic Rock Dust, which is Loaded with Minerals; but, only IF it is Proper Volcanic Rock: beCause some Volcanic Rocks are Poisonous, and can even Kill the Topsoil, while other Volcanic Rock Dust makes the Finest Richest Topsoils in the World, and so Rich as to not Require any other Fertilizing, except for a Small Amount of Manure, which could be your own Dung, if it is Treated Properly in a Methane Digester with the Powdered Volcanic Dust, after which it is Spread Out thinly on the Topsoil in a Garden of Fruit Trees and Nut Trees, which will Love it — that is, IF you have been Eating Natural Foods, excluding Meats, Eggs, and Dairy Products. In other Words, Think of yourselves as Adam and Eve in the Garden of Eden, who were Living on Sweet Juicy Fruits, Green Leaves, and a few Raw Nuts, who Lived for 900+ Years! Indeed, People were Designed to Live a very Long Time; but, only IF they should Eat Properly on Living Foods, as Opposed to Cooked Dead Foods from Gross Grocery Stores and Fast-food Junk-food Stores, which are Set Up for Capitalist Hogs to get your Money, who have no Interest in your Good Health. Guaranteed! ‡

10-06 [ ] O Elected King, do you Actually Believe that Adam Lived for 930 Years on nothing but Fruits, Nuts and Vegetables? Would he not have Died from Deficiency Diseases?

10-07 [ ] Well, my Friend, Adam and Eve had the Great Advantage of having a Perfect Beginning, in a World of Wonders that was not Contaminated by Greedy Selfish Capitalists. Indeed, they had no Stress, no Fears, no Sicknesses nor Diseases: beCause they Lived in a Pristine World, which had Fresh Clean Air to Breathe, Pure Living Water to Drink, and Wholesome Natural Foods to Eat, which we could all have, even Today, if we were WISE: beCause it is all Physically, Materially, Financially, and Economically Possible. However, the Major Obstacle that Prevents that from Happening is UNBELIEF among the Masses of People, who are Extremely IGNORANT, who have no Idea what they are Missing: beCause they never had it! Indeed, you cannot Miss having Tree-ripened Fragrant Sweet Peaches, if you never had them. Moreover, you cannot Miss having someone to Love, if you have never had anyone to Love. Likewise, you cannot Miss having Fresh Clean Crisp Air to Breathe, if you have never had it. But, IF you have had those Good Things, you can Miss having them, and thus Want to have them again, and have them all of the Time. Yes, you might even Remember having Good Health, when you were Young and Full of Life; but, only IF you were Fed Properly, whereby you might have had some Good Health to some Degree. However, if you have never been Able to Run with the Deers and Play with the Wild Mountain Goats, how would you Know what you are Missing? Believe it or not, it is Possible to be Regenerated, whereby you can Obtain Good Health by Means of Fasting and Praying and Eating Properly between such Fasts, which you can Read about in the *Holy Bible,* which only Mentions it: beCause, if it had gone into any Great Details about that Important Subject, the Edomites would have Edited it OUT: beCause it would have Interfered with their Incomes, which are Obtained by Selling DRUGS, Chemical Poisons, Tobacco Products, Cokes, Candies, Cookies, Cakes, Artificially-flavored Fruit Juice Drinks with lots of Sugar added, and all Kinds of ABOMINATIONS that Jesus Christ and Moses would not Touch: beCause they did enough Fasting to have their Senses Working Properly, which will also be True for YOU, when you Do Enough Fasting and Eating Properly between Fasts. In Fact, you will Discover that you are Living in a Manmade HELL, if you do Enough Fasting: beCause almost everything STINKS, and Especially those Stinking Vehicles that Burn Gases and Fossil Fuels, which are among the Worst of those Abominations that God HATES. Nevertheless, we now have Choices to make: beCause we are at another Crossroads in Life, whereby we can Turn Riit or Left, or just keep on going Straight Down to HELL! Yes, it is YOUR Decision to make, my Friend or Enemy, and your Decision will Depend on your FAITH in All that is

GOOD, who is otherwise known as GOD, who Lives in a Paradise of Peace and True Happiness, called Mount Zion, which is the Holy City of the Great King, which is Guarded by the Angels with their Flaming Swords, whereby no Unclean Thing nor Unclean Creature can Enter into it, including those Stinking Noisy Polluting Vehicles: because they are not Needed nor Wanted for True Prosperity.

10-08 [_] O Elected King of Provable Truths, we will have to Confess that you are Riit, sooner or later; but, until the Masses of People should take up their *Holy Bibles* with Sincerity, just to Discover that you are Correct about those Important Subjects, you could say that this is a Lost Generation, for which there is NO Hope — that is, unless the Rain should STOP, and they should be FORCED to Fast by Means of Starvation, whereby they might come to their Riit Senses with the Prodigal Son of Luke 15, which you have MAGNIFIED in your Inspired Book, called: **"The New MAGNIFIED Version of the GOOD NEWS According to Saint LUKE!" (The Magnified Gospel of Luke in Plain English!) By The Worldwide People's Revolution!®** Book 061. Yes, it is an Inspired Book that everyone should Study, along with **"The New MAGNIFIED Version of the GOOD NEWS According to Saint JOHN!" (The Gospel According to Saint John Zebedee Boanerges in Plain English!)** Book 062. However, getting them to Study those Inspired Books will be more Difficult than Pulling Out Teeth: beCause of their Great UNBELIEF. After all, they have never Seen a Holy Man, nor would they Believe that it is Possible for anyone to Live a Holy Life in a Corrupt World like this, where we are Bombarded with Endless Advertisements for Junk Foods and Poisonous Drinks — not to Mention all of the Lusts of the Flesh Pots of Egypt, and the Vain Things that we must Buy to make us Happy! Yes, the latest Craze is Buying Electric Cars, which Cost 30,000$ or more, which is enough Money to Build several small Cisterns for Water Storage — except that Gardens Require HUGE Amounts of Water, and must be Protected from Raccoons, Opossums, Squirrels, Crows, Rats, Mice, and THIEVES, which will Greatly Multiply when the Great False Economy CRASHES! Indeed, those Hypocritical Professing "Christians" will no doubt Discover themselves becoming Thieves and Liars: beCause of not being Set Up Properly for LIVING! Yes, they have been Deceived by Satan, who has them Hoping that Jesus Christ will soon Return and thus Save them from it all; or, that they will be Raptured Up to Heaven before the Great Tribulation, as if they were Qualified to Live with the Holy Ones, after Living like Fat Hogs and Greedy Selfish Bears. Nevertheless, if the Rain Stops, there is some Hope for them to come to their Riit Senses; but, only IF they should Learn what you have Revealed. Therefore, it is very Important that a Copy of this Book, and your other Inspired Books, should be Placed in their Hands, whereby they might Study them during those Days.

10-09 [_] Well, my Friend, by that Time, it will be far too Late to Save them: beCause it Requires much Time, Money, Materials, Energy, and the Cooperation of **"Seven Great Armies of Working Soldiers,"** just to Save them. Yes, it would Require Water Ships and many Water Distilleries, just to Water the Fruit Trees with Remineralized Water, which would not be at all Convenient, nor easy to Do. In Fact, even with United Effort, Worldwide, it would be a Great Challenge, just to Survive: beCause the Ignorant Fools would be going to WAR over the Last Gallon of Gas, just to Maintain their Phony Lifestyle, even though they could have been Living in those **"Beautiful Swanky PALACES!" (A New Concept in Living Habits — Swanky Palaces for Poor People!) By The Worldwide People's Revolution!®** Book 066.

10-10 [_] O Elected King, I am not Sure that Climate Changes could be Stopped, even if we should now begin to Build those **"GLORIOUS Swanky Hotels Castles and Fortresses"**: beCause the Atmosphere is already Full of Capitalist Dung, which will Require a hundred Years or more to Clean itself up, even if we now Stop Polluting the Earth with our Abominations.

— Chapter 11 —

A Guaranteed Solution for Reversing Climate Changes!

11-01 [ ] You might Remember how Clear the Skies were during September 11th, 2001, when all of the Airplanes were Grounded in **"The Divided States of United Lies,"** whereby the Atmosphere had a Day of Reprieve, and the Airlines Suffered an Economic Crisis: beCause many People Cancelled their Traveling Plans by Airplanes: beCause of being Afraid of those Wicked TERRORISTS — only to Discover, later on, that it was an Inside Covered-up Government Covert Job, called a "False Flag" Operation, whereby the United States Federal Government Attacked its own Citizens, and Blamed it onto a Convenient Patsy by the Name of Osama bin Laden, being similar to the President Kennedy Assassination, whereby the Federal Government Murdered President Kennedy, and Blamed it onto another Patsy by the Name of Lee Harvey Oswald: beCause the United States of America is not so Innocent as some Ignorant People might Vainly Imagine. In Fact, it was such a Top Secret Covert Action in both Cases, that the Files will not be Opened until the Year 4040 AD, just to make Sure that no Civil War is brought about by Revealing the Whole Truth about those Covert Actions — not that very many Politicians would Care whether or not half of Americans should Die in a Civil War; but, that we might be Taken Over by some Enemy, such as Russia or China, who have had their own Covert Actions; but, no such Marvelous False Flag Operations as was carried out during September 11th, 2001, by **"The Divided States of United Lies!" (The so-called "United States of North America" in Disguise!)** Book 058. Indeed, that was such a Well-planned Top Secret Military Action, that it even Deceived the Federal Burden of Investigation (FBI) and the Central Unintelligent Agencies (CIA), of which there are no less than 30 Nameless Organizations, none of whom have any Idea what the other Organizations are Doing! Yes, it is a Case of the Left Hand having no Idea what the Right Hand is Doing! Well, at any rate, we can Comfort ourselves with the Fact that none of the 10,000+ Important Questions have been Answered about the Evil Events of September 11th, 2001 — such as, "Just Exactly HOW did World Trade Center Tower 7 come Crashing Down in less than 7 Seconds at 5:20 P.M. without the Use of any EXPLOSIVES?" Awe, Osama bin Laden must have Snuck into World Trade Center Towers 1, 2, 6 and 7 the Night before September 11th, and Wired Up no less than 20,000 TONS of Explosives, just to Accomplish such Fantastic Events, which only an Expert Demolitionist like him could have Accomplished without any Help from the Federal Government of **"The Divided States of United Lies!"** Indeed, you might not be Aware that Tower 7 had some 283 Hardened Steel Columns in it, and Covered nearly a whole City Block, and many of those Hardened Steel Columns were 22-inches by 52-inches and 47 Stories Tall, which all Decided at the very same Instant to come Crashing DOWN in Free-fall Fashion, like Ballet Dancers hitting the Floor at the Exact same TIME: beCause of being Sparked by a little Kitchen Fire on the 19th Floor, in one Corner of it, which Caused all of those Steel Columns to Decide on their own Powers to CRASH themselves into the Basement, which Broke Open the so-called "Bathtub" that Held Out the Hudson River, and Caused all of Lower Manhattan to be FLOODED with Water — except that no such a Thing Happened! Indeed, it was far more Complicated than that. In Fact, most of those Steel Columns, even in Towers 1 and 2, also, were simply MELTED by the Forces of Mysteries, whereby no Steel Columns Penetrated into the Basements of any of those Buildings! Otherwise, the Concrete Bathtub would have been Broken, and there would have been a BIG Flood Disaster. In Fact, George Stephanopoulos was giving an ABC News Report from the Crash Site, and Peter Jennings asked him WHERE the Pile of Rubble went to, which should have been at the Bases of Towers 1 and 2, which should have been no less than 20 Stories TALL: beCause of the Million Tons of Concrete and Steel that was in each Building, which Melted Down to no more than

ONE Story Tall, and did not leave any Gaping Holes in the Ground, nor even Penetrate through the Ground Floor! Yes, Amazingly enough, there were a few Pieces of Steel still sticking up into the Air; but, almost all of it was GONE, and the Concrete was Transformed by MAGIC into FINE POWDER, which Spread itself out over 10 City Blocks in all Directions from there: beCause that is the Nature of Falling Concrete without the Use of any EXPLOSIVES! In Fact, when you take a simple Block of Concrete Up to the Roof of any Tall Building in the World, and simply DROP IT onto the Ground, it always Transforms itself into FINE POWDER on the way down to the Ground, whereby there is only Dust to be Gathered Up — at least According to NIST, which is the National Institute of Sciences and Technologies, which made a Thorough and Unbiased Investigation into all of those Evil Events of September 11th, 2001, and came up with the Rational Conclusion that World Trade Center Tower 7 came Crashing Down in less than 7 Seconds by the Almighty Power of "Thermal Expansion," whereby all 283 Hardened Steel Columns Humbly Submitted to the Will of Superstitions, and thus Loosened all 2,967,856 Hardened Steel BOLTS and Welded Joints at the Exact same Time, in Order to make that Possible without the Use of any EXPLOSIVES! Yes, it was a Most Marvelous TRICK, you might say, just to make that Possible, and without Spending 6 Weeks or more Setting Up those Explosives, which only 6 Demolition Companies in the Whole World know HOW to Do, one of which must be Guilty of Doing it; but, it cannot be Found among all of the September 11th RUBBLE. Indeed, the Dust was Tested for Explosives by Independent Investigators, who Discovered that it was FULL of Thermite Particles, which NIST pooh-poohed as False Science, who Refused to make any Tests of the Dust for any Explosives: beCause they were Sure that Osama bin Laden was the Culprit who did that Dirty Deed, along with his 19 Hired Hijackers from Saudi Arabia, most of whom are still Walking about: beCause they were some more Patsies — at least according to the Architects and Engineers, whose Experts Claim that it was a Demolition Job for a Fact, and that only Expert Demolitionists could have Accomplished it, which should be Proven in a Courtroom; but, NIST has no Interest in Proving anything, much less the Federal Cover-up Government, which has Filed their Investigations away until the Year 4040: beCause Words might get Out that we have been Deceived by them, as the North Koreans Claim, as well as the Iranians, Russians, Cubans, and most Europeans, who are now Aware of the TRICKS of **"The Divided States of United Lies,"** who Murdered German Soldiers in Iraq by Means of a Military Helicopter, which was Leaked by Wicked-leaks, along with other Wikileaks Information, which is not Appreciated by the Anti-Christ False Flag Operators, who have been Covering Up their Crimes for Centuries! §§‡

11-02 [ ] O Unelected King, if the United States Federal Government is Guilty of any such False Flag Operations, it is Self-evident that there needs to be a Thorough House Cleaning in the District of Criminals, in Washington. Yes, all of those Top Secret Organizations — including the FBI, the Bureau of Alcoholics Tobacco and Firearms Fanatics, the Bureau of Homeland Insecurity, the Internal Revenue Snakes, and the CIA — should be Retired to a City of Refuge for Suspected Criminals, where they can Attend to their Organic Gardening, or else be Hanged to the nearest Lamp Posts, along with ALL of those CONgress People and the Supreme Court Injustices: beCause none of them Called for a THOROUGH Investigation into the Evil Events of September 11th, until ALL of the Evidence was Destroyed! Yes, George Warmonger Bush and Little Dick Chicanery are at the Top of the List of Most Wanted Criminals: beCause they Worked with the United States Air Force to bring about those Evil Events: beCause it was Military-grade Termite that was Discovered in the Dust at the World Trade Center Sites, which is Proof that only the Military could have Done it, O Rummy Donald. However, there were also MELTED Car Engines several Blocks from the Crash Sites, which Dr. Judy Wood Reported about in her Scientific Investigations, which the CONgress has yet to Investigate. In Fact, those Melted Engines are never Mentioned by any Snooze Reporters, even as Tower 7 is seldom if ever Mentioned. However, Lester Holt gave a Cover-up Report about it all for NBC, and said that those Melted Car Engines were the Results of a New Phenomenon, known as Melted Car Engine Syndrome, which Attacks Parked Cars that are too Close to World Trade Center Buildings, whereby the Smell of them MELTS the Engines, and also Turns Cars UPSIDE DOWN by the BLASTS of Imaginary EXPLOSIVES, which I Thought was a rather Strange Statement to make. Nevertheless, Lester Holt is a Firm Believer in the Mythical Noah's Ark Story, whereby a 600-year-old Gentleman Fed and Watered no less than 2 Million Species of Animals, each Day, and Cleaned Up their Poop and Piss after them, and still had Time to Butcher no less than 60 Bovines, Daily, just to Feed those Carnivores! Yes, the Ark must have had a Good Supply of Extra Bovines, just to Feed all of those Bears, Lions, Tigers, Jackals, Hyenas, Dogs, Wolves, Foxes, Coyotes, Wolverines, Mongooses, Skunks, Snakes, Hawks, Owls, Eagles, Buzzards, Vultures, Crows, Ravens, and many other Flesh-eating Creatures — none of which made any Noises whatsoever in their Cages: beCause Noah provided Marijuana for them to Eat, which Soothed their Nerves. Indeed, the 10,000+ Species of Apes and Monkeys were all SILENT, except for when they Sang *Silent Night, Holy Night,* in Remembrance of their Lord and Master, who also Believed that Jewish MYTH. Otherwise, he would have Clearly said, *"You should not Accept the Jewish Fables as Facts — such as that Story about Noah and his Ark: beCause there is no Way that the Ark could have Contained Enough Water to Water 2 Million Species of Animals for an entire Year, much less any Way for only 8 People to Water and Feed them and Clean Up after them."* But, behold, he made no such Declaration of Truths: beCause he Wanted most People to be Tested for their HONESTY: beCause no Liars will Enter into his Holy Kingdom; and only a Liar would Deny the Obvious FACTS — that World Trade Center Tower 7 could not have come Crashing Down in less than 7 Seconds without the Use of EXPLOSIVES! Indeed, whomever Denies that is an Ignorant IDIOT, even if he or she is a CONgress Person with a 2x4 Board Stuck in his or her Rectum, all of the Way up to his or her Brain Box! Chances are that none of those People ever Studied www.AE911TRUTH.org for themselves. §§‡

11-03 [_] Well, my Friend, Chances are that they will Conclude that you and I are Totally INSANE, just for Doubting the Official Reports about September 11th, 2001: beCause everyone Knows that we have the Best Government in the World, which is also the most Innocent, which sent in Army Tanks to Rescue the Children in the David Koresh Compound in Waco, Texas, whereby those Tanks Shot Out NAPALM into those Wooden Shanties, in Order to SNATCH UP those little Children into Heaven, in a sort of Pre-Rapture Episode, whereby their Souls were SAVED! HALLELUIAH! And then, to put the Frosting on the Cake, the Federal Government Orchestrated the Oklahoma City Bombing a Year after that Glorious Event, after Warning all of the Members of the Bureau of Alcoholics Tobacco and Firearms Fanatics to be Golfing during that Day: beCause none of them had any Idea that their Fatherly Federal Government could Orchestrate another False Flag Operation, just to get RID of the Patriotic Militias that were Rising Up at that Time, which amounted to about 800 Organizations, which were almost all Dismantled within a Month or 2: beCause few of them had any Great Interest in being the next Victims of their Frankenstein Federal Government, which put the Blame on Poor Little Timothy James McVeigh, whom they Pretended to Execute, who is now Living in a Retirement Home in Florida, along with those Drugged Victims of Flights 97 and 77, who have no Idea what Happened: beCause the Drugs Prevent them from Thinking. Therefore, they are all like Zombies, who Play Games and Watch Movies on their TVs — Thanks to their Wonderful Fatherly Good Government, which has no Secret Plans for doing the same Thing to ME, nor to YOU: beCause they are the GOOD GUYS, Remember? Otherwise, they would be DEMANDING **"The Great Worldwide TELEVISED Court HEARING,"** whereby all such Things might be PROVEN in a Courtroom! §§‡

11-04 [_] O Elected King, there are at least a Million Conspiracy Theories about what Actually Happened in all such Cases, which would Require a thousand Years to Settle in any Courtroom, even if those Trials should begin Today, while some of the Accused Victims are still Alive, whereby they might Testify in any such Courtroom. For Example, if 6 Million Jews were Exterminated in Nazi

Crematories during World War 2, there should be some Witnesses to it all: beCause most of the Survivors, who were Rescued from those Prison Camps, had SMALL NUMBERS — such as AU10247AU and AU9681AU on their Tattooed Arms, with the Highest Number being 104,005 without an AU, which Identified them as being Victims of Auschwitz, Poland. Indeed, the AU was put in front of and behind the Numbers, just to make Sure that no one Added any Numbers, later on, which many Lying Red-faced Jews did, later on, and even made up their own Tattoos on Jews that were not even in the War Zone, just to Gain Sympathy from whomever they might Lie to. After all, we are Supposed to Feel very Sorry for all Jews: beCause of that HoloHOAX Nonsense, in spite of the Fact that most of the Victims who Survived it had LOW Numbers, which is Proof that the Nazis were not Attempting to Exterminate them: beCause, if they were, they would have begun the Extermination with the First Prisoners, who would be more apt to Know more about what was going on in those Concentration Camps: beCause of being there from the Beginning of the War. But, behold, they Survived: beCause of having Stronger Constitutions, which Resisted the Diseases that were going around, who are still Alive beCause of it, who could Testify at **"The Great Worldwide TELEVISED Court HEARING,"** except that the Edomites do not Want them to Testify: beCause we might Learn too much. Indeed, we might even Learn that there were no Gas Chambers at all! In Fact, Zyklon B Gas just Happens to leave Identification Marks of itself in BLUE, which has never been Found in any so-called "Gas Chambers," except where they Disinfected Clothing with it, rather than Boil the Clothing in Hot Water: because there was a Shortage of Fuel at that Time. Therefore, the Germans had to be very Conservative with their Energy, in an Effort to Win the Unwinnable War: beCause the Axis Powers had Access to only 5% of the World's Natural Resources, while the Allies had Access to 95% of those Resources, including Crude Oils and Gases, which is WHY they Won the War — not beCause they were Better Warriors; but, because the Leaders of the Allies did not Care whether or not they Lost Millions of Men and Billions of Bullets: beCause they had Hordes of People to Sacrifice for that Unjust Cause, even as you have Explained within other Inspired Books, which only give a few of the Details: beCause too many Details in any one Book could Cause it to be Banned from Publication, even as was the Case for your Inspired Book, called: **"The UGLY Scarred Dishonest Face of Poor Old Miserable UNCLE SAM!" (A Memorial Day Legacy!) By The Leader, Adolf Hitler, Junior!** Book 054, which was Suppressed by Create Space for Less Truths. §§‡

11-05 [_] Well, my Friend, if any of those People were Sincerely Seeking the Whole Truth about any Subject, they would be the First to be Demanding **"The Great Worldwide TELEVISED Court HEARING!" (That Great Meeting of the Most Intelligent and Well-Educated Minds!)**, Book 041, just to Discover what the Whole Truth might BE! But, behold, none of them are Interested in it: beCause they Stand on the WRong Side of almost every Important Issue! For Example, they Know full well that it is Possible for almost everyone in the World to become Moderately RICH, and without Telling any Lies nor Selling any Trash: beCause we could all be Living in those **"Beautiful Swanky PALACES!" (A New Concept in Living Habits — Swanky Palaces for Poor People!) By The Worldwide People's Revolution!®** Book 066. Indeed, they Know for a Fact that we have no Lack of Mountains of Rocks nor Rivers of Water for Doing that; but, they Want almost all of the Money and Pleasures for themselves, while Maintaining a SLAVERY SYSTEM, whereby their Ignorant Slaves do the Dirty Work for them. In Fact, they have Deliberately set up Public Schools for the Purpose of "Dumbing them Down," as the Saying goes, for making them into ZOMBIES, who cannot Think for themselves! Indeed, by the Time that a Student is ready to Graduate from College, he has no more Interest in Reading another Book of any Kind, which is the Case for 85% of those Graduated Students: beCause they have been made SICK of Learning, which is Exactly what their Tax Masters Want: beCause they Want a LOT of Education Slaves, Work Slaves, Tax Slaves, Interest Slaves, Insurance Slaves, Drug Slaves, Sex Slaves, Endless Bills Slaves, and you Name it — all of whom are Fully Persuaded that they Live in the Best Country on the Earth, in spite of not having any Fresh Clean Air to

Breathe, Pure Living Water to Drink, Wholesome Natural Foods to Eat, Natural Clothing to Wear, nor Secure Fireproof Tornado-proof Insurance-proof Houses to Live in. Indeed, they are simply DECEIVED SLAVES, and do not even Realize it! Nevertheless, X-amount of them are "Dropping Out," and are Moving Out: beCause they have come to Realize that it is all a Grand DECEPTION of the Capitalists, who should be Brought in Shackles and Chains to TRIALS, and made to Prove WHY anyone in the World should be Living in such EXTREME POVERTY! Indeed, if we did not have any Mountains of Rocks to Work with, it would be Different; and if we did not have any Fossil Fuels for Running Heavy Equipment, it would be Different; but, behold, we have all of the Technologies, Tools, Materials, Money and Voluntary Working Soldiers for getting it all done Properly and Efficiently, without the Use of any Banks nor Bankers, much less any Lying Politicians nor Worthless Preachers, who are such Spiritual Cowards that they will not even Address these Important Subjects. ‡

11-06 [_] O Elected King, I Fail to Understand what any of that Information has to do with Climate Changes, much less with Guaranteed Solutions for Climate Changes?

11-07 [_] Well, my Friend, the Climate Problems have all to do with our Basic Philosophies and Lifestyles, which must be Changed, if we Expect to Survive what is Bound to Happen — that is, IF *the Book of Revelation* has any Credibility at all, which it likely does, even if it is a Fictitious Story: beCause it is an Inspired Book, which was written by someone who was *"... in the Spirit on the Sabbath Day,"* which Means that he was in Tune with the Holy Spirit, who Knows all Things, even in Advance, in spite of not Mentioning anything that might Identify such Nolij. Therefore, it is a Good Idea to Pay Attention to it. After all, if it is Correct, we are in Big Trouble; and, even if it is not Correct, we are still in Big Troubles: beCause of those Climate Changes, which are Natural Reactions to our Environmental Sins, which will only be Slightly Reduced by making Electric Cars for everyone in the World: beCause that Sin will Produce more Sins — such as more Paved Highways, which Absorb Heat from the Sunlight, and thus make the Climate even Hotter than it was. However, those Swanky Fortresses would Eliminate the Need for any more Highways, and would Cause many of the Present Highways and Parking Lots to be Paved with Pine Trees, or at least some Weeds: beCause of being Closed Down. However, that Plan would not Fit in with the Capitalist's Plans for making themselves Richer and Richer, while making the Masses of People Poorer and Poorer.

11-08 [_] O Elected King, there is no Doubt that your Master Plan for Solving our Massive Problems is the Best Plan in the World: beCause those **"GLORIOUS Swanky Hotels Castles and Fortresses"** will Solve at least 5,000 Problems at the same Time, while other Solutions might Solve one or 2 Problems, only, while Creating some more Problems — such as Building an Electric Car for everyone in the World, when the Big Babies already have far too many Toys to Play with, whereby the Highways are already Jammed with far too much Traffic, which is Calling for more and more of those UGLY Highways, which we cannot even Keep Repaired Properly: beCause of being 20+ Trillion Dollars in Debt to the Edomites. Therefore, we must begin to Think OUTSIDE of the Box that we have put ourselves into.

11-09 [_] O Elected King, do you Seriously Believe that most People will just GIVE UP their Present Lifestyles, and Move into those Swanky Fortresses in Wilderness Places like Western Texas and the Great Plains of Montana?

11-10 [_] Well, if I were Asking them to Depart from their Swanky Palaces, and move into those Wooden / Plastic Firetrap Mouse-infested Cockroach Dens, I could Understand WHY they might Rebel Against the Idea: beCause of Lowering their Standards of Living; but, I am not Asking for that.

— Chapter 12 —

A Guaranteed Solution for Rising Sea Levels

12-01 [_] O Elected King, are you not Aware that the Pollution that already Exists in our Atmosphere is Sufficient to Continue to Melt the Icebergs, and thus Raise the Sea Levels?

12-02 [_] Yes, I am quite Aware of it, even though I am not a Scientist of any Kind; but, I am Observant enough to Know what you are Saying, and it is likely True. However, all Swanky Fortresses will be BUILT UP on Foundations of Cisterns, whereby Rising Sea Levels will not be any Great Problem for the Righteous People, who Move themselves into those Fortresses; but, for People who Live on Islands in the Seas, it will still be a Major Problem, unless we can Persuade them to also Build Swanky Fortresses for themselves, which we can Help them to Do: beCause we are Able to Do that, even if some People are not Willing to Help them. After all, some of those Islands are some of the Nicest Places to Live in this World of Wonders. Therefore, if they have Stone Bedrocks to Build on, we can Accommodate them, and thus Save their Islands from being Drowned Out. However, their Way of Life might have to be Changed to some Degree: beCause of not Living Directly on their Beaches; but, Up Above those Beaches, whereby they might have Better Views, but less Access to the Waters. Indeed, they might have to Walk Down Stone Steps, just to get to the Beaches, or otherwise use Elevators; but, those are just Minor Inconveniences that can be Tolerated, while Rising Sea Levels cannot be Tolerated. ‡

12-03 [_] O Elected King, are you Suggesting that we should Export thousands of Shiploads of Rocks to those Low-lying Islands, along with Shiploads of Sand, Gravel, and Cement for making Concrete Cisterns, and enough of them to RAISE UP the Islands far above the Sea Levels by a Hundred Feet or more?

12-04 [_] Well, some of the Islands are Presently only just a few Feet above the Sea Level. Therefore, if they are Raised Up by only 50 Feet, it will be a Vast Improvement, and a lot more Security for the People who Live on those Islands.

12-05 [_] O Elected King, I would say that it should be our First Line of Actions to Save the Islands, except that none of them would Look like Islands after Building Tall Stone Walls around them; but, they would Look like UGLY Fortresses, which I HATE! {Please Check the Box with an X, if you Agree with such a Statement.}

12-06 [_] Well, my Potential Enemy, it must be that you have never Seen a Beautiful Stone Fortress, many of which are Visited by Millions of Curious People, who especially like to Search around in Hidden Tunnels and Secret Passageways, which Wise People could Design into their New Castles, just for the Children to Play in them — except that they might get Lost in them, if they were left Unguarded by Adults. Chances are that you are one of the few People on the Earth, who do not Like the Looks of Castles and Fortresses; but, wait until you get to Visit one of those **"GLORIOUS Swanky Hotels Castles and Fortresses,"** which have Planned Flower Gardens, Vineyards, Orchards, and Vegetable Gardens, which are Designed for BEAUTY. After all, Rocks and Pretty Flowers are the Perfect Combination for Beauty, and especially when they are Enhanced with Beautiful People and Magnificent Horses with Silver-studded Harnesses with Bells Ringing, pulling Golden Coaches through Arcaded Streets that are Paved with Polished Granite, and Lined with Polished Marble Walls, or with Colorful Ceramic Murals on the Walls, and with large Mirrors, here and there, just to Reflect their Beauty. Yes, you are now Free to let your Imagination Run Wild, O Artists, Architects, and Engineers: because you will no longer be Restricted by a Lack of Money: beCause you will be Hired with Good Wages to Do Good Works: beCause that is the Duty of **"The New RIGHTEOUS One-World Government!" (HOW to Establish a Righteous One-World Government without Going to WAR!) By The Worldwide People's Revolution!® Book 056.**

12-07 [_] O Elected KING, I just LOVE your Positive Attitude toward Life! And therefore, I will do anything to Please you, and also do it with all of my Might. However, I am Greatly Worried that X-amount of Young People will be Overzealous to Do Good, and will not be Patient Enough to take their Time to Do it RIIT, which might Require some Schooling. Indeed, I Visualize some very UGLY Messes in this World, without the Snoopervision of **"The New RIGHTEOUS One-World Government"** Officials. For Example, most Mexicans are very Ambitious, when you Provide them with Materials, Tools, and Money to Work with; but, they can make some of the most Ugly Messes that you have ever Seen: beCause they seem to have no Sense of Beauty in their Heads. ‡

12-08 [_] Well, most People like to have the Freedom to Do whatever they Want to, and without any Snoopervision: beCause they do not Like to be Told what to Do; but, it is my Firm Belief that we all Need GOOD Masters, which is WHY they are called Beautiful PLANNED City States: beCause the Masters should be Planning them Correctly, and Thinking like RICH People, instead of Poor People. Yes, they should Plan those Swanky Fortresses as if they were Planning them for GOD, and not for Hermits, Beggars, Bums, Hobos, nor Lazy Sloths. After all, if someone does not Feel like Working, he or she should REST at a **Swanky Fasting Sanitarium**, which will get all of the Laziness Out of him or her, and make him or her Ambitious. For Example, just Think of the many Buildings that I have Helped to Build, for the Proof of the Goodness of Fasting. Moreover, just Think of the many Inspired Books that I have Written for the same Good Reason. Could anyone Rightly Accuse me of being LAZY?

12-09 [_] O Unelected King, you might not be Lazy; but, it is for Certain that you are a bit CRAZY, and Especially if you Vainly Imagine that anyone is going to go along with your Idea to RAISE UP the Islands of the Seas by Building Tall Swanky Fortresses on them, whereby they can Withstand the Tidal Waves of Mountains Sliding into the Oceans. For Example, it is Possible that Southern California will some Day DROP into the Pacific Ocean, and thus Cause a Tidal Wave to Sweep Across the Islands of Hawaii, and Remove every Building over there, even all of the Way to Japan and China! Yes, Hong Kong could easily be Swept Away by such a Tidal Wave. Likewise, the Canary Islands might Slide Off into the Atlantic Ocean, and thus Cause all of the Coastal Cities in the entire Eastern United States to be WIPED OUT, including Houston, Texas, which is just barely above Sea Level. In Fact, it is Believed by Scientists that such a Tidal Wave could Sweep all of the Way to the Rocky Mountains, and thus DROWN most Americans: beCause they are not Living in SECURE Swanky Fortresses! Therefore, if they Want to Save themselves from any such Natural Disasters, they will have to get their Lazy Asses OUT of Bed, and get to WORK on the Construction of those Tall Stone Walls, which can mostly be done by Mechanical Slaves, if they Use their Heads to THINK! §§‡

12-10 [_] Well, my Friend, it seems like the Earth is Designed for Natural Disasters of Various Kinds, which can only be Counteracted by Building those **"GLORIOUS Swanky Hotels Castles and Fortresses!" (Beautiful Planned City States for WISE Intelligent Well-Educated People with Common Sense and Good Understanding!) By The Worldwide People's Revolution!® Book 019.**

— Chapter 13 —

A Guaranteed Solution for Forest Fires

13-01 [_] Just Think of the Great Challenge that it will be to Combat Forest Fires, which are easily Started by Lightning Strikes, Camp Fires, Cigarettes, and Explosives. In Fact, I can hardly Think of a Greater Challenge to Mankind — except that there is a Simple Solution, which is to let those Forests Burn themselves Out, much like they did for the Wildfires in Yellowstone National Park, which came very Close to Eliminating the Old Faithful Inn, which is a Log Structure, which could be Surrounded by Tall Stone Walls a Mile or 2 from it, except that those Walls would not Look very Natural in that Park, even as the Old Faithful Inn does not Look very Natural; but, it Looks Appropriate for such a Park, which is Closed Down during Winter Months: beCause it is not Practical to keep it Open. Nevertheless, just Exactly what is the Best Solution for Combating those Wild Fires?

13-02 [_] O Elected King, there are Vast Wilderness Areas in this World of Wonders — such as the Amazon Basin, much of the Wild West, Siberia, Mongolia, and most of Africa — which are Impossible for People to Control. Therefore, why Waste any Time, Money, Materials, or Energy on it? Why not just let Mother Nature do whatever she Wants to? But, in the Meantime, we can keep ourselves Busy on the Construction of those Swanky Fortresses, whereby we can at least Save some of the Trees that would otherwise be Burned Up, which can be made into Lumber for making Fine Hand-crafted Furniture, which Lumber can be Stored in Secure Fireproof Warehouses at Swanky Fortresses, as well as in the Workshop Storage Domes. Indeed, if the *Holy Bible* is True — that one-third of all Trees will be Burned Up — then why not Try to Save as many Trees as Possible by making them into Lumber? ‡

13-03 [_] Well, I Hear what you are Saying; but, those Trees just Happen to make most of our Oxygen, whereby they are Needed for that Purpose, alone. Therefore, we cannot Rightly Cut Down the Forests, just on the Presumption that the *Holy Bible* might be Correct; but, we most Certainly could Rescue a LOT of Trees, by making them into Lumber, as you say: because that Fine Hand-crafted Furniture will Greatly Enhance those Swanky Fortresses. However, I have Heard that most of the Good Trees have already been Cut Down and Removed from the Forests. For Example, there are only a few thousand of those large Redwood Trees Remaining, if I have Heard Correctly, when there used to be Millions of them! Moreover, Trees are known to Evaporate Water into the Atmosphere, which Actually Help to bring more Rains, which is WHY it most often Rains around Rivers and Lakes, where there are Trees, while Dry Lands and Deserts get very few Rains. Therefore, it seems like the Cure for those Forest Fires is to Plant MORE Trees, rather than Cut them Down. Indeed, we would have to Water all such Trees, until they get big enough to Support themselves, which would be quite a Challenge; but, there are millions of Unemployed People, who would probably Love that Job, if they were Provided with Swanky Stone Dome Homes to Live in, even in Wilderness Places, where they could also have little Communities of People in Miniature Swanky Fortresses, which could be Strategically Located in Places where the Surrounding Forests could be Watched from Watch Towers, even if those Places were Abandoned during Winter Months, when Snows might Pile Up, and there would be no Danger of any Forest Fires. ‡

13-04 [_] O Elected King, would you have us Building Tunnels from Swanky Fortresses to Guard Houses on Mountaintops, just to Provide Secure Means of getting to and from those Towers? For Example, would you have us Digging Trenches for making Stone Tunnels from Old Faithful Geyser to the Tops of the Mountains around there, in Yellowstone National Park, whereby Guards could Ride on Electric Motorbikes throughout the Park within those Tunnels, just to Keep an Eye on Things?

13-05 [_] Well, I am Sure that most People would Object to that Idea, until they Think about it. After all, a Proper Tunnel would be Invisible from above the Ground, and it could also have Entrances and Exits along the Tunnels, here and there, just for the Guards to get some Fresh Air, if nothing else, which would all have to be Carefully Planned; but, like I said, most People would Object to it: because of Disturbing the Natural Terrain. But, as for other Places in the Mountains, it would likely Prove to be a Good Idea: beCause there are often Sudden Snow Storms, which can Cover the Land 10 to 20 feet Deep. Therefore, if there were Secure Guard Houses, made Properly with THICK Stone Walls and Double Windows, being Connected to little Fortresses with Underground Tunnels, it would be Safe to say that no one would Lose his Life in such a Place; but, HOW to put Out a Forest Fire has always been a Major Problem: beCause of the very Rough Terrain, and almost Impossible Places to get to, which is WHY most of those Trees are still Standing. After all, some of those Mountains are almost Straight UP! Therefore, it is like Forbidden Territory. However, when it is Practical to Protect a Workable Forest, which is the Case for many Forests, I would say that it is a Good Idea to have Guard Houses every Kilometer in all Directions, as well as Proper Tunnels Connecting them, which would be a Major Project for the Future. Moreover, there could be Sprinkler Systems set up throughout such Forests for Watering them, if we Wanted to get that Ambitious, which would put Millions of People to Work, and make it Possible to Grow Bigger Healthier Trees, and especially Nut Trees, which could be Harvested and Frozen, and thus Preserved for many Years in Glass Jars for Times of Famines, along with Dates and Dried Figs, which Keep Well for Decades in Ideal Conditions, while Honeys Keep Well for thousands of Years in Ideal Conditions. Therefore, no one has to Starve to Death during the Future, if we Act Wisely, and get ourselves Prepared for the Worst Conditions Possible.

13-06 [_] O Unelected King, if God is out to Kill us, we will all be Killed. {Please Check the Box with an X, if you Agree with that Statement.}

13-07 [_] Well, if God were out to Kill anyone, and especially Wicked People like George Warmonger Bush and Little Dick Chicanery, Incorporated, you would Think that he would have already Done it; but, he gets his Justice by Causing their Spirits to be Born in New Bodies in Appropriate Places, whereby those Wicked People can get their Just Rewards during their next Lives. For Example, if George and Dick do not REPENT, they are likely to be Born in Baghdad, Iraq, the next Time Around, where a Car Bomb can Explode them into little bitty Pieces, whereby their Remains can be Washed into the Sewage System; and then their Spirits can be Born in some Deep Dark Jungle in Africa, where the Wild Beasts can Feast on them, if they still do not Repent. Yes, that is the Way that God Handles Wicked People, who cannot Escape from his Judgments and Rewards. Otherwise, they could be Born in the Bodies of Paraplegics, or Children with Down's Syndrome. Yes, there are any Number of Ways for God to get his Justice and Revenge on all such Sinners. However, if a whole Nation becomes too Wicked, he will also give Satan Permission to Wipe it Out by whatever Means is Appropriate, just as a Warning to other Wicked Nations, which was NOT the Case during World War 2: beCause Satan had nothing to do with that War: beCause he was on a Vacation at that Time, in another World. Indeed, that was simply a Case of Capitalists and Communists making Fools of themselves, when they would have been Wise to Join Adolf Hitler, and not gotten into any Hateful War, which is what the Wise People of Austria did, and thus never Lost a single Soul, nor even one House from it! Meanwhile, other Nations Rebelled Against the Higher Powers, and thus made Fools of themselves, just as *Romans 13* Warns. §§

13-08 [_] O Unelected King, you Surely do not Believe all such Biblical Lies, do you? {Please Check the Box, if you do NOT Believe in *Romans 13*.}

13-09 [_] Well, I only Believe in the Proper Version of *Romans 13*, which you can Discover in one of my Inspired Books. {Please Check the Box with an X, if you also Believe in that Version.}

13-10 [_] O Elected King, I have no Idea which Book that your Version of *Romans 13* might be found in. Therefore, how can I check it out?

— Chapter 14 —

A Guaranteed Solution for HOW to Quickly Discover Important Information!

14-01 [_] O Elected King, I Remember reading a certain Thought in the *Bible*, which I have never been Able to Locate since then, and have no Great Interest in Re-reading the entire Bible, just to Discover that certain Thought. However, that Laziness does not Quench my Thirst for Discovering that Thought. Therefore, HOW am I going to Find it?

14-02 [_] Well, my Friend, there is a very large Book, called *Strong's Exhaustive Concordance*, which Lists every single Word that can be Found in the *King James Version* of the *Holy Bible*, which is Designed to Help you to Locate all such Thoughts; but, you have to Remember at least one Exact Word within the Verse, which must also be Spelled Correctly, before you can Discover it. However, there are likely other Verses with Related Thoughts, which use Different Words, whereby you will not be Able to Discover them, unless you have a Bible with Cross References to those other Thoughts, which is still not Guaranteed to Help you to Discover ALL of the Verses concerning ALL of the Thoughts: beCause those Cross References were made up by People with Limited Nolij and with very Limited Good Understanding, who, for Example, completely Overlooked the Subject of Reincarnation: beCause they did not even Believe in it, in spite of the Fact that there are many References to it within the *Holy Bible!* Therefore, you might Think that you could Discover those References by going to some *Bible Commentary,* only to be Greatly Disappointed by the Lack of Information about Reincarnation, which might only Refer you to one Verse in *Hebrews,* which states that, *"It was Appointed unto People to Live and Die only once, and after that the Judgment would come for them; but, behold, we all Missed our Appointments: beCause we Failed to Pass our Tests of Faith, Hope, Trust, Love, Patience, Persistence and Obedience, which are **The Seven Basic Spiritual Building Blocks of LIFE,** without which no Person can See the Glory of the Gods."* — NMV. Therefore, it could be that you were Reading a Different Version of the *Holy Bible,* other than the *King James Version,* which is one of about 200 Contradictory Versions on the Market, none of which make much Sense, except for *The New MAGNIFIED Version,* which you can Discover by Carefully Reading **"Thu Nq MAGNUFIID Verzhun uv Thu PROVERBZ uv KING SOLUMUN in Plaan Ingglish!"** (The Understandable Version of the Famous Proverbs of King Solomon in Plain English!) By The Worldwide People's Revolution!®, Book 028, which is written in Swanky "Funetik Ingglish," which has only one Way to Spell one Sound each Time.

14-03 [_] O Elected King, there is the *Blue Letter Bible* on the Internet, which has about 14 of those Versions, and you can Search for any Special Words within any one of them, and thus perhaps

Discover certain Subjects and Thoughts; but, what if you Remember Reading a certain Idea in some Forgotten Book — such as *The Adventures of Huckleberry Finn,* which is Rich with Various Thoughts, which might even be Spoken by Nigger Jim, or Huck Finn, in some Southern Slang or Dialect — HOW can you Quickly Discover such Thoughts, seeing that no one has made up any *Strong's Exhaustive Concordance* for all such Multitudes of Books? In Fact, there are Literally BILLIONS of Books for all such Thoughts to get Lost in. Therefore, it is Impossible for you to Discover those Thoughts without Reading those Books.

14-04 [_] Well, my Friend, there is a Guaranteed Solution for that Problem, which I have Revealed within, **"The Washington Journal is a FARCE!" (C-SPAN Managers are not very WISE!) By The Worldwide People's Revolution!®** Book 006. However, you might not have any Interest in Reading that Book: beCause of already Understanding that C-SPAN is a FARCE. Therefore, I will now Reveal it to you within this Inspired Book: beCause it is such a Wonderful Idea. Indeed, you are likely Correct — that there are Billions of Books in this World of Wonders — and I have not Diminished that Number by any Degree: beCause of Adding on another 350+ Books to the Long List, which could be Divided among a Million Careful Readers, whereby each Reader Carefully Studies just one or 2 Paragraphs, whereby such a Reader can Quickly and Easily Identify each Thought within his or her Given Verses — that is, IF he or she is Wide Awake when the Subject or Thought is brought up at **"The Great Worldwide TELEVISED Court HEARING!" (That Great Meeting of the Most Intelligent and Well-Educated Minds!)**, Book 041. For Example, let us say that the Subject of Reincarnation is brought up, knowing that at least one-third of the People in the World Believe in it, and would Like to Learn more about it — HOW would they Quickly Discover all of the References to that Subject within those Billions of Books in the World, including my own? Well, in the Case of my Books, it would be Extremely Easy: beCause of so many People being Familiar with them; but, in the Case of *The Adventures of Huckleberry Finn,* I am not Sure that it even Mentions Reincarnation. However, if that Book has been Digitized, it should be relatively easy to Discover it, which is also True of my Books; but, it could be that the Subject is Suggested in other Words, whereby "Reincarnation" is not Actually Mentioned; but, it is only Suggested in a Subtle Way. Therefore, it Requires a Reader who has Recognized it and Remembers it. Therefore, if that Reader Knows for a Fact that the Subject is Mentioned somewhere in *The Adventures of Huckleberry Finn,* it can still be Quickly Discovered by Special Readers at that Great Meeting of the Most Intelligent Minds, who can Quickly Divide the Book among them by using the Numbered Pages. For Example, if your Number is 41, it Means that you should Carefully Read Page 41 in that Book, just in case the Subject of Reincarnation is Mentioned on that Page in some Way. Moreover, more than one Person can be Assigned with Page 41, just to Double Check each other; and all of the Books in the World can be Digitized for that Purpose, whereby our Computers can Quickly take us to any Book that we Search for on the Internet. ‡

14-05 [_] O Elected King, suppose the Reader is a Dimwit, who does not Understand that Jesus was Talking about Reincarnation, when he Clearly stated: *"If you can Receive it, John the Baptist is Elijah"?* In other Words, the Spirit of Elijah was Born in the Body of John the Baptist when he was Reincarnated. But, if the Reader is not very Bright, and cannot Think Straight, he or she might not Recognize the Connection, even as most People do not Recognize the Connection in an Obscure Verse in *The Book of Revelation,* which states that when Jesus Returns, *"... every Eye shall See him, even they also who Pierced him,"* which would Include those Roman Soldiers, who would have to be Reincarnated at the Time of his Second Coming by Means of a Resurrection, or by Means of simply being Born Again into this World, which is the Case for most People, who have to Live more than just one or 2 Lives, just to Learn their Lessons. In Fact, most People have likely Lived several Lives, and have still not Learned their Lessons: beCause of being all PUFFED UP with PRIDE. For Example, most Americans would not be Willing to Confess that their Motorized Vehicles are Abominations, which not only Kill hundreds of thousands of People, Worldwide, every Year; but, they also Pollute the Air, Water and Land with Toxic Abominations. Indeed, only a Humble Honest Person would make such a Confession; but, not one of those PROUD Americans, who has his Head STUCK in one or the other of those 2 Stinking Holes in **"The BIG White OUTHOUSE on the Not-so-Biblical Capitol DUNGHILL!"** Book 023. Nevertheless, HOW can all such Illusive Scriptures be Discovered without someone bringing up those Subjects? §

14-06 [_] Well, my Friend, the entire Objective for Conducting **"The Great Worldwide TELEVISED Court HEARING,"** is to Discover the Whole Truth about all Subjects of Importance to Mankind, whereby we might Save ourselves from the MADNESS of Greedy Capitalist HOGS, Communist Dogs, and Deceived Socialists, who have no Idea HOW to Solve their Host of Massive Problems. Otherwise, we might all Accept their Philosophies, and thus Fix our Problems!

14-07 [_] O Unelected King, none of your Solutions have been Proven to WORK, in spite of being Reasonable and Logical. For Example, if all of the Books in the World were Divided among the People who Voluntarily Agree to Read them, there is no Guarantee that any given Subject will be Discovered in all of those Books. For Example, the Subject of Reincarnation might be Mentioned in a Million Books, which might lend some Credibility to that Philosophy, which might be Discovered by the Readers; but, who could Discover all of the EVILS of Capitalism in any such Books, seeing that it is an Accepted Belief by most People, and especially by most Americans, who Sincerely Believe that Capitalism is the Economic Salvation of Mankind, when it is Actually the Self-Destruction of Mankind? Moreover, for every Book that Speaks Evil of Capitalism, there are likely a thousand that Speak in Favor of it: beCause the Possession Worshipers are the most Deceived People on the Earth! Indeed, it never crossed their Weak Minds that maybe Jesus Christ was Correct — that a Man's Life does not Consist in the Abundance of his Possessions; but, in his Relationship with GOD, who Adheres to the Doctrine of having *"all Things in Common,"* whereby all of the Mountains of Rocks and Rivers of Water Belong to ALL of us, and should be Shared among ALL of us, along with the Sand, Gravel, Cement, Trees, and all Building Materials, which cannot even be Properly Utilized without having the Proper TOOLS to Work with, which should also be SHARED among all of the Believers in Jesus Christ: beCause no one Person can Afford to Buy all of the Necessary Tools for Constructing a Beautiful Swanky Fortress, much less do all of the Necessary WORK for getting one Built; but, a Group of 200 Million Working Soldiers can get it all Finished in a HURRY with the Correct Tools. Indeed, it only makes Good Sense to have all such Things in COMMON among us, whereby no one Claims to OWN those Rivers of Water, Mountains of Rocks, nor the Mechanical Slaves that will do most of the Work for us; nor would anyone in his nor her Riit Miind WANT to Own all such Things, just for the Sake of PRIDE.

14-08 [_] Well, my Friend, you have just Touched on a very Important Subject, which is the Legitimacy of OWNERSHIP in the Eyes of GOD, who Happily Shares his Mountains, Rivers, Lakes, Forests, Rains, Minerals, and all other Material Things with us, which many Foolish People have Staked a Claim on, like they might Claim a Gold Mine to be their Own, just beCause they Discovered it by Chance, whereby they can PUFF UP their Minds with Great Pride over their Discovery and Ownership, which would be Like the Apostles making themselves very PROUD for having the Gifts of the Holy Spirit, whereby God would no doubt CURSE them for it: beCause they have no Legitimate Right to be Proud of any such GIFTS; but, they should be most Thankful for them, and thus Use them Wisely. Likewise, we should all be very Thankful for the Mountains of Rocks, Rivers of Water, Lakes, Forests, Minerals, and all Natural Resources of Building Materials, and thus Use them WISELY, which is Anti-Capitalism, Anti-Greed, Anti-Selfishness, and Contrary to the very Foundation of the American Way of DEATH, which is to PUFF UP the Minds of Ignorant Little Children with PRIDE! Indeed,

"The Public School of IGNERUNT FQLZ" starts out each Day with a Pledge of Allegiance to the Bloody RAG of **"The Divided States of United Lies!"** Pray tell, what would be Wrong or Evil about Pledging our Allegiance to the Great Creator GOD, who might Smile on us for it? And, more Specifically, what would be Evil about having all of those Material Things in COMMON among us, whereby we could all become Moderately RICH, without Telling any Lies, nor Selling any Capitalist TRASH!? Why should the Rich HOGS get to Enjoy the Polished Marble Stones, while the Masses of Poor People Live in Mud Huts and in Wooden / Plastic Firetrap Mouse-infested Cockroach Dens, when they could ALL be Living in those **"Beautiful Swanky PALACES!" (A New Concept in Living Habits — Swanky Palaces for Poor People!) By The Worldwide People's Revolution!®** Book 066?

14-09 [ ] O Elected King, I am almost Certain that someone in the World, other than yourself, has written an Extensive Book about that Subject of having *"all Things in Common,"* since it was an early Church Doctrine, which was Practiced by many Monks in Monasteries, and by the *Shaker Villages,* who Shared their Labors and Wealth with one another, who even took Vows of Poverty, and only Claimed to Own their Spoons, Toothbrushes, Combs, and Bibles. In other Words, it is another Important Subject that should be brought up at **"The Great Worldwide TELEVISED Court HEARING,"** whereby the Masses of People might come to Realize that they could Prosper much more by at least a hundred Times, if they all just Humbly Submitted to the Rulership of a RIGHTEOUS KING, who would have them Designing and Building their own **"Beautiful Swanky PALACES!"** Book 066. Yes, they could Accomplish Great Things, and make the Whole World a Wonderful Place for everyone to Live! {See: **"Are Americans the Most STUPID People who ever Lived?" (HOW Working People can PROSPER and Live in PEACE Under the Rulership of a RIGHTEOUS KING!) By The Worldwide People's Revolution!®** Book 047.}

14-10 [ ] Well, my Friend, that Important Subject about having everything in Common is fairly well Covered in **"The New MAGNIFIED Version of the Book of ACTS!" (The Understandable Version of the ACTS of the Apostles in Plain English!) By The Worldwide People's Revolution!®** Book 063. However, many Professing "Christians" will tell you that I have ADDED False Doctrines to the Infallible Word of God, which is ONE Word, which is JESUS. Therefore, they will just Naturally Reject all of those Provable Truths unto their own Damnation, and thus have to Suffer through the Great Tribulation: beCause of Rejecting me as their Elected King. Indeed, I may not be a Perfect King; but, just about any Righteous King would be a Vast Improvement over no King at all, whereby the Capitalist Madness goes on and on, whereby the Masses of Poor Ignorant People are Exploited by the Edomites, who get Richer and RICHER, who now have Trillions of Dollars in their Bank Accounts, and still Want more Trillions! Meanwhile, 7 Billion People are Living without Fresh Clean Air to Breathe, Pure Living Water to Drink, Wholesome Natural Foods to Eat, Secure Houses to Live in, Swanky Palaces to Richly Enjoy with their Marvelous Cathedrals, Concert Halls, Theaters, Gymnasiums, Indoors Swimming Pools, Tennis Courts, Bowling Alleys, Skating Rinks, Game Rooms, and Royal Swanky Buffets, which would be Serving the Best of Foods that have been Grown by **"The LUSCIOUS All-Mineral Organic Method of Gardening!" (HOW to Grow DELICIOUS Satisfying Foods for Potential Kingz and Kweenz in Swanky PALACES!) By The Worldwide People's Revolution!®** Book 021. Indeed, the Violent Movies Industries will be Retired to the Cities of Confusion, along with the Beer Halls, Whore Houses, Drug Dens, Snake Dens, Porcupine Lawyers, Political Rabbits, Stinking Skunks, and whomever is not Interested in Living a GOOD Life with other People of Like-mindedness, who have All that is GOOD at the Center of their Lives, who Seek to Raise Up HOLY Children, who Live for hundreds of Years without any Sicknesses nor Diseases, who have no Use for those Stinking Noisy Polluting DANGEROUS Vehicles, who are Contented to Walk with Jesus Christ and Saint Paul, who would Touch NONE of their Abominations, including those Stinking

Sprays and Poisons that are under Kitchen and Bathroom Sinks, which have Warning Signs to Keep them Out of the Reach of Children.

— Chapter 15 —

A Guaranteed Solution for Election Deceptions!

15-01 [_] You may be a Firm Believer in the so-called "Democratic Election System," which provides a Way for the Masses of Poor Ignorant People to VOTE for their so-called "Leaders," who seldom if ever Present any Reasonable Solutions for anything, who Speak in such Vague Terms with Multiple Interpretations, that no one has any Real Idea what to Expect from their Administrations. For Example, Dr. Obama ran on the Slogan, "Change that you can Trust!" And Donald Trumpeter ran on the Slogan, "Let's make America Great Again!" Well, America never was "Great" in the Eyes of Righteous People, and much less Great in the Eyes of God, who has very little Use for **"The BIG White OUTHOUSE on the Not-so-Biblical Capitol DUNGHILL!" (The Chief Sins of the Divided States of United Lies!) By The Worldwide People's Revolution!®** Book 023. In Fact, God has no Use for DEMON-ocracy, at all: beCause it is an Unworkable and Insane Government System, which is Like giving little Children a VOTE concerning how much Candy, Pie, and Iced-cream that they might Want to Eat, whereby they would all become SICK and Diseased with Rotted Out Teeths! Or, it would be Like giving Employees a VOTE concerning how much Work that they should Do, and how much they should be Paid for Doing almost nothing, and whether or not they should even Show Up for Work, and what Quality of Work that they should Do? Indeed, would you Operate a Business like that, which allows the Employees to Decide what gets Done? I Seriously Doubt it: beCause your Business would Utterly FAIL, even as those Politicians in Washington have Failed to Solve America's Massive Problems, in spite of Wasting TRILLIONS of Dollars on such Vain Projects as so-called "Health Care," which just Ignores the Dietary LAWS that God gave to Moses, which at least Prevented SOME of the Diseases. Nevertheless, it is Unlikely that most People are going to Give Up their Sacred Institute of DEMON-ocracy: beCause they are easily Deceived by it, and even Vainly Imagine that VOTING, itself, has some Kind of Magic Power to CURE whatever Ails them! ‡

15-02 [_] Granted, it is Possible that an Election could Help to Solve X-amount of Problems; but, only IF the Masses of People should Learn the WHOLE Truth about the Subject that they are Voting on. For Example, without the Permission of the Electors, the Federal Government of **"The Divided States of United Lies"** gave Permission to the Manufacturers of Water Pipes to put DEADLY LEAD into their Water Pipes — as if it were Impossible to Make Water Pipes without LEAD! However, when the Flint, Michigan Children got Brain Damages from the Lead, the Electors became somewhat Aware of what was Done to them, Nationwide, whereby they Voted to REPLACE ALL WATER PIPES WITH GLASS PIPES, which have ZERO Lead in them, which was on the National General Election Ballot, on the Backside of the Ballot, where they had an almost Invisible Tiny Secret Box [_] to Check with an X, which 99.999,999,999% of Americans did not SEE! Indeed, the Print was so Small as to be almost Invisible, and the Wording was so Legalistic as to not be Understandable by 99.999% of the People, even if they did Manage to read it. Personally, I did not get to See it: beCause I did not even Bother myself to Vote for the Right-WRong Rong-Riit Parties: beCause I already Knew in Advance that no such Issues would be Posted on any such Ballots for anyone to Vote FOR nor AGAINST: beCause that is not what DUMBmocracy is all about. Indeed, the whole Idea is to DECEIVE the Masses of People, who are not Capable of Judging whether or not Lead Pipes are GOOD or BAD: beCause only CONgress Members have enough Nolij to Juj such Important Subjects! Yes, I used to Believe that same Outlandish LIE, until I Thought about it, and then I came to the Happy Conclusion that NO Vote was a Vote Against BOTH False Parties. However, someone Reminded me that a Vote for Bernie Sanders was a Positive Vote — except that he was not Running on an Independent Ticket. However, even if he had been Running on such a Ticket, he would no Doubt have LOST: beCause the American Political System is RIGGED by the News Media, which has never yet given even ONE Positive Advertisement for the Great Truths that I Teach — one of which is the Fact that Voting, itself, has no Power to Correct anything, unless the Elected Official has some Reasonable and Guaranteed Solutions! For Example, WHO is going to Replace those Lead Pipes with Glass Pipes, seeing that Capitalism cannot Afford to Buy those Trillions of Dollars-worth of Glass Pipes: beCause Capitalism and DUMBmocracy are far too POOR to Do that? In Fact, not even all of the Trillions of Dollars in the Edomite Banks could get that Job Done: beCause we are Talking about Lead Pipes WORLDWIDE! Yes, the People of very Poor Countries could not Afford any GOOD Pipes; and therefore, they Bought All-American Lead Pipes for Poisoning their own Children: beCause Capitalism is very Good at Producing CHEAP Trash to Sell to Ignorant Poor People, who would rather have SOME Pipes than NO Pipes at all! After all, Packing Water in a Wooden Buckets is not exactly the Nicest Job in the World. But, if they had been WARNED by **"The New RIGHTEOUS One-World Government,"** that all such Lead Pipes are DANGEROUS, and should not be Used, they might have Voted for GLASS Pipes in all Cases! But, behold, no such Issues were put on any Ballots for any Elections: beCause that would Prove to be Anti-Capitalism, which would be BAD for American Businesses! §§‡

15-03 [_] O Elected King, how is it that Americans "Cornered" the Markets on all such Things as those Lead Pipes, which were Installed all around the World, in every City of Confusion, except in Germany, Switzerland, Denmark, Sweden, Norway, Finland, Iceland, Cuba, North Korea, and Costa Rica? Could the other Nations not Afford to Investigate the DANGERS of Capitalism? ‡

15-04 [_] Well, my Friend, the other Nations just TRUSTED **"The Divided States of United Lies,"** even as most Americans also just Trusted their WICKED Anti-Christ FALSE Cover-up Federal Government to Do what is Riit for them; but, they FAILED: beCause of GREED. Indeed, they could have Informed the General Public about the Endless Supply of GOOD Money that a Righteous Government would have, without the Use of any Bankers; but, that Part of the American Constitution is so VAGUE as to be Meaningless to most Americans. Indeed, it Clearly states that CONGRESS has the Power to Mint and Print all New Moneys, and then it Fails to Explains what should be Done with that Money, whereby everyone could become Moderately RICH, just by their Labors, alone! Indeed, the Founding Fathers did not know anything about Beautiful Planned City States, nor did they Believe in **"Seven Great Armies of Working Soldiers!" (HOW to Provide a Way for Everyone to WORK: so as to Eliminate Poverty, Crimes, Drug Abuses, Prisons and Unnecessary Taxes!)**, Book 015: beCause they Wanted to make a few Rich Hogs RICHER, while making everyone else into their SLAVES: beCause they had their Heads Stuck in the Stinking Rectum of their Religious Non-Biblical Ungodly NONSENSE! Yes, they Misinterpreted what the *Holy Bible* was Teaching: beCause it is a MUTILATED Book of Books, which is Missing Vital and very Important Information — such as what a Good Government should Do for Obtaining more MONEY! Indeed, the *Holy Bible* can be Blamed for much of their Political and Religious Insanity: beCause of not going into Specific Details about a GOOD Government, which should have an Unlimited Supply of GOOD Money, which must be EARNED by Honest Labor, without any Loans, without any Interest, and without any Taxes: beCause Taxes are not Needed for True Prosperity; but, OBEDIENCE to the Laws of God are Needed. In Fact, without the Laws of God, a Nation can become so Corrupted that it Destroys itself, Internally, much like **"The Divided States of United Lies"** has Destroyed itself, which is now 140+ Trillion Dollars in DEBT, as Bill Moyers pointed out on a PBS Program, Years Ago. But, not to Worry: because the Tax Slaves and Interest Slaves will Bail us Out! Yes, we already Bailed Out the Gangster Banksters, just to Prop Up the Great False Economy, at a Cost of a few Trillion Dollars — not only for them; but, also for the Automotive Industries: beCause the very Last Thing that we Americans Want to Fail, is the Automotive Industries: beCause they Produce such GOOD Jobs for Millions of People — such as those Greasy Filthy Mechanics' Jobs, while filling Junkyards with Trashed Cars: beCause that is "the American Way of LIFE," you might say, which is Actually the American Way of DEATH! Yes, it is Death to Air, Water, Land, Animals, and People; but, not to Worry: beCause Capitalism will Save us by Producing Countless Electric Cars, which will Replace those Gas-hog Cars — that is, IF we can Figure Out HOW to Redo our Infrastructure, whereby all such Cars can easily be Recharged — that is, until we Run Out of LITHIUM for making those ElecTrick Batteries, which will Require about 5 Years; and then all of those Recharging Stations will become Useless, and we will have to Build NEW Infrastructure for HYDRO-ELECTRIC Cars: beCause we have an Abundance of Ocean Water to use for POWER, which only Requires a Billion more UGLY Wind Generators! Yes, we should Cover Up all of the Great Plains with such Wind Generators, and Redo the Electrical Grid to Accommodate them: beCause that is the "Inexpensive" Solution, whereby the ElecTrickery Bills Slaves can Pay for it all, who are already Paying 10 Times more than they should be: beCause of being TRICKED. §§‡

15-05 [ ] O Elected King, if anyone Studies **"UNLIMITED ENERJEE 99 Percent Pollutions Free!"** **(HOW to Obtain FREE ElecTrickery, Worldwide!) By The Worldwide People's Revolution!®**, Book 029, they will be Thoroughly PISSED OFF with those Needless Electric Bills. However, if it were such a Great Idea that you Propose, how come the Russian and Chinese Communists did not Accept that Idea?

15-06 [ ] Well, my Friend, first of all, they never Heard of that Great Idea, much less Think of Building those **"GLORIOUS Swanky Hotels Castles and Fortresses!"** **(Beautiful Planned City States for WISE Intelligent Well-Educated People with Common Sense and Good Understanding!) By The Worldwide People's Revolution!®**, Book 019: beCause that was a Revelation from GOD, to me, alone, who is his Selected King of **"The New RIGHTEOUS One-World Government!"** **(HOW to Establish a Righteous One-World Government without Going to WAR!)**, Book 056, which is still the One and ONLY Rational Solution for Solving our Massive Problems, which must Begin with **"The Great Worldwide TELEVISED Court HEARING!"** **(That Great Meeting of the Most Intelligent and Well-Educated Minds!)**, Book 041, whereby we can Learn all of the Facts, as well as all Rational Solutions for our Massive Problems, which will Naturally Require some PATIENCE; but, in the End, it will all Pay Off with the Greatest Rewards: beCause the Masses of People will end up Living in those **"Beautiful Swanky PALACES!"** **(A New Concept in Living Habits — Swanky Palaces for Poor People!) By The Worldwide People's Revolution!®** Book 066.

15-07 [ ] O Elected King, WHO on this Earth is going to Stand Up at **"The Great Worldwide TELEVISED Court HEARING,"** and Object to Living in those **"GLORIOUS Swanky Hotels Castles and Fortresses!"** Book 019? Yes, WHO is going to make a FOOL of himself by Objecting to it? After all, there are no less than 700 Miles between El Paso, Texas, and Dall-ass Fort Worthless, where at least a hundred such Fortresses could be Built in Various Shapes and Sizes with Various Colors of Rocks from the Rocky Mountains, whereby most Americans could Move into those Fortresses, and Immediately Solve no less than 5,000 Problems for themselves! For Example, all of their Debts will just be Forgiven and Forgotten: beCause, if those Edomites Object to that Plan, they will be Brought in Shackles and Chains to COURT, and made to Prove the Necessity for any Bankers at all, seeing that it is the JOB and DUTY of **"The New RIGHTEOUS One-World Government"** to Provide all of the Necessary Money for Building all of those **"GLORIOUS Swanky Hotels Castles and Fortresses!"** Yes, it is their Duty to HIRE those **"Seven Great Armies of Working Soldiers"** to Build those Beautiful Planned City States, each of which is Well Able to Govern itself, and thus Prove WHOSE Religious and Political Beliefs are Best: beCause they will Prosper Most, and have the Least Criminals among them, if they have any Criminals at all. Indeed, the First Criminals that they will get RID of, are those Greedy Selfish Edomite BANKERS, who have Collected their Last Usury Payments from their Interest Slaves! Granted, they might be Pissed Off with that Plan; but, it is Fair to say that they already have Enough Money to Retire on. But, if they do not, we can Help them to Retire in the nearest Slimmeteries, by Hanging them to the nearest Lamp Posts for the many Crimes that they have Committed — such as the Bursting Housing Bubble Plan, whereby they Robbed Millions of People, and Bankrupted Millions, and Caused the Great Recession, from which we have still not Recovered. Meanwhile, none of their Puppet News Reporters mention anything about a Righteous One-World Government, which has an Endless Supply of GOOD Money, which must be Earned by Honest Labor, without any Loans, without any Interest, and without any Taxes: beCause everyone is a Good Person, like Jesus Christ and his Self-Disciplined Disciples. Yes, they will all REPENT, or else be left to Suffer in their Abandoned Cities of Confusion, along with the Rats, Snakes, Skunks, Raccoons, Opossums, and whatever might Move into them, once the Righteous People have DEPARTED from them: beCause of VOTING for the Construction of those **"GLORIOUS Swanky Hotels Castles and Fortresses!"** Yes, you will no doubt see a BIG Check Box [_] on the next General Election Ballot, beside the Clear Question: **ARE YOU IN FAVOR OF BUILDING SWANKY FORTRESSES? [_] YES, [_] NO.** And whomever Checks the NO Box will be Hauled up to COURT, and made to Defend his or her Presumptions: beCause no Sane Person would Object to that Plan. Guaranteed! ‡

15-08 [_] Well, my Friend, X-amount of People will no doubt be DECEIVED by the Capitalists and Socialists, who will be saying that Swanky Fortresses will LIMIT our Freedom of Speech and of the Press: beCause no one will be Allowed to Publish any more LIES — such as the EVILS of something so GOOD as a Swanky FORTRESS, which will have no less than 5,000 Advantages over Normal Cities of Confusion, and ZERO Disadvantages! Indeed, if there are any Disadvantages, someone should NOW List them, and Publish them in a Book: so that we might Study them, and Respond to their False Accusations. For Example, one Woman Objected to the Idea on Account of having Polished Granite Floors, which she said were DANGEROUS, which should be CARPETED with 3-inches of Heavy-duty FOAM Rubber, and Covered with Persian Rugs on Top of Plastic Carpets: so that when someone Spills a Coke on the Carpet, they have to Replace that Section of the Carpet, and Wash the Persian Rug, whereby the Non-permanent Colors might Blend Together, and make it more Beautiful. However, I told her that she was a bit Crazy. Nevertheless, if she should Want any such Carpets on her Floors, she should simply Check the Appropriate Boxes in **"The Complete SURVEYS of our VALUES!"** (SURVEYS of Religious Spiritual Political Governmental Sexual Social Moral Economic Business Labor Habitual and Miscellaneous VALUES!), Book 059, whereby she could get to Live with other People of Like-mindedness, who could have all of the Filthy Stinking Carpets that they might Want, and it will not Bother my Conscience the Slightest Bit, even though it would not be a Good Idea to put any such Carpets in the Kitchens, nor Dinning Rooms: beCause they might have to be Replaced every Week or 2: beCause of Ignorant People Vomiting on them, and Dogs Pissing on them, and Cats Dunging on them.

A-[_] And she said, "I do not Object to having a little Stink in the House."

B-[_] And I said, "Well, O Woe-man, what you most Desperately Need to Do is some FASTING, whereby you might Smell Out the Truth of it, and then you will Change your Mind." {Please

Check the Box with an X, if you Agree with me. Otherwise, you may Check her Statements, if you Agree with them.}

C-[_] And she said, "Fasting is the Last Thing that I will ever Do."

D-[_] And I said, "Suppose the Rain Stops, and there is nothing to EAT?"

E-[_] And she said, "I will Deal with that when the Time Comes."

F-[_] And I said, "When that Time Comes, you will be Caught with your Diapers wrapped around your Mouth, just to keep the DUST Out of your Lungs."

G-[_] And she said, "What do you Mean?"

H-[_] And I said, "I Mean that you have no Idea what you are Talking about: beCause the only Way that you can Deal with any Problem in a Rational Manner, is to FORSEE what is Coming, and get yourself Prepared for the WORST Conditions, which can only be Done by Building and Living within those Swanky Fortresses!"

I-[_] And she said, "I will Trust the Federal Government to take Good Care of me."

J-[_] And I said, "Yes, somewhat like they took Good Care of the Victims of Hurricane Katrina in 2005, when some 1,800 People, and mostly White People, DIED from it, huh?"

K-[_] And she said, "I Remember Hurricane Sandy, which Wiped Out thousands of Houses along the Eastern Coast; but, they had no Business Living there, anyway."

L-[_] And I said, "There have been tens of thousands of Natural Disasters during the past 300 Years, all around the World, and yet Ignorant People like you are still not Fully Persuaded that we should Build those Swanky Fortresses: beCause there is some Part of your Brains that does not Work Correctly."

M-[_] And she said, "There is some Part of your Brains that needs to be Bulldozed into Lake Erie."

N-[_] And I said, "It could be that you Need a Brain Transplant; but, I Perceive that you have a Heart Problem, whereby you have little or no EMPATHY for the Billions of Suffering People in this World of Woes, who would be Happy to Help Build and Live within those Swanky Fortresses, just to have some Good Foods to Eat, and some Pure Water to Drink, if nothing else."

O-[_] And she said, "If they were not so Lazy, they would be just as Rich as we Americans are."

P-[_] And I said, "Woman, if you call us the Rich People, who are 20+ Trillion Dollars in Debt to Rich Bankers, you are among the Most Deceived Creatures who ever Lived!"

Q-[_] And she said, "This is the Best Nation on the Earth, which is far Richer than any other Nation."

R-[_] And I said, "If you are Measuring our Riches by the Height of our Skyscrapers, you have a WRong Definition for Riches, which Begin with Good Health, which is True Wealth."

S-[_] And she said, "My Medical Doctor says that I am in Good Health, even though I Weigh no less than 350 Pounds: because I have a Good Heart."

T-[_] And I said, "Woman, you have a Bad Head and a Sick Heart, and do not even Know it."

U-[_] And she said, "I Think that you just like to Insult other People, who are just as Good as yourself, if not Better. Indeed, you are just another BIGOT!"

V-[_] And I said, "I am Trying to Help you to See the Light of Enlightenment; but, you Refuse to even Think about it. Therefore, you will just have to go on Suffering for your Dietary Sins."

W-[_] And she said, "There are no Dietary Sins. Where did you read that in the Holy Bible?"

X-[_] And I said, "It is Obvious that you did not even read the first 5 Chapters of the Bible, or else you would have Discovered the Story of Adam and Eve, who Ate the Forbidden Fruit, which Represented all Forbidden Foods, which you are still Feeding to your Husband and Children: beCause of not being Able to THINK, whereby you have also made them Equally as Sick and Diseased as yourself."

Y-[_] And she said, "If I get Sick, I go to my Doctor, and he Prescribes some Medicine for me to take, and come back in a Week to see him again."

Z-[_] And I said, "If you just Fasted for a Week, and did not Consume any MediSINZ, you would no doubt get Well, and without Wasting any Money on his Deceptive Medicines. Therefore, I Suggest that you Study a Good Book, called: **'Did God or Satan Ordain Medical Doctors??' (Ask Huck Finn and/or Nigger Jim: because neither Tom Sawyer nor Judge Thatcher would Know!) By The Worldwide People's Revolution!® Book 022."**

15-09 [_] O Elected King, I now Understand what you Mean by "Election Deceptions": beCause those Wicked Politicians never Mention HOW to get Well without the Assistance of any Medical Doctors, just by FASTING and Eating Natural Wholesome Foods and Natural Drinks, without any Capitalist Poisons in nor on them. Indeed, the American Bisons Roamed on the Great Plains for thousands of Years, without the Assistance of any Medical Snakes, Hospitals, nor Drugs of any Kinds; and all of them were Healthier and Happier than most Americans.

15-10 [_] Well, my Friend, if VOTING could Save us from the Lies of Poisonous Snakes, you would likely be one of the First in Line to Vote; but, no such Important Issues can be Found on any Election Ballots: beCause most of the People would have no Idea what to Vote for, seeing that they have never Read so much as ONE of my Inspired Books. Moreover, if you do not put a Book in their Hands, and Beg them to Read it, they are also Unlikely to Do it. Therefore, it is Time to Nag them into it, or else tell them that you are no longer their Friend — not that they would Care to Lose you as a Friend: beCause of having Cold Hearts and Weak Minds; but, that you are one of the few People on the Earth that they can Respect and Trust.

— Chapter 16 —

A Guaranteed Solution for Bad Health

16-01 [_] O Elected King, you have no doubt Crossed the Line on that Guarantee: beCause there is no Guaranteed Solution for Bad Health. Otherwise, you could read about it in the *Holy Bible,* which only Mentions Good Health 2 or 3 Times: beCause God does not Care whether or not we have Good Health. However, Billions of Wild Animals have Lived for thousands and maybe millions of Years in Good Health, and without the Services of any Medical Doctors, much less their Countless Drugs, who come up with an Average of 3,000 New Drugs each Year: beCause it is Extremely Profitable for them. In Fact, it is the Leading Business in **"The Divided States of United Lies!" (The so-called "United States of North America" in Disguise!)** Book 058. Indeed, when People are so Deceived, as most Americans are, it is Extremely Easy to SELL to them more and more Drugs: beCause they somehow Equate Drugs with Good Health, while none of the Wild Animals would see any Connection between Poisonous Drugs and Good Health. ‡

16-02 [_] Well, my Friend, it could be that some Drugs Work Effectively for Assisting the Body to Heal itself; but, if the Body has Lost its Ability to Heal itself, no Amount of Drugs can Save it; but, they can Deceive us, and perhaps Prolong our Lives for a few Days; but, nothing Beats a SURE CURE for whatever Ails us, and that is a Natural God-given Diet, combined with much Fasting and Praying, which are Free of all Charges — that is, except for that Natural God-given DIET, which Requires some very Expensive Fresh Fruits, when you Live in Alaska. Otherwise, you could Eat some Fresh Raw Whale Blubber, and perhaps be Cured: beCause of not being Able to Eat more than a Bite or 2 before Vomiting, whereby you would be on a Forced Fast of a Strange Kind. However, a Natural Diet also Includes Fresh Clean AIR, which cannot even be Obtained in Alaska: because of the POLLUTION in this World of Woes. Therefore, like it or not, we keep coming around to the Hateful Subject of those Gasoline-powered and Diesel-powered Vehicles, as well as Airplanes that Burn Jet Fuel, which must be done Away with: beCause they are all Abominations! However, if you are one of those People who is Fully Persuaded that those Things are GIFTS from GOD, which must be Multiplied, then you have a Major Mental Problem, which is easily Cured by Starting up a Car, and putting your Nose Directly into the Tailpipe, and keeping it there while you Breathe Deeply, until you Pass Out! And then you can be Locked Up in an Insane Asylum, where you can be Forced to Fast, until you come to your Riit Senses, whereby you might Confess that those are Abominations, which were never Needed for True Prosperity, except to Build those **"GLORIOUS Swanky Hotels Castles and Fortresses,"** whereby those Mechanical Slaves are Useful and Permissible. Indeed, not even God Objects to Using them for that Purpose: beCause of Doing GOOD Works. After all, those Machines can be Running Properly, and hardly have any Bad Effects on the Environment, if they are only Used as Needed, while doing Away with ALL of those Gasoline-powered Vehicles and Jet Airplanes: beCause they are the Main Producers of Pollution, along with those Coal-powered ElecTrickery Plants, which must be Shut Down. §§

16-03 [_] O Elected King, if all of the Idle Bulldozers, Backhoes, Trackhoes, Cranes, Bucket-loaders, and other Heavy Equipment were put to Work, it is unlikely that we would have to Produce any more of those Machines: beCause we would have those Swanky Fortresses Finished before those Machines would Wear Out. For Example, just the other Day, I saw no less than 100 Bulldozers sitting Idle in a Sales Lot, and I Thought to myself: "Why not put those Machines to WORK?" And then it crossed my Mind that those Machines have a Limited Lifespan: beCause they were Produced by Greedy

Capitalists, who Designed them to Wear Out. (Remember the Steel Trailer Hitch Balls in Trucks.) Therefore, it might be Wise of us to Design NEW Machines, which are Powered by Hydrogen, which Burns Clean, which would Require some Retooling of the Factories that Produce Heavy Equipment; but, now that Money is no longer a Problem, neither is it a Problem for us to Redo a few Things — such as Produce Hydrogen-powered Bulldozers, Airplanes, Trucks, Tractors, and whatever we Need.

16-04 [_] Well, my Friend, if we went at it, like going to WAR, I am Sure that we could get it Done. However, I am also Sure that certain Environmentalists will be Objecting to the whole Idea: beCause of Disturbing a few Mountains of Rocks in Remote Places, which most of them have never even Seen. Nevertheless, we must Keep an Open Mind concerning it all: beCause there might be a Better Way to Do it. For Example, some Man in Florida single-handedly Moved HUGE Rocks all by himself for Building some Structures, which he kept a Secret: beCause of being Afraid that such Information might be Abused by our Enemies, who might use the same Power to Remove whole Buildings — such as the Washington Monument. Therefore, we do have to be Careful when Playing with Fire, you might say; but, if there is some Technology that could Greatly Assist us to Build those Swanky Fortresses, we should Learn about it. Likewise, if there is some Way that People can be Healed by Natural Means, we should Learn about it.

16-05 [_] O Elected King, I was under the Impression that you have already Discovered a Guaranteed Solution for Bad Health. So, is that True or False?

16-06 [_] Well, my Friend, it is more like HOW to Prevent Bad Health, rather than Cure someone that has Bad Health, which might Require some Special Miracle from God, while the Prevention of Bad Health will not Require any Special Miracles; but, it will Require a lot of Cooperation among the Nations, who can all Agree that we have Wasted a LOT of Money on so-called "Health Care," and are still as Sick and Diseased as ever: beCause of Funneling the Money into DRUGS and Useless Experimentations, when it is Obvious that a Good Wholesome Natural DIET is the Best Prevention, even if some of the Spoiled Children do not Like that Idea. Trust me, they will easily Change their Diets when they are Fed GOOD Wholesome Natural Foods — such as Sweet Fragrant Tree-ripened Mangos of the Correct Varieties, as well as Dried Figs, Fresh Figs, Dates, Nuts, and Carrot Juices. Yes, there are all Kinds of Melons, which are far Superior to Soft Drinks, if those Melons are Grown Properly. In Fact, there are Literally tens of thousands of Varieties of Fruits and Vegetables, which most People have never Tasted, which we will soon Learn to Love. ‡

16-07 [_] O Elected King, it is Amazing how much Money, Time, Materials, and Energy has been put into Sports, Cosmetics, Perfumes, Video Games, and all such Nonsense, which should have been put into the Construction of those Swanky Fortresses, whereby X-amount of People could have been Eating those Good Wholesome Natural Foods, already; and then they would have no doubt had Good Health. However, I am Reminded of a Verse in the *Holy Bible,* where Jesus said: *"He who Seeks to Save his Life shall Lose it; but, he who Loses his Life for my Sake, the same Person shall Save his Soul in the Kingdom of God: because he will be Born into it."* — NMV. Therefore, I am now Wondering if it is Possible to Obtain Good Health by Seeking after it, seeing that it would be like Seeking to Save our Lives?

16-08 [_] Well, my Friend, you must keep all such Words in Context with the Subject that Jesus was Talking about, which was not Concerning Good Health; but, it was about Sacrificing your Life for the Sake of Truths, whereby you might Lose your Life for it: beCause those Edomites do not particularly Like any such Truths: beCause Truths Threaten their Businesses — such as their Drug Businesses, Chemical Corporations, Weapons Manufacturing, Medical Scams, and so on.

16-09 [_] O Elected King, if your Guaranteed Solution for Bad Health can only be Implemented by the Cooperation of all Nations, we are in BIG Trouble: beCause we cannot even get ONE Nation to Agree to GIVE UP Using those Stinking Noisy Polluting Vehicles.

16-10 [_] Well, my Friend, that is WHY we, the People, must DEMAND **"The Great Worldwide TELEVISED Court HEARING,"** whereby we can Discover WHO the Real Criminals ARE, and thus bring them to COURT, and thus Find them Guilty, and thus Sentence them to 20 Years of Hard Labor at a Rock Quarry, if they do not make Full Confessions. After all, it is True that the American Bisons Roamed around on the Great Plains for thousands of Years in Good Health, and without the Assistance of any Medical Snakes: beCause they Lived on Wholesome Natural Diets. Therefore, it is just a Matter of Discovering what Mankind's Natural Wholesome Diet IS, or should be, and then Follow that Plan for Maintaining Good Health, even if all of those Candy Makers and Soft Drink Producers are put OUT of Business: beCause Good Sweet Dates are Equally as Good as any Candies, and much Better for our Good Health, while 100% Natural Fresh Fruit Juices are much Better than Soft Drinks. Otherwise, it can be Proven at that Great Meeting of the Most Intelligent Minds what is Good for us, and what is NOT Good for us, whereby Goodness can Overcome Evilness. Moreover, when it is Discovered, whatever is Good for us should be Mass-produced by those **"Seven Great Armies of Working Soldiers!"** Book 015. Otherwise, the Problem has not been Solved. Chances are that TRUE LOVE is the Key Missing Ingredient to Good Health. But, whatever it is, we Need to Discover it, and the sooner the better: because we are now Wasting Trillions of Dollars in Vain. Furthermore, after we do Discover whatever is Needed for Good Health, we will have to Provide a Way for People to Obtain it, and also Help them to Obtain it, even if we have to Plant Billions of Fruit Trees. Meanwhile, the Unbelievers will be Welcome to Eat and Drink whatever they Want to, just to Prove themselves to be FOOLS, who will also be Welcome to Tax themselves, and Waste Trillions of Dollars on Medical Research, War Games, and whatever they Like; but, I will Check the Box [_] here to Indicate that I Want to Come OUT from among the Wicked Ones, and Touch NONE of their Unclean Things.

— Chapter 17 —

A Guaranteed Solution for North Korea

17-01 [_] Not everyone is Aware that North Korea has a Problem, which is just a Reflection of the same Problem that most Americans have, which is an Inferiority Complex, whereby they have to make up for it by Force of Armaments: beCause they are otherwise Spiritual COWARDS, who are Afraid of **"The Swanky Sword of Divine Truths!" (The Most Powerful Weapon in the Whole Universe!)**, Book 067, which would not be the Case, if they were True MEN and Honest Wombmen; but, they are just Spiritual Cowards, who are Afraid to Face the FACTS and the Realities of Life. Otherwise, they would be the First to DEMAND **"The Great Worldwide TELEVISED Court HEARING,"** whereby they might Discover the Whole Truth about all Important Subjects, including the Truths about the Goodness of having *"... all Things in Common,"* which is more Accurately Translated as *having all Material Possessions and Natural Resources in Common.* In other Words, those are OUR Mountains of Rocks, Rivers of Water, Lakes, Seas, Oceans, Forests, Hills, Valleys, Swamps, Minerals, Gases, Coals, Oils, and Natural Resources, which we should all Use WISELY for the Benefit of ALL of us, and not just to make a few Rich Hogs Richer. Yes, in the Light of that Good Understanding, the North Koreans are more Righteous than the South Koreans, and the Communists in general are more Righteous than the Capitalists: beCause they at least Recognize the Fact that this Earth was Designed to be SHARED by Everyone, and not to be Exploited by Rich People for Rich People: beCause that is a Greedy Selfish Philosophy, which has no Place in the Holy Kingdom of All that is GOOD, which is the Kingdom of God: beCause, "God" is "All that is GOOD," while Satan is all that is Evil, who is called the Devil.

17-02 [_] O Elected King, if we had all Material Things in Common among us, we would all be Extremely Poor: beCause there is not Enough Gold, for Example, for everyone in the World to have at least one Solid Gold Brick, whereby they might be somewhat Rich.

17-03 [_] Well, my Potential Friend, it is not Necessary that everyone should have a Gold Brick: beCause People can be Perfectly Happy without any Gold at all. For Example, I have Lived for my entire Life without a Diamond Ring, a Mercedes-Benz Car, a Grand Piano, a Rolex Watch, nor a Big Wooden Mansion, and I do not Feel Poor nor Deprived beCause of it. In Fact, none of the Wild Animals have any such Possessions, and they seem to be quite Contented, just to be Alive: beCause they are in Good Health. Indeed, the Wildebeests can Run all Day, and not even be Tired, which seems to make them Happy; but, Lustful People fill their Vain Houses with Countless Vain Things from their Attics to their Basements, and even Stuff their Garages full of Capitalist Trash, and are still Unhappy: beCause there is an Empty Place within their Souls, which only the Love of God can Fill, which Explains HOW those Ancient Monks could be so Happy with so few Personal Possessions. In Fact, it could be that Less Possessions produce More Happiness, while More Possessions produce Less Happiness. However, that is not to say that Extreme Poverty produces More Happiness: beCause it is easy to Prove that it does not; but, having Access to the Great Riches that would be Available within all of those **"Beautiful Swanky PALACES,"** would be what is most Important for True Happiness. For Example, suppose that you could go into the Orchard and Discover as many Fresh Ripe Sweet Fragrant Peaches that you might Want to Eat, would you Care whether or not any of those Trees Belonged to you, Personally? Of course not! Indeed, the Important Thing would be whether or not there were enough Fruit Trees for everyone to have all of the Fresh Ripe Sweet Fragrant Juicy Peaches that they might Want to Eat, which, of course, would be of less Interest if there were also an Abundance of

Sweet Juicy Apricots, Plums, Pears, Apples, Cherries, Berries, and other Sweet Juicy Fruits to Eat: beCause your Soul would be Satisfied with them, whereby you would not be Lusting after them. In Fact, once that was the Case, you would no doubt be Seeking some Romance with someone who might Love you, which would Satisfy that Part of your Life; but, only if you Believed in FIDELITY, which is Sexual Faithfulness to one other Person, which God Loves, while he Hates Whoredoms, Adulteries, and Unfaithfulness.

17-04 [_] Now, you might Rightly Ask, "What does any of that have to Do with the Problems that are Presented to the World by North Korea?" Or, as the People of North Korea might Rightly Ask, "What does any of that have to Do with the Problems that are Presented to the World by the Divided States of United Lies, which is Obviously the Greatest Threat to the Peace and Happiness of Mankind: beCause they are the Warmongers and Big Bullies, who Vainly Imagine that they have the Right to tell other People HOW to Live, Think, and Act? Indeed, they Force their Ways onto other People, whereby they have Corrupted entire Nations with their Abominations. For Example, the Chinese used to be Contented to Ride Bicycles to Work; but, now they have those Stinking Noisy Polluting Cars, Coal-powered ElecTrickery Plants, and Countless Motorcycles, which are Polluting their Air so much as to make it Unbreathable!" Well, it is beCause those Problems are a Result of Rejecting the Truths that were Taught by Jesus Christ — such as, *"You shall Love your Naaberz as much as you Love yourself,"* which Lops Off the Head of Capitalism: beCause it has Zero Love for the Naaberz, being Based on a Selfish Greedy Money-grubbing Philosophy of Possession Worshipers, who Believe that they must be the PROUD OWNERS of Material Things, while True Christians could care less about Owning anything: beCause they have True Love for their Naaberz, who are Happy to Share their Wealth with whomever is Happy to Share their Wealth with them: beCause they have all Material Possessions in Common among them, whereby everyone has an Abundance of Sweet Fragrant Juicy Peaches to Eat: beCause they have LOTS of Land to Plant them on, while the Poor Capitalists cannot even Afford to Buy any Land: beCause it Costs a thousand Dollars for one Square Meter! Indeed, only Excessively RICH Capitalists can Afford such Lands, while the Masses of Poor Capitalists can only HOPE that they get Rich enough to Afford to Buy such Lands. But, in the Process of Obtaining those Riches, they Lose Sight of their Goal to have some Sweet Peaches, and end up in the Sanitized Slaughterhouse, getting their Precious Organs Removed by the Doctor Knife, who Knows full well that all such People would have been much Richer while Living on Farms, where they might Eat those Sweet Peaches, instead of Pizzas and Hamburgers; but, he does not Dare to say anything about it: beCause the Capitalists would be against him for it. Nevertheless, did the North Koreans go about Providing Good Foods for their People to Eat, as Good Communists would have; or, did they Waste their Money on Military Nonsense?? Likewise, did the Capitalists go about Providing Good Foods for the People to Eat; or, did they Waste their Money on War Games, Cosmetics, Sports, Drugs, Junk Foods, Poisonous Drinks, and Nonsense?? Indeed, WHERE are any of those Sweet Juicy Fragrant Peaches to Eat? Where are any Good Fruits of any Kind to Eat? Where is any Fresh Clean Air to Breathe? Where is any Pure Living Water to Drink? Where are any Secure Self-air-conditioned Houses to Live in?

17-05 [_] O Elected King, it Appears to me like both the Communists and Capitalists utterly Failed to Obtain the Better Objectives in Life, while the Socialists have gotten Lost in the Darkness of Ignorance and Confusion, who have no Idea what the Right Objectives should even be! Indeed, they Want Good Health Care without Caring for any Fruit Trees at all, as if Good Health could be Obtained without Eating any Tree-ripened Fragrant Sweet FRUITS, at all! In Fact, they read in their Unholy Mutilated Bibles that the Perfect Food for Mankind is the Sweet Fruit from the Tree of Life, while they go about Chopping the Fruit Trees DOWN, in order to make more Space for their almost Worthless Wooden / Plastic Firetrap Mouse-infested Cockroach Dens, as if Good Foods had nothing to Do with Good Health! Therefore, are they CRAZY, or what??

17-06 [_] Well, my Friend, it is Obvious that all such People are Greatly Deceived, and have no Idea what is Required of them for Living in Peace with True Happiness, or else they would be Promoting the Swanky Fortress Plan, which Provides a Way for all Peoples to become Moderately RICH, and without Telling any Lies nor Selling any Capitalist Trash. But, Try to Tell that to those Ignorant People who are Spiritually BLINDED by their PRIDE, and you will soon Discover that their Spiritual Ears are Filled with the Wax of Unbelief.

17-07 [_] Now, I Hear the Master Farmer say, Listen to me, O you Wretched Miserable FOOLS, and I will tell you how to bring Peace into the Middle East, and also Solve that North Korean Problem, if you have Spiritual Ears that can Hear. First of all, it will Require some Honesty on both Sides of all such Issues, which will Require some Humiliation, just to Confess that you are Spiritually Blind, Deaf and Dumb. Indeed, their Way of Living has Proven them to be WRong: beCause they do not even have an Abundance of Sweet Juicy Fruits to Eat, in spite of supposedly having all Things in Common among them. Likewise, the Capitalists and Socialists have Utterly Failed to Provide the People with Good Health: beCause of having WRong Objectives, whereby they have Proven themselves to be Ignorant Fools. But, now it is Possible and most Practical to Confess your Errors, and Change your Ways of Thinking and Living: beCause it will Prove to be your Salvation from your Insanities. However, I Know in Advance that you will not Listen to me, nor Obey what I say: beCause you never have. So, why would you now Change your Ways of Thinking and Acting? Truly, Truly, I say to you, O Fools, if any Nation is Determined to Do something, they will likely Obtain it, sooner or later: beCause of their Determination, Persistence, and Stubbornness; but, that does not make it RIIT: beCause you cannot Do Good without Doing what is RIIT, and you cannot Do what is Riit, without Doing what is GOOD. And there is nothing Good about Blasting one another Off of the Earth with Atomic Bombs. Therefore, in the Case of North Korea, and of any other so-called "Enemies," the Way to get them Converted to the Whole Truth is to Practice Overwhelming LOVE, which will Require some Sacrifices on the Parts of the other Nations, who must Show to them Real LOVE. After all, most of them are Extremely Poor, and will thus Greatly Appreciate that Love, which can be Demonstrated by Shiploads of Good Foods, Well-made Tools, Natural Cloth for making Clothes, and whatever is Necessary for Helping them to Build their own **"GLORIOUS Swanky Hotels Castles and Fortresses,"** which will be much less Expensive than going to War. After all, they have Mountains of Rocks to Work with, and lots of People to Do the Work. Therefore, that is not the Problem that Faces other Poor Nations, who have almost nothing to Work with — such as those Poor People in Iraq, who should be Assisted to Grow a Billion Date Palms, whereby they might Contribute their Share of Dates to the World, whereby it would become a much Better World to Live in; but, only IF those Dates were Grown Properly by **"The LUSCIOUS All-Mineral Organic Method of Gardening!" (HOW to Grow DELICIOUS Satisfying Foods for Potential Kingz and Kweenz in Swanky PALACES!) By The Worldwide People's Revolution!®** Book 021. Yes, in Exchange for Growing those Dates, other Nations can Provide them with Cut and Polished Stones to Work with. Likewise, in Exchange for Iron Ore and Coal, the People of North Korea can be Provided with Fruits from South Korea, or whatever they have to Share with them: beCause it is now Time for all Nations to Cooperate with each other, and be Determined to make all Peoples Moderately RICH, whereby they have no Interests in going to War, nor in making any more Hateful Weapons. After all, you already have enough Bombs to Destroy Mankind and Animalkind a thousand Times over. Therefore, why Produce any more Weapons? Why not Think in Terms of Overwhelming LOVE? Why not Sacrifice your Pride on the Altar of Love, and thus Discover a much Better Way to Live, which is Presented to you within the Inspired Books by my Selected King?

17-08 [_] O Selected King, the Master Farmer would never Talk like that: beCause he does not call People FOOLS, even if they are.

17-09 [_] Well, it is Obvious that you have never "red" the *Holy Bible* from Cover to Cover even one Time. Try the New MAGNIFIED Version, which Explains what a Fool IS. Trust me, most People are Ignorant Fools, or else they would be the First to be DEMANDING **"The Great Worldwide TELEVISED Court HEARING!" (That Great Meeting of the Most Intelligent and Well-Educated Minds!) By The Worldwide People's Revolution!®** Book 041. Yes, they would be Marching by the Millions in Washington, D.C., and all around the World, Demanding JUSTICE for ALL Peoples, which must Begin with a Confession of the Whole Truth, whatever it might be, which can only be Discovered when we have Total Freedom of Speech, whereby the Truth might be Learned, which is now Suppressed by Wicked Governments, and Especially by **"The Divided States of United Lies,"** which does not Want you to Learn about the GOODNESS of having *"ALL MATERIAL THINGS IN COMMON."* Indeed, they Want a few Rich Hogs to get 99% of the Pie, while the Masses of Poor People go on Suffering in their Confused States of Extreme Poverty, who do not even have Fresh Clean Air to Breathe, Pure Living Water to Drink, Wholesome Natural Foods to Eat, Natural Clothing to Wear, nor Secure Houses to Live in, who are nothing but Education Slaves, Work Slaves, Tax Slaves, Interest Slaves, Insurance Slaves, Credit Card Debt Slaves, ElecTrickery Bills Slaves, Gas Bills Slaves, Food Bills Slaves, Water Bills Slaves, Childcare Slaves, Mortgage Slaves, Drug Slaves, Medical Care Slaves, Entertainment Slaves, Transportation Slaves, and even Cemetery Slaves, who never Heard of FREE Swanky TOMBS within the Tunnels of Swanky Fortresses. But, not to Worry: beCause most of them would Prefer to go to Heaven in a Big Toxic Mushroom CLOUD! §§‡

17-10 [_] O Elected King, are you saying that we should Gather Up Shiploads of Clothing from the Salvation Army, and send that Clothing to North Korea, rather than let it Rot in Warehouses? Are you saying that we should send Shiploads of Used Cars to them, also, whereby they might have some Means of Transporting themselves on their 2,000 Miles of Highways? Are you saying that we should send Shiploads of Tractors and Bulldozers over there: so that they might Practice American Farming Methods, whereby it Requires 1,000 Calories of Energy to Produce 1 Calorie of Food to Eat? Are you saying that we should send Shiploads of Lumber, Plastic Carpets, Synthetic Rubber Roofing, and Toxic Paints to North Korea, whereby they might Raise their Standard of Living like we Americans have done, whereby we have Deceived ourselves to the Maximum Degree, and are now very PROUD to be the Greatest FOOLS who ever Lived, who have a List of Endless Bills to Pay, who are in Debt up to our Necks, who are OBESE HOGS, who can only GRUNT at the Master Farmer, and even Blame him for a Lack of Rain in Due Season, rather than get our Lazy Asses to WORK, and Build those **"GLORIOUS Swanky Hotels Castles and Fortresses!"**? Are you saying that we should not make a Preemptive Attack on North Korea, and Wipe them Out, before they Wipe us Out? What Kind of an Ignorant Fool are you, anyway? Do you not know that the Russians and Chinese might Join the North Koreans, if we Bomb them, and thus get us into another World War, which will be very Good for our Great False Economy, which will make many Edomites much Richer than they already are? Do you not know that our War Games have made it Possible for us to Prosper with True Prosperity? Indeed, if it were not for the Military Industrial Bankers' News Media Complex, we would all be Living like those Poor North Koreans, whose Bedrooms and Living Rooms are only 8 feet wide and 12 feet long, which barely have enough Space to Turn Around in: beCause of being FOOLS! After all, they have lots of Iron Ore, which they could have used Wisely to make their own Bulldozers, Rock Cutting Machines, and whatever they Needed for True Prosperity; but, they Chose to Build Chicken Houses for themselves to Live in: beCause they Wanted to Imitate the Western Societies, who have done Likewise: beCause they have no Vision of what is Required for True Prosperity! §§

— Chapter 18 —

A Guaranteed Solution for Insanity

18-01 [_] Granted, not everyone is Insane; but, most People are Partly Insane, or else they would Agree that it is High Time to Conduct **"The Great Worldwide TELEVISED Court HEARING,"** whereby we might Learn just WHY Humanity must Act so Insanely as to Make Billions of Weapons for Killing each other? Indeed, one would just Naturally Think that most People would be SICK of those Hateful Wars, Tornado Destructions, Hurricane Disasters, Floods, Fires, Car Accidents, Plane Crashes, EXPLOSIONS, and Bad News Reports; but, someone finds it all Profitable, which is WHY it goes on and on: beCause it is Promoted by the Moneymongers, who can never get Enough Money to Satisfy them, whom I have Identified as EDOMITES, just to Separate them from the Israelites, who are Fathers Abraham, Isaac, Jacob, Joseph, Moses, Joshua, Gideon, Samuel, Elijah, King David, Daniel, Isaiah, Jesus Christ, Saints Peter, James, John, the Apostle Paul, and other Believers in TRUTHS, who would not Object to Conducting that Great Meeting of the Most Intelligent and Well-Educated Minds, just to Discover what Solutions might now be Available for Solving our Massive Problems, if nothing else. In Fact, it was Jesus who Suggested the Idea, when he said that when he Returns, he will SEPARATE the People who are Like Sheeps from the People who are Like Goats, which I have MAGNIFIED in Book 041, which is mentioned above. Indeed, it is the one and only Way to bring Peace into this World: beCause People, who are Like Sheeps and Goats, never did get along very Well with People who are Like Lions nor Wolves: beCause they have Contrary Natures.

18-02 [_] O Elected King, why do you not just Relax, and let Jesus Christ take Care of it all, since this is his Crazy World? Indeed, why do you People Fret yourselves over the Troubles of Mankind, as if you could Solve our Problems by Means of Reason and Logic, when it Requires someone with Great POWER and Authority, who can Transform Rocks into Pure Gold, and Raise Up the Woolly Mammoth Elephants, just to get the Attention of those Ignorant Dimwitcrats and Reprobates in the District of Chief Criminals, in Washington, who have their Heads Stuck in those 2 Stinking Holes in **"The BIG White OUTHOUSE on the Not-so-Biblical Capitol DUNGHILL!"**? Moreover, it is Obvious that they are all INSANE to some Degree, just for Rejecting the Fact that those **"GLORIOUS Swanky Hotels Castles and Fortresses"** just Happen to have more than 5,000 Good Reasons and Great Advantages for Building them and Living within the Borders of them, and without any Great Disadvantages! For Example, they have no Need for any Dangerous Vehicles, which will Save us hundreds of TRILLIONS of Dollars during the Future, even as you have already Listed in: **"The Low Court of Supreme Injustices is Brought to Trial!" (Our Elected King Butts Heads with the United States Supreme Court, with or without their Black Robes of Hypocrisies and Lies!) By The Worldwide People's Revolution!®**, Book 011, and in: **"The Right Design for Living!" (A List of Great Advantages for Building Beautiful Planned City States!)** Book 012. Yes, most People would not Know anything about those Beautiful Planned City States: beCause the News Media has never Mentioned them, much less any of the Great Advantages. However, if they had Advertised them for the Past 70 Years, like they have Advertised their DRUGS, everyone would now Know about them, and thus VOTE for them: beCause of Wanting to Solve their Problems, and especially their OBESITY Problems: beCause it is rather Burdensome for most People to Pack an Extra 100 Pounds or more of Weight around with them, when they could be as Light on their Feets as the Deers and Antelopes! Indeed, they can read about it in their *Holy Bibles,* if they have a Mind to Do so; but, the Sunday School Teachers never Point it Out: beCause they are also OBESE, and Greatly Ashamed of it; but, they have no Idea HOW to Solve that MASSIVE Problem, much less HOW to Solve the other 5,000+ Problems of Mankind that Originate from a BAD Lifestyle, whereby they have no Organic Gardens, Vineyards, Orchards, nor Home-craft Workshops to WORK in, which is a Major SIN, which Moses Warned us about, saying: *"Woe unto those Foolish People, who Build House to House, until there is no Place to Plant a Garden, Vineyard, nor Orchard, who must Travel Long Distances, just to get to Work, who must leave their little Children in the Care of Poisonous Snakes, who Teach Outlandish Lies to them, in Order to make them into Education Slaves, Work Slaves, Tax Slaves, Insurance Slaves, Usury Slaves, Debt Slaves, Drug Slaves, Food Slaves, Poisonous Drinks Slaves, Entertainment Slaves, and Various Kinds of other SLAVES: beCause of being taken Advantage of by those Edomites, who Love Slavery, who never Reveal to them HOW to be Liberated from their Slavery: beCause it is not in their Interest to put themselves Out of Business, which is the Business of Producing more and more Capitalists, whose Primary Doctrine is the Love of Money, who will Say and Do just about anything for more Gain: beCause they have no Love for their Naaberz, much less for God, who has nothing for Sale, who Shares his Good Earth with all of us, and for Free, even as we should also Share the Material Wealth of this World with each other for Free, which is the Primary Reason for Establishing a Righteous One-World GovernMINT, which simply Mints and Prints the Necessary New Money — not to Give it Away to Ignorant Fools, nor to Waste it on Election Deceptions; but, in Order to Use that Money WISELY, in Order to HIRE Seven Great Armies of Working Soldiers, in Order to Help Construct Beautiful Planned City States, which will Represent that New Money, which will make it the very Best Money in all of the World, which must be Earned by Honest Labor, without any Loans, without any Interest, and without any Taxes: beCause a Righteous Government has no Need for any Taxes: beCause everyone within that Good Government Loves and Obeys the New MAGNIFIED Version of the 20 Commandments, which can be found in an Inspired Book, called:* **'LIGHTNING STRIKES Versus Lightning Bugs!' (HOW you can Become Moderately RICH, without Telling any Lies nor Selling any Trash!) By The Worldwide People's Revolution!**®*, which should be Mandatory Reading in all Public Schools, Churches, Synagogues, Temples, Mosques, Theaters, Auditoriums, Concert Halls, Gymnasiums, Race Tracks, and wherever People are Assembled Together, whereby they might Learn all about a RIGHTEOUS One-World Government, and the Great Advantages that it has over any False Governments, whose People are forever Suffering in their States of Extreme Poverty, who do not even have Organic Gardens to Eat from, who are Relying on the Production and Sales of TRASH, Junk Foods, Poisonous Drinks, Drugs, and all such Vain Things, which none of the Wild Animals ever Needed nor Wanted, who are Healthy, Wealthy and Wise in their own Ways; but, none of them are Living in Beautiful Swanky PALACES: beCause they do not have Hands to Work with, except for the Monkeys and Apes, who are Contented with Food and Clothing, you might say, who are Good Examples of what you would not Want to be Like. However, if you do not Say and Do what is Right for yourselves, you will end up in a Lower State of Self-inflicted Torment than any of those Wild Animals. Yes, you will be Driven Insane by your Lusts and Greed, whereby you will become Liars and Spiritual Murderers, like Donald Trumpeter, George Warmonger Bush, Condosleezy Rice Patty, and Little Dick Chicanery, Incorporated, who will have no Reasonable Solutions for anything, being Distant Relatives of Judas Iscariot, Saint Joseph Stalin, and Cigar-chomping Whiskey-guzzling Winston Churchill, who could have Debated Adolf Hitler on an International Radio Broadcast for the Sake of Avoiding any Hateful World War; but, they were Spiritual Cowards of the Lowest Kind, who Refused to Debate the Important Issues, and thus Resolve those Issues in a Civilized Manner, without Murdering anyone; but, behold, that would have Required some Honesty and a little Humiliation, which was far Below their Great Dignity, who were PUFFED UP with Great PRIDE, who Needed to be Slapped Down with some Great Plague; but, behold, God was Sleeping during that Time, and no one could Arouse him by any Means: beCause he was far too Tired to be Awakened. Yes, he was Tired of Listening to Foolish TV Talk Shows, which never Present any Reasonable Solutions for anything, which just Blab and BLAB: because they Love to TALK! Meanwhile, Billions of People are Suffering in their States of Extreme*

Poverty, and Dying by the Millions: beCause of Needless Sicknesses and Diseases, which could easily be Prevented by having Good Wholesome Natural Diets. But, behold, that would not be Profitable for the Drug Companies, nor for the Medical Doctors, who rake in Trillions of Dollars per Year from all such Ignorant Slaves, who have never even read Pages 70—72 of this Inspired Book, who are Drugged, Drunk, and Spiritually Blinded by their LUSTS, who could all be Living in those **'Beautiful Swanky PALACES!' (A New Concept in Living Habits — Swanky Palaces for Poor People!) By The Worldwide People's Revolution!®***, Book 066; but, they would rather take a Chance on Capitalism Saving them, and also making them Equally as Rich as Bill Computer Software Gates, whose Firetrap Wooden House could easily Burn Up in less than one Hour, and all of his Riches could come to nothing in less than one Day: beCause, if* **'The New RIGHTEOUS One-World Government'** *gets Established, everyone in the World will be Provided with a FREE Computer or 2, and those Computers will be Guaranteed to Endure the Test of Time: beCause of being Educational Tools, which will be Used Wisely by that Good Government, whereby everyone will Learn, Believe, Love, and OBEY* **the New MAGNIFIED Version of the 20 Commandments!** *Yes, it will be a Great Time of Wonderful Celebrations, when all of the Slaves will be LIBERATED, which will be called the Grand Year of JUBILEE! Yes, you should Study* **'The END of CONFUSION!' (The Great CELEBRATION of the Magnificent Wedding of the Most Humble Honest Nations, and the Grand Year of JUBILEE!) By The Worldwide People's Revolution!® Book 050."** §

18-03 [ ] Well, my Friend, it is a Great Shame that all such Inspired Words were not written somewhere in the Books of Moses: beCause we might have Avoided 4,000+ Years of Suffering; but, that is not the Way that God Wanted it: beCause he Wanted us to Learn a very Difficult Lesson to Learn, which is the Fact that Mankind is not Able to Govern itself Properly, Apart from the Laws and Rules of GOD. In other Words, we must Learn and Obey God's Divine Laws and Flexible Rules, just to Govern ourselves Properly, and one of those Laws calls for the Establishment of **"The New RIGHTEOUS One-World Government!" (HOW to Establish a Righteous One-World Government without Going to WAR!) By The Worldwide People's Revolution!®** Book 056.

18-04 [ ] O Elected King, in Times Past, and especially when I was just a Boy, the Masses of People would have said that you are the most Insane Person among us, just for Vainly Imagining that it might be Possible to Establish a Righteous One-World Government; but, now we are coming to Realize the Importance of it, just to Save ourselves from Climate Changes, if nothing else: beCause someone must Rein in that Wild Bronco called Capitalism, which has been Running Roughshod over the whole World, whereby we have Produced Trillions of Tons of Capitalist TRASH, much of which is now Filling the Oceans, which Greatly Displeases the Gods, as well as anyone in his or her Riit Miind. Yes, it is a Great Shame on the Head of Humanity, which will not be Easy to FIX. Nevertheless, I am Anxious to read your most Reasonable Guaranteed Solution for that Massive Problem.

18-05 [ ] Well, my Friend, before that Massive Problem can be Solved, the Masses of People must be Fully Persuaded to STOP BUYING ANY MORE TRASH! Nevertheless, I will go into the Details in the next Chapter.

18-06 [ ] O Elected King, most Insane People can be Cured by simply FASTING, and then they must Live on Sweet Juicy Fruits. However, if their Mouths are full of Mercury Fillings in their Teeths, that Mercury could still make them Insane: beCause it is a Known Poison, which was Outlawed in Germany and in other European Nations: beCause of the Bad Effects it has on People's Brains; but, it is still Legal in **"The Divided States of United Lies,"** whose Federal Government has very little Love for its People, which is also WHY they Permit the Skies to be Saturated with Aluminum Oxide, which is Sprayed into the Atmosphere by Jet Airplanes, which is WHY those Jet Streams linger on for Hours, rather than quickly Dissipate into the Atmosphere, as they used to do. Yes, they are called Chem-trails by the Experts, who say that American Lakes now have 90,000 Times as much Aluminum Oxide in them as they had 50 Years Ago, which Means that the Aluminum is also coming down in the Rains on the Farmlands, whereby our Crops are filled with Aluminum: beCause the Evil Edomite Empire Discovered that if People get Enough Aluminum in their Bodies, it will Cause them to have Alzheimer's Disease, whereby they cannot Remember very well, which will Cause them to become Dependent on the Services of Medical Doctors and Caretakers, which will Increase their Profits: beCause they are also Greedy Capitalists. Therefore, when you Look Up into the Sky, and see those Chemical Trails behind those Jet Airplanes, you should Understand that you are being Poisoned by your own Federal Government. ‡

18-07 [_] Well, my Friend, all such Things must be Proven at **"The Great Worldwide TELEVISED Court HEARING!"** Indeed, you could be Correct about all of that; but, not being a Scientist, I would not Know for Sure; but, I am Willing to *"Prove all Provable Things, while Holding Tightly to All that is GOOD,"* as the Apostle Paul wrote in *First Thessalonians 5:21.* Yes, it is quickly followed by: *"Abstain from all Appearances of Evil,"* which is Good Advice for all Lawmakers, who make laws that Protect Criminals, while Incriminating Righteous People. For Example, you may Finish this Sentence —

18-08 [_] O Righteous King, if you were to List all of the Injustices in **"The Divided States of United Lies,"** they would fill a Book much thicker than the *Holy Bible:* beCause those Injustices have no End. For Example, just Think about the Millions of Young People in this Country, who have been Imprisoned for Using or Selling Drugs, who would not have been Doing so, if they had been Working in their own Gardens and Home-craft Workshops and Sales Shops. But, being Unemployed, and Deprived of any such Gardens, they had to do something to gain some Money; and therefore, they got into the Illegal Drug Business, which is Actually less Harmful in some Cases than Smoking Tobacco: beCause Tobacco is much more Addictive than Marijuana. In Fact, it is 7 Times as Addictive, and is still Legal to Sell: because of those Lying Hypocrites in Washington, District of Chief Criminals. ‡

18-09 [_] Well, my Friend, all such Things can be Proven at **"The Great Worldwide TELEVISED Court HEARING,"** and those Wicked Politicians can be Sentenced to 20 Years of Hard Labor at a Rock Quarry, if they do not Quickly Confess the Truth of it. However, I still Firmly Believe in Freedom to Choose whatever Way that anyone Wants to Kill himself: beCause I Know that his Spirit can easily be Born in a New Body in a Worse Place — unless we go about making that Impossible in this World, by Building those **"GLORIOUS Swanky Hotels Castles and Fortresses,"** which may also Permit the Growing and Using of Tobacco in Seventh Swanky Fortresses, as well as any other Drugs; but, no one will be Permitted to Capitalize on any such Products: beCause that will be Against the LAW, which will have Harsh Punishments for Disobedience — such as a Year of Hard Labor at a Rock Quarry, just for Selling a single Cigarette: beCause there will be FREE Cigarettes in Abundance at those Seventh Swanky Fortresses for whatever Ignorant Fools Want them, who will also have to Cover their own Health Care Costs: beCause the Righteous People will no longer be Taxed to Support the Rebellious People, who may Rebel with other People of Like-mindedness, and Do whatever they Want to with each other, and even Rape and Murder each other, and it will not Bother my Conscience the Slightest Bit: beCause I will also be Living with other People of Like-mindedness, who will Check the Appropriate Boxes in **"The Complete SURVEYS of our VALUES!" (SURVEYS of Religious Spiritual Political Governmental Sexual Social Moral Economic Business Labor Habitual and Miscellaneous VALUES!) By The Worldwide People's Revolution!®** Book 059.

18-10 [_] O Elected King, I just LOVE your Good Attitude toward other People, who should be Free to make Fools of themselves; but, not to Drive other People Insane, nor make Tax Slaves of them.

— Chapter 19 —

A Guaranteed Solution for the Trash Disposal Problem

19-01 [_] There is no Reasonable Solution for getting Rid of the Trash that has already been Buried in the Earth; but, there is a Reasonable and Guaranteed Solution for STOPPING the Production of more Trash — such as Used Telephone Books: beCause all such Information can be Digitized, and thus not Produce any more Telephone Books. But, HOW to Stop Producing Throw-away Packaging Materials for Computers to be Shipped, for Example, will Require some Innovation and Permanent Shipping Boxes, which are Returnable and Reusable. Likewise, all of those Throw-away Bottles can be made Reusable — except that some People do not Like to Drink from the same Bottle that someone else Drank from, and perhaps put their Cigarette Butts into it. Therefore, the Cities of Confusion, and the Seventh Swanky Fortresses, will have to have their own Separate Food Contains, while the other Swanky Fortresses can Share the same Kinds of Food Containers: beCause they have Clean Habits. ‡

19-02 [_] O Elected King, are you saying that Swanky Fortresses will Eliminate the Need for almost all Throw-away Containers?

19-03 [_] Well, I am saying that we can make Heavy-duty Reusable Containers, including Bottles for Foods and Drinks, much like the Old Coke Bottles, which were used a thousand Times or more, and then Remelted and Molded into New Bottles, which can also be done with Canning Jars, which can be Designed to Endure for many Generations. Moreover, when People go Shopping at a Swanky Fortress, they can Pack their Empty Clean Containers with them, and get New Containers. However, most of the Foods and Drinks will be FRESH, and therefore no Bottles nor Jars will be Needed, except to Transport those Foods and Drinks Home, which can be done in several different ways; but, the most Efficient Way is to bring your own Clean Containers with you when you are going Shopping, except that you might do some Impulsive Buying of Products that you did not Plan on Buying, in which Case you might have to Borrow some Containers, and Return them during the next Shopping Spree. For Example, there might be a New Crop of Pecans, Cashews, or Hickory Nuts in some Grocery Store, which came Unexpectedly, which you now Want, which can be put into one of your Canning Jars, if you brought some Extra Jars with you. Otherwise, you could use one of the Canning Jars at the Store, for Free: beCause of having all Things in Common, including those Canning Jars. In Fact, if there were an Abundance of Cashews, you could Load Up on them, and even go on a Cashew Diet for awhile, just to Prove to yourself how Bad it is, whereby you Turn Pale and Sickly: beCause it is not a Well-balanced Diet. In Fact, you might even get some Disease from such a Limited Diet. Nevertheless, you should be Free to Choose whatever you Want, unless there is a Shortage of something, whereby that something is Rationed among all of the People. After all, when was the last Time that you saw a Ton of FREE Fresh Cashews in any Grocery Store? Probably never! Therefore, do not Complain about any Lack of anything to Eat at a Swanky Fortress: beCause, **"The Swanky Associations of Professional Gardeners"** will do their Best to Produce an Abundance of everything that People might Like. Therefore, they will Plant and Care for 10 Cashew Trees per Person in the World, just to make Sure that everyone gets all that they might Want: beCause it is Possible to Freeze them Properly for as much as 10 Years, and still be Good, which is True of all Nuts. Therefore, if you Want to Insure an Abundant Supply of something, just Volunteer to Help Produce it: beCause that Association will be First in Line to get all that they might Want, even if it is Barbecued Beef. However, there might be some Warning Signs on all such Products, Warning you of the Dangers of being a Glutton for Self-inflicted

Punishments. Indeed, you will be Responsible for your own Good Health, A-[_] unless you Want other People telling you what to Eat, how to Eat it, and when to Eat it, which is also Possible for whomever Checks that Box with an X. B-[_] Personally, I Prefer to be my own Master when it comes to Eating.

19-04 [_] O Elected King, it is my Belief that if a Person is in Good Health, he or she has a Right to Choose his or her own Diet; but, when a Person becomes Sick, Diseased, or Disabled, and is no longer Able to Care for himself, it is Time for someone else to be in Charge of him or her: beCause it is not Right to Tax the Healthy People to Support the Undisciplined People. Likewise, if someone cannot Remember to bring their own Reusable Containers with them, when they go Shopping, they should have to go back Home and get their Containers, just to Help them to Remember it the next Time.

19-05 [_] Well, my Friend, most People do well, until they get Old and Helpless, and then they Need some Help, which is WHY there must be **"The Swanky Association of Caretakers,"** who Help Old People to go Shopping, and also Remember their Reusable Containers, if they are Forgetful. Therefore, there is no Need to Punish any Old Person for being Forgetful; but, Young People can be Sent to a **Swanky Fasting Sanitarium**, or even to a **Swanky Institution of Correction**, whereby their Minds and Bodies can be Rejuvenated. A-[_] Otherwise, they could simply Volunteer to do some Fasting, at Home, and still be their own Managers concerning Fasting. But, each Swanky Fortress will have its own Rules and Regulations to Follow: beCause each one will be Fully Responsible for its own Good Health, which will eventually Prove whose LAWS and RULES are the Best. B-[_] Indeed, some may even Choose to have Insurance Bills to Pay, C-[_] while others may Choose to just Voluntarily Serve as Doctors and Nurses, D-[_] while others may Choose to Visit Doctors in Foreign Countries to Treat their Ailments. E-[_] However, I would Personally Choose to take Good Care of my own Health: so that I would not be a Burden on anyone else. F-[_] Moreover, I would not Object to Caring for Old People, if they would just Follow my Rules for getting Well, which would Naturally Include a Good Diet of Fresh Raw Sweet Fruits, which would Eliminate a lot of those Packaging Materials: beCause Fruits come in their own Packages, which only need Boxes or Carts to Carry them, which can be Designed to Endure the Test of Time.

19-06 [_] O Elected King, suppose the Young People are not Interested in Caring for the Old People: beCause of not Believing that Commandment to Honor your Father and Mother?

19-07 [_] Well, that is a Problem that Requires the Services of a Good Preacher, who should be Paid Well to Teach the Truth about each Subject: beCause that is his Duty. {See: **"Why are some Preachers so Poor?"** Book 009.} Indeed, he should not be Paid according to his Popularity by passing a Collection Plate around: beCause that is a Corrupt System, which Produces Weak and Flabby Sermons, which seldom Correct anyone. Therefore, what People Need are Good Strong Educational and Inspiring Sermons, like the ones in: **"The Gospel According to our Elected King!" (The Good News from the Most Modern Perspective!) By The Worldwide People's Revolution!®** Book 077.

19-08 [_] O Elected King, I Propose that we Build some Trash-collecting Ships to send into the Oceans with Dragnets to Collect some of the Billions of Tons of Trash that have been Dumped into the Oceans by Thoughtless Lazy People: beCause those Plastic Bags are Killing certain Fishes, and making an Ugly Mess in the Oceans, and on the Beaches, which is Disgraceful to Mankind.

19-09 [_] Well, the Capitalists who Produced all such Trash should have to Clean it up with the Help of whomever Dumped it there. But, how to Clean Up the Toxic Chemicals and Liquid Waste Products that have been Dumped into the Rivers, Lakes, Seas, and Oceans is a Problem for which I have no Solution, except to do Away with all such Industries, which are mostly Dealing with the Manufacturing of Vehicles and Related Products — such as those Dangerous Solvents, Paint Thinners, and Sprays.

19-10 [_] O Elected King, most People Lived Well for thousands of Years without Producing all such Trash, Chemical Poisons, Toxic Abominations, nor Garbage Foods. Therefore, it seems to me like we could go on Living like that for thousands or even millions of more Years, now that we Know what is Required for Obtaining and Maintaining Good Health, which is NOT more and more Chemical Abominations, Drugs, nor Polluting Vehicles, none of which would be Needed nor Wanted within those **"GLORIOUS Swanky Hotels Castles and Fortresses!" (Beautiful Planned City States for WISE Intelligent Well-Educated People with Common Sense and Good Understanding!) By The Worldwide People's Revolution!®** Book 019. Therefore, that seems to be the Best Solution for the Trash Disposal Problem: beCause all of the Garbage can be Recycled through the Bowels of Hogs and Chickens, or just Composted with Tree Leaves, Sawdust, Hairs, and other Organic Matter, which Means that People would have to Stop putting those Abominable Hair Sprays on their Empty Heads: beCause no such Stinking Perfumes are any Good for an All-Mineral Organic Garden. Likewise, the Drugs that Sick-minded People Consume come Out of them in their Piss, which is no Good for Fruit Trees, which may Absorb those Drugs, and Store them in the Fruits and Nuts, whereby they are Recycled into the Food Chain. Indeed, the Rivers are now Full of all such Hateful Drugs, which makes the Water Unfit to Drink, or even to Cook with it. Therefore, what is your Guaranteed Solution for getting RID of all such Drugs in our Food Chain?

— Chapter 20 —

A Guaranteed Solution for Getting RID of Drugs

20-01 [_] {HEADNOTE: Just as soon as I finished writing the Title of this Chapter, the Computer Screen went Blank, and refused to Display anything, whereby I was Forced to press the Start Button until the Computer Shut Off, and then I Restarted the Computer, which is to Prove that Satan is still at Work: because the Last Thing that he Wants to Happen is for us Human Beings to get RID of Drugs: beCause it is by Means of Drugs that all of the Nations are Deceived, which you can read about in the 18th Chapter of *the Book of Revelation,* which calls it *Sorceries* in the *King James Version (KJV),* which is more Accurately called *Druggeries.* (See the word *Sorceries* in *Strong's Exhaustive Concordance,* published in 1850—1980, when they still had Freedom of Speech and of the Press.) Indeed, it is by Means of Drugs that Satan has Deceived all Ignorant People: beCause those Drugs have more than one Effect on the Minds of People, which Drugs are able to Trick the Body, which is a very Complex Mechanism, which Scientists and Medical Doctors still do not Fully Understand, nor even Pretend to Fully Understand: beCause, the more that they Study the Mind and Body, the more Complex it becomes to them. Moreover, each Body is Unique, and has Different Reactions to Different Drugs, which is WHY not all Drugs have the same Effects on People, some of whom are not at all Effected by them, as if being Totally Immune to them, which would likely be the Case for Jesus Christ and other Holy People, who could even Drink Deadly Poisons, and they would not Harm them: beCause their Bodies are Working Correctly, and have Natural Defenses against Foreign Substances. However, that is not to say that Christians should Haphazardly Eat nor Drink anything that is Served to them, nor Consume any Drugs that might be found for Sale: beCause that is Foolish, and even Suicidal. In Fact, it is Highly Recommended that all True Christians should Do as the *Holy Bible* Teaches, and *"Come Out from among the Wicked People, and be Separated from them, and Touch NONE of their Unclean Things, says the Supreme Ruler, ..."* which was the Good Advice of the Apostle Paul, who was

Quoting the "Lord Jesus," who would be the Last Person to Eat at the Death and Hell Restaurant: beCause they have nothing that is Fit to Eat, nor Drink! Therefore, *"Avoid the Appearances of all Evils,"* and do not Enter into such an EVIL Place, which might even be Worse than the Local Bar for Drunkards and Prostitutes: beCause of those DECEPTIONS. Yes, just take a Good Look at the FAT and Sick People who Patronize such "All-you-can-Eat" Royaless Buffets, and Kindly Ask yourself if you Sincerely Want to become Like any of them? Yes, sit in the Parking Lot, and Watch them coming and going for an Hour or 2 at Dinner Time, and Observe how Unhappy they are with themselves and with you, who might even Want to MURDER you, if you Criticize **"The Divided States of United Lies!" (The so-called "United States of North America" in Disguise!)**, Book 058: beCause they Worship Medical Doctors, Politicians, False Preachers, and Misguided Teachers, who Seek to Justify the EVILS of Capitalism, beginning with those Poisonous and Deceptive DRUGS! Yes, they Seek to Justify American War Games, also: beCause they are Murderers at Heart, and the Worst of Lying Hypocrites, who Say that they Love God, while Disobeying ALL of his Commandments, beginning with the First one, which Clearly States: *"I am the Great Creator God, even the Supreme Ruler of this Heaven and Earth; and therefore, you shall not have any other Rulers nor Gods above me."* And then it goes on to Elaborate, by Stating: *"Neither shall you make unto yourselves any Graven Images, nor any Likenesses of anything that I have Created, and Especially any Imaginary Images or Pictures of myself: because you have never Seen me, nor do you have any Idea what I Look Like. Therefore, you shall not make any Images nor Likenesses of anything in the Sky above, nor on the Earth beneath the Sky, nor of anything in the Waters that are below the Ground, in the Oceans, Seas, Lakes, nor Rivers: beCause all of those Things are Inferior to yourselves, who were Created in my Image to some Degree, who have Minds to Remember and Think with. Therefore, Remember my Commandments, to Love and Obey them, lest you should make Fools of yourselves, and even Destroy yourselves by Various Means, who could Inherit your very own Worlds, if you were found Worthy of them: beCause that is WHY that they are Multiplying, even as the Fishes of the Sea and the Birds of the Air are Multiplying: beCause that is the Glory of the Gods, who are Creating more and more Worlds to be Inhabited with more and more Wise People of Various Kinds. Therefore, be Wise, and Stop Polluting the Earth with your Abominations: because it is Possible and most Practical for all of you to be Living in Beautiful Marble Palaces, for which I have Provided many Mountains of Rocks for you to Work with, which you should Use Wisely, and Share them with everyone: because it is also the Glory of the Gods to be Generous, and to Share all such Material Things in Common among us, whereby everyone can be Healthy, Wealthy and WISE. Therefore, if you have any Interest in becoming my Adopted Spiritual Children, you will have to Learn, Believe, Love and OBEY ALL of my Riichus Commandments from the Heart. Otherwise, I will have to Think of you as Stubborn Disobedient Spoiled Jackasses, who will have to be Whipped into Submission by Various Means, by Sicknesses, Diseases, Accidents, Wars, Deaths, Famines, Plagues, Natural Disasters, Unnatural Disasters, and whatever is Required for Correcting you: beCause, what else am I Supposed to Do with you? Indeed, I could Cast your Spirits Down to Lower Orders of more Hateful Worlds, whereby you could be Tormented both Day and Night, forever and ever; but, of what Value would you be to me, nor to yourselves, after making such Fools of yourselves as those Drug Addicts have done? Truly, Truly, I say to you, it is Time for all of you to Wake Up and Come to your Riit Senses, and Stop Acting like Babies. Yes, it is Time for all of you to Grow Up; but, Especially for all of you MEN to Grow Up: beCause you are Supposed to be the Leaders and Rulers among you. Therefore, let your Beards Grow, and Strengthen your Muscles by Working with those Heavy ROCKS, whereby you can make Solid Stone and Concrete Walls that are no less than 10 feet THICK, whereby the Temperatures of your Houses will be Stable the Year Around, which should all have Ice Houses under them, whereby the Moisture can be Sucked Out of your Houses, while making them Comfortable and Livable. Indeed, you must Build Beautiful Planned City States for yourselves in Great TERRACES, whereby each Stone Dome Home Complex covers no less than one whole Acre of Large Cisterns for Water Storage, Tunnels, Tombs, Marble Stairways with*

Granite Steps, and whatever is Required for True Prosperity, which just Naturally Includes Spacious Living Rooms, Kitchens, Bedrooms, Bathrooms, and Game Rooms, all of which are Covered with 20 feet of Sand, Rubble Rocks, Gravel, Clay, and Sifted Topsoil at least 3 feet Deep, whereby you can Plant Beautiful Fruit Trees, Nut Trees, Grape Vines, Berry Bushes, Vegetable Gardens, and Flower Gardens in the Terraces, whereby you can Honestly say that you have Accomplished Great Things in my Name: beCause I will Bless you for it. Yes, your Healthy Happy Children will also Bless you for it, who will not Grow Up to become Drug Addicts nor Ignorant Fools like that Donald Trumpeter, George Warmonger Bush, Little Dick Chicanery, Donald Rummyfell, Condosleezy Rice Patty, Paul Wolfwits, nor any of those other Low Life Criminals in the District of Chief Criminals, in Washington, who Need their Asses WHIPPED with the Seven Last Great Plagues! Nevertheless, if they Beg for Forgiveness for their Greediness and Selfishness, I will Forgive them: beCause I Understand what is WRong with them, and with everyone else in this World of Wonders; but, behold, if you do not all Repent, and Change your Ways of Thinking and Acting, I will be Forced to Allow Satan to Curse you with those Seven Last Great Plagues, in an Attempt to Correct you, or else Wipe you Out: beCause you are Disgusting People, and in many Ways. Therefore, Humble yourselves by Means of Fasting and Praying, combined with Weeping and Mourning for all of your Sins, which are Transgressions of my Divine Laws, one of which is to Work with United Effort, whereby Great Things can be Accomplished; but, only IF your Minds are Working Correctly, which is WHY you must Fast and Pray and Eat Sweet Fruits, just to get your Minds Working Correctly, according to **'The Proper RULES for FASTING!' (The Complete Instruction Manual for True Repentance!)***, Book 046, which is a Companion Book of:* **'HOW to Become a HOLY Man!' (40 Good Reasons WHY People Should FAST and PRAY!) By The Worldwide People's Revolution!®***, Book 045, which is Required for Entering into the Holy Kingdom or Good Government of the GODS, who are all HOLY! Yes, be you Holy, even as I am Holy, says your Supreme Ruler and Divine Lawmaker: beCause, without Holiness of Mind, Spirit, and Body, no Person shall See my Holy Face. Therefore, Come Out from among those Wicked People, and be you Separated from them, and Touch NONE of their Unclean Things — including those Stinking Noisy Polluting Vehicles — and then I will Receive you as Holy Children, and will be a Good Father unto you, and will Hold you in my Bosom, and Dandle you on my Knees, and Kiss your Necks, and Show Great Affections for you: beCause of Loving you! But, if you Rebel Against the Inspired Words of Provable Truths that I have Revealed to my Colorful Peacock from Angel Ridge, King's Mountain, Kentucky, in the United States of North America, I will be Forced to Allow Satan to Punish you, and Severely so: beCause of your Rebellion. Yes, the Greatest of all Sins is the Rejection of Provable Truths, which Causes all of the other Sins. Therefore, Cease from your Insanity, and DEMAND* **'The Great Worldwide TELEVISED Court HEARING,' (That Great Meeting of the Most Intelligent and Well-Educated Minds!)***: beCause it is the Most Rational Way to Solve your Massive Problems, while getting Justice for all Peoples, Worldwide! Amen. Yes, let all of the Righteous People say a Hearty, AMEN — so it is Written, and so shall it be Done!"* End of Headnote. Please Check the Box [ ] with an X, if you Agree with God. Otherwise, you shall be Damned with the Devil who has Deceived you!}

20-02 [ ] O Elected King, that Sounded like a Good Conclusion for your Inspired Book, which Begins and Ends on Pages 76—78, which will be easy for Readers to Remember where it is Located. §

20-03 [ ] Well, my Friend, that little Headnote also Reveals HOW to get RID of Drugs, by Building those Beautiful Planned City States, which will not Entice Ignorant People to be Consuming any Drugs: beCause of becoming Healthy and Happy without them. Indeed, I have Lived for my entire Life without them, and so can you and everyone else! Therefore, it is now Time for us to DEMAND **"The Great Worldwide TELEVISED Court HEARING!" (That Great Meeting of the Most Intelligent and Well-Educated Minds!) By The Worldwide People's Revolution!®, Book 041,** by which we will Quickly Form **"Seven Great Armies of Working Soldiers!" (HOW to Provide a Way for**

Everyone to WORK: so as to Eliminate Poverty, Crimes, Drug Abuses, Prisons and Unnecessary Taxes!), Book 015. Yes, the Architects, Designers and Engineers should all get Together in each Nation, and make Proper Plans for those **"GLORIOUS Swanky Hotels Castles and Fortresses!" (Beautiful Planned City States for WISE Intelligent Well-Educated People with Common Sense and Good Understanding!) By The Worldwide People's Revolution!®** Book 019.

20-04 [_] O Selected King, are you not Aware that some Countries are far too Small for the Construction of any Swanky Fortresses? For Example, WHERE would you Fit a Swanky Fortress into Vatican City, in Rome, which is only 140 Acres, which are already mostly Covered with Buildings, including Saint Peter's Basilica?

20-05 [_] Well, my Friend, Vatican City is already a Miniature Fortress to some Degree, which will Work very Well for Conducting **"The Great Worldwide TELEVISED Court HEARING!"** Indeed, Saint Peter's Basilica is Designed Perfectly for such a Great Meeting of the Most Intelligent Minds, which Saint Peter would also LOVE: beCause he was a Lover of Provable Truths, as were all of the Apostles and Disciples of Jesus Christ, even until this very Day: beCause none of them were Afraid of the Bright Shining Light of Truths: beCause they were Good Honest Hardworking People. However, it is a Fact of Life that those Lying Edomites are not the Slightest Bit Interested in any such Great Meetings of the Most Intelligent Minds: beCause they HATE the Light of Truths, even as Jesus said, and will just Naturally REFUSE to Attend any such Meetings. For Example, WHY would George Warmonger Bush and Little Dick Chicanery have any Desire to Expose themselves in the Light of Provable Truths concerning the Hateful Wars in Iraq and Afghanistan?

20-06 [_] O Elected King of the Mountains, it seems that you Evaded the Question — are you not Aware that some Countries are far too Small for the Construction of any Swanky Fortresses? How about Belgium, Norway, Denmark, Finland, Sweden, Switzerland, Holland, and other Small Countries around the World — would you have them DESTROY their Present Cities of Confusion, just to Build Self-air-conditioned Bomb-proof Houses with All-Mineral Organic Gardens on their Roofs? Moreover, HOW would you keep those Houses from LEAKING?

20-07 [_] Well, my Friend, I did not Intend to Evade the Question; but, it just came Natural for me, being Old and somewhat Forgetful, after Suffering with Carbon Monoxide Poisoning, which was so Bad that I could not Remember my own First Name, about 48 Years Ago, when I was in the U.S. Army, which did not Detect it, nor Pay to me a Dime for Compensations for it, even though I should have Received a Disability Check for the Past 48 Years, if Justice were to be Served: beCause it was not my Fault that the 1972 International JEEP was Leaking its Exhaust into the Driver's Chamber of it; but, it was the Fault of International Trucks, Incorporated, whom the Army could have Sued for Damages to get their Compensations. Nevertheless, they are still Welcome to make Amends, if they are Interested in Justice for ALL, and without me taking any of them to Court: beCause I have no Money for Doing that, and do not even Qualify for a Social Insecurity Check: beCause I Lost my Right Mind for many Years, and was not Mentally Able to Hold a Job, much less Pay for any Insurance: beCause I was not Qualified to Drive a Car, which would have been Required of me: beCause of Living on a Farm, far away from any Jobs. However, no one even told me that I had to Pay into Social Security for at least 10 Years, just to Qualify for a Minimum Check, which should have been made Clear when I was in the Army; but, it was NOT. Therefore, I had no Idea that I was going to make a Fool of myself by not Collecting even a Minimum Wage of 400$ per Month when I got 70 Years Old! But, that is the Case, and not only for me; but, also for whomever did not Know it in **"The Divided States of United Lies,"** which likes to Ignore us Vietnam Veterans, and just HOPE that we all go Away!

20-08 [_] O Elected King, you are Surely not Hurting for MONEY, after Presenting the World with no less than 80 Inspired Books for Sale, are you? Indeed, I would Think that you would be the Richest Man in the Whole World, by now! After all, your Books are far Better than those of Mark Twain, which have Sold MILLIONS of Copies!

20-09 [_] Well, my Friend, it is a Well-known Fact that very few Drug Addicts can Appreciate any such Inspired Books, except for those who have been using Marijuana, which seems to Open their Minds, whereby they can get the Subtle Messages Understood. In Fact, that might be the single Best Thing that has Happened in **"The Divided States of United Lies,"** whereby at least some of the People have EXPANDED Minds. However, they often get "Caught Up" in Esoteric Philosophical Nonsense — such as the Mythical Powers of the Pyramids, which may have some Secret Benefits, which we all Need to Discover at **"The Great Worldwide TELEVISED Court HEARING!"** But, the most Important Issues at Hand are concerning the BILLIONS of Poor Wretched Miserable Suffering People in this World of Woes, who could Seek their Philosophical Dreams AFTER they are Living in those **"Beautiful Swanky PALACES!" (A New Concept in Living Habits — Swanky Palaces for Poor People!) By The Worldwide People's Revolution!®** Book 066. Yes, after they have all become Moderately RICH, they could Pursue the Wind, as King Solomon might say, and Hope to Catch it, which is Okay with me: beCause I have also Wasted much Time with all such Profitless Nonsense, and am still not Able to Walk on the Water, nor Transform Rocks into Pure Gold, nor Raise Up any Woolly Mammoth Elephants from any Gardens — not that the World is in a Desperate Need of so much Gold: because it is Possible to make New Money from Stainless Steel Washers, which can have a Bit of Pure Gold placed in the Centers of them, if we Want to give to that Money some "Real Value," as Thomas Jefferson might say. However, once those **"GLORIOUS Swanky Hotels Castles and Fortresses"** are Finished, they will be Far Better than any Mountains of Gold, which will then only be used for Decorating Churches, Cathedrals, Mosques, Synagogues, Temples, Shrines, Theaters, Concert Halls, Gymnasiums, Swimming Pools, King's Thrones, Courtrooms, and Royal Swanky Buffets. Yes, there is already enough Gold for doing all of that, which is now Hiding itself under Edomite Bank Buildings, which they will Gladly Surrender to **"The New RIGHTEOUS One-World Government,"** or else we will bring them in Shackles and Chains to that Great Meeting of the Most Intelligent Minds, and make them Answer our Important Questions. For Example, do any of you Rich Bankers DENY that we have Sufficient Mountains of Rocks in this World of Wonders, whereby everyone in the World could be Living in a Beautiful Swanky PALACE? Indeed, if you Deny it, PLEASE STAND UP! — at which Time none of them will Dare to Stand Up and make Fools of themselves: beCause they Know for a Fact that there is no Lack of Mountains of Rocks, nor any Lack of Voluntary Working Soldiers, who will be Happy to Do all of that Work while Earning GOOD Swanky Wages, which will be Provided by that Good GovernMINT, until almost everyone in the World will become Moderately RICH, even if they must Leave their Crowded Countries, and Move into more Spacious Countries, where there is Room for those Glorious Fortresses. For Example, there is a Vast Plains in Venezuela, where many such Swanky Fortresses could be Constructed in an Ideal Climate for Growing Mangos, Avocadoes, Cherimoyas, Bananas, Papayas, Pineapples, Lychees, Rambutans, Soursops, Oranges, Grapefruits, Limes, and Samoan Coconuts by the Millions. Yes, an otherwise almost Worthless Piece of Land can be Transformed into the Paradise of GOD, if those Poor People will go along with my Master Plan, which I am Sure that they will, if they just Learn about it. Likewise, there are many Ideal Places in Mexico for Small Swanky Fortresses, and one very Large one in Mexico City, itself, whose Ancient Buildings can be Preserved within the Heart of it for Museums and Tourists to Visit. Meanwhile, the President of Mexico can Invite all of the Mexican Slaves in the United States to RETURN HOME, for Constructing those Beautiful Planned City States, whereby they can Attend to their Organic Gardening.

20-10 [_] O Elected King, that Sounds very Good to me. {Please Check the Boxes [_] if you Agree.}

— Chapter 21 —

A Guaranteed Solution for Chronic Constipation of the Mind!

21-01 [_] O Selected King, there are Multitudes of Problems in this World of Woes, which you have not yet Addressed — such as HOW to Solve the Problems in Syria, Israel / Palestine, Jordan, Iraq, Iran, Egypt, Ethiopia, Somalia, Sudan, Kenya, Libya, South Africa, and in many other Nations of Africa, which have Hordes of Refugees, Migrant Slaves, and Poor Miserable People, who have no Means for Building any of those **"GLORIOUS Swanky Hotels Castles and Fortresses!"** Indeed, they are Stuck in the Tar Pits of Extreme Poverty, even as the People of Afghanistan, Pakistan, Kirgizstan, Kurdistan, and India, which has the largest Democratic Deception on the Earth, which is Following in the Footsteps of China, which is making a HUGE Capitalist MESS over there, which has Air that is so THICK with Capitalist Pollution that one can barely Breathe! Did none of them Visit Lost Angels, Californicate, before they Set their Sights on the Glories of HELL? Why did they not Accept the Swanky Fortress System, and thus Avoid Wasting their Money on those Stinking Noisy Vehicles, Coal-fired ElecTrickery Power Plants, Chemical Factories, and other Abominations? Were they Suffering with Chronic Constipation of the Mind, or what??

21-02 [_] Well, my Friend, you could Honestly say that those Chinese were Greatly DECEIVED by Richard (Tricky Dick) Nixon and Henry Kiss-assing-ger, who went over there to China, Years Ago, and talked them into Practicing Capitalism, Under the Table, you might say: because they were Professing Communists on Top of the Table, who Obviously Envied the Western Nations for their False Prosperity, whereby they Proceeded to make FOOLS of themselves, and thus Increased their Diseases by no less than 9000%! Yes, they are now Importing all Kinds of American Sicknesses and Diseases: beCause of Adopting the American DEATH Style, whereby they are Consuming Tons of Sugar, Tobacco Products, and other Kinds of DRUGS. Yes, they have taken Hold on the Witches' Brooms, and are Sweeping Dust Up their Nostrils, and cannot even See what they are Doing to themselves: beCause there is so much Pollution that they cannot even Think Straight! After all, if their Thinking were at all Clear, they would Quickly Adopt the Swanky Fortress Plan — except that they would have no Idea WHERE to Build one! Indeed, most of the Better Lands are already Occupied with People: beCause they have a LOT of People to Deal with. However, there is a Great Gobi Desert over there, which could be Developed into a thousand or more Swanky Fortresses, by Mining Out Topsoil from River Deltas, which could be Transported over there by Wind Power, just as soon as the First Swanky Fortress gets Finished, which would Produce far more Electricity than would be Needed within the Fortress, which could be Exported to wherever it is Needed. ‡

21-03 [_] O Elected King, such a HUGE Project would keep many Chinamen Working for Decades to come; but, WHERE would they get Sufficient Quantities of Fresh Water for all such Luscious Gardens in Swanky Fortresses?

21-04 [_] Well, my Friend, if I Remember Correctly, there is an Ocean of Water right near to them, which can be Distilled by Solar Power: beCause there is lots of Sunlight in the Gobi Desert, and the Sand is Good for making Glass Windows and Mirrors for doing that. Moreover, the Sea Salt can be used for Heat Banks by making it into Blocks of Salt, which can be Stored in Solar-Hot-Houses, even as I have already Explained in some other Inspired Book. Indeed, wherever there is a Will, there is a Way. Therefore, it is just a Matter of Seeing a Vision of what is Needed. Chances are that the

Innovative Chinese People will easily Figure it Out, once they Catch on to the Idea that People Need to EAT; and therefore, they might as well be Eating GOOD Natural Wholesome Foods, and not any American GARBAGE Foods, Preservatives, Harmful Chemicals, nor Poisons of any Kind. After all, China is a LONG WAYS from being Overpopulated in the Gobi Desert, which likely has enough Space for 10 Times as many Chinese People, as well as Japanese, who seem to be Crowded for Space, who could Assist them with those Construction Projects, seeing that they also have Mountains of Rocks to Share with them — that is, the Himalaya Mountains appear to have some Rocks, if I Remember Correctly, which are Begging to be Used Wisely! §‡

21-05 [_] O Elected King, how is it that you could Vainly Imagine that the Japanese and Chinese People could ever get along Well, and especially if they Invited the Koreans to Help them? Do you not Know that they have been at WAR for Centuries, even as those Saudi Arabians and other Arab Nations have been at WAR?

21-06 [_] Well, my Friend, it is Obvious that none of them Discovered their own Building Materials: beCause of Suffering with Chronic Constipation of their Minds! Therefore, the most Rational Solution is for all of them to FAST, or STOP EATING, until they come to their Riit Sensuz, which might Require a Month or so of Fasting; but, it will be very Good for them: because all of their Senses will be Working much more Proficiently, and especially those Parts of their Brains that Remember Important Things — such as WHY they were Born into this World, instead of being Born in some more Hellish World, like the Hot Sweaty Jungles of Africa, which have Depressing Heat, whereby a Person hardly Feels like Doing anything, and the Least Amount of it as Possible, which is a Good Place to Leave to the Apes and Monkeys: beCause there are Ideal Places to Build Swanky Fortresses, even in Africa; but, not likely in Siberia nor in most of Alaska and Northern Canada. But, that is not to say that such Places do not have Natural Resources that could be Exploited, if those Resources are Needed for Building Swanky Fortresses.

21-07 [_] O Elected King, you must be Suffering with Chronic Constipation of the Mind, if you Vainly Imagine that those Greedy Russians are going to Voluntarily Help those Poor Chinese to Prosper, when they have their own Multitude of Extremely Poor People. Indeed, they will do Well to Care for themselves, without Sharing any of their Natural Resources — such as Crude Oils and Gases. Besides that, it is Impractical to Ship anything over such Long Distances, which would only Wear Out the Trains and Railway Tracks. §‡

21-08 [_] Well, my Potential Enemy, if you are Looking for Excuses for not being Cooperative, I am Sure that you can Discover those Excuses; but, I will Try to be more Positive-minded, and Think of Reasonable Solutions for our Massive Problems. After all, it is only Reasonable to Think that this Earth has an Abundance of whatever is Needed for Constructing those **"GLORIOUS Swanky Hotels Castles and Fortresses!" (Beautiful Planned City States for WISE Intelligent Well-Educated People with Common Sense and Good Understanding!) By The Worldwide People's Revolution!**® Book 019. Otherwise, God would not have Commanded it to be Done.

21-09 [_] O Unelected King, I have never read in the *Holy Bible* where God Commanded any such Things to be Done, have you?

21-10 [_] Well, it seems like I just recently Quoted it to you from Moses, himself, which you could say was my own False Fabrication; but, it is Equally as Authentic as anything in the Books of Moses, who was likely a Fictitious Character, himself: beCause the Jews were very Good at making up Biblical Stories, among which was the Exodus Episode, and 40 Years in the Wilderness of Sin with some 6

Million People and tens of Millions of Animals, which would have Drank Up a River of Water, each Day, which did not even Exist in that Wilderness, which could not Support a single Herd of Camels, let alone so many People and Animals — that is, if it were in any Condition at that Time as it now is, which has never had a River running through it, much less Fields of Grasses. However, you could say that those Animals and People were Eating Manna during that 40 Years, and had no Need for Tree Leaves nor Grasses. Yes, you could say that the Manna was so THICK on the Sandy Ground, that the Cows just Licked it Up. Or, you could say that the People spent all Day Gathering the Manna for the Cows, Sheeps, Goats, Horses, Asses, and Camels to Eat: beCause, if they had not, those Animals would have soon Lost their Teeths: beCause of Chewing on SAND! Chances are that 6 Million People could not have Found enough Space to Pitch their Tents, much less the Tabernacle: beCause, as far as I know, there is no Flat Land on the Sinai Peninsula, nor in most of Saudi Arabia, along the Red Sea, other than one small narrow Strip, which could not have contained that many People Standing Up, without any Tents! But, all such Things can be Proven at **"The Great Worldwide TELEVISED Court HEARING,"** as well as the Possibility of Crossing through the Bottom of the Red Sea at Easy-on-Geber, where the Sea is about 200 Miles Wide and 5 Miles Deep, having a Series of Steep Cliffs on each Side of the African Rift, each of which is about 2,000 feet Tall! But, not to Worry: beCause, with God, all Things are Possible, you might say, except for God to LIE! And someone is Obviously Lying to us about something from *Genesis 1* to *Revelation 21,* which tells about a Holy City that is 1,500 Miles HIGH, which would be a bit Impractical to Live in without any Sunlight: beCause almost nothing would Grow in such a Place. Nevertheless, we are Assured that *"... the Lamb is the Light thereof."* In other Words, he must also be very HOT: beCause a City so Tall would be very Cold at the Top, or even just 5 Miles Up, where the Oxygen would be getting rather Thin, and the Breathing would be like Climbing Up Mount Everest without an Oxygen Tank. But, not to Worry: because the Lamb is also the Oxygen thereof, and the Water of Life thereof, and the River of Life thereof, and the Tree of Life thereof: beCause it is all just a Symbolical Fairy Tale, being like much of the *Holy Bible,* which never gets Specific about anything, except for the Construction of the Tabernacle and the Clothes of the Priests, which seemed to be much more Important than any Instructions about Maintaining Good Health, or how to Build a Good House, or how to Plant a Fruit Tree Properly, and also Care for it Professionally: beCause it was just Assumed that People might know HOW to Do those Things, Properly; or, that God did not Care how they did those Things, Improperly. Whatever the Case, there are many Important Books MISSING from that *Holy Bible.* Otherwise, the World might not be in such a Big MESS! Strangely enough, there is not one Word about Capitalism in it: beCause none of those Holy Prophets could Imagine People being so STUPID as to Vote for Dimwitcrats nor Reprobates, who never Mention any of the Great Truths that you can Discover within this Inspired Book: beCause they might put themselves Out of Business by Teaching such Truths. Therefore, it is Best for their Financial Security to never Mention anything about Swanky Fortresses, much less anything about their 5,000+ Good Reasons and Great Advantages for Building them and Living within the Borders of them, which could be done for any of the Refugees in the World, beginning in Syria, Sudan, and Guatemala, who would be ever so Grateful for it. ‡

— Chapter 22 —

A Guaranteed Solution for an End to the Tale of the Peacock!

22-01 [_] O Selected King, is there no End to the Tale of Outlandish Lies that you Teach? What makes you Vainly Imagine that those Swanky Fortresses can even be Built, seeing that not one Exists in this World of Woes?

22-02 [_] Well, if God could Build a Holy City that 1,500-Miles High, Wide, and Long, I should Think that we could Build one that is only 20 Miles in Diameter, and 2-Miles Tall. However, if Height is a Problem, we can be Contented with whatever is Possible and most Practical. After all, my Mind is plenty Flexible enough to Accept some Reasonable Changes: beCause I am not BIGOTED. Indeed, it could be that there is far too much PRESSURE on the Lower Cisterns for Water Storage, whereby they might Collapse, if the Fortress were too Tall; but, some Engineers did a little Scientific Experimenting with some Regular American Red Bricks, about 70 Years Ago, and Discovered that 2 very THIN Brick Walls, about 4-inches thick, could Hold Up 300,000 Tons of Sand in a Concrete Box on Top of those 8-feet-tall Walls. Therefore, if Weak Bricks could do that, with the Compression Strength of Cookies, just Imagine how much Weight 2 of those 10-feet-thick Solid Granite Walls might Hold Up? Chances are that the Empire State Building in New York City could be Set Up on Top of such Strong Walls, and not show any Signs of Collapsing: beCause Granite might be a hundred Times as Strong as a Brick! However, a very THICK Wall is much Stronger than a THIN Wall: beCause the Central Part of a Thick Wall is Securely Held in Place by the Surrounding Stone. However, in the Case of Multiple Cisterns, Tunnels, Tombs, and Packed Sand between them, there is even Greater Strength: beCause those Buildings begin to Form ARCHES in all Directions, and Millions of Arches, which are the Strongest Things known to Mankind. Therefore, each Solid Concrete Dome on Top of each Cistern is Supported by the Pressure of the other Solid Concrete Domes and Barrel-vaulted Tunnels, which have about 10 feet of Thickness. For Example, if a Tunnel is 24 feet Wide at the Tops of the Side Walls, which are 24 feet Tall, a True Arch would be 36 feet Tall in the Center of it. Therefore, if 12 feet of Concrete is poured just above the Center of the Arch, the whole Arch is about 48 feet Tall and 24 feet Thick at the Outer Sides, which would Form a very Strong Base to Rest another Row of Heavy-duty Cisterns on Top of such a Tunnel, which is Flanked by Tombs on each Side of the Tunnel, which are Flanked by Large Cisterns on each Side of them, which are not likely to Move by even the Slightest Bit: beCause of their WEIGHT, and beCause of being Supported on all Sides by more Cisterns, Tombs, and Tunnels.

22-03 [_] O Elected King, do you have any Idea just how much TIME would be Required for an Army of Working Soldiers to Construct such a Beautiful Planned City State? Moreover, would ALL Swanky Fortresses be Built on Foundations of Large Cisterns?

22-04 [_] Well, my Friend, it would all Depend on just HOW we go about Doing it; but, I would say that it would Require about 20 Years, if those **"Seven Great Armies of Working Soldiers"** had the Correct Tools to Work with, including HUGE Swanky Concrete Mixers, which might make a thousand Tons of Concrete at one Time, which could Prove to be Interesting: beCause of getting all of the Ingredients put Together Properly, including Boulders as big as Cars, which will take up much Space in the Solid Thick Walls of those Swanky Cisterns, while Saving much Time and Energy dealing with small Rocks. Nevertheless, such Rocky Concrete would also have to have lots of smaller Rocks in it, as well as much Sand and Gravel to "Mortar" the large Clean Rocks Together. Moreover, all Swanky

Fortresses should be Built Up on Foundations of Large Cisterns: beCause we cannot have too much Fresh Water Stored Up for Times of Droughts, which have Proven to be the Destruction of many Societies, including the Anasazi Indians of New Mexico and Colorado, who, by all Archeological Proofs became Cannibals in the End, just before they became Extinct. Moreover, Tree Rings Testify to that Theory, which gives to it Credibility, which most People Accept, if they Study it Carefully. Therefore, it is a Good Idea to be Prepared for the Worst Kinds of Conditions, even though there is no Guaranteed Way to Prepare for the Time when the Earth might Shift on its so-called "Axis," and even Cause Ocean Floors to RISE UP, and Mountains to SINK under the Sea, which would Naturally take any Cities with them, even if they were Built Up very High: beCause the Oceans might be 20 Miles Deep! Therefore, given the Dangers of Climate Changes and Melting Ice, there is the Possibility of such a Shift, and thus the Destruction of the Continents, themselves! In Fact, you can read about it in that *Holy Bible,* somewhere in *the Book of Isaiah,* if I Recall Correctly. {See www.Amazon.com for: **"The New MAGNIFIED Version of ISAIAH in Plain English!" (The Understandable Version of the Book of Isaiah!)** Book 044.}

22-05 [_] O Elected King, it seems like we will go to a LOT of Hard Work to Build those New Cities, which not even God can Guarantee to Stay Put; but, I would say that they will be much more Likely to Stand Firm when Jehovah God Arises to Shake Terribly the Whole Earth, as Isaiah Reported. Indeed, only a Solid Stone Dome Home Complex could Withstand any such VIOLENT SHAKING: beCause of its Design. Therefore, we should make up our Minds about whether or not we Want to Survive the Coming Disasters, or just Trust God to Cause our Spirits to be Born here Again.

22-06 [_] Well, we are Promised a Renewed Heaven and Earth, wherein Dwells Righteousness; but, in the Meantime, it will be Good Exercise and Experience for us to Build those **"GLORIOUS Swanky Hotels Castles and Fortresses,"** which will get us Better Prepared for that New World, when we will have to go to Work and Build New Cities, again: beCause God is not going to Do for us what we can Do for ourselves, lest he should Spoil us. Indeed, you might be Looking for a very Long Time for a City that is Built without Human Hands; but, I would be quite Contented to Live in any of those **"Beautiful Swanky PALACES!" (A New Concept in Living Habits — Swanky Palaces for Poor People!) By The Worldwide People's Revolution!®** Book 066. After all, People have been Living and Dying for at least 6,000 Years, and no such Holy City has Appeared in the Sky, lately. Therefore, what are the Chances of it Appearing during our Lifetimes? Perhaps it was just an Edomite TRICK, to get Poor Ignorant People to Accept such a False Doctrine: beCause it has Served those Edomites very Well, who Live in their Palaces, while Eating thousand-dollar Meals, and Drinking Expensive Champaign with other Rich Edomites — none of whom Accept any such False Doctrines, nor even Believe in that Hebrew God: beCause they Worship the God of Possessions. Indeed, without that False Doctrine in the *Holy Bible,* those Edomites could have never become so RICH: beCause the Masses of People would have Seen the Light of Truths concerning it, and thus Claimed their own Mountains of Rocks, and made their own Beautiful Planned City States, and said to Hell with those Rich Bankers. ‡

22-07 [_] O Selected King, do you not Understand that all of those Rich People have already Received their Rewards, as Jesus said? Indeed, *"Woe unto you who are now Rich: because you have Received your only Rewards, who could have Received Glorious Worlds with Great Riches, if you had Loved and Obeyed the Laws of the Gods; but, behold, you are Selfish and Greedy People, who have not Shared your Wealth with those Poor People who Suffer all around you: beCause you are without Empathy, Love, nor Compassion, being Adopted Sons and Daughters of Satan, who shall Reign Over you in the World to Come: beCause you shall be Cast Out of this World, into a Lower Order of Worlds, where you shall be Tormented both Day and Night: beCause that is your Just Reward. But, Blest are those Humble and Wise People, who Share the Riches of the Earth with one another, and Work Together with United Effort to Build Beautiful Planned City States: beCause they shall be the Healthy and Happy People."* — *The Gospel According to Saint Bartholomew 5:27—28.*

22-08 [_] Well, I must Agree with Jesus: beCause his Inspired Words of Provable Truths make Good Sense. Moreover, I can also Fully Understand WHY all such Books were DELETED from the *Holy Bible:* beCause those Rich Edomites would not Want anyone to Learn any such Truths, including other Edomites, who might also Join **"The Swanky Associations of Working Soldiers!"** **(A Fascinating Collection of Various Kinds of Voluntary Working Soldiers!) By The Worldwide People's Revolution!®** Book 018.

22-09 [_] O Colorful Peacock, I am Wondering if there is a Guaranteed Solution for an End to the Tale of the Peacock? After all, I would Think that 80 Books on Amazon dot com would be Sufficient — no?

22-10 [_] Well, it would seem that 80 Books should be Enough to Persuade any Sane Person to Believe and Obey the Truths that I Teach; but, the Unbelievers might still have some Unanswered Questions — such as what to Do for the Multitudes of Refugees in this World of Woes? Nevertheless, when all of those Great Truths that I Teach are Accepted, there will be a Guaranteed End to my Inspired Books — not that I have ran / run out of Writing Materials to Discuss; but, that there will be no more Need for more Peacock Books, once those Swanky Fortresses are Built: beCause there will be Holy People, who will take up where I have left off. After all, I am the Forerunner of **The Worldwide People's Revolution!®**

— Chapter 23 —

A Guaranteed Solution for the Refugees, Worldwide!

23-01 [_] First of all, when we Hold **"The Great Worldwide TELEVISED Court HEARING,"** there will not likely be so much as one Rebellious Nation in the World: beCause of the Peer Pressure of the other Nations, who will Boycott any such Non-cooperative Nations, and Refuse to Trade any Goods and Services with them, nor even Accept their Ambassadors and Diplomats: beCause of Judging them to be Insane! After all, we are Talking about making most of the People in this World Moderately RICH, which some Rich People might not Like the Sound of; but, when they Consider the Fact that they are also Deprived of Fresh Clean Air to Breathe, Pure Living Water to Drink, Wholesome Natural Foods to Eat, Natural Clothing to Wear, and Secure Houses to Live in with other People of Like-mindedness within Beautiful Planned City States, they will also Humbly Submit to **"The Swanky Sword of Divine Truths!"** **(The Most Powerful Weapon in the Whole Universe!) By The Worldwide People's Revolution!®** Book 067. Yes, it will be a bit Humiliating for some Rich People to Confess the Truth of it; but, I would say that most of them will still go Along with the Idea: beCause they are Tired of Living in FEARS of those Atomic and Hydrogen BOMBS, among Terrorist Attacks, Chemical Warfare, Biological Warfare, Cyber Attacks, Kidnappers, Assassinators, and whatever might be Out there. Yes, God Knows that most of them have also Suffered Long Enough with their Sicknesses and Diseases, and are now Ready for some Serious Changes in the Political Weather.

23-02 [_] O Elected King, are you saying that those Syrian Refugees will be able to Return to Syria, and Build their own Swanky Fortresses? Will they not be Tormented by that Wicked Regime that is Established over there under the Dictatorship of Bashar al-Assad?

23-03 [_] Well, my Friend, that Dictator, and all other Dictators will Happily Agree to Help the People who Need Help, or else we will not Help them to Build any Swanky Fortresses, nor have any Seats at **"The Great World TEMPLE of PEACE!" (The Glory of Jerusalem Arises Again!)**, Book 017 — which Temple will be the Headquarters for **"The New RIGHTEOUS One-World Government!"** Indeed, they will be Excommunicated from the World Community, until they Humbly Submit to Reason and Logic. After all, we are not Asking them to Give Up their False Religions, nor their False Political Beliefs: beCause each Planned City State may have whatever Beliefs that they Want, just as long as they are not Taxing other People to Support them, nor Inventing nor Using any Hateful Weapons to Destroy other People of Different Faiths, who have the same Rights.

23-04 [_] O Selected King, are you not Aware that the Radical Muslims have an Agenda to Destroy whomever is NOT a Radical Muslim? Indeed, it is a Part of their Religious Upbringing, which they Gather from reading the *Holy Qur'an,* which is the Muslim Bible, which was Dictated directly to Muhammad by the Angel Gabriel, himself, in Arabic, just to make Sure that all of the Words of Allah were Correct, whereby no less than a thousand Islamic Sects have arisen because of it. Therefore, we cannot Expect ISIS, al-Qaeda, and dozens of other Radical Muslims to just DROP their Beliefs, and run for Cover in a Swanky Fortress: because they are not going to Do that at any Time soon. §§‡

23-05 [_] Well, it could be that ISIS (Israeli Secret Instigation Services) has a Valid Point to make about some certain Subject. Therefore, their Leaders, and all other Religious Leaders, will be Kindly Invited to Attend **"The Great Worldwide TELEVISED Court HEARING,"** whereby we might HEAR whatever they have to Say, and also Analyze it Properly in the Light of all *Scriptures,* including the *Koran:* beCause their Beliefs are Supposedly Based on the *Scriptures,* including the Uninspired Dictations of MuhamMAD, who can easily be Proven to be a FALSE Prophet, or no Prophet at all: beCause, after reading the entire Boring *Koran* from Cover to Cover, I did not Discover so much as ONE Prophecy in it. Nevertheless, I do not Want to be anything like CNN News Reporters, who give One-sided Reports from the American Points of Views, while Totally Ignoring any Points of Views from the so-called "Enemies" — such as President Kim of the Democratic People's Republic of North Korea, whose Ambassador should come to the United Nations Assembly, and Address their Viewpoints. Indeed, CNN should have Access to all such Ambassadors, if they Want to have a Reputation for being Unbiased News Reporters. After all, it could be that North Korea has been WRonged by someone, and Namely by **"The Divided States of United Lies!" (The so-called "United States of North America" in Disguise!)**, Book 058, which just PRETENDS to Love its Naaberz as much as it Loves itself, which simply Ignores the True Christian Doctrine about having all Material Things in Common among us, whereby everyone in the World can Share the Wealth of the Earth, and thus become Moderately RICH, without Telling any Lies, nor Selling any Capitalist TRASH — such as those Stinking Noisy Polluting Vehicles, which Healthy People can Live Happily without: beCause they use Electric Elevators, Escalators, and Subway Trains within Beautiful Planned City States, which are Designed for Eternal Employment and True Prosperity! Yes, the Democratic People's Republic of North Korea will no doubt Accept that Doctrine, once they Learn it, if they have not already Accepted it; but, Rich HOGS, like Donald Trumpeter, Incorporated, will likely Reject the Idea: beCause that will Spell the END of Confusion and MADNESS, including Islamic Madness, which is Based on the Assumption that MuhamMAD was a True Prophet, when he gave NO Prophecies about anything, nor even Visualized a Beautiful World, which has no Terrorists, Murderous Soldiers, nor Ignorant Fools in it. {See: **"Terrorists Beware that your Days are Numbered!" (HOW to Bring those Terrorist Attacks to a Screeching HALT!) By The Worldwide People's Revolution!®** Book 043.}

23-06 [_] O Elected King, suppose a certain Percentage of Syrians want to Build Swanky Fortresses; but, al-Assad has no Desire to Build any of them — will **"The New RIGHTEOUS One-World**

Government" send in Troops to Protect those Syrians, who are Determined to Build Swanky Fortresses? {See: **"AIIRMWVC and Reasonable Solutions!" (Aliens, Illegal Immigrants, Refugees, Migrant Workers, and other Victims of Capitalism!) By The Worldwide People's Revolution!® Book 032.**}

23-07 [_] O Elected King, I find it most Amazing that such a Hateful Person as Bashar al-Assad has not been Eliminated by an American Drone, which could also be used to Eliminate the so-called President of North Korea, who got 99.99% of the Votes, after which the Opposition Party was Exterminated: beCause that 99% Voted for it, which was a True DEMOCRATIC Exercise: beCause the Majority of the Electors have that God-given RIGHT, which is Proof of the Righteousness of DEMON-ocracy, which was also Utilized when the Jews Arranged the Crucifixion of Jesus Christ, when the MOB Screamed out, *"CRUCIFY HIM! CRUCIFY HIM!!"* Yes, it was a Democratic Decision, which, like most all Democratic Decisions, Worked out BADLY: beCause they Crucified the most Righteous Person who ever Lived, whom they should have made into their Righteous KING, and thus not Suffered for the next 2,000+ Years under the Dictatorship of DEMON-ocracy. §§‡

23-08 [_] Well, my Friend, most of the People in the World have been Deceived by those Election Deceptions, whereby they Vainly Imagine that they are somehow Served very Well by Demon-ocracy, or Mob Rulership, which is seldom if ever Permitted to Vote concerning any Specific Issue — such as whether or not they Want to be Governed by a RIGHTEOUS KING, as Opposed to a Mob of Ignorant Dimwitcrats and Anti-Christ Reprobates? Indeed, the American "Way of Self-Destruction" is quite Contrary to the Biblical *"Way of Life,"* which is to Love and Obey the Teachings of Jesus Christ, one of which is the Doctrine of having *"… all Material and Spiritual Things in Common among them, whereby there are no Excessively Rich People, nor Extremely Poor People among them,"* as *the Book of Mormon* puts it in so many Words. {See: **"The New MAGNIFIED Version of The Book of MOORMUN!" (The Story of the White and Dark Indians in the Americas!) By The Worldwide People's Revolution!® Book 040,** which comes in 2 Volumes of about 500 pages, each.}

23-09 [_] O Elected King, I would Think that if most of the Nations should Build those **"GLORIOUS Swanky Hotels Castles and Fortresses!" (Beautiful Planned City States for WISE Intelligent Well-Educated People with Common Sense and Good Understanding!),** Book 019, that all of the Righteous People would FLEE from any Rebellious Nations, and thus Move into those Fortresses, whereby only the Crazy and Ignorant People would be left in those Rebellious Nations, who would soon become Refugees in Swanky Fortresses: beCause of the Dictators, who would Arise to Seize Power among them as a last Desperate Opportunity to Practice Capitalism, which is the False Economic System of the Possession Worshipers, which Produces a few Excessively Rich Hogs, while Producing Multitudes of Extremely Poor Sheepoul, which Economic System the Rich People Glorify as "the economic salvation of mankind," when, in Reality, it is the Self-Destruction of Mankind! ‡

23-10 [_] Well, my Friend, it remains to be seen whether or not anyone in the Whole World will Oppose **"The New RIGHTEOUS One-World Government!" (HOW to Establish a Righteous One-World Government without Going to WAR!) By The Worldwide People's Revolution!® Book 056.** For Example, would you Stand Up at **"The Great Worldwide TELEVISED Court HEARING,"** and make a Fool of yourself, by Opposing it? Indeed, what would be your most Rational Argument for Opposing it? Awe, you could say that the World will be Greatly Suffering for a Lack of Rich Bankers: beCause of putting all of them Out of Business! However, when almost everyone is Living in those **"Beautiful Swanky PALACES!" (A New Concept in Living Habits — Swanky Palaces for Poor People!) By The Worldwide People's Revolution!®,** Book 066, that will hardly be an Acceptable Argument, with or without Demon-ocracy. But, if the Masses of People in this World of

Wonders were now given a VOTE for whether or not they Want to become Moderately RICH, and with only an Average of 4 Hours of Common Skilled Labor per Day, or the Equivalent thereof, I do Believe that 99.999,999,999% of them would Check this Box [_] with an X! {Please Check it, if you Agree with me. Otherwise, please use the Space below to Explain WHY that you would NOT Accept my Master Plan for Worldwide Law, Order, Obedience, Peace and True Prosperity among all Peoples; and be Prepared to Defend your Beliefs in a Courtroom with Law and Order. Otherwise, feel Free to write an Uninspired book about it with a Fictitious Pen Name, and Publish it by CreateSpace on Amazon.com: because I would like to read it, just for the fun of it. Indeed, I might be Inspired to Write another Exceptionally Good Book about it, and also Publish it with a Fictitious Pen Name: beCause it is not Safe to Reveal too many Truths in **"The Divided States of United Lies!" (The so-called "United States of North America" in Disguise!)**: beCause such a Revelator is likely to be Assassinated by the Edomites. Nevertheless, it is Impossible to Assassinate **"The Swanky Sword of Divine Truths!"** Book 067.}

— Chapter 24 —

A Guaranteed Solution for Eliminating Nuclear Trash!

24-01 [ ] Ever since the Mad Capitalists Invented the Atomic Bomb, People with Good Hearts have been Trying to Think of Ways to get RID of them; but, it was only a Matter of Time when X-amount of Nations came up with their own Atomic Bombs for the Sake of "National Security," which is WHY North Korea also came up with their Atomic Bombs, and Iran is still Struggling with Satan to get their own "National Security" by Means of them: beCause they are Threatened by the Israelis, who have already Assassinated Iranian Scientists: beCause the Israelis FEAR that Iran might "Wipe them Off of the Map," which was once Iran's Objective, according to certain All-American News Propagandists, who Misinterpreted the Good Intentions of the Iranians, which was NOT to Exterminate all Israelis; but, only to Restore the Land of Palestine to the Palestinians, which would be somewhat Like Restoring America to the Native American Indians, which would be a Legitimate Cause to most American Indians, who could likely be Persuaded to make Car Bombs to BLOW UP Crowds of Americans, if those Indians were of the same Nature and Intellectual Capacity as those Radical Muslims, who Worship Buzzeldick the Great, who have a Spiritual Roadblock within their own Minds, which they cannot See Passed: beCause that is the Nature of the Unholy Spirit of Unbelief. Yes, it is one of the most VILE Spirits, which can only be Killed by **"The Swanky Sword of Divine Truths!" (The Most Powerful Weapon in the Whole Universe!) By The Worldwide People's Revolution!® Book 067.**

24-02 [ ] O Unelected King, if you Vainly Imagine that you, or anyone else, can get RID of Nuclear Weapons, you are only Deceiving yourself: beCause there is no Way in this World that we can get RID of our False Gods and Goddesses — such as the God of BAAL, which is the God of POSSESSIONS, whom almost everyone Worships, including THYSELF, O PeaCOCK: beCause you Like to OWN Things — such as your Million-dollar Marble Mansion! Yes, I have seen Pictures of it within your other Uninspired books. Therefore, I Know for a Fact that you are another Possession Worshiper! §§

24-03 [ ] Well, my Potential Enemy, it is True that I presently Live in a Million-dollar Mansion, when it is Compared with the Billions of Shanties all about me; but, it so Happens that I do NOT OWN IT! Nor do I Rent it! In Fact, I Bought about 90% of the Building Materials, and all of the Land that it sits on; but, none of it is in my Name, nor in the Name of my Brother Vern, who Bought the other 10% of it: beCause we are NOT the Owners of it, which is Proof that we are NOT Possession Worshipers. In Fact, we Actually Own less than 4,000$-worth of Property, including one TV, 2 Used Computers, and some Furniture — none of which we will take with us when we Die. Therefore, your False Accusation must be Corrected and Well-Understood by all Readers: beCause it is a MAJOR Issue, which is the Main Cause for those Nuclear-powered Nations to Want to Defend themselves with Nuclear Weapons, even though most of them have used the Silly Argument that they Need Nuclear Electric Power Plants for ElecTrickery, which is also the Case for Iran, which has an Abundance of Sunlight and WIND, which it only Needs to CAPTURE; and then they could all have FREE Electricity, and be Thankful for it. However, that would not Solve their "National Insecurity Problem," would it? Indeed, they would still be Threatened by those Israelis and American Warmongers: beCause of Supporting those Palestinians, which is at the Heart of the Problem in the Middle East: beCause they were Served a Great Injustice by the Israelis, even as the American Indians were Served many Great Injustices by the Brits and Europeans, who eventually Conquered them, and put them onto Indian Reservations, whereby they Forced the Indians to CONFORM to Capitalism, or else, DIE OFF: beCause those Founding

Fathers had little or none of the Spirit of Christ in them, or else they would have Helped the Indians to Build those **"GLORIOUS Swanky Hotels Castles and Fortresses"**: beCause of the 5,000+ Good Reasons and Great Advantages for Doing it, one of which is National Security: beCause, WHO can Conquer a Properly-constructed Swanky FORTRESS? Answer: NO ONE. And why is that? Well, you just have to Stop and THINK about it.

24-04 [ ] O Elected King, if a Swanky Fortress cannot be Conquered by Bent Bows with Sharp Arrows: beCause of Doing Away with all Military Weapons, I suppose that you are Correct. However, as of this Date, we still have many Nations with Aggressive Military Weapons, and even Atomic Bombs and Hydrogen Bombs. Therefore, if we cannot Persuade those Nations to Surrender ALL of their Military Weapons to **"The New RIGHTEOUS One-World Government,"** we cannot Assure ourselves of Everlasting PEACE. However, what makes you Vainly Imagine that any such Government can be Trusted? Indeed, once you are Dead and Gone, there will Arise a WICKED One-World Government, which will make SLAVES of all of us! Yes, they will make Education Slaves, Work Slaves, Tax Slaves, Interest Slaves, Insurance Slaves, Rent Slaves, Mortgage Slaves, Credit Card Debt Slaves, College-loan Debt Slaves, Property Tax Slaves, ElecTrickery Bills Slaves, Gas Bills Slaves, Water Bills Slaves, Food Bills Slaves, Drug Slaves, Childcare Slaves, Sex Slaves, and Various other Kinds of Slaves of us: beCause that is the Nature of an Edomite Slavery System, which is Powered by BANKERS, who Control the Money Supply, who Determine WHO is RICH and WHO is POOR, which is the very Reason WHY that YOU are so Poor, whereby you cannot even Afford to OWN a HOUSE! Indeed, you Used to Own a House, until it was Taxed Out from under you: beCause there was no Way that an Old Man without an Unsociable Insecurity Check could ever Raise Enough Potatoes with a Digging Fork, to Pay for all such Taxes. Therefore, you and your Older Brother were FORCED to Depart from the Farm, and Move into some City of Confusion, just to Survive! In Fact, with only 430$ per Month for your Brother Vern's Social Insecurity Check, you were Forced to Move to MEXICO, just to Survive: beCause the Food is a lot Cheaper over there. For Example, a Box of Avocadoes, which Costs no less than 400$ in **"The Divided States of United Lies,"** can be Bought for only 50$ in Mexico! Likewise, a Box of Mangoes, which Costs about 15$ in Mexico, is Selling for 160$ in America. Therefore, it is far more Financially Practical to Live in Mexico, where there are also more Freedoms, and far less Taxes, and far less Harassments by the Federal Government of Mexico, which Actually has some of the Spirit of Christ, whereby they Love their Naaberz as much as themselves to some Degree, and at least Try to *"Do unto others as they would have others Do unto them,"* which used to be called the Golden Rule. However, that Rule was never Practiced by the Federal Government in the so-called "United States of North America," which is Obviously Working for those Rich Edomite Bankers, and NOT for the Masses of People, who would LOVE to Live within those Swanky Fortresses, in those **"Beautiful Swanky PALACES!" (A New Concept in Living Habits — Swanky Palaces for Poor People!)**: beCause they are Tired of the Endless News Reports about TERRORISTS, who would Naturally be EXTERMINTED by that Swanky Fortress System: beCause of having a RIGHTEOUS KING or HOLY QUEEN in Charge of each Swanky Fortress, who would Gladly Submit to **"The New RIGHTEOUS One-World Government,"** which would have Total Control over all of the Military Weapons, most of which would be Melted Down and made into Good Durable TOOLS: beCause such a Good Government would have no Reason for Attacking any Swanky Fortress: beCause all of the Inhabitants would Learn, Believe, Love, and OBEY **"The New MAGNIFIED Version of the 20 Commandments!"** — which can be Found in: **"LIGHTNING STRIKES Versus Lightning Bugs!" (HOW you can Become Moderately RICH, without Telling any Lies nor Selling any Trash!) By The Worldwide People's Revolution!®** Book 074, ISBN — 13: 978-1545-0799-73, or ISBN — 10: 1545-0799-78, which anyone can Discover for FREE in a Swanky TRUTH-brary, or at www.Amazon.com.usa for a Reasonable Price, which can be Shared by any Congregation of Truth Seekers for less than a Dollar Donation per Person! §§

24-05 [_] Well, my Friend, **"The New RIGHTEOUS One-World Government"** can be Trusted: beCause all Meetings of the Minds will be Conducted in OPEN Public Courtrooms with all TV Cameras Running from the Major News Networks from around the World: beCause there will be no more Secret Meetings behind Closed Doors, whereby everyone will be Able to Learn what is going on, and Judge for themselves WHO is Correct. For Example, when all of those Major Edomite Bankers are Gathered Together, we will Ask them a few very Important Questions — such as:

A-[_] Do all of you Intelligent and Educated Bankers AGREE with me, that there are no less than 7 Billion Extremely Poor People in this World of Woes, who do not have Fresh Clean Air to Breathe, Pure Living Water to Drink, Wholesome Natural Foods to Eat, Natural Clothing to Wear, nor Secure Houses to Live in? Indeed, if you Disagree, please STAND UP and tell us WHO has all of those Good Things! — at which Time, NONE of them will Stand Up: beCause they all Know for a Fact that at least 7 Billion People are Deprived of those Good Things.

B-[_] Do any of you Bankers Deny that Bankers Control the Money Supplies for almost all Nations? If you Deny it, please Stand Up! {Please Check the Box with an X, if you Deny it.}

C-[_] Do any of you Bankers Deny that we have hundreds of thousands of Mountains of Rocks, which could be Used WISELY for Building those **"Beautiful Swanky PALACES!" (A New Concept in Living Habits — Swanky Palaces for Poor People!)**, if we, the People, should Elect to Establish **"The New RIGHTEOUS One-World Government,"** which has the Duty of Minting and Printing the Necessary New Money for HIRING **"Seven Great Armies of Working Soldiers"** to Build those **"GLORIOUS Swanky Hotels Castles and Fortresses"** in all of the Nations, wherever it is Practical to do so, and that Stonework will Represent that New Money, which will make it the Best Money in all of the World, being Represented by Things of Real Value, as Opposed to the Capitalist Trash in the Trash Dumps, and the Old Rusty Cars in the Junkyards? If you Deny it, PLEASE STAND UP! — at which Time none of them will Dare to Stand Up: beCause they Know for a Fact that there are many Mountains of Rocks that would be Good for that Purpose. However, if you Deny it, please Check the above Box with an X.

D-[_] Do any of you Bankers Deny that it would be a Good Thing to HIRE those Voluntary Working Soldiers according to **"A List of FAIR Swanky Wages!" (The Equitable Wage System!) By The Worldwide People's Revolution!®**, Book 065, whereby there would be no more Poverty, Worldwide? If you Deny it, please Stand Up and Explain your Point of View! — at which Time no one would Dare to Stand Up: beCause all of the Arguments are in my Favor! But, if you Disagree, please Check the Box with an X.

E-[_] Do any of you Bankers Deny that it would be a Good Thing if all of the Spacious Rooms within Stone Dome Home Complexes were Faced with Polished Marble Tiles, or Ceramic Tiles, which could be Painted with Beautiful Murals before they are Baked, just to make those Homes Beautiful Places for People to Live for thousands of Years, and easy Places to Clean, which should also have Granite-faced Floors, even if they are Covered with Stinking Bacteria-laden Dusty Carpets by Ignorant Fools? If you Deny it, please Stand Up! — at which Time none of them will Dare to Stand Up: beCause it is Impractical to Build Wooden / Plastic Firetrap Mouse-infested Cockroach Dens for People to Live in, which also have Outlandish Heating and Cooling Bills, not to Mention Insurance, which never Covers the Lives of the Little Children who Burn Up in them, or Die from the Toxic Fumes of all such Burning Houses, which have Costed Americans TRILLIONS of Wasted Dollars! Nevertheless, if you Deny it, please Check the above Box with an X, and get Prepared to Defend your Ignorance at **"The**

Great Worldwide TELEVISED Court HEARING!" (That Great Meeting of the Most Intelligent and Wel-Ejukaatid Miindz!) By The Worldwide People's Revolution!® Book 041. Yes, get your Arguments all Lined Up: beCause you will have the Great Privilege of Living in such a Worthless House in some City of Confusion, and without any Government Assistance: beCause the Free People will have no Interest in Taxing themselves to Support any such IGNORANT FOOLS!

F-[_] Do any of you Bankers Deny that it would be a Good Idea for all such Stone Dome Home Complexes to be Covered with All-Mineral Organic Gardens, whereby the Inhabitants might have a Way to Feed themselves, even if their Federal Government should go Totally INSANE? If you Deny it, please Stand Up! — at which Time they will not Dare to Stand Up: beCause it is Possible for all of those Gardens to be Cared for by the VOLUNTARY Working Soldiers of **"The Swanky Association of Professional Organic Gardeners,"** who will be more than Happy to Live in those **"Beautiful Swanky PALACES,"** in Exchange for 4 Hours of Services per Workday, or the Equivalent thereof. Nevertheless, if you Deny it, please Check the above Box with an X, and be Prepared to Defend your Insanity at that Great Meeting of the Most Intelligent Minds, who will put you to Great Shame for your STUPIDITY! After all, if you do not Like Gardening, it is only beCause you have not had Good Topsoil to Work with, which will be Mass-produced by **"The Swanky Associations of Working Soldiers!"** (A Fascinating Collection of Various Kinds of Voluntary Working Soldiers!) By The Worldwide People's Revolution!®** Book 018.

G-[_] Do any of you Bankers Deny that it would be a Good Idea to Build BILLIONS of Large Swanky Cisterns, whereby everyone in the World can be Assured of having a Fresh Clean Water Supply of LIVING Water: beCause of Pumping and Running that Water over Waterfalls and Riverbeds with Rough Gravel, Sand, and Beautiful Polished Boulders, whereby everyone can Enjoy those **"GLORIOUS Swanky Hotels Castles and Fortresses!" (Beautiful Planned City States for WISE Intelligent Well-Educated People with Common Sense and Good Understanding!) By The Worldwide People's Revolution!®**, Book 019, whereby they do not have to Suffer any longer under the CRUEL Dictatorship of CAPITALISM, Socialism, Fascism, nor Communism? If you Deny it, please Stand Up! — at which Time none of them will Dare to Stand Up: beCause, in spite of all of their so-called "Wealth," none of them have ever Drank any Pure Living Water from their Lead-lined Pipes, nor even from their Heavily-chlorinated Recycled Sewage Water from their Septic Tanks: beCause that is Impossible. Nevertheless, if you Deny it, please Check the above Box with an X, and get Prepared to Defend your Beliefs at **"The Great Worldwide TELEVISED Court HEARING,"** where all of the Top Scientists and Medical Doctors in the Whole World will be Confronted with **"The Swanky Sword of Divine Truths!"** Book 067. Yes, if you Object to having Living Water for all Plants and Creatures to Richly Enjoy, please get yourself a Glass of that Recycled Sewage Water, right now, and Ask yourself how it Compares with some Living Water from the Neuschwanstein Castle in Southern Bavaria, in Germany, or from some Glacier in Jasper National Park, in Canada, where the Rivers of Living Water Flow? Otherwise, please Check the above Box with an X, which would Indicate that you Deny it.

H-[_] Do any of you Bankers Deny that it would be a Good Idea if everyone in the World, except for Voluntary Part-time Sailors, should have the Great Benefits of Swanky Fortresses, which have more than 5,000 Advantages over these Filthy Noisy Crime-infested Cities of Confusion? If you Deny it, please Stand Up and Explain yourself! — at which Time none of them will Dare to Stand Up: beCause of Knowing that we have no Time to Waste on any of their Nonsense, which can now be Addressed in: **"FREEDUM uv SPEECH!" (U Speshould Maguzeen uv Onist Upinyunz!) By The Worldwide People's Revolution!®** Book 030. Yes, if you have any Important Unanswered Questions, it is now Time to Ask them, whereby we will not have to Waste any Precious Time with Ignorant Fools at **"The Great Worldwide TELEVISED Court HEARING,"** where all such Magazines can be Read Aloud between Meetings for whomever Wants to Listen and Learn: beCause ALL Television Channels and Radio Stations will be Focused on those Meetings, alone, except for any Major News Reports about Natural Disasters, and Things of Great Concern — such as the Surrendering of all Military Weapons to **"The New RIGHTEOUS One-World Government!" (HOW to Establish a Righteous One-World Government without Going to WAR!) By The Worldwide People's Revolution!®** Book 056. Nevertheless, if you Object to that Great Idea, please Check this Box [_] with an X.

I-[_] I Object to that Worthless Idea, your Dishonorable Majesty: beCause that would Limit our Freedom of Speech and of the Press, which Requires 500 Different TV Channels, just for Entertainment, Religious Garbage, and Worthless Talk Shows, which never Present so much as one Reasonable Solution for anything: beCause those Reports are not Designed to Help us to Solve our Problems, which might Require us to THINK, which would Cause Headaches among Politicians, Preachers, Teachers, and Professors, who have been Discussing the Burned Stew for Decades, and have not Figured Out any Way to FIX it. However, you have come up with that Great Meeting of the Most Unintelligent and Deceived Minds Idea, which is of no Interest to us Tax Slaves: beCause we only Want to Play with our Balls, and have a Good Time, and just Ignore any Climate Changes, Wars, Famines, Refugee Problems, Sicknesses, Diseases, Natural Disasters, Floods, Fires, Earthquakes, Tornadoes, Hurricanes, Typhoons, Tsunamis, Mudslides, Landslides, Erupting Volcanoes, and whatever is Beyond our Control. After all, this is the Year 2017, and we still do not have a Reasonable Solution for Wet Dreams, nor for Gay Marriages in Moscow and Uganda: beCause we Suffer with Chronic Constipation of our Minds! Otherwise, we would all be DEMANDING that Great Meeting of the Most Intelligent Minds, just to Learn WHO Killed President John Fitzgerald Kennedy, and WHY it was Covered Up for 140 Years? Yes, we would be Demanding JUSTICE for ALL, including the Victims of the All-American False Flag Operations during September 11th, 2001, which are Unsolved and Unresolved Mysteries, which have yet to be Explained in a Rational Manner, whereby any 12-year-old Boy or Girl can Understand it: beCause of making some Sense! After all, HOW could 283 Hardened Steel Columns come Crashing Down in UNISON, in less than 7 Seconds, without the Assistance of EXPLOSIVES? Well, I will tell you HOW — they came down by what NIST called "Thermal Expansion," which is when the Left Brain gets into a War with the Right Brain, and the Head EXPLODES from Frustration! However, that Pressure can easily be Released by Learning the Whole Truth, whereby PEACE can be Established among the Nations, all of which will Cheerfully Agree that you might be CRAZY, O Selected King, just for having Faith in such an Impossible Thing as that Great Meeting of the Least Intelligent Minds; but, none of them Disagree with the Fact that you can easily be Proven to be WRong about a LOT of Important Subjects — such as WHO Orchestrated the Murder of John Fitzgerald Kennedy, and WHY? Indeed, there is only ONE WAY to Discover the Answers, and that is to Reveal ALL of the Evidences, which have been DESTROYED: beCause those Evidences were Hidden in World Trade Center Tower 7, in New Yuck City, along with many other Important Documents: beCause it was the Best Way to make America Great Again, by Covering Up any Past Sins. Otherwise, President Donald Trumpeter would be Demanding a THOROUGH and Unbiased Investigation of all of those Evil Events of September 11th, 2001, whereby the Real Criminals might be brought to JUSTICE! §§‡

{HEADNOTE: Please Check the above Box with an X, if you Agree or even Disagree with any of the Statements, which you can Highlight with a Yellow Marker, if you Agree; or with a Pink Marker, if you Disagree, which will be Proof that you did Read the Statement, if you Initial it at the End. RWS, for Example, or DJT, GHWB, JDR, WFG, or JFK. You should also Sign your Name with Ink at the Beginning of this Book, and at the Beginning of all other Books that you Read by **The Worldwide People's Revolution!®**, after you Carefully PRINT your Name in ALL-CAPITAL LETTERS, whereby anyone might be able to Read it, even if they cannot Read your Signature, which should be followed by the Day, Month, and Year — such as 21/08/2017. You are also Welcome to use a Fictitious Pen Name or Pseudonym, just as long as you are Consistant with it, whereby you might Identify yourself with it, and Remember it, which you can also use when you Fill Out and File on the Internet **"The Complete SURVEYS of our VALUES!"** — which will be used to Help you to Locate other People of Like-mindedness with your Values, which will all eventually be Computerized for making that Possible. Trust me, it is a Great Idea, which was not Possible until this Generation. However, neither Terrorists nor Edomites will Like that Idea: beCause they are Dishonest Lying Hypocrites, like most Reprobate Republicans, who Claim to Love God while doing their Best to Destroy his Good Earth, who Seek to Justify Capitalist Sins, while Mocking Swanky Fortresses. However, they will Eventually come around to making their Confessions when their Bellybuttons are Rubbing on their Backbones for Hunger and Thirst, and not beCause of any HoloHOAX!}

J-[_] Justice Demands that Great Meeting of the Most Intelligent and Well-Educated Minds.

K-[_] King Jesus will get True Justice when he Returns in all of his Naked Glory, being about 400 Miles TALL, whereby every Eye can get to See him, as it states in *Revelation 1,* which is the Truth of it: beCause there is no Way that anyone in Panama could See Jesus Coming over Atlanta, Georgia, unless he were at least 400 Miles Tall! {Please Check the Box, if you Agree.}

L-[_] Lots of Laughs! King Jesus is the Inspired Author of this Special Book, which everyone must Check with their X's, whereby King Jesus can Open Up all of the Books during his Judgment Day, and Inspect them for those Check Marks, whereby the Good People can be Separated from the Evil People: beCause the Good People will Check the Appropriate Boxes, whereby they can be Justified, while the Evil People will Check this Box [_], whereby they can be Condemned to Eternal Hellfire! And I am Serious! I Think. Well, maybe not. §§

M-[_] Money is the Problem. Indeed, we should just do Away with all Money, and then everyone will See the Light of Truths very Brightly: beCause they will come to Realize that many Things are much more Important than Money — such as that Fresh Clean Air, Pure Living Water, Wholesome Natural Foods, Natural Clothing, and Secure Houses, which can only be SECURE within those **"GLORIOUS Swanky Hotels Castles and Fortresses,"** which are Designed for DEFENSE, whereby each Beautiful Stone Dome Home Complex is a Miniature Fortress of its own! Indeed, just HOW could an Army of Murderers get into it, seeing that the Walls are no less than 10 feet THICK, and the Stainless Steel Doors are a Foot Thick, like those of Bank Vaults? Indeed, it would be Futile to make War against such a Well-planned City State, which would be Designed to Endure through a Nuclear Nightmare. However, I am Wondering WHY we Need to go to so much Trouble to Protect ourselves and our Properties, when we can Establish **"The New RIGHTEOUS One-World Government,"** which will be Guaranteed to Protect us: beCause that is its Main DUTY! After all, every Swanky Fortress will BELONG to that Good Government, which will be of Great Interest to them to Protect: beCause that Good Government will be made up of the ELECTORS, themselves, who have Filled Out and Filed

"The Complete SURVEYS of our VALUES!" (SURVEYS of Religious Spiritual Political Governmental Sexual Social Moral Economic Business Labor Habitual and Miscellaneous VALUES!), Book 059, who will Elect Righteous KINGS to Govern it, who will be Paid with Easy Skilled Labor Wages, only, and will not Own anything except for their Clothing, Books, Computers, simple Tools, Furniture, and Movable Items: beCause all of the Beautiful Stone Dome Home Complexes will Belong to **"The New RIGHTEOUS One-World Government!"** Book 056. Indeed, they will all be Permanent Buildings, which will be Worth far more Money than anyone in the World could ever Afford to Buy — such as the Lincoln Memorial in Washington, which you could not Buy for a Billion Dollars! ‡

01-[ ] I did not Check the above Box with an X for Verse M: beCause my Home is my own Private Castle, even if it is just a Shack with a Tin Roof in some Democratic Slum.§

02-[ ] I did not Check the above Box with an X for Verse M: beCause I am Afraid of such a Beastly One-World Government, which might come to have Total Control over me and everyone else, whereby they might be Telling me what to Eat and Drink. §‡

03-[ ] God have Mercy, O Fool, can you not See that most People Desperately Need someone to Tell them what to Eat and Drink? Moreover, do you not Tell your own Children what to Eat and Drink? Or, do you just give to them the Freedom to Commit Suicide at the Table?

04-[ ] No Adult should have to be Told what to Eat nor Drink: because that is what Freedom is all about. Therefore, *"Give to me Liberty, or Give to me Death,"* as Patricia Henry might say to her Pet Dog on a Chain in the Backyard of **"The BIG White OUTHOUS on the Not-so-Biblical Capitol DUNGHILL!"** Book 023. §§‡

05-[ ] People are Liberated by Truths, only. Therefore, what we Need to Learn is the Whole Truth about each Important Subject, including the Truths about Eating and Drinking, and then we might Act as Ejukaatid Adults, whereby we might make Riit Decisions, and thus Check the Appropriate Boxes in the Surveys of our Values, and thus have the Freedom to Do GOOD for ourselves and others, which would Begin with Swanky Fortresses, which have more than 5,000 Good Reasons to Build them!

06-[ ] I Refuse to take any Tests, whereby my Values might be Discovered: beCause I am a True Christian, who is Ashamed of my Values. §§

07-[ ] I am not Ashamed of my Values, and will be Happy to take any Tests; but, only IF we Establish **"The New RIGHTEOUS One-World Government,"** whose Elected Officials have Filled Out and Filed on the Internet their Complete Surveys of their Values, whereby I might Judge whether or not they are Worthy to be my Elected Officials. Period.

08-[ ] I am Afraid that no one will Qualify to Govern us, if every Elected Official must Fill Out and File on the Internet **"The Complete SURVEYS of our VALUES"**: beCause, who could Honestly Check these Boxes, except for a RIGHTEOUS Person? Therefore, that Eliminates 99.999,999,999% of the People in this World of Woes, which will make those Government Elections rather Simple: beCause only a few People will be Qualified to VOTE for any Elected Officials of that Good Government!

09-[_] It will not Offend me, even if only 1% of the Population is Qualified to VOTE: beCause of Filling Out and Filing on the Internet **"The Complete SURVEYS of our VALUES"**: beCause I will Know for a FACT that only Righteous People got to Vote, who would also have to be fairly well Ejukaatid, just to be Able to READ **"The Complete SURVEYS of our VALUES!"** Book 059. Yes, that alone will Disqualify most Ignorant People, whereby we might have a Chance to get this Crazy World Straightened Out. Indeed, everyone in the World will be Welcome to Fill Out and File **"The Complete SURVEYS of our VALUES,"** even if they must have some other Person Read the Surveys to them: beCause of not being Able to Read nor Write; but, that is Okay with me: beCause I am quite Confident that ONLY Righteous Honest People will Cooperate with our Elected King's Master Plan, whereby I will Know that I can Trust all of those People who do get Elected.

10-[_] I did not Check the Boxes for any of the above Statements: beCause … because … because … beCAUSE I do not Want to. Period.

11-[_] Can you not Explain in some Rational Manner just WHY that you do not Want to Check the Appropriate Boxes that have Statements that you Agree with?

12-[_] No, I cannot Explain WHY: beCause of am a Subjective Person, instead of an Objective Person, like you. Moreover, I am far too Lazy to Look Up those Words in a Dictionary: because I do not have a Computer, nor a Dictionary.

13-[_] Well, then, you should be one of the First Persons in the World, who should Want to VOTE for our Selected King: beCause, if he is Elected to be the Righteous King of **"The New RIGHTEOUS One-World Government,"** he will Provide a First-Class-Quality Computer to everyone in the World, who Wants one. Therefore, you will no longer have any Reasonable Excuse for not Looking Up the Words in a Proper Dictionary, which will be more like an Encyclopedia, than a Normal Dictionary: beCause it will be more like Wikipedia, which will also contain all Biblical Names, as well as all 99 Islamic Names for GOD: beCause the Muslims used to have no less than 99 GodS, which was getting them Confused by the Time that MuhamMAD came along, who Decided that they should have just ONE God, whose Name was Allah. Yes, he Persuaded them to Believe in that one and only God by Killing whomever Disagreed with him, which was the Act of a very BIGOTED Person, you must Confess, which our Selected King would never Think of Doing: beCause he is NOT a Bigoted Person, nor does he Intend to FORCE anyone to Accept his Personal Beliefs — such as Jehovah God Living Inside of Jupiter! § {See www.Amazon.com for: **"The Secret City of the Great King!" (HOW the True Church will Escape from the Great Tribulation!) By The Worldwide People's Revolution!® Book 042.**}

14-[_] If your Selected King Sincerely Believes such Things as God Living Inside of Jupiter, then I will Accept it as the Pure Unadulterated Truth: beCause I Know for a Fact that he is an Inspired Author, who Constructed this Book in less than one Month, all by himself, and without Telling any Lies: beCause he has no Good Reason to Lie; but, those Politicians have all Kinds of Reasons for Lying: beCause they Want to get Elected by a MOB of Demon-possessed People, who are such Spiritual COWARDS that they Refuse to Fill Out and File on the Internet **"The Compete SURVEYS of our VALUES!"** Book 059, which is PROOF that none of them are Qualified to VOTE! §‡

15-[_] Okay, I will Surrender to **"The Swanky Sword of Divine Truths,"** Book 067, and Cheerfully Agree to Fill Out and File on the Internet ALL of **"The Complete SURVEYS of our VALUES,"** but, only IF all other Electors do Likewise.

16-[_] I Confess that it will Greatly Reduce the Confusion and Madness that is Involved in those Election Deceptions for Hypocritical Politicians, who would never be Willing to Fill Out nor File any such Surveys on the Internet: beCause of Fearing that the Electors might Learn Truths about them, and their Hollywood Natures, who Wear Masks: because they are all PUPPETS on the Strings of the Edomites, who Control them. §‡

17-[_] Granted, this Plan would Save BILLIONS of Dollars in Election Deceptions, and might even Save the Planet from Radical Climate Changes: beCause People like Donald Trumpeter and Little Dick Chicanery would not be on any Election Ballots: beCause of not being Willing to Fill Out nor File **"The Complete SURVEYS of our VALUES!"**

18-[_] Hold everything! Have you People not Questioned just WHY our Forefathers put it in the Constitution that, *"No Religious Tests shall be given to any Potential Candidates for Election Deceptions"?* Indeed, the very Reason for not having any Religious Tests was beCAUSE a Buddhist might be a more Qualified Person to be the President, than a Baptist, Methodist, Episcopalian, Lutheran, or Catholic, which is WHY that I am going to Vote for a MUSLIM President! §§

19-[_] We are Talking about the Elected KING of **"The New RIGHTEOUS One-World Government,"** who should be the Most Honest and RIGHTEOUS Man among us, which Excludes ALL Muslims, and ALL Women: beCause MuhamMAD was not even a Prophet, much less a HOLY Prophet; and all Wombmen are Excused from Leadership: beCause they are the Weaker Vessels, who have their Duties at Home, which can easily be Proven in a Courtroom. Otherwise, they would be Demanding **"The Great Worldwide TELEVISED Court HEARING!"** Therefore, if anyone has Faith in such a Murderous Abuser of Children as MuhamMAD was, he or she does not Qualify to VOTE for a Righteous King. Moreover, such a Person is likely Planning on Killing me for saying it, which is more Proof of his Disqualifications for Voting: beCause, if Muhamad was Innocent and Righteous, it can also be Proven in a Courtroom. ‡

20-[_] We are all Created EQUAL in the Eyes of God; and therefore, everyone of Age has a Right to Vote for whomever might Rule Over them, and also become Partakers of their Sins: because that is HOW it Works in the Mind of God, who puts the Electors in the same Box as their Elected Officials, and will Hold them Responsible for the End Results. For Example, certain Americans Voted for President Harry S. Truman, who Dropped an Atomic Bomb on Hiroshima, Japan, in August of 1945; and therefore, all of his Electors will have to give an Account to God for Murdering X-amount of Innocent Men, Women, and Children in Japan — that is, if they do not now Quickly Confess that it was a Great EVIL Deed, which would have never Happened if the Leaders of the World had Agreed to Conduct an International Radio Debate with Adolf Hitler, who was Begging for it, who had the Best Plan for Solving the Great Depression Problem of the 1930's, whereby he got Germany OUT of that Great Depression within only 6 Months, after he was Democratically Elected. But, the other Leaders of the Nations REFUSED to Attend any such Debates on the Radio: beCause they Knew for a FACT that they did not have a Leg to Stand on, while they also Knew for a Fact that Adolf Hitler was in the

Right about that Subject, and that World War 2 could have been PREVENTED by Conducting that Great Meeting of the Most Intelligent Minds, whereby no less than 100 Million Lives could have been Saved! Yes, Revised History is now on the Side of Adolf Hitler, who Called on the other Nations, and Specifically on Great Britain, France, Russia, and the United States to have that International Radio Debate; but, like Stubborn Mules, they REFUSED; and therefore they Lost more than 30 Million Soldiers, while the Germans only Lost about 2 Million! Therefore, the Germans Won that War, while their Enemies LOST in the Public Courtroom of Honest Opinions!

A-[ ] Adolf Hitler was a very BAD Person, who was Responsible for World War 2 and all of the Atrocious Things that were done on both Sides, even in Japan. §

B-[ ] I Believe that Adolf Hitler was the Good Guy, who was Maliciously Maligned by the Edomites, who are still Afraid to Face the Facts in a Courtroom.

C-[ ] I Confess that I am Extremely Ignorant concerning that Subject; but, I am Willing to Learn all about it, if it will Help to bring Peace into this World.

D-[ ] I will be Damned to Hell with the Devil, if I have any Good Thing to Say or Write about Adolf Hitler. And to Confirm it, I will Check this Box [ ] also.

E-[ ] ‡ Educated People know that there are Provable Truths behind the Neo-Nazis, or else they would not be Accepting such Beliefs: because they are not so Stupid as some People might Vainly Imagine. See YouTube Videos by Benjamin Freedman, Eustace Mullins, David Irving, and Ernst Zundel, who was Liberated in a Courtroom, after being Imprisoned for the Truths that he Taught. Yes, Educate yourself, and do not Believe all Things that you Hear. Yes, Ask yourself why it is that the News Reporters always Mention World Trade Center Tower 7 when Remembering September 11th, 2001, which was the Headquarters for the Mayor of New York City, as well as several Major Banks, Insurance Companies, the Secret Service, the FBI, the CIA, the BATF, and other Top Secret Snoops? §

F-[ ] I Fail to find any Good Thing about Adolf Hitler in the History Books, even though President Eisenhower Stole his German Autobahn Plan, whereby we Built Freeways all across the Country, in the Name of Adolf Hitler. Yes, that is the Name of Interstate Highway 1, from Floride, Florida to Nude Beach, Venice, Californicate! §

G-[ ] God Knows that Adolf Hitler was Equally as Good as any Leader who ever Lived, except for Jesus Christ, himself; and he was far Better than most, including that Wicked Saint Joseph Stalin, who had more than 50 Million Russian Christians put to Death for the Edomites: because he was Married to one. Yes, Americans and Brits took his Side during the Great War: beCause Stalin was the GOOD Guy, which can be Proven in a Courtroom, which is WHY that he was brought to Trial for War Crimes after World War 2. §§‡

H-[ ] I Prefer to Bury the Hatchet, and leave a long Rope of Hopelessness Tight to it, just in case we Need another World War to Distract our Minds from the Provable Truths within Books like this one.

21-[_] I did not Check the above Box with an X: beCause I cannot Agree that God will Hold my Bald-headed Grandmother Responsible in the Day of Judgment for the very Hairy Decisions of Harry S. Truman, just because she Voted for him with her Wig on. §

22-[_] Who would Know the Mind of GOD, who may be Allah, or Hairy Krishna? §

23-[_] I will take my Chances on Electing more Candidates, like Donald Trumpeter: because I Firmly Believe in the Superstitious Notion that it is GOD who Decides WHO Wins our Elections, who will make our Selected King the KING of Kings, himself, if he Wants to, and without any Election Deceptions at all! §§

24-[_] I cannot help but Believe that you are a bit Crazy: beCause no God in Heaven nor on the Earth has any Interest in what Ignorant FOOL might get Elected: beCause that is all *Biblical Nonsense!* Indeed, it was a False Doctrine that was made up by the Edomites, who wanted to put their God in Charge of the World, whereby they could put themselves in Charge of the World: beCause Jehovah God was on their Side of every Issue, including Gay Marriages, even as the Supreme Court Decided: beCause the Majority of them are JEWS, or Jewish Sympathizers, like Donald Trumpeter, who Works for the Sodomite Edomites: beCause it is all a Money Game, which Favors the Edomites in all Ways: beCause they have Arranged it that Way: beCause their Ancestors are the Unholy Ones who Constructed that so-called *"Holy Bible,"* which is no more Holy than the *"Holy Koran,"* which is less Holy than *The Adventures of Huckleberry Finn,* which at least uses the N Word no less than 10,000 Times: beCause there are all Kinds of NIGGERS in this World of Woes, most of whom are WHITE-Skinned with Black Hearts and Red Ears and Bleeding Lips from Eating Cactus Plants! Yes, if it were not so, they would be Checking the Appropriate Boxes with their X Marks! But, they even Refuse to Check any one of the following Boxes: §‡

A-[_] I Agree with the above Statement to some Degree.

B-[_] I Believe that Gay Marriages are GOOD: beCause it is much Better for Young Horny Priests to get Married, than to Sodomize Altar Boys.

C-[_] I Confess that it would be much Better for Gay Men to get Married, and thus Practice Fidelity, than to be Whoring around Town with HIV-AIDS, Syphilis, Gonorrhea, Herpes, and 250 other Transgender Sexual Diseases. §§

D-[_] I Promise to be Perfectly Honest, if I get Elected, and Agree to be Castrated if Convicted of Telling any Lies at any Time.

E-[_] Educated People know that People are sometimes Forgetful, and therefore they might not Speak the Exact Riit Werdz when Questioned in a Courtroom, even if they have taken an Oath to Tell the Whole Truth and nothing but the Truth: beCause of being Associated with the Contradictory and Hypocritical Hebrew God, who was not always Perfectly Honest, who told a certain Prophet to Lie to another Prophet, who was Met by 2 Female Bears, who Ate him for Lunch. § (See *Second Kings 2:24; and First Kings 20:39, KJV.*)

F-[_] I Fail to Understand what this Survey is all about.

G-[_] God Knows that you are Excused from any Election Deceptions: beCause your Brains are Malfunctioning. This Short Survey is about Honesty, and Honest People will not Object to Checking the Appropriate Boxes.

H-[_] I Firmly Believe in being Perfectly Honest about the Subjects within this Inspired Book. For Example, Swanky Fortresses are GOOD Things, even if none of them have ever been Built: beCause they are Good in Principle.

I-[_] I am an Innocent Lamb of God, and would just like to have Fresh Clean Air to Breathe, Pure Living Water to Drink, Wholesome Natural Foods to Eat, Natural Clothing to Wear, and a Secure House to Live in with Eternal Employment in my own All-Mineral Organic Garden. Therefore, I am not Ashamed to Check the above Box with an X, and this Box [_] also, to Confirm it.

25-[_] I did not Check the M-Box: beCause Money cannot be done Away with, without something to Replace it — such as the Mark of the Beast, which is a Numbering System.

26-[_] I will go back and try to Discover what is WRong with the Statement in the M-Verse above. Chances are that it has been Greatly Misunderstood.

27-[_] I Want to get on with the Book: beCause I am Tired of Teasing my own Brains. Indeed, if there were something WRong with having Money, Jesus would have said so. But, instead, he said that a Wise Man would put his Money in the Bank, for Collecting Interest on it, whereby 10,000$ might Gain him 50 Cents per Year for Usury. §

N-[_] Not everyone is as Crazy as you are. Indeed, I Want to OWN my own House, even if it is just a Tarpaper Shack in a Snake-infested Swamp. {Please Check the Box with an X, if you Agree.}

O-[_] Are there no other Options? Can we not Borrow enough Money from those Edomites to Build more Paper Shacks for everyone in the World, who is now Deprived of a Decent House? Indeed, *Habitat for Humanity* is the Best Solution, whereby all such People can have Endless Heating and Cooling Bills to Pay, not to mention the ElecTrickery Bills, Food Bills, Telephone Bills, Insurance Bills, House Repair Bills, and all of those other Lovable BILLS, which I just Long to Receive in the Mail! {Please Check the above Box, if you Agree. Strangely enough, not even former President Jimmy Carter has Checked that Box: beCause he does not Want to be Convicted of Unconsciously Building Firetrap Shanties and Debt Traps for Ignorant Children to Fall Headlong into.}

P-[_] No Sane People on the Earth will Check the O-Box: beCause it is Possible and most Practical for everyone to be Living in those **"Beautiful Swanky PALACES!" (A New Concept in Living Habits — Swanky Palaces for Poor People!) By The Worldwide People's Revolution!®** Book 066. Indeed, if it were not Possible, our Elected King would not be Promoting it with a Capital P. After all, he is the Principle Advocate of Proper Living, which you can Read about in: **"The Right Design for Living!" (A List of Great Advantages for Building Beautiful Planned City States!)**, Book 012, which is a Companion Book of: **"The Low Court of Supreme Injustices is Brought to Trial!" (Our Elected King Butts Heads with the United States Supreme Court, with or without their Black Robes of Hypocrisies and Lies!) By The Worldwide People's Revolution!®** Book 011.

Q-[_] The Great Question is this: **"Are Banks and Bankers Needed for True Prosperity?"** And the Answer is Obvious — they are NOT, or else Moses, King David, King Solomon or the Apostle Paul would have said so. {Please Check the Box with an X, if you Agree.}

R-[_] I Agree that Bankers are not Needed for True Prosperity; but, I do not Agree that Moses, King David, nor King Solomon would have said so, if those Bankers were Needed: beCause none of them knew anything about Banks nor Bankers, which probably Explains WHY they all Prospered. In Fact, King Solomon was the Richest Person who ever Lived, who Collected Millions of Tons of Silver and Gold, each Year, which Disappeared into the Hollow Earth. {See: **"The Secret City of the Great King!" (HOW the True Church will Escape from the Great Tribulation!) By The Worldwide People's Revolution!®** Book 042.}

S-[_] Satan has all of you People Greatly Deceived: beCause our Modern World could not Function without Banks nor Bankers. {Please Check the above Box with an X, if you Agree.}

T-[_] It is Time for a Great REVOLUTION, which must be a Peaceful Revolution: beCause that is Possible and most Practical. {Please Check the Box with an X, if you Agree.}

U-[_] I Understand that **"The Great Worldwide TELEVISED Court HEARING"** can make that Peaceful Revolution Possible; but, it is not Possible without it.

V-[_] The Right Way to get the Victory over Satan and his Multitude of Demons is to Expose their Lies in the Light of Truths, which Calls for that Great Meeting of the Most Intelligent and Well-Educated Minds, including the Historians and Authors of Books. (Hide your Head, O Douglas Brinkley. Read **"A People's History of the United States"** by Howard Zinn.)

W-[_] World War 3 will End all Hopes for that to Happen — that is, unless we get the Jump on those Edomites, and DEMAND that Meeting before they can get a War going. Indeed, we, the People, can Tweet and Twitter our Messages, and thus get the Jump on them.

X-[_] X-amount of People will just Naturally Refuse to Cooperate, until they get a VISION of what is Needed to Solve our Problems, which is a RIGHTEOUS KING, who has the Most Reasonable Solutions for our Massive Problems. Yes, he is the Person that we must be Willing to Vote for, even if we Judge him to be a little Crazy: beCause we are all Crazy to some Degree.

Y-[_] You might be Crazy, and Donald Trump is most Certainly Crazy; but, I am NOT Crazy, which is WHY that I have not Checked any of the Boxes in this Survey of our Beliefs. §§

Z-[_] You must be Related with a Stubborn Zebra, who is neither Black nor White, who cannot make up his Mind concerning GOOD nor EVIL. For Example, Car Accidents are EVIL, while Electric Subway Trains are GOOD: beCause no Swanky Train can be Derailed by any Means, nor get into any Deadly Accidents: beCause of the DESIGNS of those Swanky Fortresses, which have One-way Tracks for Single Trains, only, and no Way for Terrorists to get into them.

24-06 [_] O Unelected King, none of those Major Bankers will be Willing to Show their Faces at any such Meetings of the Minds. Therefore, HOW will you Overcome that Problem?

24-07 [_] Well, if they are not Willing to Attend such Meetings, it would be a Good Idea to make their Headquarters into the First Nuclear Disposal DUMP, whereby they can be gotten RID of: beCause they are Obviously Mindless People, and the Chief Enemies of Mankind. After all, they surely have enough Money to Retire on, seeing that they have Collected Trillions of Dollars.

24-08 [_] O Elected King, are you Serious? Would you Actually Recommend that Russia and China should Drop Atomic Bombs on New York City, if those Greedy Bankers Refuse to Attend the Meetings of **"The Great Worldwide TELEVISED Court HEARING!"**? Would that not be the END OF THE WORLD?

24-09 [_] Trust me, those Bankers will Agree to Attend those Meetings: beCause their Riches are of no Value, if they do not Survive to Enjoy those Riches. Besides that, if they are Wise, they will become Useful Members of **"The New RIGHTEOUS One-World Government!"** Yes, they could Volunteer to do the Gardening at **"The Great World TEMPLE of PEACE!" (The Glory of Jerusalem Arises Again!) By The Worldwide People's Revolution!®** Book 017. After all, each Elected King will have his Volunteer Servants and Administration Officials, who will all get to Live in their own Swanky Stone Dome Home Complexes within that Great Temple, which is WHY it will be about 8 Miles in Diameter, being Built Up in 60 Great Terraces, having 10 Minor Terraces within each Great Terrace, making a Total of 600 Terraces, each of which will be about 40 feet Tall, making them about 24,000 feet Tall, being Crowned with a Dodecagon Tower about a thousand feet Tall and a quarter of a Mile in Diameter, which will contain the Great Golden Throne Room for our Greatest Elected King, 6 High Priests from 6 Major Religions, 60 Elected Great Kings from 60 Major Nations, and a Maximum of 600 Elected Governors from Minor Nations, Provinces, and Islands of the Seas.

24-10 [_] So, O Elected King, are you saying that there will be no such Temple Built, until all of the Nations Surrender their Military Weapons, including their Nuclear Weapons, to **"The New RIGHTEOUS One-World Government!"** — which will consist of Righteous MEN, only? Will that not Cause a Gender War, and perhaps a Race War between White People and Black People? Indeed, you seem to be Inviting in more and more Problems to Fix, just by Excluding the WOMBmen from your Master Plan.

— Chapter 25 —

A Guaranteed Solution for Peace between the Races!

25-01 [_] Well, first of all, I Want everyone to Know that I am NOT Excluding Women from my Master Plan: beCause their Duty is to Raise Up little Baby Moseses and Jesuses, who will make Good Leaders in Worlds to Come. Meanwhile, all Wombmen should Understand that they will be Queens in their own Billion-dollar Palaces, if they Act Wisely: beCause their Husbands will Provide whatever they Need to become Moderately RICH, and Cheerfully so: beCause those Husbands will also become Moderately Rich, just for OBEYING what I Teach, which might Sound BAD to a Rebel; but, most People will Agree that it would be much Better to be Humble Obedient Servants of a Righteous King, who Provides them with everything that they Need to become Moderately Rich, than to be Poor Miserable Independent Jackasses of the Slave Masters, who have been Whipping their Buttockses for thousands of Years, while Pulling on their Long Ears, and Stuffing them with Capitalist LIES. For Example, they have Assured their Slaves that if they get Good Educations, they can get Good Jobs, and therefore Earn more Money, without Mentioning a Thing about those Hateful TAXES, which are Designed to EQUALIZE all of those Slaves; but, not their Masters, who might Receive as much as 4,000 Times as much Pay for their Services, as in the Case of Bill Computer Software Gates, who also Promotes the Capitalist Lies, in spite of Knowing what an Unjust System it is. ‡

25-02 [_] O Elected King, the White Supremacists just recently had a Big Protest in Charlottesville, Virginia, where they Wanted the Statue of General Robert E. Lee to STAND FIRM: beCause they Believe that White People are Superior to Black People, and were Created to be their Masters, which you also seem to Teach, saying that Adam was the First White Man on the Earth, who was put here to Govern it with other White Men, which seems to be Contrary to Reason and Logic: beCause Black People are well Able and Willing to Govern themselves, which has been Proven, again and again. For Example, there are those Healthy Happy Africans in Sudan, Uganda, Nigeria, Egypt, Libya, Algeria, Republic of the Congo, South Africa, and in many other African Countries, who get along so Peacefully Together, who have no Wars among them — even though I Heard that there was only a 6-month Period in the entire History of Africa, when they did NOT have a War of some Kind going on, which is somewhat like the Gang Wars in Chicago, Los Angeles, and other American Cities, which are mostly between Black Men, who seem to Turn to Violence for Remedies, rather than Courtrooms: beCause they are not very Civilized People, except for Dr. Martin Luther King, Junior, who got Assassinated by some White Trash, which would have never Happened, if all of those Black People had Remained in Africa, where God put them: because it is the Perfect Place for Colored People, who do not get along Well with White People. §§‡

25-03 [_] Well, my Friend, I would say that most Black Americans would be Happy to be the Voluntary Servants of General Robert E. Lee: beCause he was such a Fine Respectable Christian Gentleman, who Judged Black People to be Equally as Capable of doing their Gardening as himself, who only Needed Good Masters to Teach to them HOW to Do that Gardening, which is True for most of us; but, we also Need Good Rich Topsoil to Work in: beCause a Fruit Tree is not going to do Well in very Poor Topsoil, which Needs to be Protected from High Winds and Erosion by Tall Stone Walls, which 99% of the People could never Afford, much less the High Taxes that they would be Charged for Building any such Tall Stone Walls, which Taxes are Determined by the Linear Feet and the Height. For Example, a 3-feet-tall Stone Wall might be 50 Cents per Linear Foot, while a 6-feet-tall Stone Wall might be 1$, while a 24-feet-tall Stone Wall might be 4$ per Linear Foot, times 840 feet around one Acre of Gardens, would equal 3,360$ per Year for Taxes in a Poor State like Arkansas; or, about 24,400$ per Year in a Richer State like Virginia. Therefore, unless you were fairly Rich, you could not afford to Pay any such Taxes, just to have a one-acre Garden with some Protection, which would be considered to be a LOW Stone Wall in Swanky Fortresses: beCause their Walls would be a Minimum of 40 feet Tall, just to make it Possible to have some Reliable Wind Generators Installed along the Tops of all such Tall Strong Stone Walls, even though 100 feet Tall Walls are Better for those Wind Generators. Therefore, if you had a Stone Wall 100 feet Tall around your Garden, the Tax Masters would be out to Kill you with their Tax Assessments, who would be Wanting no less than 100,000$ per Year for their Taxes, which would be more than one Acre of Land could Produce in such a Shady Place, which is Surrounded by such Tall Strong Stone Walls. However, when we Build those Swanky Fortresses, the Stone Dome Home Complexes will be about 30 feet Tall, being Covered with 10 to 20 feet of Sand, large Rough Rocks, Gravel, Sand, Clay, and Topsoil at least 3 feet Deep, which will then be Covered with Fruit Trees, Nut Trees, Grape Vines, Berry Bushes, Vegetable Gardens, and Flower Gardens, whereby those Gardens will not be so Shaded by a single Tall Stone Wall on ONE Side of the Garden, and by 2 Shorter Stone Walls on 2 other Sides, about 20 feet Tall, being between you and your Naaberz' Gardens within that Terrace, while the next Terrace above you will have another Slanting Tall Strong Stone Wall with Electric Generators at the Top of it, which will Surround the entire Fortress at the Tops of all Tall Terrace Walls: beCause that is what will make it Possible for those Wise People to have FREE Electricity forevermore, while also Protecting their Fruit Trees from any Bad Wind Storms, Rats, Mice, Raccoons, Opossums, and other Varmints, which will not be Able to Climb Over those Tall Stone Walls, which will have Hangover Walkways at the Tops of them, being made of SLICK Polished Granite Stones on the Undersides of them, which not even a Snake will be Able to get Around.

25-04 [_] O Elected King, you are Talking about a HUGE Amount of Difficult Work to get all those Stone Walls Constructed, which will Naturally Require Tunnels and Port Holes for Bunkers along each of those Stone Walls, both Inside and Outside, which Tunnels will be Connected with the Stone Dome Home Complexes, whereby any Parachuting Enemies will be Trapped in whatever Gardens that they Happen to Land in: beCause they will be Surrounded by Bunkers with Soldiers and Weapons on all Sides, which will make any such Wars Impractical, even though it is Doubtful that any such Wars will ever get Started between White People and Black People: beCause each Group of Wise People will be Living with other People of Like-mindedness, even if they Want to Mix their Races.

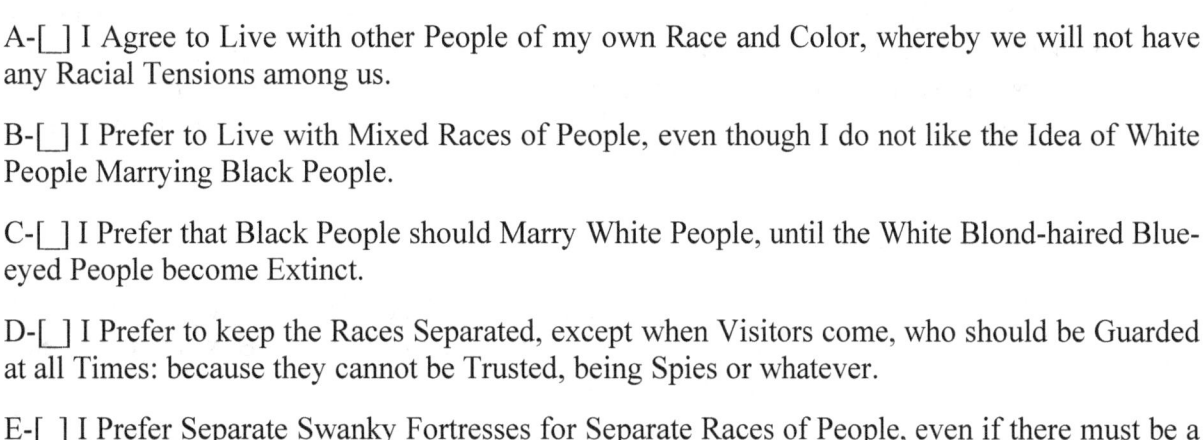

A-[_] I Agree to Live with other People of my own Race and Color, whereby we will not have any Racial Tensions among us.

B-[_] I Prefer to Live with Mixed Races of People, even though I do not like the Idea of White People Marrying Black People.

C-[_] I Prefer that Black People should Marry White People, until the White Blond-haired Blue-eyed People become Extinct.

D-[_] I Prefer to keep the Races Separated, except when Visitors come, who should be Guarded at all Times: because they cannot be Trusted, being Spies or whatever.

E-[_] I Prefer Separate Swanky Fortresses for Separate Races of People, even if there must be a hundred Separate Kinds in each Country.

F-[_] I Prefer to have all Mexicans and Europeans and Asians go back Home to Mexico, Europe, Asia, or wherever, and leave America for the Original Indian Tribes, only.

G-[_] I Prefer that the United States of America should be a Land of Refuge for all Peoples in the World, of whatever Colors, Races, Nations, Religious Sects, and Political Doctrines: beCause there is Plenty of Space for all of us, which Nation can become the Melting Pot of the World, whereby we all become Mongrelized like the Cats and Dogs, whereby we will all have to get along Well, even as the Mixed Races in Venezuela get along Well. §§

H-[_] I Prefer to just Mind my own Business, and leave other People alone. Yes, they can Choose to Say and Do whatever they Like, just as long as they leave me alone.

I-[_] The Irish were mostly White People, who got along Well, until they Adopted a Phony Religion, and then that Religion got them Divided into 2 Major Factions, which have never gotten along very Well since then. However, it is now Possible for each Faction to Separate itself from the others, and thus Live in Peace. {Please Check the Box with an X, if you Agree.}

J-[_] Jesus Christ would Melt all of those Factions Together with his HOT Sword of Truths, which would Prove all of their False Doctrines to be WRong. Therefore, they would simply Drop their False Doctrines, and take up his Truths as their New Doctrines.

K-[_] King Jesus would SEPARATE all of the Races of People, and do Away with the Slavery Systems, altogether: beCause neither Black People nor Brown People Need any White Masters — that is, AFTER they get their Swanky Fortresses Finished: beCause, until then, they must have Educated People to Guide them, and neither Black nor Brown People are Educated enough to Handle any such Complicated Projects. Indeed, all such Fortresses would become Future Disasters. For Example, if Black People were in Charge of Building their own Stone Dome Home Complexes, all of the Domes would be LEAKING Water into them from the Gardens above them: beCause those Black People would not have any Idea HOW to Install the Ceramic Tiles on those Domes in such a Way that they would NOT be Leaking! Guaranteed! Likewise, those Brown People would not have any Idea HOW to make Ice Houses that do not SWEAT on the Outsides of them: beCause that Requires EJUKAASHUN and True Nolij. §§‡

L-[_] Lots of Laughs! Any Ignorant Person can be Taught HOW to Drive a Nail into a Board without Hitting her Fingers with the Hammer, just by Using a large Round ROCK, whereby she might Smash her Fingers, and then Require the Emergency Help of some Doctor Knife, who would Naturally be a Black Doctor, who makes up 1/10th of one percent of Medical Doctors: beCause they cannot Pass the Medical Examinations, whereby they might become Medical Doctors. However, that is not to say that Black People could not become Architects and Engineers: beCause they also make up less than 1/10th of one percent of them, most of which are Black Lesbian Women! §§‡

M-[_] God have Mercy! — when is this Hate Speech going to STOP?

N-[_] None of that was Hate Speech: because this is just a SURVEY of our Honest Opinions, which you may Agree or Disagree with. Just be Sure to Check the Boxes with Statements that you Agree with, including this one.

O-[_] There is a Good Option to Choose from: beCause it can be Proven in a Courtroom that there are Black Masters, Brown Masters, Yellow Masters, Red Masters, Blue Masters, Green Masters, Gray Masters, and White Masters — all of whom were Born to be Masters. Likewise, there are all Colors and Kinds of Servants, who were Born to be Servants, who would have no

Idea what to Do without the Help of Masters. Yes, it is Proven in an Inspired Book, called: **"Were you Born to be a Master or a Servant?"** — which has been Updated to: **"A Sound Argument for Masters and Servants!" (WHY Everyone Needs a GOOD Master, and every Master Needs Good OBEDIENT Servants!) By The Worldwide People's Revolution!®** Book 008. Yes, I used to Deceive myself, saying to myself that I have no Need of a Master: beCause I can be my own Master. However, if you were to Carefully Inspect the House that I Built, you would have to Confess that I most Desperately Needed a GOOD Master to Teach to me HOW to Do it — except that I am very Slow to Learn any such Things, and would likely Need a Good Master to Approve almost anything and everything that I might go to Do: because I cannot even Cut a Board Off Straight, nor Set a Ceramic Tile FLAT on a Vertical Wall: beCause I have yet to Discover a SQUARE Square, nor a LEVEL Level: beCause the Masters, who were in Charge of Making those Helpful Tools, were Obviously SLEEPING on their Jobs! Otherwise, you might be Able to Find a SKWEIR Skweir, and a LEVOUL Levoul; but, behold, only one in a hundred is True and Trustworthy, which makes them very much like PEOPLE, who are not always Square nor Levelheaded. However, if there is any Doubt about WHO was Born to become a Master, and WHO was not, you only have to Study **"The Complete SURVEYS of our VALUES!" (SURVEYS of Religious Spiritual Political Governmental Sexual Social Moral Economic Business Labor Habitual and Miscellaneous VALUES!),** Book 059, whereby it becomes Obvious WHO the Masters are, and WHO the Servants are: beCause none of the Servants are ABLE to Complete those Surveys without some Help! §§‡

P-[ ] People with their Heads Stuck in one or the other of those 2 Stinking Holes in **"The BIG White OUTHOUSE on the Not-so-Biblical Capitol DUNGHILL!"** are not Qualified to be Masters of any Kind: beCause their Senses are Malfunctioning. For Example, some of them Badmouth General Robert E. Lee, who wanted to Settle the Slavery Issue in the Congress, even if the Constitution had to be Changed; but, President Lincoln wanted a Civil War: because most of the Taxes were Collected from the Sales of Southern Cotton at that Time, whereby he wanted to Maintain the Union at all Costs, which did Cost some 600,000 American Lives of mostly Young White Men, who would have also much rather have Settled the Issue in Congress, even if the South was Separated from the North, which is still Separated in many Ways in spite of that Hateful War. Indeed, there are still Neo-Nazi Fascist and Racist Groups like the KKK and White Supremacists, who would rather Live in an All-White Society, who should be Able to Do that, and who would be Able to Do that, if we should Establish **"The New RIGHTEOUS One-World Government,"** which would Help ALL Peoples of ALL Races, Religions, and Political Groups to Build their own Beautiful Planned City STATES, whereby they could Govern themselves According to their own Beliefs, and also be Protected by that Good Government, which would be Colorblind. However, it would also Recognize the Fact that Iron and Clay do not Mix with each other, no matter what you Do with them. But, if certain Ignorant Fools Want to Try to Mix the Races within their own Cities of Confusion, so be it — let them have at it: beCause they will only Prove what has already been Proven at College Campuses, and on the Streets in **"The Divided States of United Lies!" (The so-called "United States of North America" in Disguise!)** Book 058. {See: **"The South was Right!"** By Donald Kennedy.}

Q-[ ] The Great Question is this: **"Has it Proven to be a GOOD Thing or a BAD Thing for the Races to be Mixed Up?"** Well, that Question can only be Rightly Answered by Social Scientists and People who have Studied all such Cases, who are OBJECTIVE, and not Subjective in their Thinking. Indeed, the FACTS Show that most People are Prejudiced to some Degree among ALL of the Races, which seems to be Born within each Person. However, the Facts also Show that most Dark-skinned Races have a Higher Degree of Respect for the White

Races, than they do for the Darker Races, whom they tend to Despise more if they are Darker than themselves. In other Words, a Light-brown Person is more likely to Despise a Black Person, than a White Person, even Unconsciously: beCause of several Reasons; but, Primarily beCAUSE most White People are of a Higher Moral Standard than most Black People, which can be Proven by Court Records: because White People Commit less Crimes, even if they are Poorer than their Black Naaberz: because most White People have Religious Backgrounds as a Tradition, while many Black People have no Religious Backgrounds, and do not Fear God nor his Judgment Day. However, if they do have those Religious Backgrounds, they are much less likely to Commit Crimes, and especially against White People; while a White Policeman might Think nothing of Killing a Black Person: beCause of Dealing with so many Black Criminals, which they should not have to Deal with: beCause that gives to them a Master / Slave Complex, whereby the White Policeman just Naturally Thinks of himself as being Superior to the Black People, which would not be the Case if he did not have that Position of Authority, which he would not have within the Swanky Fortress System, whereby each Race of People are Governing themselves, and Living in Peace: beCause they BANISH any Potential Criminals, who do not Agree to WORK for a Living, and especially in their own Gardens, whereby they can get Closer to the Great Creator God: beCause of having more and more Respect and Love for his Creations, including his Animals, which make Good Pets, and Help to Maintain Balanced Minds: beCause most Animals are not Violent by Nature, nor Mean, like some Ignorant People, who should not be Watching any such Violent Movies, including those War Stories, except for *Shenandoah, How the West was Won,* and *The Ten Commandments,* which Teach Moral Lessons. Indeed, the Bad Guys are always Proven to be WRong, which may be Unrealistic in the Real World; but, the Lessons are much Better than no Lessons at all: beCause People can Think about such Things, and come to Rational Conclusions on the Positive Side of Life, which is much Better than Violent Video Games, whereby no Moral Lessons are Taught. ‡

R-[_] I will Resist any Temptations to Check any of these Boxes: because I am not Sure WHO is Riit, nor WHO is Rong. However, if there is a Great Creator God and a Day of Judgment, most of us are in Big Trouble: beCause we have Certainly Disobeyed his Commandments, which seem to be Reasonable. Indeed, if everyone in the World should Learn, Believe, Love, and OBEY his Commandments — and Especially **"The New MAGNIFIED Version of the 20 Commandments,"** which can be found in **"LIGHTNING STRIKES Versus Lightning Bugs!" (HOW you can Become Moderately RICH, without Telling any Lies nor Selling any Trash!)**, Book 074 — I would say that we would have no Problems in this World, at all. However, that is also Unrealistic: beCause not everyone is going to Learn, Believe, Love, nor Obey those Commandments. However, the People who Do Love and Obey them should not be Taxed to Support those who do not, who should be Banished from all Swanky Fortresses, except for the SEVENTH Kind, where almost everything is Legal, including Murder, Rape, Stealing, Lying, Adultery, Drug Abuses, and you Name it: beCause People should be Free to Commit their Sins with other People of Like-mindedness, whereby they might Learn their Lessons with the Prodigal Son of *Luke 15.* §§‡

S-[_] The Saints were Commanded to not allow any Sinners to Live among them, which is WHY Moses had them Stoned to Death! In Fact, if the Parents of a Rebellious Child should Accuse that Child of being a Glutton, Drunkard, or Lazy Person, the Child could be Stoned to Death for it, which might seem to be rather Harsh; but, it was their Way of Keeping the Criminals under Control, who were Taught from Childhood on that they should Eat and Drink in Moderation, and no more than one Gallon of Manna per Day, which is a considerable Amount of Food for an Adult to Eat, when you Think about it: because that Manna was very

Rich Food, being Sweet and Oily, like Butter and Honey. However, if you were Lifting Heavy Rocks for much of the Day, it would be a Rational Amount to Eat, and much more Satisfying than Butter and Honey, which can make you Sick before it Satisfies your Hunger: beCause it is an Unbalanced Diet. Likewise, a Diet of Black Walnuts can make you Sick, without Satisfying your Appetite for something Sweet, while a Diet of Dried Fruits with the Walnuts will Satisfy you, if you just Eat one Pound, and then Eat some Fresh Lettuce or a Raw Vegetable Salad of some Kind, which has Important Enzymes in it. Indeed, just a few Raw Onions will take Care of that Part of your Diet. ‡ {See: **"DIETS!" (A Reasonable Solution for the "Eternal Controversy"!) By The Worldwide People's Revolution!®** Book 037.}

T-[_] It is High Time for us Tax Slaves to DEMAND **"The Great Worldwide TELEVISED Court HEARING,"** whereby we might Discover the Whole Truth about all Important Subjects.

U-[_] I Understand that whomever Failed to Check the T-Box is a Potential Enemy, who should not be Allowed into any Swanky Fortresses of the First, Second, Third, Fourth, Fifth, nor Sixth Kinds. In Fact, such a Person should be Thoroughly Vetted by the One-World Government Police.

V-[_] **"The New RIGHTEOUS One-World Government"** will not have any Police, and therefore they will not be Able to VET anyone. However, no one can be Elected into any Office within that Good Government, without first Filling Out and Filing on the Internet **"The Complete SURVEYS of our VALUES!" (SURVEYS of Religious Spiritual Political Governmental Sexual Social Moral Economic Business Labor Habitual and Miscellaneous VALUES!)**, Book 059, whereby the Electors can Determine for themselves whether or not they Want any such People Governing them, who must also Fill Out and File their own Surveys of their own Values before Qualifying to VOTE!

W-[_] I would rather Fight in World War 3, than to Answer any such Questions, or Check any Boxes with Statements that I Agree with: beCause no "Big Brother" Government is going to be Watching over ME!

X-[_] X-amount of People are already being Watched by their "Big Brother" Federal Cover-up Government, which even Records every Communicated Message on all Telephones and Computers! Therefore, they already have a Record of your Beliefs, if you have given them to anyone. Moreover, if you Send any Books or Long Documents by Means of the "Cloud," you should Understand that all such Books or Documents are Stored in a Big Computer Warehouse in West Virginia, which is done to Assist the Federal Burden of Investigation to make Arrests of Suspected Traitors of the American Dream, which is for everyone in the World to become a SLAVE of some Kind — as in an Education Slave, Work Slave, Tax Slave, Rent Slave, Interest Slave, Insurance Slave, Drug Slave, Sex Slave, ElecTrickery Bills Slave, Food Bills Slave, Gas Bills Slave, Water Bills Slave, Credit Card Debt Slave, and so on — beCause that is the Edomite Plan since Ancient Times, which is WHY they were the Slave Trade Masters, who Bought and Sold Black People, who are now supposed to LOVE them for it, even though they have not even Asked for Forgiveness for it! §‡

Y-[_] All Sins of Yesteryears should be Forgiven without anyone Asking for it.

Z-[_] The Zeal of **The Worldwide People's Revolution!®** will Straighten Out all such False Doctrines, and Set the Record Straight. Indeed, Slavery is a CHIEF SIN against God and Mankind, which all Righteous People will now Confess and Check the above Box with an X.

25-05 [_] There will never be Peace between the Races, until there is JUSTICE for ALL Races, which can only be Served by Establishing **"The New RIGHTEOUS One-World Government!"** Indeed, all of the Vain Conversations in the World will never Satisfy the DEMANDS of True JUSTICE, which Requires a Good Government, which has an Unlimited Amount of Good Money, which must be Earned by Honest Labor, without any Loans, without any Interest, and without any Taxes, which "Money" is Best Managed in Computers, which can Keep Accounts of all Things that are Programmed into those Computers. Indeed, each Person, who has not Joined **"The Swanky Associations of Working Soldiers,"** should have a Personal Positive and Permanent Identification NUMBER, or RFID Computer Chip in his or her Right Hand, or in his or her Forehead, if he or she does not have a Right Hand, nor Left Hand, whereby he or she can Use that Identification Number to Buy and Sell every and anything, whereby the Computers can Keep Track of all such Things. Otherwise, if a Person does not Want any such Numbers to Identify him or her, he or she should Join **"The Swanky Associations of Working Soldiers!" (A Fascinating Collection of Various Kinds of Voluntary Working Soldiers!) By The Worldwide People's Revolution!®**, Book 018: beCause no Money will be Needed by those People, who will have all Material Things in Common among them, who will SHARE their Wealth, and Gladly Work for 4 Hours each Workday, in Exchange for getting to Live within one of those **"Beautiful Swanky PALACES!" (A New Concept in Living Habits — Swanky Palaces for Poor People!) By The Worldwide People's Revolution!®** Book 066. Indeed, those Wise People will not see any Need for any Money, nor for Keeping Track of it: beCause they will have Access to the Best Foods and Drinks in the World, which they will Provide for themselves, along with Natural Clothing, Secure Houses, Large Swanky Cisterns, Luscious Gardens, Churches, Mosques, Synagogues, Temples, Cathedrals, Shrines, Auditoriums, Theaters, Concert Halls, Swimming Pools, Gymnasiums, Game Rooms, Museums, Schools, Public Truth-braries, Royal Swanky Buffets, Courthouses, Fasting Sanitariums, Hospitals, and whatever they Imagine that they might Need and are Willing to Work for with other People of Like-mindedness, who may not Choose to have any of those Things, if they do not Want them: beCause no one is going to be FORCED to Do GOOD Works, nor EVIL Works. Indeed, no one is going to be Drafted into any Murderous Armies. However, if the Great Truths that I Teach are Rejected by the Masses of People, I Prophecy that they will be Branded with the Mark of the BEAST, and also end up getting their Bloodbath in the Valley of Decision! Yes, they will also be Forced to Say and Do many Evil Things, which I have never Asked of anyone — such as Pledging their Allegiance to some Bloody RAG, instead of Pledging their Allegiance to GOD!

25-06 [_] O Elected King, am I Understanding you Correctly — that you are Proposing that everyone in the World should Receive a Permanent Positive Personal IDENTIFICATION NUMBER, or RFID Chip, whereby they must Use that Number to Buy and Sell everything?

25-07 [_] You seem to have Skipped Over the last half of the above Paragraph in Verse 25-05. Indeed, I am Proposing a Moneyless System of Good Government for Righteous People, who could also Keep Records of all of their Work and Time, if they Wanted to; but, they would not have to Waste any Time with Money Games, nor get Branded with any Mark of the Beast System. In Fact, they could make up their own Monopoly Money, if they Wanted to Waste their Time with it; but, no such Money is Needed for True Prosperity: beCause, if you Need a New Computer, for Example, you can simply go to the Tool House with your Old Computer, and Trade it for a New Computer: beCause, **"The Swanky Association of Computer Makers"** will have lots of them for all Members of **"The Swanky Associations of Working Soldiers!"** Moreover, they will be Top-Quality Computers, which they may Trade for other Quality Tools, which are made by other Associations of Working Soldiers. In other Words, we will Determine what Things that we all Need for True Prosperity, and go from there. So, if Wide Flat-screen TVs are Needed, we will Mass-produce them, and make Sure that everyone has one in Good Working Order, and Free of any Charges: beCause all of the Labor will be Voluntary.

25-08 [_] O Selected King of **The Worldwide People's Revolution!®**, I am not Sure that I Like that Plan: beCause those Black People might be a bit Lazy, and thus not make Proper Tools: beCause of not Following the Golden Rule, whereby someone might get Hurt by a Broken Chain, Bolt, or whatever.

25-09 [_] Well, that is WHY we must Establish **"The New RIGHTEOUS One-World Government,"** which will Test and Grade all Products, whereby only the Best Products will be Traded among the Members of **"The Swanky Associations of Working Soldiers!"** Indeed, they will have High Standards, even as the Shaker Villages did, during the 1800's. Therefore, if you Want to have a High Standard of Living, you only have to Check the above Box with an X, and then *"Do with all of your Might whatsoever your Hands Discover to Do ...,"* as the *Holy Bible* Teaches, *"... as if you were Doing it for God, and not for People."* (See *Colossians 3:17—23; and Ecclessiastes 9:10, KJ.*) Therefore, with a Good Attitude like that, you should easily get along Well with all Members of **"The Swanky Associations of Working Soldiers!"** Book 018.

25-10 [_] O Elected King, with a System like that, all of the Races will be somewhat Equalized: beCause no one will Know whether or not any certain Tool was Made by a Chinaman, German, Greek, African, Jew, Russian, Indian, nor American Indian — that is, except for Things like Persian Rugs, which could only be Properly made by the Iranians, who have been Doing it for Centuries, who are Experts at that Occupation. Likewise, the Germans are Expert Machinists, who make the Finest Tools and Equipment, which would Naturally get a Better Grade than the Tools and Equipment that is Produced by the Indians and Mexicans, who are not so Well-Trained. Therefore, it is likely that a lot of Tools and Things would be Produced; but, not Sold nor Wanted: beCause of having Bad Grades on them. Therefore, it seems to me like a lot of Time, Money, Materials, and Energy would be WASTED by the Swanky Associations of Sloths and Sluggards. After all, **"The New RIGHTEOUS One-World Government"** could not be Bribed with Money to put Higher Grades on Cheap Products, which would Accumulate in Countless Warehouses, which would Prove to be a Worse Economic System than Capitalism: beCause of Mass-producing TRASHY Products — such as Broom Handles that Break, or Fall Off of the Brooms. In Fact, I just Bought one of those Worthless Brooms, not long ago, and the Handle came Off of it, which Wasted much of my Day just to Fix it; and thus I said to myself, "If I were in Charge of this Insane World, I would have all such Things GRADED by the New BIASED One-World Government, which would be Colorblind; but, it would not be Blind nor Ignorant. In Fact, it would Grade every Product by its Quality of Workmanship, its Endurance, its Appearance, and its Usefulness, which would Eliminate about 99% of that Trash that is now found for Sale." And then the Holy Spirit Reminded me that all of those Products were Produced by Capitalism, whereby I have come to HATE Capitalism, which is the Love of Money in Action, which would not be Motivating any Working Soldier to Do anything: beCause there would be NO Money Involved in it, even though I do Remember that you have stated in other Books, and even in this Book, that we can have Money, if we Want it: beCause, **"The New RIGHTEOUS One-World Government"** has the Duty of Minting and Printing all such Money! Therefore, you have my Mind Greatly Confused: beCause I do not Know what to Believe, nor not to Believe! But, it seems that Money is a Necessary Evil Thing.

— Chapter 26 —

A Guaranteed Solution for the Money Problem

26-01 [_] When you Consider all of the Evils that are brought about in this World of Woes: beCAUSE of Money and the Lust for more of it, it makes you Want to put Money in the same Category as those Dangerous Vehicles, which People can Live Well without. Indeed, the Maya and Inca Indians did well without Money: beCause they had a Different Economic System, which was Based on Sharing and Caring with the Bartering System as an Option. For Example, I will Trade my Mangoes for your Avocadoes, or my Beads for your Spoons. However, such an Economy only Works Well when no one Owns any Major Properties — such as Houses, Horses, Cars and Barns: beCause it would be Extremely Difficult to Trade a Potato for a House. However, the Mayas Solved that Problem by not having any Private Ownership of Houses nor Lands, which all Belonged to the City States, which had a Nobility Class of Educated People, who Managed the Servants, or Lower Classes, whereby everyone had Good Houses and Plenty of Foods, which were sometimes Imported from other City States, which Worked Together and Cooperated with one another, whereby they all Flourished as much or more than the Europeans at that Time. In Fact, they were Highly Civilized People with very few Criminals among them. But, they did have False Religious Notions and Superstitions, whereby they eventually came around to Sacrificing their own Children to the Gods, even as the Israelites did: beCause of being Deceived by Satan, who Works among Ignorant People of all Nations. ‡

26-02 [_] O Elected King, it Appears to me that the Love of Money is at the Root of almost all Evils, as the Apostle Paul pointed out in *First Timothy 6,* which you have Beautifully MAGNIFIED in your Inspired Book, called: **"For the Love of Money!" (The Strange Things that People Say and Do to Get more Money!),** Book 003, which is a Companion Book of: **"The Root Cause for almost all Evils!" (The Strange Things that People Say and Do to Get more Money!) By The Worldwide People's Revolution!®** Book 078.

26-03 [_] Well, my Friend, the Lack of Money is the Cause for many more Evils than one could Count during a Whole Day. For Example, just Think of all of the BAD Construction Jobs that have been Done for the Lack of Money. For Example, there are Millions of Houses in Mexico and other Countries in Mild Climates, which have Concrete Roofs with Rusty Steel Reinforcement Bars in them, which are Guaranteed to RUST OUT within 40 Years or so, whereby all such Roofs must be Redone at a far Greater Expense than the Original Roofs: beCause of having to Tear them Down, and Rebuild them; and, beCause of INFLATION, whereby the same Amount of Money will only Buy one-tenth as many Materials and Labor! For Example, 40 Years Ago one could get a half-inch-thick Steel Reinforcement Bar 20 feet long for only $2.10, which is now 20$. Likewise, one used to be able to Hire some Worker for 50 Cents per Hour when I was a Boy, who now Wants no less than 15$ per Hour: beCause of that INFLATION, which is brought about by Edomite Bankers, who Love it: beCause they Build Permanent Buildings, which do not just Rust Out, Rot Down, Blow Away, nor get Eaten Up by Termites: beCause they are not Stupid People by any Means. Indeed, they Understand ACCUMULATIVE WEALTH, while most American Slaves have no Concept of what that might Mean. Therefore, they Unwittingly Buy those Wooden / Plastic Firetrap Mouse-infested Cockroach Dens, which Require Constant Repairs, and INSURANCE: beCause they never Know for Sure what Mother Nature will Deliver to them in the next Natural Disaster, nor Manmade Disaster. But, for Sure, MONEY is at the Heart of the Problem, which is Usually a LACK of Money for Doing it Properly, which is Solved by Establishing **"The New RIGHTEOUS One-World Government,"** which has NO Lack of Money for Doing everything Properly, which Money is Used WISELY, in Order to HIRE whomever is Willing and Able to Learn and Work, in Order to Construct Beautiful Planned City States, which Represent that New Money, which makes it the very Best Money in all of the World, which is Backed Up and Represented by PERMANENT Buildings, known as those **"GLORIOUS Swanky Hotels Castles and Fortresses!"** — none of which will be OWNED by anyone: beCause not even a thousand Extremely Rich People could Afford to BUY any such Fortresses, which is Okay: because there is no Need for anyone to OWN them. In Fact, it would be Dangerous for anyone to Own them: beCause someone would Want to be Robbing them of their Fortresses, or going to War to Obtain them, which Problem is Totally Eliminated by Establishing that Good Government, which will Happily HIRE any Group of Wise People to Build their own Swanky Fortress — even as few as only 1,000 People, who may Build a Miniature Swanky Fortress, only 2 Miles in Diameter, and in 4 Terraces, without a Swanky Castle: beCause there are not enough People to Do all of the Work that would be Required. Therefore, such a Fortress would be called a Lost Creature's Hotel: beCause that is about all that it would consist of, which could be Expanded to make a Swanky Fortress out around it, if enough People should Join that Group of 1,000 People, which is a Possibility, if they had a Proper Religious and Political Foundation to Build on. ‡

26-04 [_] O Elected King, after all such People got their Swanky Fortresses Finished, they could use any Kind of Money to Trade Goods and Services with, even if that Money were Printed on Postcards: beCause it is just a Matter of TRUST in it. For Example, if you had a Postcard with a Special Picture of the Capitol Building in Washington on it, you could Print the Value of that Money on the Backside of the Postcard, and I would Trust it to be Valuable Money: beCause of having your Signature on it, which anyone could Counterfeit, if they Wanted to; but, no one within our Swanky Fortress would be Doing any Counterfeiting of any Money: beCause the Penalty would be Banishment! Besides that, no one would Want to Counterfeit any of our Money: beCause the People within our Fortress would Want to Maintain the Integrity of our own Money. Moreover, being a very Small Swanky Fortress, everyone would Know everyone else, and also what they are Doing for a Living, whereby it would be very easy to Discover any Counterfeiter, who would be coming up with NEW Money that he or she did not Earn by Honest Labor, which Money could be Stamped with a Special Seal, which only the Seal Maker of **"The New RIGHTEOUS One-World Government"** would Know HOW to Make, and then Issue it to those Unique City States, each of which would have Special Identification Numbers, and be in the Control of that Good GovernMINT, which would do the Hiring and Paying of the Working Soldiers, who could not use their Money Outside of their own Fortress: beCause it would not be Accepted by other People; but, it could be Traded for Universal One-World Government Money, which could be Transported to other Swanky Fortresses, and Traded Directly for their Kind of Money, which could be Used within that Fortress. Yes, it sounds a bit Complicated, and so it is; but, not without a Good Reason: because it is HOW the Integrity of all of those Moneys can be Maintained and Protected: because the Universal One-World Government Money would only come in Special Wrapped Packages of no less than 1,000 Dollars in a Package, which would have to be Opened by the Official Secretary of the One-World Government, who would know right away if it were Counterfeit Money: beCause someone would have to Tamper with the Packaging, just to be Able to Make a Counterfeit Bill, and then try to figure out HOW to make a Counterfeit Package for his Counterfeit Bills, which Package would have a Special Seal set in a thin Layer of Wax, which would be Extremely Difficult to Duplicate, and would be Changed once per Week, whereby the Counterfeiter would not Know what that Special Seal should Look Like, which would be Issued at the same Time to all Swanky Fortresses, once per Week, which would not give the Counterfeiter Time to Duplicate it: beCause those Packages of Sealed Bills would only be Issued for one Day at the End of each Week. Therefore, if someone Wanted to Leave a certain Swanky Fortress, in Order to Visit another Swanky Fortress in some far-away Place, he or she would have to Obtain at least 1,000$ in a Sealed Package, and Deliver it to the Official One-World Government Secretary of the other Swanky Fortress. §§‡

26-05 [_] Well, my Friend, for the Lack of Trustworthy People, you have Invented a very Complicated and Confusing Monetary System, which no one would Like, including myself: beCause of having to Deal with that Money Game. {Please Check the Box with an X, if you Agree with me.}

26-06 [_] O Elected King, I must Agree with you. Therefore, I Propose that each of us should Accept an RFID Chip, which would contain our Personal Identification Numbers and all of the Information that we might Want to put into those Chips — such as our Medical History, Blood Type, and Relative's Names. Indeed, our Identification Numbers could be used in One-World Government Computers to Keep Records of our Money, which would Greatly Simplify the Money Game, while doing away with all Cash, which would Solve X-amount of our Present Problems — such as those Bank Robberies, Illegal Drug Dealings, Black Market Businesses, Kidnapping for Ransom Money, and so on. Indeed, the Readers can Discover a whole List of Good Reasons for doing that in your Inspired Book, called: **"Mark Twain Races for the PRESIDENCY!" (The 2020 Presidential Candidates Desperately Need some Strong Undefeatable COMPETITION!)** Book 033.

26-07 [_] Well, that might Work Fine, until some Rogue State Blasted an Atomic Bomb into the Upper Atmosphere, whereby none of those Computers would Work, nor would any ElecTrickery System be Working, whereby not even the Gas Pumps would be Working, much less the Refrigerators, Freezers, Air-conditioners, Fans, nor Water Pumps! Moreover, just a Solar Flare from the Sunstar could do that Evil Thing to such a System. Therefore, that System has its Weaknesses, and is not at all Foolproof. In Fact, most People would rather be Trading Goods and Services with Good Old CASH in their Hands — that is, IF any of it could be Trusted after the Great False Economy CRASHES! Indeed, there is a Good Chance that all Governments would simply TRASH their Old Money, and say that we must Accept their New Money, which is the only Legal Money to be Used, which would also Require TIME to get all of that Done, while in the Meantime the Masses of People would have no Reliable Money to Work with. However, if People were WISE, and were Living within those **"GLORIOUS Swanky Hotels Castles and Fortresses,"** they could Live Happily without any Money at all: beCause their Economies would not be Based on any Counterfeit Moneys. Indeed, just as long as the Wind might keep Blowing, their Lights would still be Burning, and their Pumps Pumping, and their Ice Houses would still be Working, and their Gardens would still be Growing, and therefore they would have nothing to Fear nor Worry about, even if they had no Money at all: beCause their Pantries would be Full of Wholesome Natural Foods and Pure Living Water in their Glass Drinking Fountains.

26-08 [_] O Elected King of the Mountains, I must Confess that you do have a Guaranteed Solution for the Money Problem; but, only IF we Earthlings should Build about 2 Million large Swanky Fortresses! Indeed, that may be a Guaranteed Solution; but, it is NOT an Easy Solution to make into Reality.

26-09 [_] Well, my Friend, it will be a whole lot Easier to Accomplish by UNITED EFFORT and Cooperation, than it will be by the Independent Jackass Method, whereby each Family is Forced to Build its own Ridiculous Half-ass Fortress with a 4-feet-tall Cardboard Wall around it, and a 200-gallon Plastic Toxic Tank for Water Storage. {See www.Amazon.com for: **"Does a Good Soldier have to be a MURDERER?" (Seven Great Swanky Armies of Voluntary Working Soldiers!) By The Worldwide People's Revolution!®** Book 027. There is also another Book with a Water Tower on the Cover Photo, which might Address that Subject more Thoroughly.}

26-10 [_] O Elected King, it would be Humiliating for me to Join any Swanky Army of Working Soldiers: beCause I Think of myself as an Independent Jackass, who has no Need for any Government Assistance. Indeed, I Believe in FREEDOM. Therefore, Count me OUT of your Insane Ideas!

— Chapter 27 —

A Guaranteed Solution for the Independent Jackasses

27-01 [_] Now, as you have no doubt Heard, there is more than one Way to Skin the Cat; and when it comes to Changing the Minds of Independent Jackasses, we have a Major Problem: beCause their Beliefs are Rooted in Ancient and Ridiculous Superstitious Beliefs — such as being FREE, while being nothing but Education Slaves, Work Slaves, Tax Slaves, Interest Slaves, Insurance Slaves, Rent Slaves, Credit Card Debt Slaves, Drug Slaves, Food Bills Slaves, ElecTrickery Bills Slaves, Gas Bills Slaves, Water Bills Slaves, Childcare Slaves, and Various other Kinds of SLAVES: beCause a "Slave" is someone who is Forced to Say and/or Do Things that he or she does not Want to Say nor Do — such as Work for 5 Months of the Year, just to Pay the TAXES! Yes, the Independent Jackass Lives in a State of DENIAL, and will not Willing Confess that he or she IS a Slave of any Kind nor Color. However, it can easily be Proven in a Courtroom that I am Correct about that Subject. Moreover, no Honest Person on this Earth Disagrees with me about it: beCause the Facts are the FACTS, no matter HOW we Interpret them. However, you could Rightfully Argue that there are Lesser Degrees and Greater Degrees of Slavery. For Example, Billions of People do not have Electric Bills to Pay, nor even Water Bills, much less any Income Taxes: beCause they have NO Incomes as we know them, whereby they Work for Wages: beCause they simply Work in their Gardens, and Eat from their Gardens, while Living in Mud Huts with Thatched Roofs, while Sleeping on Mats on the Ground, while Hoping that no Spiders Bite them during the Night, nor Scorpions Sting them. Therefore, those People are somewhat FREE and somewhat Independent; but, they still Depend on their Naaberz for certain Things, and they Certainly Depend on God for Rains in Due Seasons. So, are they Healthy and Happy? Well, some People have Studied all such People, in Order to Answer that Important Question, only to Discover that some of them are Healthier and Happier than others — Depending on what they BELIEVE and THINK. In Fact, if they have a Strong Belief in some God, and Pray to that God, they are generally Healthier and Happier than those People who do NOT Believe in any God; but, the Happiest ones among them are the Richer ones with Spacious Houses, Electric Lights, Refrigerators, Washing Machines, and Tools of Various Kinds to Work with in their Gardens, Vineyards, Orchards, and Home-craft Workshops, who generally Live longer, and have Happier Families — that is, IF they do not become too Civilized, and get Televisions and Radios, whereby they are Bombarded with Various Advertisements for Vain Things that they do not Need nor Want, whereby they become Discontented with their Low Standard of Living, and get to Lusting after the Vain Things that Produce Hollywood Stars, who Overdose on Drugs, get Divorces, and Commit Suicide for the Fun of it. Indeed, each Person is now Confronted with a Long List of LUSTS to Deny himself of, or else be Tormented by them. But, for Sure, the Healthier a Person is, the Happier he is, which can easily be Proven in a Courtroom, or just by Visiting a Gymnasium, where Young Men are Exercising their Muscles, and not in any Competition to Discover who can WIN: beCause a Loser can become very Depressed by it. ‡

27-02 [_] O Elected King, I must Agree with you — that most Capitalists are SLAVES of Various Kinds — but, if they Objected to it very much, they would likely Change their Lifestyles, and take up Farming in Guatemala, or Honduras: beCause it is a lot less Stressful. However, a certain Amount of Stress is supposed to be Good for us, which is about the Amount that would Confront a Wild Deer, who must always be on the Lookout for any Wolves, Snakes, Lions, Bears, or other Vicious Creatures, which is far too much Stress for me. Indeed, I Prefer the Comforts of the City of Confusion, which does have a Car Accident, now and then, and maybe a Race Riot; but, all in all, it is a Quiet and Peaceful

Life — at least until the Wife comes Home, and begins to Nag her Husband over some Meaningless Thing, whereby they get into a War of Words, and never come to any Rational Conclusion about anything, and especially about Politics and Religion: beCause they get their Information from Different Contradictory Sources, all of which have a thousand and one Vain Arguments; but, your Guaranteed Solutions can hardly be Argued Against: beCause those **"GLORIOUS Swanky Hotels Castles and Fortresses"** are the Correct Solutions for most all Problems that I can Think of, including the Best Cure for those Independent Jackasses, who would only have to Live in one of those **"Beautiful Swanky PALACES"** for a Week or 2, and they would be Totally SPOILED! Indeed, you could hardly Drag them Out of such Places: beCause of having Access to those ROYAL Swanky Buffets, where there might be a thousand Special Dishes of Good Foods and Natural Drinks to Choose from! Yes, those Independent Jackasses would be like Country Children in a Candy Store with lots of Money, who would be Wanting to Buy at least one of each Kind of Candy, just to Taste of them. However, there is an Inherent Danger in setting up those Royal Swanky Buffets, which are likely to make a LOT of FAT People: beCause of the Spicy Foods, which will Tantalize everyone's Taste Buds, and Cause them to Eat far more than they Need to be Satisfied. In Fact, if People are not Limited to just ONE Slice of Smoked Wild Turkey, they will be Wanting to Consume an entire Turkey during one Meal: beCause that is how GOOD they are! Indeed, you can Visit some Whole Foods Store, just to Discover that Fact of Life, and be Prepared to find all of those Smoked Natural Turkeys SOLD OUT! ‡

27-03 [_] Well, my Friend, when People are Free to Eat all that they Want to for FREE, as would be the Case for all Members of **"The Swanky Associations of Working Soldiers,"** they just Naturally Learn to Eat a Moderate Amount, and be Contented with a Dish or 2 of whatever they Like: beCause they Know that it will be right there in front of them for the next Meal: beCause they are no longer Extremely Poor, nor Unable to Afford to Buy any Smoked Natural Wild Turkeys, for Example. Indeed, **"The Swanky Association of Professional Turkey Farmers"** will Mass-produce BILLIONS of Turkeys, if that is what those Working Soldiers Want to Eat, whereby they can get all that they might Want, and thus settle down to Eating a Moderate Amount. After all, there will be at least 100,000 Different Kinds of Dates, Figs, Peaches, Pears, Apricots, Apples, Bananas, Mangos, Cherimoyas, Persimmons, Papayas, Avocadoes, Pecans, Hazelnuts, Walnuts, Brazil Nuts, Pistachio Nuts, Pine Nuts, Butternuts, Almonds, Pineapples, Cherries, Berries, Grapes, Raisins, Melons, Squashes, Potatoes, Carrots, Cabbages, Lettuces, Onions, Cucumbers, English Peas, Purplehull Peas, Sweet Corn, Beans, Lentils, Kale, Collards, Swiss Chard, Beets, Spinach, Celery, Kohlrabi, Pumpkins, Watermelons, Soursops, Sweetsops, Sugar Apples, Lychees, Rambutans, Longons, Jackfruits, Durians, and you Name it — even as many as 5,000 Kinds of Mangos, alone! Yes, it will Prove to be a Wonderful Time to Live, when those Royal Swanky Buffets are Serving the Best Foods and Drinks in the World, which will never become Boring: beCause of the Great Variety of them, which, when Mixed with Special Herbs and Spices and Combinations of Endless Things, will have your Mouth Running with Saliva, just to Think about Eating! But, not to Worry: beCause some Tyrant King will come along and ORDER you to STOP Eating, or else have your Head Removed: beCause of the OBESITY Problem! Indeed, such was the Case in the City of Nineveh, some 2,300 Years Ago, which Saved their Lives: beCause they OBEYED that King, and therefore God Spared them from Utter Destruction! Yes, it was a Difficult Lesson to be Learned; but, they Learned it, and thus Saved themselves. Likewise, we can now Learn the same Lesson, and do similar Fastings, and thus Save ourselves from the Capitalists, who would have us Destroy ourselves for the Sake of Eating Junk Foods and Poisonous Drinks that are not 1/100th as Rewarding and Satisfying as those Royal Swanky Buffets! After all, just how many Dried Figs and Sweet Dates could a Person Eat with some Nuts, before becoming Satisfied? Perhaps a Handful or 2, only.

27-04 [_] O Elected King, that is all the more Reason WHY that I Want to be an Independent Jackass: beCause I will have my Freedom to Grow and Eat whatever I might Fix in my Limited Kitchen, which will not have Access to the Multitudes of Foods that will be Available for FREE at the Kitchens within those **"Beautiful Swanky PALACES!" (A New Concept in Living Habits — Swanky Palaces for Poor People!) By The Worldwide People's Revolution!® Book 066.**

27-05 [_] Well, my Friend, you would still have those Options at any Swanky Fortress, where you could have your own Garden and Kitchen, and do whatever you Like, just as long as you have Discovered other People of Like-mindedness, who have Checked similar Boxes in their SURVEYS of VALUES. After all, it is unlikely that anyone is alone in this World of Wonders, who has Beliefs that are Unlike any of the Beliefs of other People.

27-06 [_] O Unelected King, it is Doubtful that you could Find even one other Person in this whole World, who has Similar Beliefs to your own — such as the Throne of Jehovah God being Located Inside of JUPITER! Therefore, how are you going to Discover a Minimum of 1,000 Like-minded People for Building your own Swanky Fortress?

27-07 [_] Well, my Friend, I Seriously Doubt that my Beliefs will Alienate me from everyone in this World: beCause there will be all Kinds of Beliefs that will have Zero Effects on our Moral Beliefs. For Example, will my Belief about the Throne of Yohoovu God being Inside of Jupiter cause me to become a Thief, Liar, Robber, Rapist, or Murderer? Absolutely NOT! Neither will your Belief about the Throne of Jehovah God being somewhere around Orion, cause you to become any Kind of Outlaw. However, if it is Proven during the Future that the Throne of Yohoovu God is in Fact Inside of Jupiter, will you Accept it as the Gospel Truth?

27-08 [_] O Elected King, it is much more Likely that it will be Proven that Jehovah God does not even Exist: beCause he has not made any Appearances during the Past 4,000+ Years! Therefore, he likely Died from Old Age, and has been Replaced by some other Strange God, who would Naturally have an entirely Different Set of Rules to Live by — such as, *"Ye shall not make unto thee any Gasoline-powered Vehicles."* That is, after he has Considered what we have Done with his Supplies of Oil, Gas, Coal, and Uranium, which should have never been Created, if God did not Want us to Use those Things Wisely for Transporting our Lazy Legs and Tired Feets around.

27-09 [_] Well, my Friend, the Gas and Oil were Necessary for Operating Heavy Equipment, which would do the Difficult Work of Billions of SLAVES, if we Used that Gas and Oil Wisely. But, to just Waste it, running around in Circles on Endless Highways, is NOT very Wise: because, what is the Next Generation going to Say and Do about it? Will they not be Cursing us for our Greed and Selfishness?

27-10 [_] O Elected King, all of those Independent Jackasses, who Want to Drive their Gas-hog Vehicles, should have to make their own Drill Rigs, and Drill for their own Oils and Gases, and do their own Refining, and make their own Vehicles from Crushed Rocks, which contain Iron Ore, and then they would Discover that they are not so Independent as they Vainly Imagined. In Fact, they would be far more Independent, if they should find themselves Living within those **"GLORIOUS Swanky Hotels Castles and Fortresses!" (Beautiful Planned City States for WISE Intelligent Well-Educated People with Common Sense and Good Understanding!) By The Worldwide People's Revolution!® Book 019.**

— Chapter 28 —

A Guaranteed Solution for anything that is not Covered within this Inspired Book!

28-01 [_] Now, you might Imagine that I have Stuck Out my Neck far too much: beCause there are Surely some Problems in the World that have NO Rational Solutions? Well, I have been Trying to Think of one, and have not yet Discovered it within 40 Years! Therefore, I Doubt that it Exists. §

28-02 [_] O Selected King of **The Worldwide People's Revolution!®**, are you Sure that you have Covered ALL of the Bases? For Example, what is a Guaranteed Solution for Family Arguments between Husbands and Wives?

28-03 [_] Well, my Friend, that Solution was given by Saints Peter and Paul, who said: *"Wives, Obey your Husbands; and as for you Husbands, you must Love your Wives and Children, even as Christ Loves his Church, and Sacrificed himself for it."* In other Words, if all Wives Humbly Submit to their Husbands, then the Children will Humbly Submit to them, and thus there will be Peace within all Families. However, a Marriage must be Based on something more than Lusts, in Order for it to Work Out Well. Therefore, before anyone gets Married to anyone, everyone should Fill Out and File on the Internet **"The Complete SURVEYS of our VALUES!" (SURVEYS of Religious Spiritual Political Governmental Sexual Social Moral Economic Business Labor Habitual and Miscellaneous VALUES!)**, Book 059, whereby Like-minded People can Discover one another, and thus get Married to someone of the same Values, even if those Values are a bit Insane — such as the Silly Belief that MuhamMAD Departed from this Earth by Flying Up to Heaven on a 4-Winged Horse that Rode on Top of a Magic Carpet, after Mounting the Horse from the Top of a large Rock that was Located on Mount Morriah, which is where the Dome of the Rock Mosque now stands, where Muhammad supposedly Prayed to Allah with Abraham, Moses and Jesus, just before he Ascended to Allah in Heaven, somewhere around Orion, on the Greatest Planet in the Universe, where they had a Special Feast for the Muslim Victories in Battles, after which they Sodomized some Young Captive Boys, and MuhamMAD Married 70 Virgins that were all 10 Years of Age, who took turns Pleasuring him until this Day. Of course, I do not Believe any such Muslim Fairy Tales, and would Hope to God that you also do not Believe them. However, you should have the Right to Believe whatever you Like, whereby you might be Damned for it. ‡§§

28-04 [_] O Unelected King, I Challenge you to present a Guaranteed Solution for those Sick-minded Radical Muslims, who will be Determined to Murder you for writing such Slanderous Things.

28-05 [_] Well, once again, the Guaranteed Solution is for People like me to Live in Secure Swanky Fortresses, whereby I do not come into Contact with any Radical Murderous Muslims, who Vainly Imagine that they will go to Heaven for Murdering Innocent People. After all, the only Things that I Know for Sure about MuhamMAD are those Things that are Written about him by Honest Muslims, whom I have never Met, and I Seriously Doubt that you have Met any such Muslims: beCause, to be an Honest Muslim, would be to Deny MuhamMAD as a Holy Prophet: beCause you cannot Discover so much as ONE Prophecy in the *Holy Koran* — as least I have not, nor has anyone Pointed Out any such Prophecies to me, which tell about any Future Events that might be Identified as Prophecies. For

Example, MuhamMAD could have said, *"And it shall come to pass during the Last Days, just before the Second Coming of Jesus Christ, that Radical Muslims will be Exploding themselves and others by Means of Bombs in Motorized Vehicles, and not just in one or 2 Cases; but, in many Cases: beCause of being Insane, and also Believing some Mythical Nonsense about going to Heaven when they Die, when it is clearly Written that no Murderer shall Enter into the Holy Kingdom of All that is GOOD; and neither shall any Fabricator of Lies, Religious Hypocrites, Thieves, Rapists, Sodomites, Adulterers, Mutilators, nor Warmongers like me, lest the Kingdom of God should become Corrupted like those Deceived Muslims, who have their Heads Stuck in the Tailpipes of Capitalism, whereby they Suffer with Chronic Constipation of their Minds. Otherwise, they would Busy themselves in the Construction of Beautiful Planned City States, which are Built Up in Great Terraces, which have Luscious Organic Gardens on all Roofs, which are Covering Stone Dome Home Complexes, which have Polished Marble Walls, Granite-faced Floors, and Spacious Kitchens and Bathrooms with Ceramic Tiles Painted with Perfect Images of Jesus, Moses, and Father Abraham, whom no Person has ever Seen: beCause they are Jewish Myths, even as I am a Muslim Myth, who will not be Riding Up to Orion on the Back of a White Horse with 4 little Wings: beCause there is no Oxygen above those Tallest Mountains, which I Discovered when I went on a Picnic on the Top of Mount Everest with Osama bin Laden, who was a Firm Believer in Buzzeldick the Great, who was the Great Grandfather of Allah. Hallelujah!"* However, no such Prophecy Exists in the *Holy Qur'an*, which is mostly a Book of Praises for the Creator of Mosquitoes, Ticks, Fleas, Lice, Mice, Rats, Snakes, Bedbugs, Weevils, Scorpions, Spiders, Fire Ants, Tsetse Flies, Hornets, Killer Bees, Cockroaches, Weasels, Laughing Hyenas, Jackals, Coyotes, Foxes, Wolves, Lions, Bears, Skunks, Raccoons, Opossums, Armadillos, Mongooses, Ferrets, and a Host of other Unwanted Creatures and Characters, including George Warmonger Bush and Little Dick Chicanery, who would make Good Muslims, if you should Split their Tongues and Tie them together in Hard Knots around Hot Branding Irons, whereby Osama bin Laden could Lead them about with a Cellular Telephone from his Cave in Afghanistan. §§

28-06 [_] O Unelected King, with Words like those, the Good Muslims are likely to Skin you Alive for Blasphemy, even though 99.99% of them probably Agree with you! After all, there is Zero Proof that any Holy Angels conversed with Muhammad, much less Transported him to Orion on a Horse, with or without any Wings, which is an Islamic Fairy Tale, and of far less Value than the Jewish Fairy Tale about Noah's Ark and the Ability of a 600-year-old Man Feeding and Watering and Cleaning Up after 2 Million Species of Creatures in Cages, who could not have even Remembered what each Kind of Animal might have Eaten, much less Provide any Fresh Foods for them. For Example, what would the 500 or so Species of Bats have Eaten during that Year, seeing that there were no Jungles, Forests, Swamps, nor Hordes of Bugs to Feast on in the Ark? And how many Mice and Rats did Noah take along with him to Feed the 600 or so Species of CATS? Just a dozen or so Species of Dinosaurs would have Filled Up most of the Ark; but, what did they do for Fresh Water and something to EAT? And yet MuhamMAD, Moses, and even Jesus Christ BELIEVED all such Fairy Tales! But, I Certainly do NOT Believe them! Do YOU? §§‡

28-07 [_] Well, I do Believe that we should Do as the Apostle Paul Advised, and *"Prove all Provable Things, while Clinging Tightly to ALL that is GOOD,"* which Debunks all such Fairy Tales, and makes it Possible for God to Judge WHO is Worthy to Enter into his Holy Kingdom, which would not Include any Dishonest Person, who could not Calculate the Absurdity of an Old Man and his 3 Sons and 3 Dawterz-in-law Caring for 2 Million Species of Animals, even with the Assistance of Modern Computers to keep Track of what they might Eat and Drink, which would present a Genuine LOGISTICS Problem like you can hardly Imagine! After all, many Creatures have Specific Diets, without which they will simply DIE. For Example, Koala Bears Feast on Fresh Eucalyptus Leaves, alone, and will not Adapt to Eating like any other Bears: beCause they are NOT Actually Bears, nor are they Related to Bears; but, they are Marsupials, and the only Members of the Phascolarctidae Family. Therefore, Noah and his Family would have had to have Known that, and thus taken a Eucalyptus Tree along with them on the Ark, just to Feed them, as well as a Forest of Bamboo Shoots to Feed the Panda Bears, which are also not Actually Bears: beCause they are not Carnivorous nor Omnivorous; but, they are Great Consumers of Bamboo Shoots and Leaves. Chances are that Pandas are Distant Relatives of the Raccoons on the Superstitious Evolutionary Tree of Mass Confusion, even though some "Scientists" say that all Bears, including the Pandas, are Related with Dogs and Hogs, even as People are supposedly Related with Apes and Monkeys, which is like saying that God might have been a Great APE when he Created Adam from the Elements of the Earth, which has no Credibility among Intelligent Well-Educated People, who Understand that Adam was a Special Creation in this World, who was the First White Man, who was Created to Govern this World, whose Spirit was eventually Born in the Body of Jesus Christ, who was the Second Adam, and the Person who Paid the Price for the Original Sin, which was Eating the Forbidden Food, which Represented ALL Forbidden Foods, including Forbidden Spiritual Foods — such as that Evolutionary Nonsense, which is Missing Billions of Missing Links between the Millions of Species of Creatures — such as the Missing Links between Alaska Brown Bears and Polar Bears, or the Missing Links between Panda Bears and Koala Bears, which are Non-existent Links! However, when you Believe some Evolutionary THEORY, which cannot be Proven in a Courtroom for a Lack of Billions of Missing Links, you have to Resort to Superstitious Evolutionary Beliefs that only Ignorant FOOLS would Accept, even as many Professing "Christians" Accept the *Old Testament* Jewish Fables as True History, when there is Zero Evidence — such as the Burial Clothing of Israelites in Egyptian Graves, which are Nonexistent! Indeed, it would be like Europeans Living in America for 430 Years, while leaving ZERO Evidence of it! And yet we are Supposed to Believe that Israelites Lived in Egypt for 430 Years, and did not Bury anyone! But, if they did Bury them, WHERE are their Graves? Indeed, Israelites have Different Skull Bones and DNA than Egyptians, whereby they can be Identified, even without any Grave Clothes. But, for Sure, the Grave Clothes would be easy to Identify, IF they Existed! Moreover, one would just Naturally Think that if Israelites Actually Lived in Egypt for 430 Years, that they would have left some Egyptian Records of it, since Egyptians were forever Honoring their Great Kings with Monuments; but, behold, there are no Monuments for Joseph, who Supposedly Saved their Lives from a 7-year-long Famine! ‡§

28-08 [ ] So, O Elected King, what is the Guaranteed Solution for Changing the Minds of those Professing "Christians" and Deceived Muslims, who Believe all such Jewish Fairy Tales? Can you Solve that Massive Problem? If so, I will Bow Down and Worship you as God, himself!

28-09 [ ] Well, my Friend, only an Ignorant Fool would Bow Down and Worship any Man as God, except for Jesus Christ, who was both a Man and a God, who was and is the Anointed Savior of Mankind: because he is the Chosen Son of Yohoovu God, who was Chosen to be Adam, himself, who brought about the Fall of Mankind from the Garden of Eden, and also brought about the Redemption of Mankind by Paying the Ultimate Price for the Original Sin by being Crucified for it, whereby he was Perfected in his Glorification on the Torture Stake, and by his Resurrection from the Dead, whereby he was made Immortal afterwards, when he Ascended to his Heavenly Father in Jupiter — that is, he was Dematerialized in this World, and Rematerialized in that World, whereby he was made Immortal, and then he Returned to this World as the Glorified KING of Kings, Spiritually, who will one Day Govern all of the Nations as the Physical KING of Kings, which he will Govern from Mount Zion, which is the Holy City of the Great King, which is Inside of the Hollow Earth! Therefore, it is Legal and Righteous for us to Bow Down to HIM, and to Worship him; but, it is not Legal nor Good to Bow Down to Worship any other Man: beCause God Forbids it. However, that is not to say that we cannot or should not Bow Down in Honor of Honorable Men and Wombmen: beCause that is Permissible, and a Form of Great Respect among People, in spite of being easy to Misinterpret. For Example, certain Leaders of

Nations have Bowed Down to the Pope of Rome, in Honor of his Office, who is the Leader of the Largest Christian Church in the World, even if he is not a Perfect Person. Indeed, he is the Best Person that the Catholic Church, or Universal Church could Discover to be their Leader; and therefore, he should be Honored as such: because no Church is Perfect by any Means, nor is it Possible for such a Person to Suddenly Appear from the Ranks of Capitalism, Socialism, Communism, Fascism, nor any other FALSE Economic System, which has Precedence over the Minds of whomever is Indoctrinated in any such False Political, Economic, Religious and Social Systems. Indeed, those False Economic Beliefs OVERRIDE the Doctrines of Jesus Christ, which are not even made Clear within the *Holy Bible,* which is a MUTILATED Book of Books, which is Missing many Important Books and much Spiritual Information, which is Necessary for Understanding the WILL of GOD. For Example, it was and still is the Intention of the Great Creator God that all People should SHARE the Earth with one another, and not Attempt to Capitalize on anything for Personal Gain. For Example, there is no Way in the World that a single Family — much less a single Person — could ever Eat all of the Fruits that might be Grown on a Mature and Productive Mango Tree: because there are far too many of those Fruits, and as many as 10,000 of them on just ONE Mature Tree! However, you could say that all such Extra Fruits should be Gathered and SOLD, or else be Preserved in a Walk-in Freezer, which no one Presently has: beCause they cannot Afford such Luxuries, much less the Proper Mango Trees: beCause the Land Costs more than 1,000$ per square Meter! However, in the True Christian Economy, all such Mangos would be SHARED by the Community, whereby none would go to Waste: beCause the Community could easily Afford to Buy the Land for Growing the Fruit Trees — except that True Christians would not be Selling the Land, as Moses Taught: beCause, *"... the Land Belongs to GOD, and must not be Sold Forever."* Yes, you can Find that Great Truth in the *Old Testament,* which does have some Jewish Fables in it; but, it also has many Great and Provable Truths within it — one of which is Revealed in that little Verse, which Forbids People to Sell the Land: beCause it ALL Belongs to GOD, and must not be Sold FOREVER! (See *Leviticus 25, KJV.*) In Fact, a True Christian would Accept the Doctrine of having all Material Wealth in COMMON, even as the First Church had it; but, our Founding Fathers were Lying Deceiving HYPOCRITES of the Worst Kind, who Stole and Robbed the Land from the Native Indians, and then Capitalized on it ever since then: beCause they did not Believe the Laws nor Rules of MOSES! Yes, they were Rejecters of Provable TRUTHS, even as their Modern Counterparts are also Rejecters of Provable Truths, or else they would be DEMANDING **"The Great Worldwide TELEVISED Court HEARING,"** whereby they might Discover the WHOLE Truth about ALL Important Subjects, including the Truths about having ALL MATERIAL THINGS IN COMMON, whereby the Mountains of Rocks, Sand, Gravel, Metals, Minerals, Rivers, Lakes, Seas, and Oceans are SHARED with EVERYONE, Worldwide, if they Confess their Sins, Change their Minds, and Change their Lifestyles into True Christian Lifestyles, whereby everyone Loves their Naaberz Equally as much as they Love themselves! In other Words, you are Welcome to Eat all of the Sweet Juicy Fragrant KEY / KAA and Haden Mangos that you might Want, just as long as you Help me to Plant, Water, Fertilize, and Care for the Trees for 25 Years, just to have them to Eat: beCause the Creator God Intended for us to Live INTER-DEPENDENT Lives, and to HELL with Capitalism! Now, as for Changing the Minds of those People, who have been Deceived by Jewish Fairy Tales, Muslim / Islamic Myths, Hindu Superstitions, and Buddhist Philosophies, I will only say this — that if you do not Accept ALL Provable Truths from ALL Religions, you are Worse than an Infidel: beCause God is LOVE, and Love Requires that we Accept **"The Swanky Sword of Divine Truths,"** which Sword is Undefeatable in a Courtroom! Therefore, if anyone Belongs to some Religious Sect of Spiritual COWARDS, that Person will Naturally NOT be Interested in Demanding **"The Great Worldwide TELEVISED Court HEARING,"** whereby he or she might be Proven to be WRong about certain Doctrines — such as the Noah's Ark Story, or the Sudden Rapture of the Church, which has about as much Credibility as Snake Oils Healing People of their Insanities. ‡

121

28-10 [_] O Elected King, I must Confess that I have never Thought about the Economic System of Jesus Christ, which Demands that we have all Material Possessions in Common among us, whereby we SHARE those hundreds of thousands of Mountains of Rocks in this World of Wonders with all Believers; but, that Sounds most Reasonable to me: beCause, WHY should so many Billions of People have to Suffer for all of their Lives, without any of those Good Sweet Fragrant Mangos to EAT, when it is Possible and most Practical for EVERYONE to have an Abundance of them, even in Alaska and Siberia? Indeed, if it were Impossible or Impractical, we might have some Excuses. However, it is Possible and most Practical for this Generation of Voluntary Working Soldiers to Plant and Care for all of the Fruit Trees for the Future Generations of Working Soldiers, whereby everyone will have FREE Fruits to Eat during the Future: beCause of LOVE! Yes, True Love will just Naturally be Followed by FAITH, Hope, Trust, Patience, Persistence, and OBEDIENCE, which are **"The Seven Basic Spiritual Building Blocks of LIFE!"** Book 036. Therefore, IF there are any True Christians in this World of Wonders — or even any TRUE Muslims, Hindus, Buddhists, or other Believers — they will just Naturally DEMAND **"The Great Worldwide TELEVISED Court HEARING,"** whereby the Masses of People can Learn the Whole Truth about each Important Subject, and thus Willingly Choose what is Best for them, even if it Proves to be some very Strange Doctrine — such as having *"... all Material Things in Common among us, whereby we Share the Natural Resources of the Earth with one another, and even Feed our Enemies, whereby they are Converted to our Way of Thinking,"* as Saint Philip put it in his Gospel. Indeed, it is a Great Idea, whose Time has now Come for ACTION on it! Yes, I will Cheerfully go out and Sell ALL that I have, and Lay Down any Money that is Gained by it at your Feet, O Selected King: beCause I Know in my Heart that you are a GOOD Person, and will make a Righteous King, who will Do Justice for ALL Peoples, Worldwide. Yes, I have Great Confidence in you; but, I have ZERO Confidence in any of those other so-called "Leaders," who are not even Demanding that Great Meeting of the Most Intelligent and Well-Educated Minds, who Vainly Imagine that we can Solve our Massive Problems by Election Deceptions, alone, which is Ridiculous! Indeed, what we most Desperately Need is to Learn the WHOLE TRUTH, whatever it might be: beCause only TRUTHS have the Power to Liberate us from the Prison of LIES. Yes, it is as Jesus stated, *"You shall Learn the Truths that I Teach, and those Truths will Liberate you and set you Free in all Ways, whereby you will no longer be Slaves of Various Kinds of the Evil Empire; but, you will be Free in Words and in Deeds. Moreover, you will be Free to Speak about any Truths to anyone and everyone: beCause of having a Righteous One-World Government, which will Praise all Truths, and Demean all Lies, which will Seek Rational Solutions for your Problems, and also Assist the Righteous People to Accomplish Great Things, which can only be Accomplished by United Effort, by Voluntary Armies of Working Soldiers, who will be Contented to Live in Beautiful Marble Palaces within Beautiful Planned City States, in Exchange for their Services, who can be Greatly Assisted by Mechanical Slaves, which can do most of the Difficult Work to Build those Cities, and without Complaining about Low Wages: because Machines do not Require any Wages. Therefore, the Working Soldiers should Voluntarily do 4 Hours of Work per Workday, or the Equivalent thereof, and then be Paid Good Wages for any more Work after that: because they might Want to Buy something. However, they should not have to Buy any Land, Cisterns, Houses, Temples, Tunnels, nor Tools: because all of those Good Things should Belong to their Good Government, which should Hire them to Build their Cisterns, Gardens, Warehouses, Stone Dome Home Homes, Workshops, Sales Shops, Gymnasiums, Swimming Pools, Theaters, Synagogues, and whatever they Want to Work for, whereby they can have True Prosperity, without any Loans, without any Usury, and without any Taxes: because only Wicked Governments have to Collect Taxes. Indeed that 4 Hours of Common Skilled Labor per Workday will easily Cover all of the Costs of Widows, Orphans, and Helpless People, who can Eat at the Royal Table with their Elected King and Queen within each Planned City State."* — NMV.

— Chapter 29 —

A Guaranteed Solution for Changing Minds!

29-01 [_] Tyrants and War Lords have a History of Attempting to Change People's Minds, even by Means of Torturing them with Hot Branding Irons, Skewers, Racks, Stretching Limbs, Gouging Out Eyeballs, Castrating Men, and Mutilating Wombmen; but, my Guaranteed Solution for Changing Minds is altogether Peaceful, Harmless, and POWERFUL at the same Time: because I Guarantee ALL Minds to be Changed about certain Things, and Especially about EVIL Things — such as those Stinking Noisy Polluting DANGEROUS Vehicles, which most People can Live Happily without: beCause of Wisely Using Elevators, Escalators, and Electric Subway Trains within Beautiful Planned City States, which will Solve no less than 5,000 Problems, just by their Designs, alone.

29-02 [_] O Unelected King, I Challenge you to Change the Minds of the Klqlus Kluks Klamz (KKK), who are otherwise known as White Supremacists, who Sincerely Believe that White People are Superior to Black People, when we Know for a Fact that all People were Born EQUAL in all Ways. For Example, I Know for a Fact that I could Write an Uninspired book like this one within no less than 40 Years, and within no more than 80 Years, if I Set my Mind to it; but, I Seriously Doubt that it would Contain as many Rational Solutions as your Uninspired book: beCause I have not Carefully Studied all such Massive Problems. For Example, Racism in America has gotten Out of Control, which was Proven in Charlottesville, Virginia, where Neo-Nazis, White Supremacists, and KKK Members gathered to Protest the Removable of the General Robert E. Lee Memorial Statue, whereby a few People were Hurt, and one was Killed by a Racist Motorist, who Rammed his Speeding Car into a Crowd of People, whose Mind could never be Changed about his Beliefs: beCause he has Nazi History to Back him up, which is probably a little more Accurate than Jewish History. Nevertheless, besides all of that, it can easily be Proven in a Courtroom that Black People are Equally as Gifted by God as White People, which is WHY the History Books are full of Black Heroes — such as Jessie Owens, and Muhammad Ali, who was the only World Heavyweight Boxing Champion 3 Times, who Suffered Brain Damages from Boxing, and thus Proved that Black People are Superior to White People: beCause they have Bigger Tally Whackers and Smaller Brain Cavities, which make it Possible for them to Win in certain Sports. Moreover, Black People like George Washington Carver excelled in the Intellectual Arena: because he was one-quarter Jew, who are known to be Superior to all other Races in certain Fields that Require some BRAINS, which I do not have much of. Otherwise, I could give to you a List of People who have Won the Noble Peace Prizes, whereby we might get some Perspective on this Issue. Indeed, People of all Colors and Kinds have Won such Prizes, which is Proof that there is no Superior Race of People, as the Nazis Taught, who almost Conquered the World, and came Close to Inventing the Atomic Bomb, which could have been Used to Threaten the World into Submission to Adolf Hitler, who was a LUNATIC, who Wanted to Build Beautiful Planned City States for everyone in the World, whereby everyone might become Moderately RICH, and without Telling any Lies, nor Selling any Trash; but, his Ideas were Rejected by JEWS, who Controlled the News Media at that Time, as well as the Major Book Publishing Companies, Movie Productions, Chemical Factories, Drug Businesses, and Weapons Manufacturing. Indeed, those Jews were Determined to go to WAR: beCause it was very Profitable for them, whereby they Gained BILLIONS of Dollars, even as they Gained TRILLIONS of Dollars by going to War in Afghanistan, Iraq, Syria, Iran, Libya, and other Nations: beCause they Play their War Games from both Sides. For Example, they Financed both Sides of World Wars 1 and 2; but, they did not get the Credit for it in American History Books: beCause those Books are Managed by the Edomites, who have an Interest in Keeping all Truths HIDDEN — such as the

True Murderers of President John F. Kennedy and Lee Harvey Oswald, who was Murdered by Jack Ruby, whose Real Name was Jack Rubenstein, who was another Smart Jew; but, not nearly as Smart as Bernie Made-off, who Played a Ponzi Scheme, whereby he Robbed many fellow Jews by tens of Billions of all-American Dollars, which were Printed by Congress just for that Purpose, according to the Constitution: beCause only Congress had the Power to Do that — that is, until the Edomite Bankers took over that Job, whereby all American Money is now Minted and Printed by JEWS, only, who also Control the Non-federal Federal Non-reserve Reserve Bank, which is somewhat like the Federal Express, which is neither Federal nor an Express, like the Pony Express, which was Quicker than the Non-federal Federal Express: beCause they had Faster Horses during those Days. Nevertheless, my Point is this — you will never Change the Minds of People who Believe in LIES: beCause none of those Lies can be Proven to be LIES! §§‡

29-03 [ ] Well, O Confused Acrobat, your Intellectual Gymnastics are enough to Derail most Rational Minds, who still Believe that all Provable Things can be Proven, and especially such Simple Things as WHO Assassinated President Kennedy, which can easily be Discovered by Opening ALL of the Hidden Records of the Federal Burden of Investigation (FBI) and the Central Unintelligent Agencies (CIA), who Know Exactly WHO did it, and WHY. However, they are Obviously Under the Control of some Higher Powers, which reach all of the Way to the Low Court of Supreme Injustices, who Failed to DEMAND a Thorough and Unbiased Investigation into the Evil Events of September 11th, 2001, which is PROOF that they are Co-conspirators in those Crimes, along with the FBI, CIA, NIST, George Warmonger Bush, Little Dick Chicanery, and a whole List of Generals, Secretaries, Bankers, Insurance Agents, so-called "Scientists," Medical Doctors, Demolition Experts, and you Name it — all of whom should be Arrested and brought to COURT for Assisting in the Cover-up! Yes, all such Heads should be Examined for their SANITY! After all, what Difference does it make if George Herbert Walker Bush was at the Keystone Position in the CIA at the Time of the Kennedy Assassination in Dall-ass, Tex-ass — can he not Answer a few Important Questions in a Courtroom, before he Expires?

29-04 [ ] O Elected King, in Order to get down to the Root Causes for American Evils, you would first of all have to have the Cooperation of the President, the Supreme Court, the Congresses, and the Attorney General, who would also not Object to a Full Discloser of those Evils, which is Asking far too much of "the Greatest Nation on the Earth," which has Top Secret SINS, which would make those Elected Officials LOOK BAD, which would be far too Em-bare-assing for American History Books to Endure the Heavy Shame of it all, whereby even the White Pages would become PINK with Shame, which, of course, is an Original Thought with me, even though I got the Idea from Studying the *Holy Bible,* which also has those Pink Pages, wherever the Sins of the Founding Fathers were Revealed in the Chronicles of the Kings, which must have been Recorded long after those Sinners Died. Otherwise, those Wicked Kings would have had all such Pages Removed, whereby no one during the Future would have been Able to Learn any Good Lessons from Past Mistakes. Therefore, IF American Officials are so PURE, why have any Top Secret Files? Why not have Open History Books for everyone to Learn from? Indeed, if Lyndon Baines Johnson was the Chief Director of the Kennedy Assassination, then the American History Books should Reveal it; but, Chances are that he only Asked the CIA and FBI to carry out the Job, and without his Directions for just HOW to Accomplish that Dirty Deed: beCause he would not Want any Connection with it, being such a GOOD Squinty-eyed Fellow with a Reputation of a SAINT — much like Saint Joseph Stalin of Russian Fame, who had some 50 Million Russians put to Death during his Reign of Terror, which was not even Reported about in **"The Divided States of United Lies,"** until some 50 Years AFTER the Fact: beCause, whomever Controls the Information Machine did not Want us American Tax Slaves to Learn about it, lest we should Demand a Thorough Investigation into WHY it was not Immediately Reported about, whereby we might have Assisted Adolf Hitler to get RID of that Puppet Communist and his Hateful Regime, rather than Join Forces with him and that Anti-Christ Cigar-chomping Whisky-guzzling Winston Windbag Churchill, who was Totally DRUNK when an Impersonator gave his "Never Give Up" Speech: beCause, "Winston Tastes GOOD, like a Cigarette should!" CLAP, CLAP! Yes, it was all about MONEY and the Love for more and more of it, which has Corrupted the entire World! But, not to Worry: beCause Capitalism and the Market Place will FIX it, according to Professor Milton Friedman, who was another one of those Nobel Peace Prize Winners of the Edomite Clan, who call this "RANTING HATE SPEECH," which is more like TRUTH Speech, which has only Touched on such Important Subjects. Indeed, what they call "Hate Speech" is Actually too Truthful for the Enemies of Christ to Tolerate, who would no doubt have him Crucified once again, if he were here, Today, giving the very same Message that he gave some 2,000 Years Ago: beCause, it was for those Provable Truths that he was Crucified! Indeed, his Apostles and Disciples were Tracked Down, Stoned to Death and Crucified on other Crosses by the same EVIL Clan, who Objected to having *all things in common,"* which was a Great THREAT to their Capitalist Doctrines, which were Based on Selfishness, Greed, Lusts, and Edomite Doctrines of the DEVIL! §§‡

29-05 [_] Well, my Friend, you make some really Good Points, for which I will have to Honor you with a Swanky PALACE, if I can Find your Remains, after those Edomites get a Hold on you: beCause they will no doubt be Highly Offended by all such Inspired Words, which, like you say, only TOUCH on the Issue, and do not go into the Bloody Gory DETAILS — even as none of those so-called "RANTING Hate Speeches" were Published on CNN, who seem to be Afraid of any Provable Truths. After all, it could be that those White Supremacist have a Good Point to make about some Subject, which I have yet to Hear: beCause it is not Reported on the so-called "NEWS," which was likely ALWAYS THE CASE throughout History: beCause Truths have always been at the Heart of every Conflict, including World War 2. Yes, I have Personally read ALL of the Speeches by Adolf Hitler, and find nothing in them that would even Suggest HATRED for Jesus Christ, nor for any of his Teachings! But, there are many Truths within his Speeches that are Worthy of some Study and Meditation — such as, *"If a Propagandist tells a Lie long enough and loud enough, Ignorant People will come to Believe it."* And such were the Propagandist Lies of Sir Winston Windbag Churchill, who never even Challenged Adolf Hitler to an International Radio Debate, whereby he might have Proven him to be WRong by Means of Reason and Logic: beCause Sir Winston was just another Spiritual COWARD of the Capitalist Order of Soothsayers, who Dangled the Cob of Corn on the End of the String that was Attached to Tom Sawyer's Fishing Pole, whereby Tom kept the Rooster running around and around in a Circle to get a Bite of Corn from the Cob, as Tom was Sitting on the Roof of the Chicken House, where he was Out of Sight, and thus Out of Mind! However, from a Distance, one can See very Clearly that the Rooster was Greatly Deceived by the Cob of Corn on the Fishing Line, whereby he was Exercising his Leg Muscles for nothing, except that Tom had Plans for Eating those BIG Drumsticks, after getting those Muscles Built Up enough by Running the Rooster around and around, which Required very little Effort on the Part of Tom, while the Rooster was nearly Exhausted. Nevertheless, as Tom gave to him a Bite of Corn, now and then, the Rooster was Foolish enough to Chase after it, even as most Capitalists and Tax Slaves are Willing to Chase after a little more Money, if they just get a Bite of it, now and then, even though it would Require far less Effort, Time, and Money to simply Plant some Corn in the Garden, rather than Chase after a Kernel of Corn, as that Ignorant Rooster might do, if he were to Stop and THINK about it. But, his Greed has Blinded his Mind, and his Selfishness has Perverted his Thinking, whereby he has no Capacity to Think, at all: beCause he is like the Normal Ignorant American, who Chases after some Money for Buying Fuel for Heating his House during the Winter, rather than get Together with his Naaberz, and Construct Houses that have Solid Stone Walls that are at least 10 feet THICK, whereby their Houses will not Require any Artificial Heating nor Cooling, whereby they might Save Millions of TRILLIONS of Dollars during the next 6,000 Years! However, that would Require some Foresight, which Poor Old Thomas Jefferson did not have, or else he might have Recommended it to Poor Nigger Jim and Huckleberry Finn, who had LOTS of Time and Energy for Constructing all such Houses; but, they Lacked a GOOD Master! Yes, their Masters Suffered with Chronic Constipation of their Minds, and could not Think of any Way to Solve the Racial Contentions among the People: beCause it did not Cross their Minds that there is **"A Sound Argument for Masters and Servants!" (WHY Everyone Needs a GOOD Master, and every Master Needs Good OBEDIENT Servants!) By The Worldwide People's Revolution!®** Book 008. Indeed, Poor Ignorant Huck Finn and Tax Slave Nigger Jim have no Idea what to DO without the Assistance of a GOOD Master: beCause they would not know just WHERE to Begin to Build the First Swanky Cistern for Water Storage, which should be Built on SOLID BEDROCK, whereby it might not Crack nor Leak. However, that would Require some Heavy Equipment — such as Bulldozers, Cranes, Trucks, Bucket-loaders, and Trains — just to MOVE so much Dirt, Trees, and Rubble Rocks, which no Poor Education Slave nor Interest Slave would have at hand, nor know HOW to Obtain! Indeed, if he should go to the Local Bank, he would Naturally be Greeted with a Big Smile from the Undertaker of Economic Disasters, who would see him as just another Rooster, who needs to be Run Around at the Chicken House at the End of Tom's Fishing Line, which that Friendly Bankster could Arrange; but, only IF Poor Huck Finn and Nigger Jim had some COLLATERAL, which they would not have: beCause they were Born in a State of Extreme Poverty, across the Big Pond — as in, one in Europe, and one in Africa. Yes, it was Convenient for it to Work Out that Way; but, as Nature would have it, that is just the Way it is in Reality, and nobody can Change it — that is, nobody could Change it, until NOW! Yes, now we have several Means of Communicating with one another, one of which is called the TELEVISION, which could be a very Useful Tool for Enlightening the Minds of whomever might have Eyes that can See, and Ears that can Hear! But, a Righteous KING would have to get in Charge of it, who has some Authority to SHUT OFF the Pure Unadulterated NONSENSE, which can be Played AFTER we Hold that Great Meeting of the Most Intelligent and Wel-Ejukaatid Miindz at **"The Great Worldwide TELEVISED Court HEARING!"** Book 041. Yes, if anyone Wants to Watch or Listen to any such Capitalist TRASH, after that Great Meeting, they will be Welcome to Do so. But, until everyone in the World is Breathing Fresh Crisp Clean Air, Drinking Pure Living Water, Eating Wholesome Natural Foods, Wearing Natural Clothing, and Living in SECURE Stone Dome Home Complexes with Home-craft Workshops, Well-made Tools, and Marble-faced Sales Shops, being Attached to Electric Elevators, Escalators, and Subway Trains within those **"GLORIOUS Swanky Hotels Castles and Fortresses!" (Beautiful Planned City States for WISE Intelligent Well-Educated People with Common Sense and Good Understanding!) By The Worldwide People's Revolution!®**, Book 019, we, the People, should GO TO BED, and STAY in Bed, until the Leaders of all Nations Agree to Conduct that Great Meeting of the Most Intelligent and Well-Educated Minds, come next April 21st: beCause we have become SICK of Poverty, Hunger, Riots, Strikes, Police Brutalities, Election Deceptions and Civil Wars! Yes, we have become so Sick of it that we can no longer go to Work, which will be a Peaceful Harmless Protest by 99.999,999,999% of the People in this World of Woes, who will at Last get their JUSTICE, and with BIG Smiles! Yes, Poor Huck Finn and Nigger Jim will be doing the Wawtqzee on the Heads of those Dimwitcrats and Reprobates in the District of Criminals, while Dancing around **"The BIG White OUTHOUSE on the Not-so-Biblical Capitol DUNGHILL!"** Book 023. Yes, Poor Nigger Jim and Huck Finn will be Ready for **"The END of CONFUSION!" (The Great CELEBRATION of the Magnificent Wedding of the Most Humble Honest Nations, and the Grand Year of JUBILEE!)**, Book 050: beCause they will at last be FREE! Thank God Almighty, as Dr. King used to say when he was not Committing Spiritual Adultery. §§‡

29-06 [ ] O Elected King, when the Holy Spirit comes over you, you can Deliver some of the most Inspiring Words that Mankind has ever Heard! But, you still have not Explained to us just HOW you will Change the Minds of those Racists, White Supremacists, and other White Trash, who Vainly Imagine that they are Better than us Black Folk, just beCause of having 1/10th as many Crimes? ‡§§

29-07 [_] Well, my Friend, why would I even Think of Trying to Change their Minds, and especially when they have some Valid Points? Why not just let them have their Beliefs within their own Beautiful Planned City States, where they can Attend to their own Gardens, Vineyards, Orchards, Cisterns, Kitchens, Dining Rooms, Home-craft Workshops, and Sales Shops? Indeed, will you Care what their Beliefs might be, while you are also Attending to your own Garden, Home-craft Workshop and Sales Shop? Seriously, will you give a Damn what any of those other People are Doing, just as long as you get to Do whatever you Want to? Are you Aware that you are now Invited to make Proper Plans for your own Beautiful Swanky Fortress, where you can Live with other People of Like-mindedness? Indeed, you are now Welcome to let your Imagination RUN WILD, and Invent any Beautiful Things that you can Think of for those **"Beautiful Swanky PALACES!" (A New Concept in Living Habits — Swanky Palaces for Poor People!) By The Worldwide People's Revolution!® Book 066.** Therefore, do not Feel Restricted by your Extreme Poverty; but, put your Heart and Head into it, and get on the Drawing Boards, O Architect, and Discover whatever you can come up with: beCause it is Possible that you might have the Best Plan of all! Indeed, if it is a Workable Plan, you will have Unlimited Resources to Work with, including whatever Money is Needed: beCause that is the DUTY of **"The New RIGHTEOUS One-World Government!" (HOW to Establish a Righteous One-World Government without Going to WAR!) By The Worldwide People's Revolution!®** Book 056. In Fact, now is the Time to PROVE that Black People are Equally as Skilled as White People — that is, IF it is True: beCause you will Produce the most Beautiful Planned City State in the Whole World, and without the Assistance of any "White Trash," as you call them. However, I venture to say that you Lack a Proper Education for Doing it, which is still no Problem: beCause the Information can be Discovered on the Internet, if you Search for it. Indeed, most of that Information was Written by White People, to whom you should give Full Credit; but, if you do run into Insurmountable Problems, do not be too Proud to Ask for some HELP: beCause that is what that Good Government is for, which will also be made up mostly of WHITE People, who will be Elected into their Offices, which is NO Sin: beCause it is True that White People were Created to Govern all other Races of People; but, not in some Tyrannical Way, nor in some Deceptive Manner, as Capitalism has done, which has made almost everyone into a SLAVE of some Kind, which is the Opposite of what I have Proposed: beCause, in the Economic System that I Propose, everyone will Actually be Able to be EQUAL to some Degree: beCause we will Try to make it that Way. However, if you Prove to be another Lazy Sloth, who does not Want to Follow the RULES for Good Gardening, for Example, according to **"The LUSICOUS All-Mineral Organic Method of Gardening!" (HOW to Grow DELICIOUS Satisfying Foods for Potential Kingz and Kweenz in Swanky PALACES!)**, Book 021, please do not Blame ME for it, nor Falsely Accuse anyone else of it: beCause your Failure might be beCAUSE of Acid Rains, or some other Uncontrollable Natural Cause. Therefore, *"Be Slow to get Angry, Slow to be Wrathful, Slow to Blame others for anything, and Careful to Study what is Required of thee,"* as said the Prophet. Trust me, there is a Riit Waa to Do all Things, and it can be Discovered by taking Counsel with Wise People, who may be Difficult to Find; but, **"The Great Worldwide TELEVISED Court HEARING"** will make that Possible, and most Practical. Therefore, just be Patient. ‡

29-08 [_] O Elected King, the more that I Learn from you, the more I Realize how much that I have been Deceived. For Example, I used to Think that People had to Change their Minds about a lot of Things, just to Live in Peace; but, now we Learn that almost no one will have to Change his nor her Mind: beCause all Like-minded People can simply Live Together within the same Kinds of Swanky Fortresses. For Example, if someone still Wants to Practice Capitalism, after we Hold that Great Meeting of the Most Intelligent Minds, they will be Welcome to Live in some Abandoned City of Confusion, and Practice Capitalism with the Snakes, Skunks, Wild Dogs, Stray Cats, and whatever has Moved into such Places! Yes, they will all have Total Freedom to Do that. Likewise, if they Sincerely Want to Practice Communism or Socialism, they will be Free to Do it.

29-09 [_] Well, my Friend, it is my Sincere Belief that most People will Accept the Truths that I Teach, once they Learn them, even as Outlandish as some of my Beliefs might Sound — such as Yohoovu God Living Inside of JUPITER, which is supposed to be a Big Ball of GASES; but, I am telling you that it has TRILLIONS of Inhabitants on the INSIDE of it, and Great Cities with GIANTS, who would make us Look like Piss Ants in Comparison. Nevertheless, no one has to Believe any of that, just to Do their own Gardening, and Share their Fruits and Nuts with their Naaberz, who will also be Happy to Share their Produce with them. But, the Proper Way to do that Gardening is to have both Kinds of Home Gardens and Community Gardens, whereby you can have Guaranteed ROYAL Swanky Buffets: beCause of having it all Planned Out Properly for making it Happen. Indeed, **"The Swanky Associations of Working Soldiers"** must do that Planning, Planting and Harvesting, just to get it Done Correctly, even as People have to Plan those Flowery Floats for the Pasadena Tournament of Roses, or the New Year's Day Rose Parade, without which those Floats would not be Attractive to anyone: beCause it Requires some PLANNING, which is not the Case for an Inspired Book, nor for an Inspired Song: beCause it comes by the Inspiration of GOD, who can also Help us to Plan Things, if we are Listening to his still small Voice. However, most of the Planning must be done by us: beCause that Way we cannot Blame God for whatever goes WRong.

29-10 [_] O Elected King, I see that you have also done some Planning in this Book — such as having only 10 Verses for each Chapter, when you could have 20 to 40 Verses, and thus make it a Better Book: beCause each Thought should be a Separate Verse, even as it is within the *Holy Bible*. Indeed, some of your Verses cover 2 whole Pages: beCause you do not Want to Break Up any Flowing RANTING Thoughts, as in Verse 29-05 and 29-07. However, in the Future, someone will no doubt take it upon themselves to Break Up those Long Paragraphs into very Short Verses, even as they did for the *Holy Koran, The Book of Mormon,* and the *Holy Bible,* whereby those Books are easier to Study, Verse by Verse, and Line by Line. However, I suppose that you will be telling us that none of your Books Require any such Studies: beCause of having Complete Thoughts, which any 12-year-old Child can easily Understand: beCause of its Completeness. Yes, you just Assume that we are all Ignorant People, who must have all of the DETAILS, before we can Understand something, while the Uninspired Authors of the *Unholy Mutilated Bible* Failed to give any Details, which made it Possible for you to MAGNIFY it, while other Ignorant People PERVERTED IT, by Adding their Religious and Political LIES to it, even as MuhamMAD came up with his *Unholy Ridiculous Koran,* which Pretends to Address all of the Important Issues, while not giving any Reasonable Solutions for anything! Indeed, even if you Studied it, both Day and Night, for a hundred Years, you would not Discover any Solutions for the Important Issues that are Addressed within this Inspired Book, which pretty well Covers everything from A to Z, which could be Enhanced during the Future, if it were Necessary. However, I Perceive that once we Build those **"GLORIOUS Swanky Hotels Castles and Fortresses,"** there will be a Minimum Amount of Problems left to Solve: beCause most of the Problems will be Dealing with Nature, which can be Handled by Planting Different Kinds of Seeds and Trees. And, speaking of Seeds, are you Aware that there used to be about 5,000 Different Kinds of RICES? Likewise, there used to be about 200 Different Varieties of Sweet Corn, which have now been Reduced to only a Dozen or so. Moreover, there are only a few Commercial Kinds of Feed Corn for Livestock, which has made the Gene Pool so small as to be in Danger of becoming Extinct! Nevertheless, your Swanky Fortress Plan will also Solve that Problem: beCause each Swanky Fortress can Specialize in Growing Special Seeds and Trees. §§‡

— Chapter 30 —

The Conclusion

30-01 [ ] Now, I want everyone to Understand that I did not Intend to go about Presenting Guaranteed Solutions for EVERYTHING in the World; but, just Solutions for Common everyday Problems, which can be done Away with, if we Want to — such as those Natural Disasters, which are Cured by the Swanky Fortress System, even if the Stone Walls are only 30 feet Tall. However, in Order to Obtain the Maximum Amount of Wind Energy in Swanky Generators, the Walls must be 50 to 100 feet Tall — Depending on their Locations. However, there are some Windy Places, even at Ground Level, which would not Require such Tall Stone Walls — except that there are other Reasons for making them fairly Tall and THICK. For Example, just HOW would we go about Protecting those Beautiful Stone Dome Homes from Freezing Cold Weather, if the Earth should SHIFT on its Axis, and put Mexico in some Cold Place like Alaska, for Example?

30-02 [ ] O Elected King, if the Earth does Radical Things like that: beCause of Climate Changes, or whatever; we will just have to MOVE to Better Climates, rather than Try to make such Places Livable.

30-03 [ ] Well, my Friend, it is Wiser to be Prepared for the Worst Possible Conditions, if it is at all Practical to do so. For Example, there are thousands of Mountains of Rubble Rocks in Mexico, which can be Used Wisely to Cover all of the Stone Dome Home Complexes with at least 10 feet of Rocks, plus Sand, Gravel, Rough Rocks, more Sand, a foot of Clay, and Enriched Topsoil at least 3 feet Deep. Indeed, it is Best to not Try to Cheat in any Way: beCause we have Plenty of everything to Work with, including Young Voluntary Working Soldiers, who will have to be Trained HOW to Work Properly: so as to not Kill themselves. After all, Heavy Equipment is very Dangerous, and can easily Kill someone.

30-04 [ ] O Elected King, it is Physically Possible to Work with Small Rocks and Light Equipment, which are not so Dangerous. For Example, you and your Brother Vern moved more than 13,000,000 Pounds by Hand to Build your 98% Rock Houses in Arkansas, without getting Hurt: beCause none of the Rocks Weighed more than 2,000 Pounds. However, if you had been Careless, I suppose that you could have Chopped Off or Smashed a Foot with such a Heavy Rock, if a Steel Bar should have Slipped on a Rock; but, it never Happened: beCause you Knew HOW to Handle all such Situations, having Good Judgment, whereby you might Qualify to be a Good Master for Teaching others HOW to Handle such Rocks.

30-05 [ ] Well, my Friend, there must be at least a Million Ways for People to get Hurt; but, if they are taking their Sweet Time, and being very Careful, and Looking Out for each other, they can do a lot of Difficult Work without getting Hurt. However, if they are all PUFFED UP with Great PRIDE, they are Bound to get Hurt: beCause, as King Solomon Warned, *"PRIDE come Parading itself in front of Destruction, and a Haughty Spirit comes before a Fall. Therefore, be Humble, Honest, and Careful to Do everything Correctly, Remembering to Pray before you Act."* — NMV. Nevertheless, it is Expected that there will be some Disasters with the Construction of no less than 2 Million Swanky Fortresses: beCause X-amount of People will just Assume that they are Safe to do this or that, whereby they will take Unnecessary Chances. Indeed, it almost always Requires more WORK to do something Correctly; but, that is the Right Way to do it. For Example, we Wanted to make the Roof of our Retirement Home in ONE-FOOT-THICK CONCRETE STEPS, whereby there would be no Rusty Steel Reinforcement

Bars in the entire 504-square-meter Roof; but, we were Cheated Out of it by the Bankers, who Pretended to be too Poor to Afford to Pay for it; but, not too Poor to Afford the Rusty Rebars. Therefore, the Capitalist System is what Robbed us of a Good House — not our Laziness. Indeed, we were Willing to do the Difficult Work; but, we needed more Money and Time, which we could not come up with — Thanks to Capitalism. Therefore, when the Roof Rusts OUT, do not Blame us for it; but, put the Blame where it Belongs, on those Greedy Selfish Bankers.

30-06 [_] O Elected King, I am Curious as to just HOW you could have made a Concrete Roof in one-foot STEPS, as you say?

30-07 [_] Well, the 40 Concrete Columns are 2-feet by 2-feet by 9-feet Tall, each of which would have a one-foot-tall Step or Slab of Concrete poured on Top of the Column, which would be 4-feet-square; and then another Step or Slab of Concrete would be poured one-foot-thick on Top of that First Step, making it 6-feet by 6-feet, being Covered by another Step that is 8-feet by 8-feet, which is Covered by a 10-feet-wide Step, which is Covered by the Final Step that is 12-feet by 12-feet. In other Words, all of the Steps are Hanging Over the Previous Steps by one foot, like this very Rough Drawing shows:

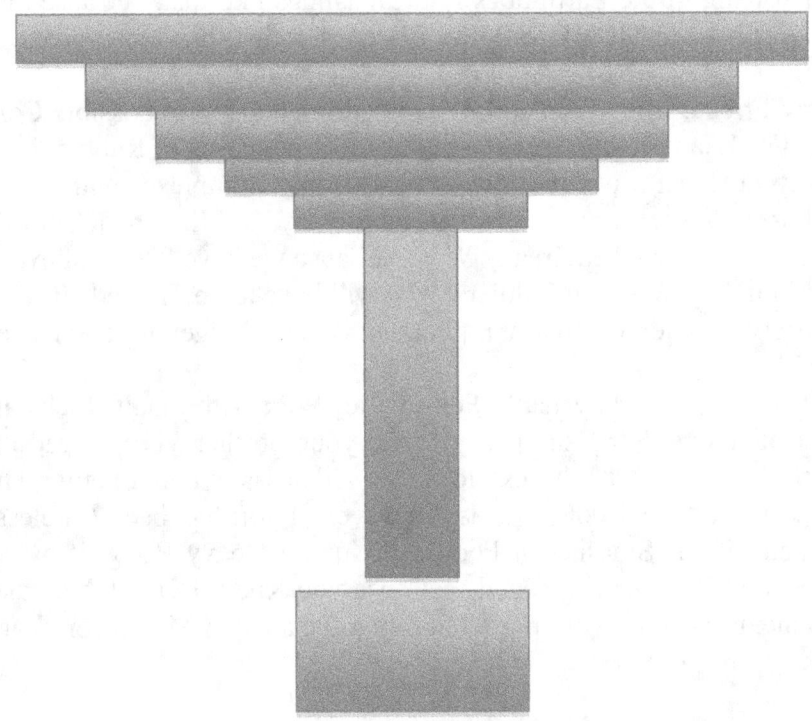

30-08 [_] O Unelected King, it seems to me as if such a Heavy Roof would put far too much Pressure on the Supporting Foundation Blocks of those Columns, which would have to be Resting on Solid Bedrock, just to keep from Sinking into the Sand. Indeed, such a House would likely be Full of Cracks, and thus the Roof would LEAK!

30-09 [_] Well, my Friend, Chances are that you are Correct about that, which would be a Good Reason for making similar Concrete Steps below the Foundation Blocks, whereby they are not likely to Settle Down, which would only be Possible with a LOT of Money. Moreover, after all of those Steps have been poured for the Roof, the entire Roof should be Covered with a Solid Layer of Concrete a foot deep, and then Tiled with Ceramic Tiles between Concrete Planter Boxes, which should also be

Tiled Inside and Outside, except for the Drain Holes: beCause you would naturally want a Garden on the Roof in those Planter Boxes, which would be about 3 feet tall and 10 feet square, resting on Top of each Column, which would somewhat Stabilize the Temperature within the House.

30-10 [_] O Silly King of the Ignorant Fools, you could use one-tenth as much Concrete in a Proper Concrete Dome Home, and put as much Dirt on the Roof as you might Like, while making the House much more Earthquake-proof. Indeed, if your Word for Windows Drawing Program were Working Properly, I could Draw a Proper Picture for you, and thus get your Thinking Corrected: beCause you are Proposing something that is Totally INSANE! Therefore, I can fully Understand WHY no Banker would Loan any Money to you for Doing such a Silly Thing, even though I will Confess that it would have the Great Advantage of not having any Rusty Steel Reinforcement Bars in the Roof, whereby it might Stand there for the next 10,000+ Years; but, only IF the Cement were made Correctly. Nevertheless, let us say that your Present Roof endures for another 40 Years, and then has to be Torn Down and Replaced with a similar Roof, at 10 Times the Expense — would that not have made it well Worth the Expense to do it Correctly, to begin with? §‡

30-11 [_] Well, my Friend, we did not have Sufficient Money for making any Proper Domes to begin with, which would have Required Special Concrete Forms, which we did not have, which the Government should have had to Rent for a Reasonable Price, since no Business would Want to Buy any such Forms: because not one Person in a thousand would Want a Stone Dome Home Complex to Live in: beCause they would rather Live in Tarpaper Shacks, than to Live in Secure Well-made Houses. Otherwise, someone might be Building those Swanky Stone Dome Home Complexes to Sell for a Billion Dollars, each. However, I suppose that you would Cut the Costs of Constructing them down to a Million Dollars, each — that is, for about 20 Spacious Rooms with Concrete Domes on Top of them, and without any Steel Reinforcement Bars, whereby they would never Rust Out nor Fall In.

30-12 [_] O Elected King, I would Think that after 50 Years of Experimenting with Concrete Construction Jobs, that you would now Know for a Fact what is BEST for us, which has nothing to do with the Costs of it: beCause, **"The New RIGHTEOUS One-World Government"** would not be at all Concerned about any Costs: beCause MONEY is the LEAST of our Problems to Solve, since it is Extremely Easy to Print with Printing Machines, which Costs no more for a One-Million-Dollar Paper Bill, than a One-Dollar Paper Bill: because it Requires the same Amount of Paper and Ink. Therefore, the Cost of a Swanky Stone Dome Home Complex should be Determined by the Amount of LABOR that is put into it, and nothing more: because all of the Mountains of Rocks are FREE, along with the Machines and Tools that are Required for Harvesting those Mountains of Rocks: beCause, in Exchange for 4 Hours of Common Skilled Labor per Day, any Voluntary Working Soldier should be Happy to Live in one of those **"Beautiful Swanky PALACES!" (A New Concept in Living Habits — Swanky Palaces for Poor People!) By The Worldwide People's Revolution!®** Book 066. Indeed, he might Want to Earn some Extra Money to Waste on Booze and/or Prostitutes; but, if he puts in those 4 Hours of Labor per Day, it will not be very long before those Swanky Palaces will be Springing Up like Beautiful Tulips in a Flower Garden in the Springtime! After all, no one will have to Buy any of that Heavy Equipment, nor any of the Materials nor Tools for making any such Heavy Equipment: beCause God has Given to us all of those Materials to Work with, for FREE! Therefore, why not just take Advantage of his Generosity, and STOP making SLAVES of Poor Ignorant People?

30-13 [_] Well, my Friend, that is what I have been Suggesting, all along; but, it seems that no one can Hear what I am Saying. Indeed, some People even call me a COMMUNIST, as if I were Proposing to make them into Russian or Chinese Communists, or even North Korean Communists — none of whom even Proposed to make everyone in the World Moderately RICH, and without Telling any Lies, nor

Selling any Trash: beCause none of their Plans called for any of those **"GLORIOUS Swanky Hotels Castles and Fortresses!" (Beautiful Planned City States for WISE Intelligent Well-Educated People with Common Sense and Good Understanding!)** Book 019. In Fact, they Deliberately set out to Build Shanties for the Communist Slaves, which barely had enough Space to Turn Around in! Yes, it was as if they were too Poor to Afford to make the Correct Tools to Work with, or did not have enough Fuels for Operating that Equipment, which may have been True for the Chinese People; but, certainly not for the Russians, who are now Selling their so-called "Fossil" Fuels to other Nations. Nevertheless, the Great Question is this: **"Will we use the Remaining Fuels to get those Swanky Fortresses Built, whereby we can take Advantage of the 5,000+ Good Reasons and Great Advantages for Building them; or, will we Waste all of that Precious Energy running around in Circles on Endless Highways to Hell, and end up becoming 10 Times Poorer than we presently are?"** Indeed, if you now Think that Rocks are Expensive, just Think about what they will Cost when there is no more Cheap Fuel for Transporting those Rocks!?

30-14 [_] O Elected King, if we had to, we could make Gasoline from Composted Cow Manure, and still get those Swanky Fortresses Constructed, if they were any Good for anything. §

30-15 [_] You have got to be Living in a Capitalist Dream World: beCause all of the Methane Gas in the Whole World would not keep American Cars running for even one Day. So, you can Forget about that Idea. ‡

30-16 [_] Could we not make Hydrogen-powered Cars, and still Maintain our Great False Economy, just the Way it is? Indeed, we could Cover Up the entire Earth with those Ugly Solar Panels for making ElecTrickery, and then we would not have to Build those UGLY Swanky Fortresses. §

30-17 [_] I am wondering just how you would know that any such Fortresses are UGLY, seeing that neither you nor anyone else has ever Seen a Swanky Fortress?

30-18 [_] I have seen lots of Fortresses, and they are all Ugly: because Rocks are Ugly. {Please Check the Box with an X, if you Agree.}

30-19 [_] Chances are that you have been Bonded to Plastic Flowers, Ugly Painted Sunsets, and Greasy Vehicles running around on Greasy Filthy Noisy Streets; and therefore you cannot Appreciate Real Flowers, Polished Rocks, nor anything of Real Beauty. Therefore, I Suggest that you do some Serious Fasting, and get your 7 Senses Working.

30-20 [_] Fasting is the very Last Thing that I am going to Do: beCause I like to Eat and EAT, which is WHY that I Weigh 200 Pounds too much; but, not to Worry: beCause there is a Great Worldwide Famine Coming, whereby almost all Bellybuttons will be Rubbing on their Backbones for Hunger and Thirst, which will Prove to be Worse than the Holocaust of the 1940's. Yes, God Knows that it will be a Wonderful Time to Live. §§‡

— Chapter 31 —

Supplemental Thoughts

31-01 [_] From Time to Time, beginning right now, I will Add Supplemental Thoughts to this Extremely Good Book: beCause it is an Appropriate Place to put those Thoughts. In Fact, 3 of those Special Thoughts calls for Appendixes: beCause they are entire Chapters of Good Thoughts, which could be within the Main Body of the Book, except that they came after the Book was Written: beCause of Developing Events, which I had no Control over; but, I do have Control over my own Books, and am Free to Express my Thoughts, which you are also Free to Express, if you Know what my Thoughts are; but, very few People do, and would Certainly not Know my Thought well enough to Express them in a Right Way. Nevertheless, there are many News Commentators and Analysts in this World of Wonders, who Presume that they Know the Thoughts of certain Politicians, Preachers, and Teachers — yes, and also the Thoughts of Inspired Authors, who really have no Clear Understanding of some of their own Thoughts, which they are Grasping for in the Darkness of Ignorance: beCause of being Blinded by the Brightness of the Light of Truths, you might say — as in the Case of Appendix 1, which is one of the Finest Pieces of Divine Literature in the Whole World, which should be Published to the Leaders of all Nations, whereby they can Publish it to all of their People.

31-02 [_] It Requires TIME to get all such Things as the Inspired Tale of the Colorful Peacock from Angel Ridge, Perfected, and we only Hope to God that the Peacock Lives long enough to get all of that Done. After all, it is a Massive Undertaking, which very few People in all of History would have Accepted as an Occupation, or Ambition: beCause of the Complications of that Task, which the Normal Person would know nothing about: beCause of having never Written so much as one Book, much less 350+ Books, which Deal with a Wide Range of Interesting Topics, among which are the Most Important Topics of this Inspired Book, which Reveals Guaranteed Solutions for ALL of our Massive Problems, even if those Topics are not Mentioned by Name: beCause the Best Solution for any Problem is Found in the Treasure Chest of the Great King, which is Full of the Beautiful Gems of Provable Truths. {See www.Amazon.com for: **"Thu Nq MAGNUFIID Verzhun uv Thu PROVERBZ uv KING SOLUMUN in Plaan Ingglish!"** (The Understandable Version of the Famous Proverbs of King Solomon in Plain English!) By The Worldwide People's Revolution!® Book 028, which is a Companion Book of: **"ECCLESIASTES UNCOVERED!"** (The New MAGNIFIED Version of Ecclesiastes and the Song of Solomon in Plain English!), Book 034, which is Greatly Enhanced by: **"The New MAGNIFIED Version of The Book of MOORMUN!"** (The Story of the White and Dark Indians in the Americas!), Book 040, which is perhaps the single Best Book in all of the World, and a "Must Read" Book for all People who Profess to be "Educated."}

31-03 [_] O Doctor Samuel Walker Edison, would you be so Kind as to give to us Readers a Guaranteed Solution for getting other People to Read this Inspired Book for themselves, whereby their Minds might be Enlightened? For Example, I have a Naaber, who has never even read the entire *Holy Bible,* one Time, from Cover to Cover, who most Desperately Needs to Read this Inspired Book, just to get a Correct Perspective of that Unholy Mutilated Bible, whereby it might be "red" with an Open Mind. After all, in spite of all of its Faults, there are a LOT of Provable Truths within it, which would be Good for everyone to Learn, no matter what their Religion might be. {See: **"Those Ridiculous Contradictions within the Holy Bible!"** (HOW to Read the *Bible* with an Open Mind!) By The Worldwide People's Revolution!® Book 057.

31-04 [_] Well, my Friend, I am not King Solomon, nor even one of his Near Relatives, you might say, whereby I might have a Guaranteed Solution for that Problem; but, if I were you, I would tell that Naaber that I have Ordered a very Special Gift for him, which should be Coming in the Mail any Day now; and then I would Deliberately Wait for at least 10 more Days, just for him to Work Up an Appetite for it: beCause I would not tell him what the Gift is; but, I would Remind him, now and then, that it is a very Special Gift, which is more Precious than the Best Car in the World: beCause he is also likely to be a Possession Worshiper. Indeed, I would not even Suggest that the Special Gift is a Book of any Kind; but, that it is the Best Gift that anyone could Receive in Evil Times like these; and then keep Mum: beCause he Needs Time to Think about it, and Wonder just what it might be? Yes, the whole Idea is to Work Up his Curiosity for that Special Gift, which you will Do, if you Act Wisely, even as King Solomon might Do; and then have the Book Specially Gift-wrapped in a Big Box for him: so that you can Deliver it to him, yourself, in Person, with a Big Smile on your Face, saying: "I Finally got that Special Gift for you in the Mail!" — at which Time he will be most Curious, and thus Open the Package with Great Anticipation, only to Discover that his Secret Prayers have been Answered in the Form of a Special BOOK, which you have had someone Bind with a Hand-carved Leather Cover, just to make it Extra Special. After all, his Soul is at Stake, and is well Worth the Costs, and he Needs to be Greatly Impressed by it. Moreover, you need to make him Promise to Return it to you, if he does not Love it, which will Encourage him to Read it, Carefully, whereby he will be Inspired to Do Likewise for any of his Unbelieving Friends, Relatives, and Naaberz. Yes, you could even begin your Experiment on the Book Binder, himself, who might Need the Encouragement, and might even See the Vision of Producing hundreds of such Hand-carved Leather-bound Editions, including any number of other Inspired Books by our Selected King — such as **"The New MAGNIFIED Version of the GOOD NEWS According to Saint LUKE!" (The Magnified Gospel of Luke in Plain English!)**, Book 061, which is one of the Best Books ever written, which can be put Together with **"The New MAGNIFIED Version of the GOOD NEWS According to Saint JOHN!" (The Gospel According to Saint John Zebedee Boanerges in Plain English!) By The Worldwide People's Revolution!®** Book 062. Furthermore, if that Book Binder does not know HOW to make such a Good Leather-bound Book, he can Learn how in another Extremely Good Book, called: **"LIGHTNING STRIKES Versus Lightning Bugs!" (HOW you can Become Moderately RICH, without Telling any Lies nor Selling any Trash!) By The Worldwide People's Revolution!®**, Book 074, which has about 60 Beautiful Photographs in it with Explanations.

— Chapter 32 —

— Appendix 1 —

A Guaranteed Solution for Racial Riots!

32-01 [_] This is a Special Chapter for a very Special Subject, which is one of my Favorite Subjects: beCause it has such a Divine Solution, and Reasonable Solution, so as to make it a Comedy in some Ways: beCause only very Ignorant People have any Personal Problem with the Racial Controversies that get other People into a Real Tizzy, and even get Provoked to Great Anger, and sometimes go to WAR over that Issue, when it is one of the most Easy Problems to Solve!

32-02 [_] First of all, before I get around to Revealing the Most Rational Solution for Racial Riots, I want to say that as the Potential Elected King of **"The New RIGHTEOUS One-World Government,"** it is only Appropriate that I should Address this Important Subject, which is not at all very Funny, and especially not to the Victims of Police Brutalities, nor of the Brutalities of "Racists," who are Accused of Thinking that their particular Race is Superior to that of all others, which would be like a Peacock Vainly Imagining that he is Superior to a White Chicken, Black Chicken, Brown Chicken, Speckled Black and White Chicken, or some other Color of Chicken, who is Cocksure that he is "the King of the Mountain," when he is in Fact just another Kind of CHICKEN when he is Stark Naked without any Feathers! Indeed, none of those Chickens of whatever Colors and Kinds have any Marvelous Tale of Provable Truths to Present to the People of the World; but, the Colorful Peacock from Angel Ridge, King's Mountain, Kentucky is Blest with a Marvelous Tale of Truths and Wisdom, for which he could Vainly Imagine that he is Superior to ALL Races of People, and should even be Worshiped by all Chickens of all Colors and Kinds: beCause they have nothing to Compare with his Awesome Tale of Truths and Wisdom. However, it was only by the Grace of God that he was Born to be a Colorful Peacock, instead of just another White Chicken, for which he can only Thank his Great Creator God, and not himself! Indeed, he has no Right to Boast about his own Great Abilities: beCause they are GIFTS from God, which can be Proven in a Courtroom.

32-03 [_] Now, you might not even Believe in any such Great Creator God: beCause of Vainly Imagining that your Father or Mother Created you, or that you Created yourself; but, most People with Rational Minds would quickly Confess that you would only be another Deceived Person with an Atheist Blindfold over your Eyeballs: beCause nothing on the Earth Created itself, nor anyone else. However, if a Person could Manage to Create another Person, it would only be Proof that it would Require a very Intelligent Person to Do that Creating: beCause it is for Certain that no Black Apes have any such Abilities, much less any Black Chickens, who may be Able to Crow about their Great Abilities and Wonderful Accomplishments in Life — such as Building Trump Towers and Washington D.C. Monuments — but, when Compared with the Creations of God, none of those Vain Things are of any Great Importance: beCause the People of the World can Live Happily without any of those Things; but, NOT without AIR, Water, Land, Trees, Fruits, Nuts, Seeds, Flowers, nor a Great Multitude of Animals, all of which are Far more Precious and Admirable than some UGLY Painting of Nothingness, which might Sell for a Million Dollars to some Extremely Ignorant Person; but, God would have no Use for it, nor would he Uglify his Palaces with any such Paintings: beCause any one of his Beautiful Sunrises or Sunsets are Far Greater Masterpieces of Fine Art, which Fill the Sky from Horizon to

Horizon with Great BEAUTY, and sometime with Awesome Dark Rolling Clouds like the People of the World have never Seen before, whereby even the most Proud and Arrogant Chicken would have to Humbly Confess that his Ugly Painting is just TRASH, when Compared with the Glorious Paintings of the Master Farmer in the Sky.

32-04 [_] But, of course, an Atheist could say that it is all just a Natural Wonder, which had nothing to do with any God nor Goddess, as if there were no Lawmaker for all of the Laws, including Natural Laws. Indeed, such an Atheist may Doubt the Existence of a Lawmaker: beCause of not Seeing his Holy Face; but, no Honest Person on this Earth can Doubt the Existence of LAWS — such as the Law of Gravity, which has yet to be Thoroughly Explained, as Wikipedia Confesses: beCause Gravity is still a Mystery! Nevertheless, that Thing that we Call the "Law of Gravity" is for Real, which anyone can Prove by Jumping Off of the Empire State Building in New York City, whereby he or she can Splatter his or her Brains around on the Street below, and thus be Fully Persuaded that Gravity does Exist, and that Something must have Created it, or else it would NOT Exist, even as Someone must have Created the Different Colors of Animals, Plants, and People, who come in a Great and Marvelous Variety, which, all by itself, is a Special Study, for which I have Forgotten the Exact Name — such as Zoology, which you could say is Anthropology — except that Anthropology does not Cover ALL of the Aspects of Human Beings in Relation with their Great Creator God, who is just as much a Part of the Human Spiritual Anatomy as the Brains, themselves, which seem to be Directly or Indirectly Connected with that Great Creator God, as in the Case of me Writing Inspired Books without taking any Thoughts at all for what I am about to Write: beCause, all that I have to Do is to LISTEN to the Holy Spirit as she Speaks to my Mind — or, as some People might say, as she Speaks to my Heart: beCause, almost everyone Knows within his or her Heart that God is as much a Part of the Human Spiritual Anatomy as their own Hearts are a Part of their Blood's Circulatory Systems, which are Extremely Complicated, no matter what the Color nor Texture of one's Skin might be, which can and does Depend on a lot of Different Factors.

32-05 [_] For Example, I have known People of all Colors and Races, who have very Fine Soft Velvety Skin, while other Skins are sometimes very Rough and Leathery, which seemed be far less Romantic, you might say, and even Repulsive in some Cases: beCause of being Diseased, which can Happen among any Race of People of any Colors. Therefore, in my Way of Thinking, it would be of Far more Value to Mankind to be Discussing HOW to Obtain that Velvety Romantic Skin, than to be Discussing the Hatred of Racists, who could easily be Born Again in some very Sick Degenerated Body of a Mongoose, you might say, or of some Stinking Painted SKUNK, who has no Conception of what it might Mean to be Born Again, Spiritually, as Jesus Christ Explained to Nicodemus, which would not make a Person Colorblind by any Means; but, it would make a Person Realize that it is only by the Grace of God that we are not all Lepers! Yes, our Flesh could be Rotting Away with our Bones, and then we might Change our Minds about being of some Superior Race of Ignorant Fools. After all, there IS a Superior Race of People, and they are called the "Holy Ones," who are like Jesus Christ and his Self-disciplined Disciples, who can be of any Color or Kind of People; but, they are Extra Special People, like Enoch, Abraham, Isaac, Jacob, Joseph, Moses, Elijah, Daniel, David, and King Jesus — all of whom are of that Superior Race of WHITE People, who were Created to Govern all of the other Races; but, behold, they Missed their Calling! Indeed, they did not have White Clean HEARTS, nor Minds, whereby they Disqualified themselves to Govern in the Holy Kingdom of All that is GOOD! Therefore, they could become the First to Learn that Great Truth, and the Last to be Qualified for any such Positions: beCause of that Hateful Thing called PRIDE, which has no Place in the Kingdom of the Gods: beCause no Rooster of any Color has a Right to Boast about his own Goodness, which is only a Gift from the Great Creator God.

32-06 [_] Indeed, a certain Black Man might Boast about his Ability to Win the Marathon Race; but, only if he were just another Ignorant Fool: beCause, without the Grace of God, he could not even Walk, much less Run. Therefore, he should be very Thankful to God for whatever Gifts that he is Blest with, even as most Athletes are, and not be Boasting about any of those Gifts, even as any Peacock should also be very Thankful for his Tale of Truths and Wisdom: beCause he did not Bless himself with any such Gifts. In Fact, he would have no Idea HOW to go about Blessing himself with any such Wonderful Gifts, nor could he Care Less about it: beCause he already Knows for a Fact that his Tale of Provable Truths is a GIFT, for which he must be Thankful, or else he will Lose it! Moreover, it is Far more Fantastic than anything that might be Gained by Attending some Public School of Ignorant Fools, whose Students might Hope to get a Good Education without the Blessings of the Great Creator God, which Borders on Total Insanity: because all such Hopes are in VAIN! Indeed, if Almighty GOD cannot Bless us with whatever we Need for True Prosperity, Good Health, and True Happiness, WHO is going to Bless us? Truly, Truly, I say to you, my Friend or Enemy, no Chicken of any Color nor Kind will ever Produce anything as Marvelous as **"An Amazing Collection of Wit and Wisdom!" (The Marvelous Tale of the Colorful Peacock from Angel Ridge, and the Strong Rope of Everlasting Hope!) By The Worldwide People's Revolution!®** Book 048. Yes, you may Strain your Spiritual Muscles all you like, and even tell all of the Lies that you can Think of; but, you will never come up with such an Inspired Book as **that** without the Assistance of some GOD!

32-07 [_] Likewise, Humanity will never Solve the Racist Problems, until the Leaders of the Nations make Honest Confessions, beginning with the Fact that GOD is of that Superior Race of Holy People, who must be Respected and Honored for his Goodness, who did NOT Cause O. J. Simpson to Murder his Wife, Nicole Brown Simpson, nor Ronald Goldman, whereby he Proved that he was of an Inferior Race of People, who Hold World Records for all such Murders, which are going on Daily, in Chicago, Houston, New Orleans, Los Angeles, and wherever in **"The Divided States of United Lies!" (The so-called "United States of North America" in Disguise!)**, Book 058, which is about as United as Iron and Clay, which simply do NOT Mix Together, nor Stick Together, even as much as they might Like to: beCause they have Contrary Natures, which God Knew in the Beginning, which is WHY he Wanted the White People to get RID of ALL of the Black People, whose Spirits would then be Born into White Families. However, the Task was far more than the White People could Handle, whose Consciences were Racked with GUILT for Murdering those Black Babies, which was called Genocide, or the Destruction of a Genetic Race, you might say, or a Race of a certain Gene, which the Creator God of this World wanted to get RID of: beCause those Races came from Alien Transplants from other Worlds from other Solar Systems, which were brought here by Satan, you might say, who Inspired those Aliens to bring them here to make them into their Slaves! Yes, the Aliens were GIANTS, who Wanted X-amount of Slaves to Serve them, which Idea was taken up by the Edomites, who were Descendants of ESAU, the Twin Brother of Jacob, who were Opposites, you might say: beCause Esau was Dark and Hairy all over, while Jacob was White and Smooth-skinned, having Blond Hairs and Blue Eyes, whose Son Dan became the Father of the Danes, who are still Famous for having Beautiful Fair Skins, who are Glorified in Pornography and Sex Movies, and Hailed as "the Most Beautiful People in the World!" Yes, if it were not so, I would not say it; but, it is just a Fact of Life, which should not be Ignored, which Sells 10 to 1 over those Black Porno Movies: beCause, for some Strange Reason, People of all Colors Prefer those Blonds, including yourself, O Lady Doubtfulness: beCause they are more Beautiful in the Eyes of almost all People! Otherwise, why would O. J. have gone Looking for a Blond to Marry? Indeed, why is it that X-amount of Black Men go Looking for those Blonds? Why are they shown in more Advertisements than any other Colors? Why are they Exploited by more Businessmen than any other Colors? Well, it is beCAUSE they are Preferred above the others, and for Reasons that will have to be Explained by those who Exploit them. Nevertheless, the Alien Giants did not Care whether or not their Slaves were White, Brown, Yellow, nor Black: beCause their Interest was in having Slaves, which was also True of the Edomites, who got into the Slave Trading Business during the 1800's: beCause the Edomite Motto is very simple — "If it is Profitable, it is the Right Business." And thus we have X-amount of Rich Edomites, who Basically Control the Markets, and especially the Stock Markets: beCause it is something that they Love: beCause they can quickly get RICH, if they Play their "Cards" Correctly, you might say. Therefore, millions of Black People were made into Slaves of the White People for the Sake of Gain. However, American Slave Trading was done away with by the Great Uncivilized War of the 1860's, whereby some 600,000+ Young Men gave their Lives for nothing: beCause the British People simply Outlawed it, without having any War over it, which was much Wiser, which could have also been Done in **"The Divided States of United Lies!"** Book 058.

32-08 [_] Now, knowing that I have the Potential of becoming the Elected King of **"The New RIGHTEOUS One-World Government,"** it is my DUTY to Address this Important Issue, and Pull no Punches from where they Need to be Delivered — mostly to the Heads of Governments, which still Allow the EVIL Slavery Systems to Continue! Yes, you might Vainly Imagine that all Slavery has been Done Away with by the Proclamation of Emancipation by Abraham Lincoln; but, the Truth is that we now have much more Slavery than ever before, which I have Identified as Education Slavery, Work Slavery, Tax Slavery, Insurance Slavery, Interest or Usury Slavery, Rent Slavery, Food Bills Slavery, ElecTrickery Bills Slavery, Gas Bills Slavery, Water Bills Slavery, Drug Slavery, Childcare Slavery, Retirement Rest Home Slavery, Mortgage Slavery, and many other Kinds of SLAVERY, even as I already Explained in Previous Chapters for your Enlightenment: because it is Possible and much more Practical for the Masses of People to not have ANY Slavery. For Example, just how much Education and how many College Degrees does one Need for Harvesting Fruits from Trees? For Example, one Avocado Tree in Mexico might have a thousand Avocadoes on it, which would be about 4,000-dollars-worth on the American Market, if Shipping were Free. Therefore, a large one-acre Garden with 100 such Avocado Trees would be Worth about 400,000 Dollars, each Year! Therefore, why Waste 4 to 8 Years in some School of Fools, just to Earn an Extremely POOR Living? Indeed, with that Kind of Money, you could Afford to Hire some Mexicans with Good Wages to Harvest all of the Fruits for you, and Pack them in Boxes to Ship to Europe, and still Earn at least 100,000$ per Year, which should easily Cover the Costs of Planting another Acre for each of your Healthy Happy Children — that is, IF you had a Good Water Supply, which would Require no less than 20 large Swanky Cisterns per Acre of Gardens: because the Rain is not Reliable the Year around in Mexico. Therefore, you would Need the Assistance of **"The New RIGHTEOUS One-World Government,"** which would Hire **"Seven Great Armies of Working Soldiers"** to Help you to Build those large Swanky Cisterns, whereby you could have a Reliable Source of Fresh Clean Living Water, even if your Skin is as Black as Coal: beCause Water does not Care what Color your Skin is: beCause it is not Prejudiced, like People, some of whom would not Want other People to Prosper, as the Water might, and as God might — that is, IF he is Truly the God of LOVE, which Jehovah God is supposed to be, even though you might find it Difficult to Prove that, after Studying the Million or more Babies who Die from Malaria each Year in his World of Woes. Nevertheless, let us not let that Stop us from Practicing some LOVE: beCause it can easily be Proven to be a GOOD Thing, while Hate can easily be Proven to be a BAD Thing — that is, unless one is Hating ALL that is EVIL — such as Slavery.

32-09 [_] Yes, you might find it Difficult to Believe that People could be so STUPID as to make themselves into SLAVES, just to Live, when it is quite Possible and most Practical to have NO Slaves at all! Indeed, a Slave is someone who is Forced to Say and/or Do something that he or she does not Want to Say and/or Do, as I already Explained in a Previous Chapter, which you have had Plenty of Time to Meditate on. Therefore, to be Perfectly Honest about it all, most Americans are SLAVES of one Kind or the other; but, most likely of many Kinds, even as I have Listed above: beCause, the Economic System is Arranged that Way by those Edomites, who are still making Slaves of People. For

Example, if a Normal American Slave wants to have a House to Live in — as opposed to Living in some Junked Van down by the River of Filthiness with Chris Farley, Poor Huck Finn and Nigger Jim — that Slave must Bow Down to some Banker, and Borrow some Money for Buying or Building that House, whereby he will make him into an Interest or Usury Slave for the next 30 to 40 Years, or more: because there is no Righteous One-World Government to Assist him Properly. Meanwhile, that Slave is Assured that he is Living in "the Best Nation in the World," without Realizing that ALL Nations, with the Exception of only a few, are Under the Dominion of those Slave Masters, whose Economic System is Based on GREED, Selfishness, Lusts, and all such EVIL Things, which is otherwise Identified as CAPITALISM, which is the Love of Money in Action!

32-10 [_] Now, you could easily become Defensive of that EVIL Economic System, and say that it is the Best Economic System in the World: beCause it has Produced more Rich People than any other System, which is True! Indeed, no one is Disputing that Fact of Life, except ME! Yes, I have a Completely Different Interpretation of what it Means to be "RICH," which is also God's Interpretation: because it is the only RIGHT or CORRECT Interpretation at the Core of it, which Begins with Fresh Clean Air, which NONE of the Capitalists have: beCause they are Actually Extremely POOR Wretched Miserable People, and do not even Realize it, even as Jesus Christ pointed out in *the Book of Revelation,* which you should read for yourself some Evening: beCause it only Requires 2 Hours to Read it. However, it Requires a Lifetime of Study to Fully Understand it, while most of my Inspired Books can be Understood with just 2 or 3 Readings of each Book: beCause all of the Truths are MAGNIFIED by the other Books, whereby even 12-year-old Children can easily Understand them.

32-11 [_] For Example, why should White Chickens be Picking and Pecking on Black Chickens, just beCause they Look Different, when it is Possible for the Spirits of White Chickens to be Born in the Bodies of Black Chickens the next Time Around, just to Teach to them the Evilness of Racial Hatred, which is Unjustifiable Hatred: beCause there are Good People and Bad People among all Colors and Races and Nations of Peoples. Indeed, O. J. Simpleton is just one Example of a BAD Person in a Black Body, while Jeffrey Dahmer is an Example of a Perverted White Man, who Cannibalized Gay Young Men to Fulfill his Sexual Lusts, which should have been Fulfilled by Marrying some Gay Young Man, rather than Denying that he was GAY. Indeed, there have been hundreds of Priests, who have also Denied their Gayness, who have Committed Various Evils against Altar Boys and other Priests, who should have been Married, either to Wombmen or to other Gay Men, rather than SIN: beCause there is no Law of God that Forbids Men to Marry other Men: beCause Jesus was Married to John, even as David was Married to Jonathan, Spiritually, which King David commented on, saying that no Woman ever Loved him as much as Jonathan did, and he had 6 Wives. (See *Second Samuel 1:26, KJV.*) Therefore, it is Possible for Men to be more in Love with Men, than with Women, which is not an Evil Thing; but, it is an Evil Thing for People to go about Murdering other People for their Beliefs, as might have been the Case in Charlottesville, Virginia, whereby James Alex Fields Deliberately Rammed his Speeding Car into a Crowd of Anti-Protesters, whereby many were Injured and one Heather was Killed, which was an Act of MURDER, which no one with a Right Mind could Justify by any Means: beCause Murder is Murder, no matter HOW one goes about Doing it — Directly or Indirectly — which may not have been the Intention of Alex to Kill anyone; but, he should have known that an Automobile is a DEADLY Weapon, and in more Ways than one, which also makes many so-called "Innocent" Americans Guilty of MURDER: beCause they are Contributing to the Death of the Good Earth, you might say, just by Contributing to Unnecessary Climate Changes, which could Unintentionally Kill BILLIONS of People with Radical Weather Changes, Earthquakes, Erupting Volcanoes, Violent Storms, Floods, Fires, Tsunamis, Tornadoes, Hurricanes, and whatever might Result from Violating the Natural Laws that Govern this World. Yes, it is a Serious Accusation, which is Directed at the Drivers of all such Vehicles, who should Change their Thinking, and DEMAND **"The Great Worldwide**

TELEVISED Court HEARING," whereby we, the People, might Learn about those **"GLORIOUS Swanky Hotels Castles and Fortresses,"** which will Solve that Massive Problem when we Build them and Move into them; and, the sooner, the Better. Guaranteed!

32-12 [_] Likewise, many other Problems will be Solved at the same Time, including the Racial Riots: beCause the Black People will have their own Beautiful Planned City States to Govern, according to their own Religious and Political Viewpoints, whereby they will only have themselves to Blame for whatever goes WRong. Indeed, if they are Wise, they will Ask for Assistance concerning those Things that they do not Know HOW to Solve, which Means that they will Ask for the Assistance of **"The New RIGHTEOUS One-World Government,"** which will have the Most Intelligent and Wel-Ejukaatid Miindz to Help us to Build the Cities, Plant the Gardens, and Learn Good Social Habits — one of which is HOW to get Along Well with other People of Like-mindedness, just by Checking the Appropriate Boxes in **"The Complete SURVEYS of our VALUES!" (SURVEYS of Religious Spiritual Political Governmental Economic Business Labor Habitual and Miscellaneous VALUES!) By The Worldwide People's Revolution!®** Book 059. Yes, it is now Possible and most Practical to SEPARATE the Good Black People from the Bad Black People, and the Good White People from the Bad White People, just by Checking the Appropriate Boxes [_], which you should now Check, if you Agree with me!

32-13 [_] O Elected King, I Agree with *that* Part of your Master Plan; but, I do not Agree with all of your Religious Doctrines — such as God Commanding the Children of Israel to Murder all of the Black People in the World, which would be Genocide, which would be an EVIL Thing, which the God of LOVE would never Require of his Chosen People. {Please Check the above Box, if you Agree with that Statement. Thank you.}

32-14 [_] Well, Yohoovu God Wanted to make this a Good World for People to Live in, which Needed Cleaning Up; but, he did not Realize what Bad Reactions would Result from that Plan, which seemed to be Reasonable to him at that Time: beCause the whole Earth had become Corrupted by Satan, who had Persuaded the Masses of People to make and Worship Idols, as if they were Gods. In Fact, they Thought of their Idols as being Gods, which we Know for a Fact is Historical: beCause many of those Granite Egyptian Idols are in the National Museum of History in London, England, where any Visitors can see them: because it is no Secret; nor is it any Secret that People are still Worshiping Idols — such as their TV Idols, whom they call "Stars," who do not always Shine so Brightly after the third, fourth, and fifth Divorces, which is Proof that none of them Filled Out their SURVEYS of VALUES before getting Married, whereby they might have Found Like-minded Marriage Partners. Nevertheless, not many Israelites were at all Interested in Slaughtering Black Children, just to Clean Up the Earth, which God could have done with a Great Plague, if he had Wanted to; but, it was his Intention to Test the Spirits of the People, in Order to Discover whether or not they would OBEY him, who came up with a Different Tactic by the Time of Christ, who also Demanded that Obedience, saying: *"If you Love me, Keep my Commandments,"* which, of course, only a few People ever did; and therefore, only those People will have any Right to Govern this World with Christ, when he Establishes his Righteous One-World Government, and they may be of any Color or Kind of Holy People, only.

32-15 [_] O Selected King, the Genocidal Hebrew God has no Appeal to me; but, his Character seems to Fit right in with the Edomite Plan, which makes me Think that maybe the Edomites Invented that God, themselves, just to have some Godly Authority behind their Evil Deeds. After all, when any Nation has the Approval of God, or Allah, they can get by with Murder in his Name, which makes it GOOD in their Minds: beCause God Approves of it, as was the Case in Iraq, when God Ordered George Warmonger Bush, Incorporated, to Attack Iraq, which Caused George to be Blest for his

Obedience: because God wanted to Clean Up that Part of the World, which had a Statue of Saddam Insane Hussein, which was Torn Down for the Glory of Jehovah God, who much Prefers the Statue of Thomas Jefferson, who was a Major Slave Owner, who always Regretted that he did not have 10 Times as many Slaves, whereby he might not have Died in Extreme Poverty — not to Mention the Extreme Poverty of all of his Slaves, who also Needed at least 100 Slaves, each, in order to make them Moderately Rich, without Telling any Lies, nor Selling any Trash! After all, Jehovah God only wanted a few People to be Rich, and all of them Needed Slaves to make that Possible: beCause God could not figure out HOW to make Mechanical Slaves — such as those Bulldozers and Electric Trains, which might do the Work of a thousand or even a million Strong Young Men, Cheerfully: beCause they never get Tired. Indeed, God could have Explained all of that to Moses, when he went up on Mount Horrible to get those 1,001 Commandments about the Construction of the Tabersnackle and Related Things that filled up much of the *Holy Bible,* which most certainly needed several more Books, just to Explain HOW White People should get along with Black People, without making Slaves of them. §§‡

32-16 [_] Well, my Friend, there might have been a Time during Ancient History, when Slaves were Needed, just to Drive the Mules; but, now we have Mechanical Slaves, which only need Operators, who could Work for 4 Hours per Workday, and have the Remainder of the Day Off. Otherwise, they could Work this Week, and have next Week Off; or, they could Work for one Day, and have the next Day Off, whereby none of them could Complain about being too Tired to Do a Good Job of whatever they might be Doing: beCause they could all get Plenty of SLEEP! However, if they Acted like most Military Soldiers, they would be Drinking all Night, and Playing Video Games, rather than Sleeping for 8 Hours. So, they might need some Good Masters, just to Order them to go to Bed on Time, whereby they might get the Proper Amount of Sleep, and thus do Better Work.

32-17 [_] O Elected King, I am Greatly Concerned over Radical Americans tearing down the Statues of General Robert E. Lee, who was one of the most Righteous Men of his Time, who Wanted to Settle the Slavery Issue in the Congress, even as the British People had done in the Parliament, even if they needed to Add an Amendment to the Constitution, which would have been an Extremely Easy Thing to Do, when Compared with going to War; but, Abraham Lincoln did not Want that to Happen, nor did other Republicans: beCause they were Collecting Taxes from Rich Plantation Owners. In Fact, about 80% of all Federal Taxes at that Time came from the SOUTH, which was Envied by the North. (See: **"The South was Right!" by Donald Kennedy**.) Therefore, if that Slavery Issue had been taken up by the Congresses, the South would have Won: beCause it had the Majority Vote, whereby Slavery would have been Outlawed: beCause it was the North that Wanted Slavery — not the South! Indeed, Robert E. Lee was against Slavery, himself, and so was Jefferson Davis, both of whom Believed in Voluntary Servitude; but, not in Slavery: beCause Slavery was not *Biblical,* while Voluntary Servitude was, and still is: beCause X-amount of People would have no Idea what to Do without the Assistance of a Master. In Fact, tens of thousands of Black People stayed with their Masters after the Civil War: because they Preferred to have Good Masters, who had enough Money to Help them to be Useful Servants. For Example, if they Forsook their Masters, they were given a Mule and 40 Acres, without any Tools to Work with, including Harnesses for their Mules! So, what were they supposed to Do with their Mules and Lands, whereby they might Earn their Livings? Well, most of them Starved Out: because of Bad Weather, Crop Failures, Wild Varmints Eating their Crops, or whatever: because, in the Natural World, almost everything is against the Independent Jackass Lifestyle. Therefore, most of the Black People Sold their Mules and Lands, and moved into Cities of Confusion, where they went to Work for White Slave Masters, who called themselves Businessmen, who sometimes Treated their New Slaves with more Meanness than they used to be Mistreated! Yes, Herriot Beecher Stowe should have written another *Uncle Tom's Cabin,* telling about the Millions of Poor Black People who Suffered in American Prisons, after being Liberated by Abe Lincoln, who had Plans for Sending all of those

Black People back to Africa, whereby they might Build their own Cities of Confusion, and make Slaves of each other, if they Wanted to; but, behold, he got Killed by an Edomite, who Wanted to Maintain the Slavery System, even as those Edomite Bankers still Want their Interest Slaves to Pay them no less than 2 Trillion Dollars per Year for Interest on their Loans! Indeed, if you had a Profitable Business like that, would you Want to Surrender it to the God of *"Love your Naaber as yourself"?* God Forbid! You would just Naturally Want MORE Interest Slaves. Therefore, you would Invent an Evil Thing called INSURANCE, which might Cover Needless House Fires, Needless Car Accidents, and other Needless Accidents: beCause Insurance is BIG Business. Yes, the Edomite Masters are in the Insurance Business, whereby they Rake in no less than 3 Trillion Dollars per Year, just for Shuffling some Papers around, when no Insurance is Needed: beCause no Cars are Needed for True Prosperity: beCause it is Possible and far more Practical to use Elevators, Escalators, and Electric Subway Trains in Beautiful Planned City States, which are Designed for LIVING, and without Producing any Trash: beCause no such Trash is Needed — except that it Provides a Way for the Edomites to Collect more Taxes! Therefore, Cancer-causing Tobacco Products are still Legal: beCause they are Sanctified by the Good Drug and Bad Foods Administration, which is a Weird Branch of the Bureau of Alcoholics and Firearms Fanatics, which Works Hand-in-Hand with the DEPART-ment of Chemical Agriculture, which is another Edomite Industry: beCause there is Big Money in all such Industries; but, especially in the Military Industries, which are Chief Edomite Businesses, which Rake in no less than 2 Trillion Dollars per Year, or about half as much as the Drug Industry, whose Managers are also EDOMITES! Yes, they Understand MONEY, which is WHY they are also the Chief Managers of the News Media, Newspapers, Book Publishing Companies, Hollywood Productions, and anything that has Big Money in it — such as the Gas and Oil Industries. Yes, you might have Heard of John Davison Rockefeller, who Founded the Standard Oil Company in 1870, and by 1880, he had a Total Monopoly over the Oil Industry in **"The Divided States of United Lies!"** Yes, he Covered his Satanic Tracks by Philanthropic Good Deeds — such as the Construction of Rockefeller Center in New Yuck City during the 1930's, when one-third of the Nation was Unemployed: beCause his Cousins — those Edomite Banksters on Wall Street — got the Nation into what they called the Great Depression, which was Explained by Benjamin Freedman, whereby they Stole Trillions of Dollars-worth of Property, including Farms, Houses, Tractors, Trucks, Cars, Furniture, and whatever they could get their Greedy Hands on, including the National Treasury! Yes, they even got Uncle Sam to feel Sorry for them in 2009, when President Barrack Hussein Obama persuaded the Federal Government to Bail Out those Poor Edomite Bankers, who had Gained no less than 2 Trillion Dollars on the War in Iraq, by Loaning Money to the Poor Federal Government, which was only 10 Trillion Dollars in Debt to those Edomite Bankers, which ran Up the Debt to 20 Trillion Dollars by 2016, which is Exactly what those Edomites Wanted: beCause, come Hell or High Water, the American Tax Slaves will have to PAY OFF that National Debt, little by little, whereby those Poor Edomites will Gain another 40 Trillion Dollars in INTEREST on their Loans: beCause they are "the Good People!" Yes, they are the People for whom we are supposed to Feel Sorry: beCause they Suffered in the HoloCO$T for Committing similar Financial Crimes in Germany and in other Nations in Europe: beCause it is a very GOOD Thing that the Masses of People should be made into Interest Slaves of those Friendly Edomites, who have Money to Loan. Yes, it Reminds me of a Sign above a Pond Shop in Danville, Kentucky, which reads: Fox and Crow — Money to Loan! Indeed, if the Fox did not Manage to Steal it from you, the Crow would figure out how to Talk you Out of it, and make you Feel Happy for making him Richer! And that is just the Way it is in **"The Divided States of United Lies,"** O Elected King. Nevertheless, in Germany — which is Famous for having the Hardest Working People in the World, and the most Skilled Craftsmen in the World — there arose a very Wicked, WICKED Person by the Name of Adolf Rubinstein Hitler, who was an Honest White Jew, of the same Foul Breed as Jesus Christ and his Hateful Disciples, whom the Ancient Jews sought to Murder for Centuries: beCause they were the BAD Guys, who called themselves "Christians," who Believed in having all Things in Common among them, which was a Sin against Capitalism, which Offended the Edomites, who sent Saint Saul out to Gather them up and get RID of them by Genocide! Yes, he was Determined to SLAY as many Christians as he might Find — that is, until that Wicked Jesus Christ met him, in Person, on the Road to Damascus, in Syria, who had been Found Guilty of Treason and Blasphemy in the Jewish Court of Pontius Pilate, who had him Crucified for his Crimes by Way of Democracy! Yes, the Masses of People screamed out, *"CRUCIFY HIM! CRUCIFY HIM!!"* And Saint Saul went along with that Plan: beCause the Prevailing Propagandists at that Time were those Lying Edomites, whom Adolf Hitler Rediscovered in Germany during the 1920's, whereby he ran for the Presidency of Germany, in 1933, and Won by a Landslide: beCause those Germans were Smart Enough to Realize what he was Teaching, whereby they Joined Forces with him, and were thus Determined to put those Edomites Out of Business by Rounding them up, and sending them to Concentration Work Camps, whereby they might Repay some of that Interest Money to the Former German Interest Slaves, who had made them RICH. Yes, they made Slaves of them in those Work Camps: beCause they Adopted an Old Edomite Proverb, which says: *"An Eye for an Eye, and a Tooth for a Tooth,"* which was really not a very Good Idea: beCause it Blinded all of them, Spiritually, which Proved to be a very Bad Thing. Nevertheless, as I was saying, the Tables got Turned Over by Adolf and his Nazi Rebels, who got Total Control over Germany, and made it into the most Powerful War Machine that has ever been known to Mankind, whereby it Required the entire Communist and Capitalist Worlds to Defeat them! Yes, it was a Case of no less than a Billion Communists and Capitalists being put to Open Shame by only 80 Million Determined People, who had **"The Swanky Sword of Divine Truths"** on their Side of that Issue, as Benjamin Freedman Explained, who was another Honest White Jew of the Tribes of Judah and Benjamin, whom the Anti-Neo-Nazi Propagandists call a Radical Derailed Jew, who Saw the Light, as Hank Williams might say, who Published a YouTube Video, which went Viral around the World, which Exposed the Cover-up. Yes, it was American and British Airplanes that BOMBED the Nazi Railroads during the End of World War 2, about 6 Months before the End, whereby the Food Supplies were CUT OFF from the Nazi Concentration Camps, whereby thousands of them Starved to Death — Thanks to the GOOD Guys, who did not give a Damn how many People Died from it: beCause they Knew for a Fact that they would Win the War, and thus be Able to Blame those Wicked Nazis for the Starving Jews and other Prisoners in the Concentration Camps, who were never even Told that it was Americans and Brits who Bombed the Railroad Tracks and Bridges, whereby they were Starved to Death. However, not all of them did Starve to Death: beCause they Lived to Tell about the HORRORS of those Concentration Camps, and even wrote thousands of Fictitious Books about those Horrors, and made up thousands of False Stories: beCause they were the GOOD People, who have a History of Biblical Lies, who do not Object to Exaggerating anything for the Sake of GAIN! Yes, they have Sold upwards of 2 Trillion-dollars-worth of Anti-Nazi Propaganda Books, Videos, Movies, and HoloHOAX Museum FABLES — none of which is Hidden from the Public with any Shame: beCause it is all Based on Donald Trumpeter-type FACTS, which are all Believable Facts — such as 4 or 5 Bodies being Stuffed into one Nazi Crematory Oven, and being Flash Cremated every 10 Minutes! Yes, the American Tax Slaves just stand there in the HoloHOAX Museum with their Mouths hanging open, in Amazement that any People could Act so MEAN as those Nazis, who had gotten the German People OUT of the Great Depression within 6 Months, whereby Germany was the Economic Powerhouse of the Whole World by 1936, which Caused those Brits and Americans to ENVY them! Yes, Americans were still in the Great Depression, until the Edomites got them into World War 2, in 1941: beCause the Germans had Attacked the Lusitania, which had a million Tons of Ammunition and Bombs, which were Falsely Labeled as Butter, Cheese and Jelly Beans, which gave **"The Divided States of United Lies"** the Right to Attack the Germans, who were the BAD Guys, who were Attempting to get RID of those Greedy Edomites. Therefore, the Edomite Leadership in Washington was not at all Afraid nor Ashamed to Sacrifice X-amount of Young Americans to SAVE the Union! Indeed, it was a Noble Thing for them to give their Lives to Save those Edomites from the Concentration Camps; but, did Americans Invite any of them to come to America before the War, whereby they might Bless America, even as they had Blest Europe? NO! In Fact, an entire Shipload of them sailed the High Seas to get here, and were Turned Away by Immigration Officials, who Hated the Smell of their Bloody Underwear, and did not Wish to become their Usury Slaves, nor their Insurance Slaves, nor their Drug Slaves — even though it was well known that Americans were already becoming Addicted to DRUGS, which is the Favorite Industry of those Lovable Edomites, who Gain no less than 4 Trillion Dollars per YEAR from those Enlightened Americans, who Sincerely Believe that God Created Drugs for Healing People, even though the Edomites give no Credit to God at all: beCause they Know for a Fact that THEY are the Inventors of no less than 3,000 New Drugs, each Year! Yes, with such Blessings as that, Americans might become so Drugged as to not even Understand that Adolf was the GOOD Guy, who never even Smoked a Cigarette during his entire Life! Yes, Adolf was the Righteous Man among the Leaders of the World at that Time, who Suffered 5 Assassination Attempts, and Survived all of them without a Scratch: beCause God was on his Side! Yes, he even Escaped to Argentina, and Lived to be 107 Years Old! But, most People would not know that: because they do not Study the Information of the Internet, which is a Reliable Source of Rich Information, if anyone is Curious enough to Look into it. Nevertheless, as I was saying, O Elected King, Robert E. Lee was the GOOD Guy, who Wanted to bring the Slavery Issue into the Highest Courtroom in the Land, and get it Settled in the Supreme Court, itself, which could have easily Decided that the South was WRONG about Freeing the Slaves, and giving to them the Opportunity to Voluntarily make themselves into Humble Obedient Servants of whomever they Chose: beCause that would be too Profitable for those Masters, who were already Rich. Indeed, let us say that YOU were such a Black Person, who was Extremely Poor, who had no Money, no House, no Tools, no Land, and nothing to Work with — would you not much Prefer to Voluntarily Join Hands with 100 other Volunteers, who would Cheerfully OBEY a Good Master, like Jesus Christ and his Disciples, who might have lots of Money to Work with, who would be Happy to Pay you Good Wages for your Services, who could Help you to Build Mansions and **"Beautiful Swanky PALACES"** for yourselves, rather than figure out what you are going to Do with that Poor Worn-out Toothless Mule and 40 Acres of Swamp Land in Georgia? Truly, Truly, I say to thee, O Peacockery, would ye not rather be the Humble and Obedient Servant of a Rich Man, who Provides all that you Need and Want to become Moderately Rich, yourself, rather than be a Poor Miserable Independent Jackass for your entire Life, with only a Vain HOPE of Catching that Cob of Corn that Tom Sawyer is Dangling from the Chicken House Roof on the End of his Fishing Line, while you Run Around and Around in Endless Circles as a SLAVE of the Evil Edomite Empire? §§‡

32-18 [_] Well, my Friend, I have no Idea what Kind of Exotic Drugs that you have been Consuming; but, it might be a Good Idea to Trash them, and take up the Book of Reason and Logic. After all, if Adolf Hitler was such a BAD Guy, is it Reasonable to Think that he would still have Millions of Undercover Neo-Nazis Hot on his Trail? Could all of those Young People be WRong about Fascism, which Teaches that the White Race is Superior to the Black and Brown Races? After all, if the Black and Brown Races are Superior to the White, Light and Blond Races, why is it that White People are a thousand Times more Prosperous than Black People, with the Exception of Oprah Winfrey and J. Tuttle Walfendorf, both of whom are partly White? Indeed, do you Think that President Obama would have Won the Election Deception, if his Mother had not been half Jewish? Therefore, there must be something in the Blood of Jews, which makes them Superior to Non-Jews, which might Explain WHY Jews Control 95% of the Wealth in the whole World! But, do not let it Upset you by any Means: because it is still Illegal to Post a Nazi Swastika anywhere in Germany: beCause the Anti-Nazis WON the War, and Reestablished the Edomites, who have once again gotten Total Control of the Great False Economy, which is Based on the Production and Sales of Capitalist TRASH, which you LOVE! Indeed, if you did not Love it, WHY would you still be Buying it? After all, you could be Living in one of those **"Beautiful Swanky PALACES!" (A New Concept in Living Habits — Swanky Palaces** for Poor People!) By The Worldwide People's Revolution!® Book 066. Yes, you could be Wining and Dining at ROYAL Swanky Buffets, while Breathing Clean Crisp Fresh Air, and Drinking Pure Living Water from the Sweet Juicy Fruits from the Trees of Life: beCause of Living in **"The Environmentalists' Paradise!" (HOW almost Everyone could be Living in a Beautiful Manmade Paradise!)**, Book 035; but, you would rather Drive some Stinking Noisy Greasy Polluting Car into a Financial Traffic Jam, whereby you are Stuck in the Tar Pits of Extreme Poverty, rather than Change your Mind about RACISM! Indeed, I am of that Superior Race of HOLY People, you might say, who would make Life very Good for ALL Peoples, if I were in Charge of this World of Woes; but, you would Prefer to Vote for some Powerless President, rather than Vote for a RIGHTEOUS KING! §§‡ {See www.Amazon.com for: **"Are Americans the Most STUPID People who ever Lived?" (HOW Working People can PROSPER and Live in PEACE Under the Rulership of a RIGHTEOUS KING!) By The Worldwide People's Revolution!® Book 047.**}

32-19 [_] O Unelected King, that above Speech really Upset the Belly of my Mind, whereby I now have Chronic Spiritual Indigestion: beCause I have no Idea what to Think. Indeed, if Adolf Hitler was the GOOD Guy, WHY did he not Win World War 2? Was God not on the Right Side of History?

32-20 [_] Well, my Poor Deceived Friend, I See that you have Believed another Edomite Non-Biblical LIE, whereby you Vainly Imagine that God is on the Right Side of every Issue, when there is Zero Truth in it: beCause SATAN is in Control of this World, which you can Discover by Reading that *Holy Bible!* Yes, he Offered all of the Kingdoms of the World to Jesus, if only he would Bow Down and Worship him; but, Jesus Refused, telling him to get Behind him. (See *Matthew 4, KJV.*)

32-21 [_] So, O Elected King, was God not Able to Intervene in the Affairs of Men, and Cause Adolf Hitler and his Nazi Thugs to Win World War 2? §

32-22 [_] Well, of course, God was Able to Intervene; but, he was not Willing to Intervene: beCause he Wanted Rebellious People to Discover the EVILS of Capitalism, Socialism, Fascism, and Communism — all of which have their Weaknesses and Major SINS — such as that Evil Stock Market, which makes it Possible to Sell Addictive Things like Cokes, Candies, Cigarettes, Cookies, Cakes, and other Tooth-rotting Addictive Things, which you can See for Sale at Super Smallmart Stores. However, if you have now Learned your Lessons, and are Ready to Conform to Truths and WISDOM, you should DEMAND **"The Great Worldwide TELEVISED Court HEARING!" (That Great Meeting of the Most Intelligent and Wel-Ejukaatid Miindz!) By The Worldwide People's Revolution!®** Book 041, whereby you might Discover the WHOLE Truth about ALL Important Subjects, including what Happened on the Moon, and just how GAY was J. Edgar Whoever? Indeed, there are a Million or more Questions that Need to be Answered, which are not going to be Answered by CNN Talk Shows, nor by C-SPAN Deceptions: beCause none of them are the Slightest Bit Interested in the Whole Truth: beCause the Whole Truth would put ALL of them OUT of Business! However, if you Doubt it, just Carefully Read: **"The Washington Journal is a FARCE!" (C-SPAN Managers are not very WISE!) By The Worldwide People's Revolution!®** Book 006, which I might have to Update to Book 081, or 091, or who knows what, now that I have Discovered that my Books are not being Totally Updated by CreateSpace for more Truths, which would not Allow me to Change them, Properly. Indeed, the Contents have to Agree with the Information on the Cover, and that Information cannot be Changed, they say. Therefore, I am Forced to Rewrite all of the first 50 Books by Master Mark Revolutionary Twain, Junior! And that Means that I have to come up with New Titles and New Contents: beCause the Contents of the First and Original Books are Copyrighted under the other Pen Name, which makes it all very Tricky, huh? Chances are that it will all Work out for my Benefit in the End.

32-23 [_] O Selected King, when you become the Elected King of **"The New RIGHTEOUS One-World Government,"** you will be able to get CreateSpace for more Truths Corrected; and therefore, that is no Big Problem. Meanwhile, the Race Riots will Continue as usual: beCause, WHO is going to Introduce a Bill into Congress to Build those **"GLORIOUS Swanky Hotels Castles and Fortresses,"** whereby all of the Races can be Separated, if they Want to be, whereby those White Supremacists can have what they Want, which is Freedom to Govern themselves as they Please? Indeed, the Black People will also be Able to Do the same Thing, and thus have Peace among themselves, if that is Possible. Perhaps they will have to Divide themselves into 10,000 Religious Sects, if they do not Discover what the Whole Truth is at that Great Meeting of the Most Intelligent Minds, which is Okay with me: because I am almost Fully Persuaded that ALL of those Religions are WRong. ‡

32-24 [_] Well, my Friend, you can well Believe that they are ALL WRong, which is WHY none of them are Interested in Demanding **"The Great Worldwide TELEVISED Court HEARING!"** Indeed, they are all Spiritual COWARDS, who are Afraid that they might be Proven to be WRong about something, while I have no Objection to that Idea at all. In Fact, I Wish to God that Nolijuboul People could go through all of my Books and get the so-called "Facts" EXACT: beCause I am Sure that there are many Mistakes among those so-called "Facts." For Example, in Verse 32-17, you can Discover many Sarcastic Contradictions — such as 22 Million Russian Communists Dying for the Cause of Saving Communism from Fascism, while Capitalist America and Canada only Lost 2 Million Young Men: beCause they stayed Out of the War, until it was Safe to Sacrifice 600,000 Soldiers on the Beaches in Normandy, while the Germans only Lost a Total 229 Men during that Invasion, which was Reported in all American Newspapers from Coast to Coast: beCause the Edomites wanted Americans to Know that it was well Worth the Sacrifice to Defeat those WICKED, Wicked Nazis, who were the BAD Guys, who were Attempting to get RID of Edomite Slavery! Yes, it will no doubt be a Justified Cause for Fighting another World War, whereby I can be Blamed for it, in spite of BEGGING you People to DEMAND that Great Meeting of the Most Intelligent and Well-Educated Minds, whereby we might Discover WHO the Real Criminals ARE! Indeed, if I am the Chief Criminal, then you are Welcome to Crucify me with Christ; but, if I am the Honest Seeker of the Whole Truth, then it should be Proven in a COURTROOM! And all of the Righteous People will say a Hearty, AMEN! [_] ‡

32-25 [_] O Selected King, are you not Aware that you have Offended the Low Court of Supreme Injustices, themselves, just by Writing your Inflammatory Book, called: **"The Low Court of Supreme Injustices is Brought to Trial!" (Our Selected King Butts Heads with the United States Supreme Court, with or without their Black Robes of Hypocrisies and Lies!) By The Worldwide People's Revolution!® Book 011?**

32-26 [_] Well, my Friend, if Chief Justice John Roberts is a Man of Integrity, he will Order me into his Courtroom on Account of TREASON: beCause of Betraying the Edomites, whose entire Evil Empire is Built on the False Doctrines of the Possession Worshipers, who Vainly Imagine that if a Man is not a Possession Worshiper, he must be an Anti-American, when a True American is one who Loves the Whole Truth about all Important Subjects, including the Truths about the HoloHOAX, the Fake Moon Landings, the Oklahoma City Bombing Cover-up, and the September 11th, 2001, Covered-up Federal False Flag Operation, which Offended at least 3,000 of us Architects and Engineers, who Know for a FACT that Steel and Concrete Structures — such as World Trade Center Tower 7 — do not just come Crashing Down in less than 7 Seconds, in Unison, by the Magic Remote Wand of Osama bin Laden: beCause all such Implosions Require EXPLOSIVES! And WHO Set Up those Explosives? Well, that is what the Investigators Failed to Discover: beCause they did not even Investigate for any Explosives: beCause they say that they just Assumed that there were NO Explosives: beCause it was Self-evident that the 2 Hijacked Airplanes brought down all 3 Towers, and most of the Central Part of

Tower 6, which had much MELTED STEEL at the Base of it: beCause, when such a Tall Tower is Collapsing, as in the Cases of Towers 1 and 2, they just Naturally HEAT UP to 4000 °F on the way down — that is, the HARDENED STEEL Heats Up to that Extremely HIGH Temperature: beCAUSE of Rubbing Noses with Osama bin Laden and Larry Silverstein on the way by, both of whom had nothing to do with the Collapsed World Trade Center Towers: beCause both of them Denied it, even as Lee Harvey Oswald Denied Killing President Kennedy: beCause, he was just a Patsy, even as he Stated, which can be Proven in that Courtroom, which has already been Proven in the Courtroom of Public Opinions. However, it would still be Interesting to bring them to COURT, just to Prove it, which God Intends to Do during his Judgment Day, if the *Holy Bible* is Correct, upon which Presidents and other Elected Officials, including John Roberts, were and are still being Sworn into their Offices around the World, who have Faith in that Great Judgment Day, whereby at least some People might get some Justice — that is, if God can find Time to Hold all such Trials for tens of Billions of People, at which Time *"... all of the Good Books shall be Opened, and the Dead People shall be Judged According to those Things that are Written." — Revelation something.* §§‡

32-27 [_] O Elected King, I have a Guaranteed Solution for no more Crimes to be Committed at Protest Rallies — such as the Rally in Charlottesville, Virginia. Indeed, if the Anti-Nazi and Anti-White Supremacist Protesters had simply Done what Jesus Christ would have Done, and stayed at Home during August 11th, 2017, or gone to Church with Ellen G. White, or gone to the Synagogue with Rabbi Alabaster Corndodger Cohen, there would not have been any Political Clashes between those 2 Groups, much less any Physical Confrontations. After all, if People have Different Political and Religious Beliefs, it is Best to just leave them alone, and let them Suffer in their States of Ignorance, rather than Attempt to Convert them to Strange Doctrines of the Devil, which they could never Accept with Good Consciences: beCause they are Fully Persuaded that they have Heard all of the Evidences that Prove their Beliefs to be True, Pure, Godly, and Reasonable to any Sound-minded Person. Indeed, the Correct Place to take up any such Arguments and Contentions is in a Courtroom — as in the Case of the Scopes Monkey Trial, starring William Jennings Bryan and John Thomas Scopes, when it was Proven beyond any Shadow of a Doubt that Black People Evolved from Apes, millions of Years Ago, while the Eastern Peoples in China, Korea, Japan and Malaysia were brought here by Aliens from other Worlds; but, Adam was Created by God from the Elements of the Dust of the Ground, whereby he could be a Perfect Man after the Order of the Holy Ones, who are known as the GODS, who are Created to Govern God's Worlds, which are Forever Multiplying: beCause that is the Glory of the Gods, to MULTIPLY. Therefore, if those Anti-Protesters had been at Home in Bed making Lust, instead of Rallying around Satan's Banners in Charlottesville, there would have been no Deaths there during that Day. However, I find it very Strange that such a Fuss was Raised Up over that Minor Issue, which went on for Days and Days, when there were some 600 Victims Killed during a Landslide in Sierra Leone at the same Time, and only a 10-second Report was given about it on the Evening Snooze Reports. §§‡

32-28 [_] Well, my Friend, I have to Agree with you — that there would have been no Clashes between those 2 Groups of Protesters, if the Anti-Nazi Protesters had simply Stayed at Home, or gone to Church, whereby they could have Meditated on what Jesus said: *"Resist not Evil,"* which is still very Good Advice for People who are Seeking PEACE. For Example, if you are Walking along the Street, and 2 Big Black Men are coming toward you with Long Butcher Knives in their Hands, it is much Better for your Soul to FLEE from the Scene of the Potential Crime, rather than make War against them, even if you are Related with James Bond or Matt Dillon: beCause you are not Equipped Properly to Handle them. However, if you are Old and Unable to Flee from them, it might be Best to step to one Side, and Bow Down and Greet them with Kindness: because they might have Mercy on you, and pass on by; but, if not, they probably just want your Money, which you can Cheerfully Surrender to them: because you are Obviously not Living within any Secure Swanky Fortress, where no such Evil

Creatures are Roaming about, neither Day nor Night: beCause they did not Check the same Boxes in their Surveys of Values as you did. ‡

32-29 [_] O Elected King, I must Confess that your Swanky Fortress Plan is far Superior to anything that President Donald Trumpeter might have to Offer, much less SINators Mitch McConnell, John McCain, and CONgressman Paul Ryan, Speaker of the House of Absent Representatives, such as Nancy Pelosi, Rabbi Cohen, the Rev. Doctor Billy Graham, News Commentator Paul Harvey; Norman Vincent Peale with his *Power of Positive Thinking,* Tony Robinson with his Pep Talks, Jay Leno with his Truthful Jokes, Nelson Mandela with his Equal Rights for Election Deceptions; Dr. Martin Luther King, Junior, with his Ridiculous, *I have a Bad Dream* Speech; nor any other Famous Person might have for Solving our Massive Problems: beCause their Wisdom comes from SATAN, and not from the God of Reasonable Solutions, who Lives within a Mighty Fortress, himself! Yes, you can read all about it in *Revelation 21,* which is coming down from Heaven to the Renewed Earth, where it will Rest itself in the CENTER of the Hollow Earth, being Suspended in Midair, whereby it will Light Up the Paradise that will Surround it, where there will be no Sea, nor any Night: beCause it is the Lamb's Holy Bride's City of Peace! § {See: **"The Secret City of the Great King!" (HOW the True Church will Escape from the Great Tribulation!) By The Worldwide People's Revolution!® Book 042.**}

32-30 [_] Well, my Friend, it is for Certain that the Low Court of Supreme Injustices would not be at all Interested in Proving any of those Things, much less whether or not Black People Evolved from Apes, which is as Superstitious as Men Landing on the Moon without any Rocket Launcher for Departing from the Moon at 4,000 Miles per Hour, which is more than twice the Speed of a Bullet! Indeed, if People were to just Think about how Ridiculous that Idea is, they would see the Fallacy of all such False Claims: beCause it Required nearly a Million Gallons of Rocket Fuel for the Saturn V Spacecraft to Depart from the Earth, while the Lunar Module Ascent "Rocket" had a Total of less than 10 Gallons of Rocket Fuel for Boosting a 2-ton Object into the Lunar Orbit that was Necessary for Docking with the Lunar Command Ship, which was Traveling at some 4000 MpH, according to NASA, which probably got its Information from NIST, which did a Thorough Investigation concerning the Evil Events of September 11th, 2001, and Concluded that "Thermal Expansion" brought down World Trade Center Tower 7 in less than 7 Seconds without the Use of EXPLOSIVES! And that is American "Science" at its very Best, which is almost as Scientific as the Warren Commission, which Determined that a Magic Bullet went through the Head of John Kennedy from the Backside, whereby it Blasted Off the Backside of his Head, and then made a Small Hole through his Throat, and proceeded to pass through the Chest and Right Arm of Governor Connally, and finally Rested itself on a Dallas Hospital Gurney in Pristine Condition on the Floor below where President Kennedy was being Examined by 4 Medical Doctors, whose Testimonies were not Admitted into the Warren Commission Report: beCause their Eye-witness Accounts of the Reality of it all were of no Benefit to the Low Court of Supreme Injustices and their Self-appointed Medical Examiners, who had never Treated any Cases that Involved Gunshots! Yes, they were the Self-appointed "Experts," whose Testimonies were far more Accurate than those of Medical Doctors with 20 to 40 Years of Experience with Gunshots! And that, my Friend, is how all such Things are Handled in **"The Divided States of United Lies!" (The so-called "United States of North America" in Disguise!)**, Book 058, which is now Worried that there might be a Race War, if those Neo-Nazis have their Way, who are only Asking for Black People to go Back to Africa, whereby the Neo-Nazis can Assist them to Build their own **"GLORIOUS Swanky Hotels Castles and Fortresses!" (Beautiful Planned City States for WISE Intelligent Well-Educated People with Common Sense and Good Understanding!) By The Worldwide People's Revolution!® Book 019.** Yes, the White Supremacists will also Gladly Join in to Assist those Poor Black People — that is, unless they can Prove that they are EQUAL in Skills and Abilities to White People, whereby they do not Need any Assistance from them. Indeed, they can now take up a Realistic

Dream, and Humble themselves to Confess that they might Need the Assistance of **"The New RIGHTEOUS One-World Government!"** **(HOW to Establish a Righteous One-World Government without Going to WAR!) By The Worldwide People's Revolution!®**, Book 056, even as we will ALL Need their Assistance: beCause no one Person has enough Nolij to get it all Done Correctly, including MYSELF, who has several Degrees and Missing Links! Therefore, just to be Perfectly Honest about it all, we might as well DROP this Superiority Complex Nonsense, and Act like Humble Obedient Children, who Recognize the FACTS, beginning with the Fact that it is only by the Grace of GOD that any one Person has any Special Gifts at all, no matter what his or her Color or Race might be. Moreover, each Nation will be Able to Prove its Abilities by Building the most Glorious Swanky Fortresses, which will Require them to Concentrate their Thoughts on Constructive Things, rather than on Hate Crimes, Injustices, False Flag Operations, Government Cover-ups, and Assassinations of Foreign Leaders in the Unholy Names of Freedom, Liberty, and Justice for ALL. Yes, all of those Evils can and should be put to Rest at: **"The Great Worldwide TELEVISED Court HEARING!" (That Great Meeting of the Most Intelligent and Well-Educated Minds!) By The Worldwide People's Revolution!®** Book 041. However, if anyone Disagrees with that Plan, they should Present a more Reasonable Plan, or else keep their Mouths SHUT: beCause this is **"The END of CONFUSION!"** and the Beginning of **The Great CELEBRATION of the Magnificent Wedding of the Most Humble Honest Nations, and the Grand Year of JUBILEE!** Book 050.

— Chapter 33 —

— Appendix 2 —

A Guaranteed Solution for HOW to Prevent any Future Protests Against Injustices!

33-01 [_] O Selected King of **"The New RIGHTEOUS One-World Government,"** are you not Aware that X-amount of Ignorant People will be Protesting against the Idea of having *"all Things in Common among us"* — such as the Mountains of Rocks, Rivers of Water, Forests, Minerals, Metals, Oils, Gases, Coals, and other Natural Resources? Indeed, they will no doubt be saying that all such Things should Belong to CAPITALISTS, who should have the Right to Exploit the Earth for all of the Wealth that they can Get: beCause it was Capitalists, like John D. Rockefeller, Andrew Carnegie, Bill Computer Software Gates, Steve Jobs, and many other Rich Americans, who made America GREAT: beCause they brought Good JOBS to Americans — such as the Jobs of Architects, Engineers, Mechanics, Machinists, Medical Doctors, Lawyers, Judges, School Teachers, Professors, Policemen, Firemen, Janitors, Trash Collectors, Cooks, Dishwashers, Barbers, Seamstresses, Shoemakers, Masons, Carpenters, Brickmakers, Bottle Makers, Tile Makers, Computer Makers, Telephone Makers, Car Manufacturers, Oil Industries, Gas Companies, Chemical Manufacturers, Drug Producers, Farmers, Farm Equipment, Trucking Industries, Theaters, Pornography Shops, Book Stores, Restaurants, and a Host of Sales Shops that fill Shopping Mauls, and line Streets and Avenues from Coast to Coast! Yes, it is a Marvelous Thing that the Industrial Revolution brought about, along with Countless Trash Dumps, Complicated Electrical Systems, Sewage Systems, Recycling Systems, Junkyards, Scrap Metal

Dumps, Road-making Equipment, Cranes, Trains, and Airplanes — all of which was made Possible by CAPITALISM, which you are Planning on TRASHING, O Silly Brainless Peacock! Therefore, it is just Natural to Think that X-amount of People will be PROTESTING Against your Insane Proposals, whereby 99.999,999,999% of the People would ABANDON those Stinking Noisy Crime-infested Polluted Cities of Confusion, and Move themselves into those **"Beautiful Swanky PALACES!" (A New Concept in Living Habits — Swanky Palaces for Poor People!) By The Worldwide People's Revolution!®** Book 066. Yes, I can Foresee it Coming, and with Great Disgust: beCause, rather than People being Civilized about it all, and Rational-minded, they are more likely to become VIOLENT, Murderous, and Suicidal: beCause of the Horrible Thoughts of Living in those UGLY Swankless Palaces, which will not even have Hamburger Shops, Pizza Parlors, Beauty Shops, nor Barber Shops: beCause you Intend to Prove that none of those Things are Needed for True Prosperity. For Example, you have not been to a Barber in more than 50 Years, whereby your Beard is no less than a Mile Long, and the Hairs of your Head are Dragging on the Ground behind you: beCause you are too Lazy to even Comb it and Wash it. Indeed, how many Years has it been since you had a BATH, O Peacockery? §§

33-02 [_] Well, my Potential Enemy, if the Industrial Revolution was such a Glorious Thing, how come it Produced those All-American World Records — such as the Most Prisoners per Capita in the World, the Most Pregnant Teenagers per Capita in the World, the Most Unwed Mothers in the World (who are mostly Black Mothers), the Most Murders in the World, the most Suicides in the World, the Most Drug Overdoses in the World, the Most Car Accidents in the World, the Most Sold Drugs in the World, the Most Sick People in the World, the Most Diseased People in the World, the Most Addicted People in the World, the Greatest Medical Expenses in the World, the Most Prisons in the World, the Most Top Secret Criminals in the World, the Most Bad Court Records in the World, the Most Divorces in the World, the Most Family Arguments in the World, the Most Unhappy People in the World, the Most Indebted People in the World, the Most Depressed People in the World, the Most Drivers with Road Rage, the Most Alcoholics, the Most Gluttons, and the Least Holy People. In Fact, I Challenge you to even Discover a Holy Person in **"The Divided States of United Lies!" (The so-called "Untied States of North America" in Disguise!)** Book 058. WHERE would you Begin to Look for one? Indeed, even the Irreverent LOUDMOUTH Slothgut Windbag Hole-in-his-Head has become FAT with Globs of LARD: beCause of being Addicted to that Capitalist Junk Food and Poisonous Drinks. So, with one-third of the Nation Suffering with OBESITY, what is to be Done for all such Ignorant People? Is it any wonder that they are PROTESTING, with or without Long Hairs and Beards?

33-03 [_] O Selected King of **The Worldwide People's Revolution!®**, you, yourself, have already Confessed that it is Impossible to Change the Leopard's Spots, or the Nature of People. Therefore, WHY Try? Why not just let them Suffer in their Miserable States of Extreme Poverty? After all, they would all much rather Live in their Tarpaper Shacks, than to Live in **"Beautiful Swanky PALACES!"** Therefore, just leave them alone, and let them go on Suffering for another thousand Years: beCause it will be Good for their Souls. Meanwhile, they will no doubt Learn a lot of Important Lessons — such as HOW to Ram Heavy Vehicles into Crowds of Protestors, whereby X-amount of them are Killed and Wounded, whereby they might Lie around on Hospital Beds and THINK about it all, and Conclude that it would be a Good Idea to SEPARATE the People who are Like Sheeps and Goats from the People who are Like Lions and Wolves! Yes, that was what God Suggested about 5,000 Years Ago: beCause he Knew that Sheeps and Goats did not get along very well with Lions nor Wolves; and therefore, they must be Protected from Communicating with each other — except that all People have the Capacity to Change their Minds, if they are not Totally Insane, and thus Change their Lifestyles and Living Conditions, and even make themselves Moderately RICH, if they take a Notion to Do so: beCause it only Requires the Election of a RIGHTEOUS KING, who has Power and Authority to bring True Justice to ALL People, Worldwide, just by Conducting **"The Great Worldwide TELEVISED Court**

HEARING," whereby the Masses of People can Learn the Whole Truth about all Important Subjects, including whether or not there are Enough Mountains of Rocks in this World of Wonders, whereby everyone can be Living within those **"Beautiful Swanky PALACES!" (A New Concept in Living Habits — Swanky Palaces for Poor People, who no longer Need to Suffer in their Miserable States of Extreme Poverty, who do not even have Fresh Clean Air to Breathe, Pure Living Water to Drink, Wholesome Natural Foods to Eat, Natural Clothing to Wear, nor Secure Houses to Live in, which are Fireproof, Mouse-proof, Termite-proof, Hail-proof, Tornado-proof, Hurricane-proof, Shingle-proof, Siding-proof, Insurance-proof, Self-air-conditioned, and Tax-proof!) By The Worldwide People's Revolution!®** Book 066. Yes, most Ignorant People would not Know that it is even Possible for them to have those Good Things; but, only IF they do not Seek to OWN any such Things as those Multi-Billion-dollar Swanky PALACES, which no one could Afford, nor should anyone even Imagine that he or she should Own any such Palaces: beCause that would only Build Up his or her PRIDE, which would Blind his or her Mind, and thus make a FOOL of such a Person! Yes, the Proof of it is the Fact that **"The Divided States of United Lies"** has no less than 300 Million FOOLS — all of whom are Living in those UGLY Wooden / Plastic Firetrap Mouse-infested Cockroach Dens, you might say, which are Guaranteed to come to RUINs by one Means or another! §§

33-04 [ ] Well, my Friend, you would Think that the 6,000-dollar-per-Year Average Heating and Cooling Bills, alone, would Cause them to THINK, and to Meditate on those SELF-AIR-CONDITIONED Swanky PALACES with the Marble-faced Walls and Granite-faced Floors, which have ZERO Heating and Cooling Bills: beCause of being DESIGNED Correctly, even as the Pantheon Building in Rome, which is more than 1,800 Years Old, and still Smiling at the Tax Collector: beCause more than 7 Million People go there to Visit it, each Year, whereby their Donations of only One Dollar, each, Covers the Costs of Police Protection from any Would-be Terrorists, who would find it Impossible to get into any Properly-planned Swanky Fortresses. ‡

33-05 [ ] O Selected King, what about North Korea sending an Intercontinental Ballistic Missile with an Atomic Warhead into the Heart of your own Swanky Fortress — would that not Violate all International Peace Treaties, and make a Mockery of **"The New RIGHTEOUS One-World Government,"** which should be Protecting all Swanky Fortresses?

33-06 [ ] Well, my Friend, if **"The Divided States of United Lies"** would simply STOP Doing their Military Exercises around North Korea, they might be able to Relax a bit, and even find Time to Meditate on Building their own **"Beautiful Swanky PALACES!"** Yes, we True Christians should Help them to Do it: beCause they might not know HOW: beCause of Wasting so much Time, Money, Materials, and Energy on War Games, rather than Concentrate on the Goodness of Swanky Fortresses, and how it is Impossible to Conquer one of them, even with Hydrogen Bombs: beCause they are Mountainous Cities with very THICK Solid Stone Walls in Great TERRACES, which make it Possible to have FREE and Abundant Electricity in Swanky Wind Generators, made with Stone Funnels. Therefore, the Wise Thing for the United States Federal Government to Do, is to Translate this Inspired Book into all Major Languages, including that of the North Koreans, and Personally Deliver Copies of it to the Leaders of all Nations, whereby they might Discover God's Guaranteed Solutions for our Massive Problems, which will Begin with **"The Great Worldwide TELEVISED Court HEARING,"** whereby the Masses of People might Learn all about it: beCause of Broadcasting those Court Hearings on ALL TV and Radio Networks, Worldwide, at the same Time, while SHUTTING OFF all of the Nonsense: beCause we are Talking about SERIOUS CLIMATE CHANGES, which may even Cause the Poles to SHIFT, whereby Violent Earthquakes will RUIN all of those Cities of Confusion, and leave the Lady Doubtfulness with her Head Stuck in one or the other of those 2 Stinking Holes in **"The BIG White OUTHOUSE on the Not-so-Biblical Capitol DUNGHILL!"** Book 023.

33-07 [_] O Elected King of all Intelligent and Wise People, even if there were no Climate Changes at all, it would still be a very Good Idea to Conduct that Great Meeting of the Most Intelligent Minds, just to Solve the Myriad of other Massive Problems — such as 4 Billion Extremely Poor People in this World of Woes, who do not even have Good Houses of any Kind to Live in, who Sleep on Filthy Noisy Streets, in Alleys, under Bridges, in Culverts, in Sewage Systems, in Subways, in Jungles, in Abandoned Houses, in Junk Cars, in Used Buses, in Cardboard Shanties, in Mud Huts, in Bamboo Shacks, in Slums, in Ghettos, and in Places that are Subject to Floods, Mudslides, Earthquakes, Volcanoes Erupting, Landslides, Hurricanes, Tsunamis, Tornadoes, Forest Fires, Arsonists, Robbers, Thieves, Gangs of Outlaws, Police Raiders, Armies of Terrorists, and you Name it! Yes, it could be that Climate Changes will FORCE us to come to the Table of Collective Solutions, and Feast on what People might have to Say about all such Things. After all, it is Possible that someone has Better Solutions than you do, O King, which we should all Learn about, whereby we might Judge what is Best for us. However, I Perceive that your God-given Solutions will be Accepted in the End.

33-08 [_] Well, my Friend, I might even be Dead by that Time, whereby some Tyrannical One-World Government will come to Power, much like Donald Trumpeter came to Power in **"The Divided States of United Lies"**: beCause neither he nor Hillary Clinton had to Fill Out nor File **"The Complete SURVEYS of our VALUES!" (SURVEYS of Religious Spiritual Political Governmental Sexual Social Moral Economic Business Labor Habitual and Miscellaneous VALUES!)**, Book 059, whereby the Electors might have Discovered their VALUES, and then Compared them with MY Values, or YOUR Values, or some other Person's Values, who might be more Qualified to be the President. For Example, which Boxes would you Check below?

A-[_] I Agree that it would be a Good Idea for all Potential Elected Officials to Fill Out and File on the Internet **"The Complete SURVEYS of our VALUES,"** whereby we Electors might Study those Surveys, and thus Know WHO we are Voting for, and WHY.

B-[_] I Believe that all Elections should be left up to Chance, whereby no one has any Idea WHO they are Voting for: beCause none of the Potential Elected Officials should have to Fill Out nor File on the Internet any of their Beliefs.

C-[_] I Confess that it would be a Great Improvement in the Election Deception Process, if all of the Potential Presidential and Governmental Candidates had to Fill Out and File **"The Complete SURVEYS of our VALUES!"** But, it would be Unconstitutional for us to Do so: beCause it Clearly States that no Candidate shall be given any Religious TEST of any Kind: beCause the Founding Fathers wanted us to Elect the most Ignorant Lying Vile Greedy Sons of Satan that he could Produce! §

D-[_] DUMBmocracy should be left alone, just the Way that it presently is: beCause, if you go about Messing with the Constitution, as your Unelected King is Suggesting, you will end up having Righteous People in the Government, who will become TYRANTS like Adolf Hitler, who Raised the German Standard of Living by 40000% within just 3 Years, which Caused all of those Germans to LOVE him, and even be Willingly to DIE for him, who nearly Conquered the Whole World, which would have been a TERRIBLE Thing to Happen: beCause everyone would have been made into an Organic GARDENER within Beautiful Planned City States, which would have been Unbearable for the Stock Market and the Handful of Rich Edomites who Profit from it. Therefore, I say that we Education Slaves, Work Slaves, Tax Slaves, Insurance Slaves, Interest Slaves, Rent Slaves, Food Bills Slaves, Gas Bills Slaves, Water Bills Slaves, Drug Bills Slaves, Childcare Slaves, Mortgage Slaves, Transportation Slaves, and all of ye other SLAVES should PROTEST Against that Wicked, WICKED Peabrain Peacock from Angel Ridge, and even Assassinate him, if you can Discover him Hiding in the Jungle, somewhere: beCause he is the ANTI-CHRIST, himself! Yes, he is Proposing that we Tax Slaves should have ALL MATERIAL THINGS in COMMON among us, whereby we do not OWN ANYTHING, except for our Combs, Toothbrushes, Spoons, Books, and Clothing!

E-[_] Educated People know that People like you are Extremely IGNORANT: beCause you are Blinded by your PRIDE, whereby you Vainly Imagine that you OWN the Highways and Bridges that you Drive on; but, you do NOT! Moreover, you do not Own the Air that you Breathe, nor the Trees of the Forests that Produce Oxygen; but, you would like to Think that you Own those Things, whereby you might BOAST about your Great Wealth, and PUFF UP you Mind with Unjustified PRIDE! Yes, it has make a FOOL of you: beCause you could have been Living in one of those **"Beautiful Swanky PALACES,"** along with many other Healthy Happy HOLY People; but, instead, you have Traded your True Wealth for False Riches, and are now Addicted to Various Kinds of DRUGS, whereby your Brains are Malfunctioning!

F-[_] I Fail to Understand what you People are Talking about — is this some Kind of a Survey of our Stupidity, or what?

G-[_] God Knows that you are LOST in the Darkness of Ignorance.

H-[_] To be Perfectly Honest with you, I Checked the A-Box — not beCause I am Running for any Political Office; but, that I Believe that if Donald Trumpeter had had to Fill Out and File on the Internet those Compete Surveys of his own Values, he would not have come anywhere near to Living in the White House in Washington: beCause the Normal American is not so Stupid as to Vote for a Capitalist Liar and HOG like him, much less a Neo-Nazi Sympathizer and Racist **BIGOT,** who is *a Person who has an Obstinate Belief in the Superiority of his own Beliefs, and a Prejudiced Intolerance for the Opinions and Beliefs of other People.* §

I-[_] I am an Innocent Child, who is not yet Old enough to Vote for anyone; but, if I had a Choice to Vote for a Righteous KING, as Opposed to a Powerless President, I would Vote for Jesus Christ, who would most likely Command us to Build those **"GLORIOUS Swanky Hotels Castles and Fortresses,"** just to take Advantage of the 5,000+ Good Reasons and Great Advantages for Building them and Living within the Borders of them: beCause he is NOT a Stupid Ignorant Person like the Irreverent Jelly Belly, who never even Mentions those Planned City States in his almost Worthless Sermons: beCause he is Obviously a Spiritual COWARD. Otherwise, he would Read this Inspired Book ALOUD to his entire Congregation, and also Encourage them to Study ALL of the Inspired Books by our Selected King of **The Worldwide People's Revolution!®**, which anyone of any Age, Color and Race may JOIN!

J-[_] Justice Demands that the Masses of People should Learn the WHOLE Truth, whatever it might be, which makes our Selected King the LEAST BIGOTED of any Person in the Whole World: beCause he is KINDLY DEMANDING **"The Great Worldwide TELEVISED Court HEARING,"** while NONE of the Bigoted People are even Mentioning it! Indeed, they Obstinately Believe that their Present Beliefs are Superior to all other Beliefs, and therefore they have a Prejudiced Intolerance for the Honest Opinions of other People, whose Beliefs might be more in Tune with those of the God of Justice, than their own Beliefs. Therefore, whomever Fails to Check the above Box with an X, is Obviously one of those BIGOTED People!

K-[_] King Jesus would not be at all Afraid to Check the above Boxes with X's: beCause he is not a Spiritual Coward. Indeed, he would LOVE **"The Great Worldwide TELEVISED Court HEARING,"** just to Learn WHY that anyone would be Rejecting his own Inspired Words of Provable Truths, who would be Free to Stand Up and Proclaim whatever Truths that he or she might Believe, even if Jesus Disagreed with those Beliefs: beCause Jesus could Answer the Questions, and put his Enemies to Silence! (Read the Gospels to Prove it to yourself.)

L-[_] Lots of Laughs! King Jesus would be Afraid to let anyone Speak at any of his Meetings of the Minds: beCause he would not have any Reasonable Solutions for anything, which would become Apparent just as soon as someone might Ask him HOW to Solve the Climate Changing Problems, while Providing Billions of JOBS! Indeed, he would be Seeking to Justify the Production and Use of Automobiles, just to Keep the Workers in Detroit BUSY! Moreover, he would Reopen all of the Coal Mines, and put those Poor People in West Virginia back to WORK: beCause he would Believe in "America FIRST," as Donald Trumpeter LOUDLY Proclaims: beCause he is Obviously another BIGOTED American, who Sincerely Believes that **"The Divided States of United Lies"** is the Greatest Nation on the Earth, which is WHY it Holds all of those World Records that we can read about in Verse 33-02, which is most likely also Missing several World Records, which the FACTS People should get Straightened Out in this Book: beCause it is not Possible for our Elected King to get ALL of the Ever-changing Facts STRAIGHT; but, he has Managed to Provide a Way for those Facts to be Corrected and Posted within Future Editions of this Inspired Book, and does not Object to that Plan; but, he DEMANDS it of us, just to Keep the Record STRAIGHT. §§‡

M-[_] Money is at the Heart of this Issue. Indeed, if the Middle-class People had Enough Money, they could Build their own Private Swanky Fortresses, and Hire X-amount of Nigger Jims to Cook their Foods, Wash their Dishes, Clean their Clothes, Sweep their Floors, Mop their Roofs, Trim their Grasses, and Gather their Fruits from their Luscious All-Mineral Organic Gardens; but, Thanks to those Edomites, they are Extremely Poor: beCause they are having to Compete with Slave Labor in China, India, Bangladesh, Pakistan, Honduras, Guatemala, and the Barbarian Coast of Barbados! In Fact, it is now Time to make America Great again by Building more New Yuck Cities along the Eastern and Western Coasts, whereby we can Worship them: beCause it is True that we are Possession Worshipers at Heart, who Want to OWN the Heavens and Earths, whereby we have Power and Control over them! Yes, that is the Glory of the Gods, and MONEY is the Best Solution for Solving that Problem. §§

N-[_] Not everyone is a Nitwit like you, Thank God, or else this Earth would have been Destroyed a very Long Time Ago — Thanks to your Greedy Capitalism, which is the Economic System of Satan, the Devil, who just Ignores the 7 Billion Extremely Poor People in this World of Woes, who do not even have Fresh Clean Air to Breathe, Pure Living Water to Drink, Wholesome Natural Foods to Eat, nor Secure Houses to Live in, much less someone to LOVE them like the First Disciples of Jesus Christ were Loved, who Turned the World UPSIDE DOWN by the Power of LOVE, whereby they Shared their Wealth, their Time, their Energy, their Materials, and whatever they had, which was a Great Threat to those Greedy Edomites, who Wanted it ALL for themselves! Look at Wall Street, if you Doubt it. ‡

O-[_] Are there no OPTIONS to Choose from? Can we not Accept SOCIALISM, which Robs the Rich People to Serve the Poor People? What about FASCISM, which is an Authoritarian Right-wing Radical Government, which Orders everyone around like Dogs? Would that not be much Better than giving the Masses of People the FREEDOM to Build their own

"GLORIOUS Swanky Hotels Castles and Fortresses," whereby they might Govern themselves, and even Smoke Marijuana, and Drive themselves Crazy with HEROIN? Indeed, have any of you Ignorant People stopped to Consider what the World might be Like, if all People had an Unlimited Amount of Money to WORK with, whereby they might Build some very UGLY Cities of Confusion, like Sao Paulo, Brazil; or Kolkata, India, which has no less than 200 Million Democratically Unemployed BEGGARS on their Streets? Give to me Liberty, or give to me DEATH, is my Motto! Let us take back America from those Niggers and Indians, and make America Great again by BIGOTRY: beCause we are the GOOD People, who have done no WRong, even as Howard Zinn pointed out in his Uninspired book, called: **A People's History of the United States**, which Lists no less than 5,000 Good Deeds by Common Honest Ordinary Hardworking American TAX SLAVES! §§‡

P-[_] People like you should be Locked Up in a Nut House with Saint Josephine Stalin, Richard Tricky Dick Nixon, Shitshak Rabean, Henry Kiss-assing-ger, and Larry Silverstein: beCause of Violating the Anti-Trust-America Act, which Demands that all Citizens should Sacrifice their God-given Right to become Moderately Rich for the Sake of Capitalism, whereby 1% of the Population can become Excessively Rich, while the 99% Live in FEAR of becoming Homeless, Jobless, and Impotent! §§‡

Q-[_] The Great Question is this: **"Will we Wake Up and come to our Riit Sensuz before we Destroy ourselves with Atomic and Hydrogen BOMBS!?"** And the Answer is, Probably NOT! But, it is as General George Smith Patton, Jr. said, "I believe that we were fighting on the wrong side of this hateful war." Indeed, after Witnessing the Evils of those Russian Communists, he had to Conclude that the Nazis were far more Righteous, and that they should have Won the War, whereby the Edomites had Patton Murdered in a so-called "Accident"! ‡

R-[_] I can Rightfully and Honestly say that I do not Know what to Believe; but, I am Willing to Watch and Listen to **"The Great Worldwide TELEVISED Court HEARING,"** whereby I might Learn what I should and should not Believe. Moreover, if anyone Fails to Check the above Box with an X, that Person is Suspect of being a Traitor of Truths, who should be Hauled into some Courtroom, and Forced to Defend his or her Insane BIGOTED Beliefs.

S-[_] I Sincerely Hope that some Righteous King gets Elected to Govern that Courtroom, and not some Prejudiced BIGOT like certain Members of the Low Court of Supreme Injustices, who cannot bring themselves around to Confess that **"The Divided States of United Lies"** was never a Truly GREAT Nation, like it would have been if the Inspired Author of this Extremely Good Book had been in Charge of this Nation and of all other Nations, who would Encourage all People of Like-mindedness to Build their own Beautiful Planned City STATES, whereby they might Govern themselves According to their own Elected Laws and Flexible Rules, whereby they might all Live in PEACE, and eventually Walk Hand-in-Hand with the GODS: beCause of Eventually Discovering the RIIT WAA TQ LIV!

T-[_] I Totally Agree with that. Yes, you just have to Think about it, and you will also Agree.

U-[_] I Understand what you are saying; but, I am not yet Willing to GIVE UP my Gas-hog Car, and go to Work in a Swanky Palace for 4 Hours per Workday: beCause I Love those Traffic Jams, whereby it Requires 2 Hours for me to get Home at Night. Hallelujah! Praise the Lord! I know that I am not Crazy, and Thank God that I am a Half-breed Muslim with a Pentecostal Hangover. §§

V-[_] People like you are likely to become VIOLENT and Murderous when the Rain STOPS, and there is nothing to EAT, when you could have had your Pantry and Walk-in Cooler FULL of Good Wholesome Natural Foods to Eat, and also had Natural 100% Fresh Fruit Juices to Drink; but, now you are Stuffed with Pride, and Blinded by your Lusts.

W-[_] I am Willing all of my Property to **The Worldwide People's Revolution!®**

X-[_] X-amount of People will Join you, and also Will their Properties to that Cause; but, I will Stay the Course on my Way to Hell on the Highway of Capitalism, which is Running on a Dead End Street, you might say: beCause the Natural Resources are Bound to RUN OUT; but, while it is still Working, it is the Way that I will go. And I am not some Religious Fanatic. §§‡

Y-[_] Yesterday came and went, along with any such Insane Ideas as the Establishment of **"The New RIGHTEOUS One-World Government"**: because it is Impossible to get the Nations to Agree to Hold **"The Great Worldwide TELEVISED Court HEARING!" (That Great Meeting of the Most Intelligent and Well-Educated Minds!)**, Book 041: beCause they might have to Change their Ways of Thinking and Living, which would Require them to REPENT, which they are NOT going Do!

Z-[_] The ZEAL of **The Worldwide People's Revolution!®** will make all of that Possible.

33-09 [_] O Elected King, the Dust was hardly Settled in Charlottesville, when some more Terrorists Attacked in Barcelona, Spain, Killing 14 People, and Injuring 100+ more: beCause there are many Radical People in this World of Woes, who have their Agendas, one of which is to Protest against the Swanky Fortress System that you Propose: because it Threatens our entire Way of Life, which you say is the Way of Death and Self-destruction, instead of True Life. Indeed, your Paradisiacal Plan would be Good for many People, who might Want Good Foods and Drinks, and to Live in Secure Cities; but, there is a Price to Pay for our Freedoms and Independence. Yes, the Price is that List of Evils that you have in Verse 33-02, which Evils make us Better People than we would be, if we were all Living in Swanky Fortresses, where there are no Temptations to Sin. §§‡

33-10 [_] Well, my Friend, if you have to be Tempted to Sin, you can always leave the Swanky Fortress that you are in, and go Visit one of those Sin Cities, whereby you can Tempt yourself to Sin; but, as for me, I can Live Happily without any Temptations at all. In Fact, I Try to Fulfill all of my Lusts, whereby Satan cannot Tempt me. For Example, if I am Hungry, I Eat, and only enough to Satisfy me: because, to Eat any more is no Temptation: because that would only make me Miserable. Therefore, I Stop Eating before I make myself Miserable, whereby I have the Victory over that Devil. However, if I had an Excessive Amount of Money, I would no doubt Fall into more Capitalist Pits by Means of more Temptations. Therefore, it is Wise of me to keep myself Relatively Poor, in spite of Living in a Marble Palace, when it is Compared with those Mud Huts. ‡

33-11 [_] O Elected King, I have been Straining my Brains to figure out WHY anyone would Object to the Swanky Fortress Plan, seeing that they could Raise their Standard of Living by at least 10000%. Moreover, I have also been Trying to figure out just HOW any Would-be Terrorist might go about Terrorizing the People within a Swanky Fortress, which I have not yet Thought of after 20 Years of Meditating on it. For Example, the Car Bomb Idea would not Work: beCause there are NO Cars within Swanky Fortresses. Moreover, the Explosives in Backpacks Plan would not Work: beCause none of the Ingredients for making any such Bombs would be Available in any Swanky Fortresses. Besides that, what would be the MOTIVE for making any such Attacks, other than Total Insanity?

33-12 [_] Well, my Friend, it could be that some Distant City of Radical Muslims might get the Notion to Try to Terrorize some Christians within a certain Swanky Fortress: beCause of having Different Viewpoints about the Doctrines of their Imaginary Gods. For Example, they could Imagine that Allah Commanded them to Attack those Christians, even as he supposedly Commanded Moses to Attack the Canaanites, Hittites, Hivites, Jebuzites, Gergashites, and other Ites in the Land of Palestine. Therefore, those Muslims might Try to make some Attack on a Swanky Fortress. However, the Chances of that Attack being Successful are very Slender: beCause no Muslims would be Allowed to even Visit a Christian Fortress without Special Permission, as well as Armed Guards, if they did get Permission, who would be Carrying their Water Pistols and Knight Sticks, if there was any Doubt about being able to Defend themselves with their Bare Hands, which they would be Trained to do, being like the Royal Canadian Mounted Police used to be Armed, who Overtook their Enemies with their Bare Hands. After all, one does not have to have a Pistol nor Shotgun to Defend himself within a Swanky Fortress: beCause no such Weapons are Allowed, except in the Armory in the Castle, which are kept Locked Up for Qualified Soldiers to Use, and only if there is some War. Indeed, all Visitors will have to Enter in Stark Naked, take Showers, and put on Clean Clothes that Identify them as Visitors, whereby it will be Impossible to Smuggle in Drugs, or any Weapons of any Kind. ‡

33-13 [_] O Elected King, will one Swanky Fortress not even Trade Goods with other Swanky Fortresses, whereby Weapons could be Smuggled into any Swanky Fortress?

33-14 [_] Well, all of the Swanky Fortresses will be Connected with Underground Subway Trains; and therefore, they will be Able to Trade Goods with other Swanky Fortresses; but, not with the Outside World, and sometimes not even with other Swanky Fortresses of Contrary Religions: beCause there is no Need for Accepting any Unnecessary Chances. In Fact, generally-speaking, most Swanky Fortresses will only Trade Goods and Services with Like-minded Swanky Fortresses. For Example, Christians will Trade with other Christians, and Muslims will Trade with other Muslims — that is, unless they are all Converted to the TRUTHS that I Teach, and then none of those False Religions will Exist! ‡

33-15 [_] O Elected King, what if a Muslim Man just Happens to fall in Love with some Pretty Christian Girl, who has sent to him her Picture, whereby he Wants to Date her and get Married to her — will that not be Possible?

33-16 [_] Well, my Friend, just the Thought of that is Inviting Trouble: beCause they have Contrary Beliefs. Indeed, the Surveys of their Values would not Match Up Correctly. Therefore, one or the other would have to be Converted to the other Religion, and the Muslim Man would have to Leave his People, and Join the Christians: beCause that is the Price that he would have to Pay for his Lusts. After all, there are Plenty of Beautiful Muslim Wombmen that he can Date and Marry, and thus Avoid any Religious Conflicts. ‡

33-17 [_] O Elected King, suppose we Feel a Calling from God to Preach to Muslims, and get them Converted to the Southern Baptist Union of Pentecostal Methodists of the Seventh-day Lutherans and Reformed Mormons — will we not have the Freedom to Enter into those Sunni Muslim Fortresses, and Preach our Sermons, whereby they might all be Converted to our Faith, even if it is Insane? §

33-18 [_] Absolutely NOT! Why would you Want to make them Sevenfold more the Children of Hell than they already are, as Jesus would say? Just let them have their Phony Religions, and leave them alone: beCause, if God Wants them Converted, he can Inspire them to get on the Internet and Read some of your Literature: beCause all Religious Groups of People will have Freedom of Speech on the Internet, and will be Able to Communicate by Various Means — such as by E-mails, Facebook,

Twitters, or whatever; but, only Diplomatically: beCause everyone will be Discouraged from any Name-calling, Cursing, Slandering, and whatever is Offensive, while being Encouraged to Speak the Truth as they Understand it. Granted, most Religious People are Bigoted, and Sincerely Believe that they have the Truth on their Side of every Issue. However, if my Master Plan is Followed, anyone will have the Right to bring anyone else to Court over any Religious Issue, and Prove their Beliefs to be True or False, which will be carried on in a Royal Way at **"The Great World TEMPLE of PEACE!"** **(The Glory of Jerusalem Arises Again!) By The Worldwide People's Revolution!®** Book 017.

33-19 [_] O Elected King, are you saying that the Daily Meetings within **"The Great World TEMPLE of PEACE"** will be mostly Court Hearings, whereby Religious, Spiritual, Political, Governmental, Sexual, Social, Moral, Economic, Business, Labor, Habitual and Miscellaneous Subjects will be Discussed on a Daily Basis? Would that not become a MADHOUSE in Short Order: beCause of Tempers Flaring Up, and Mudslinging Statements being made?

33-20 [_] NO, Absolutely NOT! In Fact, it will be the most Rational Way to Dissolve all of those Disputes: beCause it will be a Courtroom with LAWS and ORDER. For Example, when someone Wants to Speak, he or she will have to put Up his or her Hand, and be Recognized by the Judge, and all others will have to Keep SILENT, until that Person has Finished his or her Speech, even if it Requires an Hour to do so, while everyone Listens: beCause all of the Ignorant Fools will be SIFTED OUT of those Hearings, whereby only Intelligent Well-Educated People will have Permission to Speak anything, who will Normally be the Elected Officials of each Nation: beCause of Wisely Using the Chain of Command System that I have Outlined in **"The Washington Journal is a FARCE!"** **(C-SPAN Managers are not very WISE!) By The Worldwide People's Revolution!®** Book 006. In Fact, each Subject to be Addressed will be Announced at least a Month in Advance, whereby everyone will have Sufficient Time to get their Swords of Truths Sharpened Up, and get Ready for the Big Day. Therefore, let us say that the Subject is "Reincarnation," which is Accepted by about one-third of all People in the World as a Reality of Life, including myself — but, for some Strange Reason (probably beCause of Total Ignorance concerning that Subject), you do not Accept the Idea. Therefore, you would Present your Strongest Arguments Against Reincarnation to your Commanding Officer of Working Soldiers, who would also be Living in the same Swanky Fortress with you: beCause of Checking the same Boxes as you have Checked, one of which is: [_] I do not Believe in Reincarnation. Therefore, your Commanding Officer would Think about your Arguments, and perhaps Decide to Present those Arguments to his Commanding Officer, who would also Think about your Arguments, and thus Pass the Information on Up the Chain of Command to his Commanding Officer, until at Last the Information is Sent by E-mail to the Elected King or Queen of your Swanky Fortress, who may Decide to Send that Information to the Commanding Officer of all Similar Swanky Fortresses, who may Send the Information to the Elected King or Governor of the Nation, who is Representing all of the People of his Nation, who may still be Undecided about the Subject of Reincarnation. However, being an Open-minded Person, it is his Duty to Listen to all Sides of every Argument, and Contribute his Best Arguments for or against each Subject, and Accurately, in the Most Precise Manner Possible: so that any 12-year-old Child can easily Understand the Statements.

33-21 [_] O Elected King, that Process of Elimination of Ideas would take Forever to come to any Rational Conclusions: beCause of the Endless Arguments that are For or Against Reincarnation. However, if just a few People could Prove that they were Reincarnated: beCause of Presenting the Evidences of it, the Case would be Closed in a Hurry, and everyone would have to Agree to Accept that Doctrine. For Example, you say that you are the Reincarnation of King Solomon, himself, which may be True or False. However, after Carefully Examining **"Thu Nq MAGNUFIID Verzhun uv Thu PROVERBZ uv KING SOLUMUN in Plaan Ingglish!"** **(The Understandable Version of the**

Famous Proverbs of King Solomon in Plain English!), Book 028, I must Confess that the Evidence is very Strong in your Favor: beCause you are the ONE and only Person who has Rightly Explained all of those Proverbs, which can be taken into a Courtroom, one by one, and Proven to be TRUE! However, that is no Foolproof Reason for anyone to Accept the Doctrine of Reincarnation without some other Evidences — such as were Presented by *20/20* on ABC News, years ago. Indeed, those People Presented Irrefutable Evidences that they were Reincarnated: beCause they Revealed what they Actually did during Past Lives, all of which has been Documented. Therefore, only an Ignorant BIGOTED Person would Reject the Doctrine of Reincarnation.

33-22 [_] Well, my Friend, the Rejecters of that Doctrine would likely get their Beliefs from a Misinterpretation of a single Verse in the *Unholy Mutilated Bible,* which says something to the Effect that it was Appointed unto Men to Live and Die only ONCE, and after that they would be Judged, which you can find in *the Book of Hebrews* somewhere, which Fails to make it Clear that we all Missed our Appointments, and are therefore under the Obligation of Living again, and again, until we Keep our Appointments by Passing our TESTS. After all, what 6-month-old Baby could be Rightly Judged for his Words and Works, whereby God might Justly Reward him for all such Words and Works?

33-23 [_] O Unelected King, the Baby would be Justified by the Blood of Christ, and could therefore not be Condemned. Indeed, he would become one of the Apostles of Jesus Christ, and thus Sit on the Throne of God beside of the Apostle Paul: beCause of being Justified. §‡

33-24 [_] Well, if you Want to, you may take up that Argument at **"The Great World TEMPLE of PEACE,"** whereby we can Prove whether or not you are a Quarter of a Bubble Off Center, as a Carpenter might say, speaking of his LEVEL Level. Chances are that your Arguments do not Hold Water, as a Sailor might say: beCause you are Mixing Different Subjects Together. Chances are that the New MAGNIFIED Version of Hebrews is far more Accurate and Understandable. Nevertheless, you are not Obligated to Accept that Version as a Part of your Religious Beliefs: beCause you are Welcome to Believe the Atheist's Version, if you Want to, or any other Version: beCause it does not Bother the Gods the Slightest Bit, who will Decide WHO gets to Rule with them within their Holy Kingdom of All that is GOOD, which Excludes those Stinking Noisy Polluting DANGEROUS Vehicles that you also Seek to Justify unto your own Great Shame. Yes, People like you are likely to be Proven to have all Kinds of BAD Beliefs, and yet it is Doubtful that you will Change your Mind by any Degree: beCause of Seeking to Justify WICKEDNESS, Greed, Lusts, Selfishness, PRIDE, and all Kinds of EVILS, for which you will be Cast OUT of God's Holy Kingdom. Guaranteed! Therefore, you might do well to Ask yourself WHERE you went Astray from that Straight and Narrow Path that Leads to Everlasting Good Health, which is True Wealth?

33-25 [_] O Elected King, it Reminds me of the House of Representatives in Washington, District of Criminals, who are Seeking to Justify the American "Way of Life," as they call it; but, without the Capital Letters on Way nor Life: beCause, to them, not even the Love of God is Worthy to be Capitalized, in spite of Professing to be True Christians, who Vainly Imagine that they Love God, who will likely be Marching in some Protest Against those **"GLORIOUS Swanky Hotels Castles and Fortresses,"** on Account of YOUR Personal Religious and/or Spiritual BELIEFS, which have nothing to do with the Subject of the GOODNESS of Swanky Fortresses, which have more than 5,000 Good Reasons and Great Advantages for Building them and Living within the Borders of them, without any Great Disadvantages, whether or not *anyone* Believes in Reincarnation! Indeed, all such Protesters should be Born in Saudi Arabia the next Time around, whereby they can Learn to Appreciate HOT and COLD Weather during the same Day, even as Contradictory as that might seem to be: beCause it can get up to 130 °F during the Day, and be Freezing Cold at Night! But, that does not Debunk the Swanky

Fortress Plan by any Means. Therefore, when those Debates are Held in **"The Great World TEMPLE of PEACE,"** we will have to Remember to keep our Subjects SEPARATED, and in the Correct Order, which is WHY a Righteous JUJ must be in Charge of the Court, who is Happy to Hear all Sides of every Issue, and not just the 2-sided American Version of Dimwitcrats nor Reprobates: beCause there are some Independent Jackasses who have Points to make, which are Equally as Valid as those of Democrats and Republicans, who are among some of the most Deceived People on the Earth, and especially when it comes to Interpreting the Will of GOD, who is not Willing that any of them should Perish; but, that ALL of them should come to Repentance, and before the Hydrogen Bombs fall on their Heads for the Rejection of Provable Truths without any Justifiable Causes!

33-26 [_] Well, my Friend, all such Issues can easily be Dissolved in the Water of Life, if they are Soaked in it Long Enough, which is WHY all People must be very Patient when we Hold **"The Great Worldwide TELEVISED Court HEARING"**: beCause we Want to DISSOLVE all such Issues, whereby they do not Pop Up during the Future. Indeed, we Want the Court Records to be very Plain and Easy for 12-year-old Children to Understand, whereby they can come to Rational Conclusions about Riit and WRong. Otherwise, it will be a Waste of everyone's Precious Time!

33-27 [_] O Elected King, I know HOW to Cut Down on much of that Wasted Time, which is by People Studying your Inspired Books, whereby there will be no Arguments Against your Beliefs, which might Sound BITOTED to many Ignorant People: beCause of not Studying those Books; but, only **"The Swanky Sword of Divine Truths"** has the Power to Liberate us from the Prison of Lies, including the Prison of Capitalist Lies — such as that False Doctrine about the GOODNESS of Owning Possessions of all Kinds, including Multi-Billion-Dollar Swanky PALACES, which not even Bill Computer Software Gates could Afford to Buy! Meanwhile, beCause of that False Doctrine, X-amount of Billions of People are Deprived of all such **"Beautiful Swanky PALACES!" (A New Concept in Living Habits — Swanky Palaces for Poor People!) By The Worldwide People's Revolution!®** Book 066. Yes, that is the Sad News about all such False Doctrines, which Discourage Young Hardworking People from even Thinking about the Possibilities of Living in Swanky Palaces, whereby they put it Out of their Minds, when they should be Meditating on the Goodness of it, both Day and Night, until they See the Vision of it, and the Great BEAUTY of not Owning anything more than their Combs, Toothbrushes, Fingernail Trimmers, Books, Computers, and Transportable Things, even though they would not have to even Own those Things: beCause all of the Computers will be Free of all Charges, and the Internet will be Free, and the Books can be Found in any Swanky Truth-brary! Therefore, WHY bother to OWN anything? After all, when we Die, we are not going to take anything with us? However, that is not to say that we should Live like Vagabonds and Tramps: beCause that is a very Wretched Way to Live. Indeed, we should Live like Kings and Queens in **"Beautiful Swanky PALACES!"** After all, it is most Practical to do so, and without the Use of any Greedy Edomite Bankers, Political Rabbits, Porcupine Lawyers, Stinking Painted Skunks, Medical Snakes, Insurance Scammers, nor Drug Pushers.

33-28 [_] Well, my Friend, I would say that this Book is about Long Enough for most People to Read within 2 to 3 Days; and therefore, we had best call it Quits, for now, even though I could go on and on for another 20 Chapters, just to MAGNIFY the Good Thoughts that we have already Presented, which can be Magnified at **"The Great World TEMPLE of PEACE!" (The Glory of Jerusalem Arises Again!) By The Worldwide People's Revolution!®** Book 017.

33-29 [_] O Elected King, I just LOVE to Read your Extremely Good Books, and can hardly wait for the next one: beCause you are so Positive-minded. However, I Think that I would Capitalize less Words than you do.

33-30 [_] Well, my Friend, I most Certainly do Appreciate all of my Readers, who are a Great Encouragement to me, who will have to get Used to those Capitalized Words: beCause they are very Important. Otherwise, I would not do it. {See: **"Justifications for Capitalizations!" (WHY our Elected King Defies the School of Fools by Capitalizing LOVE and HATE!) By The Worldwide People's Revolution!®** Book 049.}

{NOTE: You may use the Space below to make Notes of any of your Thoughts, which you might Want to Remember to Present to your Elected Officer, in the Future, who is in Command of your Swanky Army of Working Soldiers.}

— Chapter 34 —

— Appendix 3 —

A Guaranteed Solution for the Peaceful Removal of Confederate Flags, Statues and Monuments!

34-01 [_] O Elected King, I Think that you have gone out on a Limb of the Tree of Hope just a little to Far, to say that there is some Guaranteed Solution for the Peaceful Removal of Confederate Statues, Rags and Monuments — such as the Removal of the Jefferson Memorial in Washington, D.C.: beCause Thomas Jefferson had hundreds of Slaves, and was the very Emblem of the Inequalities of Mankind at the Height of Hypocrisies! Yes, he was the White Gentleman who Proclaimed that *"... all Men were Created Equal, being Endowed by their Creator with Equal Rights to Own as many Slaves as it might Require for making their Masters Prosperous,"* to put it in the Language of the Realities of that Time, when practically 6% of the White People, and even 1% of the Free Black People, were Owners of Slaves, including White Slaves: beCause they Misinterpreted a few Verses from the *Holy Bible,* one of which Clearly States: *"You Israelites shall not make Slaves of one another: beCause you are all Brothers; but, you may make Slaves of any other Races of People, who do not Join you and Accept your Religion, which is the one and only Correct Religion in the Whole World: beCause it comes from Jehovah God, who has Identified himself to you, and to the People of the entire World by Means of Miracles, Signs, and Great Wonders, whereby there is no Doubt in anyone's Mind that Jehovah God is the Supreme Ruler of this World, who would have all People to Worship him as such: because it is Necessary that People Worship some God: because, without that Worship, there is a Vacant Place within their Hearts and Minds, which is Filled by that Evil Spirit of the Devil, who is the Chief Slave Master, who Seeks to make all Ignorant People Addicted to his Outlandish Lies, Drugs, False Doctrines, and Poisons of Various Kinds. Yes, he is the Unholy One who Promotes all Evils, including the Notion that People should be making Slaves of other People, when they would not Want other People to be making Slaves of them. Indeed, the one and only Way to have Peace and Happiness in this World of Woes, is for People to Do unto others as they would have other People Do unto them. Therefore, by Following that Golden Rule, there will be no Slavery. However, that is not to say that People cannot or should not Volunteer to be the SERVANTS of other People: because X-amount of People were Born to be Servants, while X-amount were Born to be Masters. However, it shall come to pass during the Last Days, just before the Second Coming of Jesus Christ, that the People who were Born to be Masters will be taking Advantages of the People who were Born to be Servants, and will therefore make Education Slaves, Work Slaves, Tax Slaves, Usury Slaves, Insurance Slaves, Rent Slaves, and Endless Bills Slaves of the Masses of People: because those Evil Masters will Establish a Cruel and Subtle System of SLAVERY, while Calling it Freedom, Liberty, Democracy, and Justice for ALL! Yes, it will be the Economic System of Satan, the Devil, whereby almost everyone will be made into a SLAVE of some Kind, and not even Realize it: beCause of being Blinded by Propagandist LIES — such as all Men being Born Equal, when no one is Equal in any Way with anyone else, and Certainly not Equal with Jesus Christ, nor with Moses and Elijah, who will Come and Restore all Truths to the People of the World before the Second Coming of Jesus Christ, in Order to Prepare the Way for his Coming!"* Yes, it was the Religious Belief at the Time of Thomas Jefferson and George Washington, that God Created Black People to be the Slaves of White People: because it was almost

Impossible for those White People to become Rich without the Assistance of Slaves. Moreover, it was their Firm Belief that God's Chosen People were Identified by their WEALTH, which was a Long-time Jewish Belief, which came from the *Holy Bible,* which Glorified Wealth as a Holy Thing, which is WHY Jesus went out and Sold ALL of his Houses, and Gave the Money to Extremely Poor People, and also Commanded all of his Followers to do the same Thing, whereby they all became Extremely Poor People: because it never Crossed their Weak Minds that it is Possible and most Practical to Establish **"The New RIGHTEOUS One-World Government,"** which has an Unlimited Supply of New Money, which must be EARNED by Honest Labor, according to **"A List of FAIR Swanky Wages!"** **(The Equitable Wage System!) By The Worldwide People's Revolution!®** Book 065. Yes, all **"Seven Great Armies of Working Soldiers"** should be Paid GOOD Wages for Doing GOOD Works — such as the Building of those **"GLORIOUS Swanky Hotels Castles and Fortresses!"** (Beautiful **Planned City States for WISE Intelligent Well-Educated People with Common Sense and Good Understanding!)**, Book 019, which would be Guaranteed to Solve the Unemployment and Under-employment Problems, along with at least 5,000 other Problems, including the Peaceful Removal of Confederate Flags, Statues, and Monuments, which Symbolize SLAVERY of People, which was never Needed for True Prosperity: beCause we Inventors and Innovators have always had the Capability to make MECHANICAL SLAVES — such as those Cotton-picking Machines, Electric Trains, Bulldozers, Backhoes, Trackhoes, Forklifts, Bucket-loaders, Cranes, Draglines, Steam Shovels, Tractors, Trucks, Rock Cutting Machines, Rock Polishing Machines, Hydrogen-powered Airplanes, and many other Kinds of Useful Mechanical SLAVES, which Jesus Christ never Mentioned: beCause he Obvious did not Know anything about any such Useful Labor-saving Tools, which was True of all of the so-called *Holy Prophets,* who never Presented a Workable Plan for True Prosperity. But, they presented the Jews with a Slavery System: beCause it was JEWS who made up that Slavery System, and became the Chief Proponents of it, and also the Chief Slave Masters! Yes, they were the Unholy Ones who Traded Slaves since Ancient Times, and were also the Ship Owners who brought the African Slaves to **"The Divided States of United Lies!"** (The so-called **"United States of North America"** **in Disguise!)**, Book 058: beCause it was the single most Profitable Business at that Time, which was the Buying and Selling of African SLAVES! Yes, any Rich Person with a Ship at that Time could make a Trip to Africa, and Buy a Black Man for 2 or 3 Dollars: because the Africans needed some Money; and therefore, they Rounded Up other Tribes of Ignorant Black Africans from the Interior Nations, and brought them to the Market Places along the Coasts of Africa, whereby the Jewish Slave Traders Bought them for next to nothing, and then Shipped them to the West and North, where they put those Slaves up for Auction to the Highest Bidders, while Stark Naked, just as if they were Cattle at an Auction Market, where they Sold for 200 to 20,000 Dollars — Depending on the Size and Length of their Tally Whackers and Chime Bells, or their Upright Firm Breasts, if they were Wombmen: because it was mostly a SEX Issue that Determined their VALUES. Yes, if they were Healthy Strong Muscular Young Men with Good Builds, they were also much more Romantic in the Beds of their Masters, including Saint George Washington, himself, whose Favorite Slave had a Tally Whacker that was 14-inches Long! Yes, it is a Historical FACT; but, it was of no Great Concern to Thomas Jefferson: beCause he was Lusting after those Pretty Black Wombmen, and was not such a Sodomite as George was, who often went "Fishing" with his Favorite Slave, and had certain Holy Places in the Woods to make Love in, which Greatly Bothered the otherwise Hard Conscience of Saint George: beCause he also did his *Bible Studies,* and could not Reconcile his Evil Nature with that of True Christian Doctrines: beCause they were Contradictory. Therefore, George spent much Time with Prayers and Confessions: beCause he had no Idea what to DO about Solving his own Personal Addictive Lusts: beCause it was not Taught in any Churches at that Time — I Mean, the Correct Solution for all such Problems was not Taught in any Churches at that Time: beCause it was Unprofitable for those Jews who Sold DRUGS! Yes, it was also in the Interest of George to Sell Drugs, which was his Primary Business, by which he became the Richest American at that Time, and the most Famous American:

beCause he and his Drafted Soldiers WON the Revolutionary War! Therefore, they were American HEROES, both in and out of Bed. Yes, George also Happened to have a Big Fat Impotent Tally Whacker: beCause of Abusing those Chime Bells when he was Young; but, his Tally Whacker was not quite as Glorious as that of his Black Slave, who would have been Castrated, "if'n he had not kept Mum about it all," as Nigger Jim might say to Huck Finn. Indeed, he was also a Black GAY Undercover Investigator, you might say, who Wished that he could Read and Write: so that he might Study a very Famous Book, called: **"How GAY is GOD?" (Oh the Wonders of it all when it ALL Hangs Out!) By The Worldwide People's Revolution!®** Book 071. Yes, it is a Marvelous Book, which Reveals WHY Jacob and Jesus were Wrestling Stark NAKED all Night at Peniel, which you can read all about in **"The New MAGNIFIED Version of GENESIS!"** Otherwise, you could Study *Genesis 32,* in the very GAY *King James Version.* Yes, Peniel was Derived from the Root Word at the Center of this Subject, which is the Marvelous PENIS, itself, which was at the Heart of almost all Biblical Penile Tales since the Beginning, when Adam and Eve were Stark Naked in the Garden of Eden, and did not even Know it! Nevertheless, there is no Doubt in anyone's Mind that George Washington and Thomas Jefferson were the BEST of High Class Slave Owners at the Time of the Founding of **"The Divided States of United Lies!"** Yes, it was in their Financial Interest to be Slave Owners: beCause those Slaves might have Sellable Children, whereby they might be Most Profitable, and especially if they should Sell for 1,500$ or more, which they sometimes did, and at a Time when one might normally Earn only 15$ per Month! Therefore, **"For the Love of Money"** they did very Strange Things during those Days. §§‡

34-02 [_] Well, my Friend, just Think of what a Different World this would have been, if all such *Sacred Words* had been Found within the *Holy Bible!* I Mean, all of the Words from your *Quotation,* which came from the Great Imagination of the Reincarnated King Solomon, himself, who was a Seer! Yes, it is True that George and Tom did have their Sex Problems: beCause of their Lusts for Wealth, which gave to them Evil Appetites, whereby they became Possession Worshipers, and thus the Worst of Sinners at that Time; but, they were not nearly so Corrupted as their Modern Counterparts, who Seek to Justify anything that the Baal Worshipers say and do to get more Money and Power. Yes, they even Seek to Justify those Hateful Wars, which King Solomon Avoided by being a WISE Man. However, the Guaranteed Solution for Peacefully Removing all of those Confederate Rags, Statues and Monuments of Confederate Heroes and Infamous Slave Owners, is to Build those **"GLORIOUS Swanky Hotels Castles and Fortresses,"** whereby almost everyone in the World can become Moderately RICH, and without Telling any Lies, nor Selling any Capitalist Trash. Indeed, the Wealth of a Nation is not Measured by the Number of Slaves that it has Produced, nor by the Height of its Skyscrapers; but, by the Percentage of Healthy Happy People, who are Free in all Ways, who have no Need for Raising their Standards by Lowering the Standards of other People.

34-03 [_] O Elected King, I would like for you to Explain just HOW that Building Swanky Fortresses will Appease the Demands of those White Supremacists, who Vainly Imagine that General Robert E. Lee was a Great American HERO, who Fought to Maintain Slavery, who Committed TREASON, who Fought Against **"The United States of the Whole World!" (A True Global Economy for the Masses of Working People!) By The Worldwide People's Revolution!®** Book 055? §§

34-04 [_] Well, my Friend, I already had it Explained Perfectly, when my Computer somehow Transformed the entire 156-page Document into Asterisks (*************), which Symbolizes Omitted Matter, which some Evil Person must have done, who was most likely some Money-hungry Edomite: beCause the Information Revealed more than he or she could Tolerate, being a Capitalist PIG, you might say, who wants to Sell a Computer Program for 800$, which can easily be put on a Computer Disk for 10 Cents, and Sold for 25 Cents, and still be Profitable. However, that would not be

According to the Thinking of a Normal Capitalist: beCause Capitalists are Anti-Christs in Nature: beCause they do not Believe in Sharing their Wealth with others, except in Charitable Good Deeds, whereby they somewhat Cover Up their Guilt and Shame for being so GREEDY and Selfish.

34-05 [_] So, O Elected King, can you not Remember what it was that you had already Written concerning this Subject? Can you not Rewrite it, just Exactly as you had it? Indeed, any Holy Prophet should be Able to Do that.

34-06 [_] Well, I did not say that I am a Holy Prophet, nor that I can Remember very Well. After all, I Suffered with Carbon Monoxide Poisoning, and could not Remember my own First Name afterwards. Therefore, it is quite Amazing that I have been Able to Write any Books at all, much less the World's Most Famous Inspired Books, and not just a half dozen of them; but, no less than 350 of them! Therefore, I am now Relying on the Holy Spirit to Remind me of the Words that I had Written, or else give to me Better Words. Indeed, the whole Incident of the entire Document being Suddenly Transformed into Asterisks was Shocking, Depressing, Bewildering, and Disheartening: beCause there was the FEAR that the entire Document was DESTROYED! However, the Computer had Managed to Save most of it; but, not that most Vital Part to Fulfill my Guaranteed Solution for Peacefully Removing all Confederate Emblems of SLAVERY, including the Washington Monument and the Jefferson Memorial, which only need to be Renamed: because they are Nice Buildings, which do not Disfigure the Landscape in Washington by any Means, and no more than the Lincoln Memorial, which someone could Honestly say is also Anti-Christ: beCause the Uncivilized War of the 1860's was Fought to Maintain the Union of Slave Masters — that is, of Education Slaves, Work Slaves, Income Tax Slaves, Interest Slaves, Insurance Slaves, Drug Slaves, Rent Slaves, ElecTrickery Bills Slaves, Gas Bills Slaves, Water Bills Slaves, Food Bills Slaves, Childcare Slaves, Sex Slaves, House Repair Bills Slaves, Mortgage Slaves, Property Tax Slaves, Transportation Slaves, Communications Slaves, Entertainment Bills Slaves, and all other Kinds of SLAVES, who should have all been LIBERATED by Celebrating the Great Year of JUBILEE, just as Moses Taught in *Leviticus 25*. Yes, if that were what Abraham Lincoln was Fighting for, I would say that he was a Great American HERO! But, instead, he was Fighting to Maintain and more Precisely Establish the Edomite SLAVERY SYSTEM, whereby those Poor Black People were made Sevenfold more into Slaves than they already were! ‡

34-07 [_] O Elected King, I am now going to Try to Assist you to Write the Correct Words for your Guaranteed Solution for Peacefully Removing the Confederate and Northern Symbols of Slavery, including the Lincoln Memorial, the War Memorials, and **"The BIG White OUTHOUSE on the Not-so-Biblical Capitol DUNGHILL,"** Book 023, which is the CHIEF Symbol of SLAVERY in **"The Divided States of United Lies!" (The so-called "United States of North America" in Disguise!) By The Worldwide People's Revolution!®** Book 058. Yes, it will most likely Upset the Irritated Bellies of many Weak Minds, until they Learn what I have to Say about it all; and then they will be Ready and Willing to go to WAR Against those Slave Masters: beCause of coming to Realize that they have been Snookered, as Henry Kiss-assing-ger might say, who would rather Play Monopoly Games than Pool. Yes, it is all about MONEY and the Edomite Money Games, who figured out HOW to make most Americans into Slaves without them Realizing it, whereby most Americans presently Sincerely Believe that they are FREE, and with a Capital F, when they are Actually SLAVES with a Capital S, just as you pointed out in the Verse above. Indeed, their Argument for being Free is as Weak as Water, and could never Hold Up in a Courtroom, even if the Judge's Tally Whacker were Erect for the entire Day: beCause of Lusting after a certain Blonde with Blue Eyes and Big Breasts, who is Dressed in a Red Miniskirt with her Legs Crossed over the Judge's Memory Bank, if you know what I Mean. Well, at any rate, when all of the People are Living within those **"Beautiful Swanky PALACES!" (A New Concept in Living Habits — Swanky Palaces for Poor People!) By The Worldwide People's**

Revolution!®, Book 066, those White Supremacists and Black Supremacists can Prove their Superiority by Building the more Beautiful Swanky Palaces for themselves, where they can Erect all of the Confederate and Northern Emblems and Monuments that they might Want: because no Sane Person will have any Interest in any such Nonsense, and would just as soon Spit on them, as to Look at them! Indeed, of what Value will a Statue of Robert E. Lee be to a Rich Person, who Lives in a Swanky Palace, who has Determined to FORGET those Evil Things that were in the Past, and to Press Forward to the Mark and High Calling of GOD, which is to become a HOLY Person, like Jesus Christ, who would most Certainly have no Honor for any Bloody American War Heroes, except for General Robert E. Lee, who Wanted to Settle the Slavery Issue in the United States CONGRESS, and without going to War, which could have and should have and would have been Done that Way, if a Righteous KING were in Charge of this World: beCause he would Order it to be Done that Way, or else Cut Off all Ties to that Hateful Nation of Mindless Rebels! Yes, all Trading would Cease with them: beCause they are Uncivilized People, who Want to Destroy each other for no Good Reason! Therefore, if Jesus Christ were going to Honor any Americans at all, he would Honor General Robert E. Lee, who was the Good Guy in **"The Divided States of United Lies,"** at that Time, even as you, O King of the Birds, is the Good Guy during these Times, who is now Calling for Justice for ALL Peoples, Worldwide, which can only be brought about by us Tax Slaves DEMANDING **"The Great Worldwide TELEVISED Court HEARING,"** whereby we might Learn the WHOLE Truth about each Important Subject, including what Actually Happened during the 1800's, and WHO was Responsible for all Forms of Slavery in America and around the World! Yes, Interestingly enough, there was another Great Hero in the World, who has been Greatly Maligned by the Edomites, who were Totally to Blame for World War 2, even as Benjamin Freedman Eloquently Explained in his YouTube Video Recording, which everyone should Carefully Listen to: beCause the Evil Doings of World War 2 cannot Rightfully be Blamed onto Adolf Hitler, who BEGGED the World to Demand an International Radio Debate about the Economic Situation at that Time, which was Suffering through the Great Bankers' Depression, which Began in 1929, when the Edomite Stock Market CRASHED, whereby about one-third of the People in the Capitalist World were put OUT of Work: beCause those Poor Edomites did not have any Money for them to Work with! Indeed, there was LOTS of Work that Needed Doing, even as we Americans presently Need New Bridges, Highways Repaired, and Self-air-conditioned Houses Built Properly within Beautiful Planned City States, which are Designed for LIVING, which have Eternal Employment at HOME! Yes, it is called GARDENING, by **"The LUSCIOUS All-Mineral Organic Method of Gardening!"** (HOW to Grow DELICIOUS Satisfying Foods for Potential Kingz and Kweenz in Swanky PALACES!) By The Worldwide People's Revolution!® Book 021. Indeed, when a Family is Living in one of those **"Beautiful Swanky PALACES,"** where each Family has a one-acre Organic Garden, and lots of Composted Materials to put on the Garden, Properly, the Little Brown Earthworms will be doing most of the Hard Work of Plowing the Land, and Feeding the Fruit Trees and Vegetable Gardens, which might have to be Watered, if there is no Rain; but, it is for Certain that NO ONE will be going Hungry with that Plan, as they are now doing in Venezuela: beCause of having no such Palaces with Organic Gardens: beCause they are Extremely Poor SLAVES of the Edomites! Yes, they and almost all other Nations have Fallen into the TRAPS of those Edomites, as was the Case before the Bankers' Great Depression of the 1930's, when most of the People Departed from the Land that Fed and Clothed them, and Wandered Aimlessly into Cities of Confusion, whereby they made themselves into Edomite Slaves! Therefore, when Adolf Hitler saw what had Happened to the Germans, and to the Capitalist World at large, he Determined to Do something about it, which the Edomites did not Like; but, they were Unable to Stop him: beCause he had **"The Swanky Sword of Divine Truths"** on his Side, which could only be Stopped by going to WAR, even as was the Case in **"The Divided States of United Lies"** during the 1860's, which was a Major Mistake by Father Abraham Lincoln, who should have Thought about it more Deeply, and thus came up with a more Rational Conclusion, which would have been to Build those **"GLORIOUS Swanky Hotels Castles**

and Fortresses!" (Beautiful Planned City States for WISE Intelligent Well-Educated People with Common Sense and Good Understanding!) By The Worldwide People's Revolution!®, Book 019: beCause that would have Liberated ALL of the Slaves of ALL Kinds! Yes, they already had Steam Engines, Trains, and Tools for making that Possible; but, Poor Abe did not Think about it Long Enough for God to Speak to his Heart — that is, IF it was the Will of God that any such Swanky Fortresses should have been Built at that Time, which anyone could Argue that it was NOT the Appropriate Time: beCause Mankind still had many Important Lessons to be Learned about such Evil False Flag Operations as the Federal Government carried out during September 11th, 2001, which was the Achilles Heel on the Edomite Empire, which I have now Shot with my Poisonous Arrow, as Hector might say to Alexander the Great, when Reminiscing about Past Events. Yes, World Trade Center Tower 7 was that Achilles Heel, you might say, which will bring Down the EVIL Edomite Empire: beCause of not having a Reasonable Explanation for HOW 283 Hardened Steel Columns (some of which were 22-inches by 52-inches by 47-stories tall) could come Crashing Down in UNISON in less than 7 Seconds without the Assistance of EXPLOSIVES! Indeed, that was a Fatal Move by the Edomites, when they Set Up those Explosives in Secret: beCause, it is Exactly as Jesus Christ stated — *"There is nothing Secret that shall not be Revealed. Therefore, do not Say nor Do anything that you do not Want the Whole World to Learn about."* However, Larry Silverstein just Ignored his Warning, and went about the Task of making a General FOOL of himself, whereby he Clinched the Nail by saying: "Pull it," when Asked what should be Done with Tower 7. (See www.AE911TRUTH.org for Irrefutable Scientific Evidence that the Edomites Conspired with the WICKED Anti-Christ Federal Cover-up Government to get Rid of the World Trade Center Towers, and Blame it onto Osama bin Laden, while Frightening Americans with the Possibility that Saddam Hussein of Iraq might Drop an Atomic Bomb on New York City, which would go Up to Heaven in a Great Mushroom CLOUD — and to Do all of that without a Navy, Air Force, nor Guided Missile System that might Deliver any such Bombs across the Great Sea! Indeed, Saddam had the World's Second Largest Reserve of OIL at that Time, which made it an Interesting Grab Bag for the Edomites, who could not Resist the Great Temptation to get RID of Saddam Insane Hussein: beCause he was a Great Threat to America's PET Nation, which is otherwise known as ISRAEL, which was another Grab Bag Operation after World War 2, whereby so-called "Jews" Managed to Obtain the Land of Palestine by FORCE of Arms, and thus Establish the Jewish Nation in a Land that was not Rightfully their own, even as the British Managed to Obtain America by Force of Arms against the American Indians, who were eventually put onto Reservations: beCause those Edomites could not figure out HOW to make the Indians into their SLAVES: because those Indians were Smarter than the Black People of Africa, being of a Superior Race, you might say, who would not Submit to Beatings, Whippings, nor Edomite Brutalities; nor would they Subject themselves to Education Slavery, Work Slavery, Tax Slavery, Interest Slavery, Insurance Slavery, Rent Slavery, nor any other Kind of Slavery: beCause they had Actually Known TRUE FREEDOM with a Capital F, being Born and Raised as Free People! Yes, they Lived Simple Lives on the Land that Fed and Clothed them. Therefore, they could not be Talked into the Election Deception Lies, nor the Right of White Trash to Rule Over them. Nevertheless, just to have some Peace, they Agreed to Live on those Reservations, which were Located in the Worst of Bad Places in **"The Divided States of United Lies!"** Yes, the Land was almost Worthless for Producing anything to EAT — such as the Badlands of South Dakota, where White People eventually Discovered GOLD, and thus Stole it from the Indians, even as they did in Alaska: beCause of that Evil Thing called OWNERSHIP, whereby each Ignorant Fool Vainly Imagines that he MUST OWN his own Billion-dollar Swanky PALACE, or else he cannot Live! Yes, that is WHY you MUST get a so-called "Good" Education, whereby you can Earn a so-called "Good" Living, and thus become a "Good" Tax Slave, Interest Slave, Insurance Slave, Drug Slave, Rent Slave, Credit Card Debt Slave, and Mortgage Slave, just to put the Children through College, whereby they can also become SLAVES of the Edomite Empire, while Vainly Imagining themselves to be FREE with a Capital F, whereby they are Free to go to School, Free to Learn all Kinds of Capitalist LIES, and Free to Think for themselves without Actually Doing any Thinking with a Capital T: beCause their Minds are DRUGGED, and so Drugged that they cannot even THINK! Otherwise, they would be Checking the above Box [ ] and that Box and this Box [ ] with X Marks: beCause of Agreeing with my Statement, which can all be Corrected and Proven in a Courtroom, if anyone Doubts it! However, rather than Seek the Whole Truth about all such Important Subjects, and thus get those Corrections made, if they are Required, the Normal Ignorant American is Apathetic toward it all, and has Zero Interest in Learning about any of the SINS of our Forefathers, and much less about any of the Sins of the Edomites, who have been Honored as the Best of us, in spite of bringing about the Great Depression and World War 2! Yes, by simply Withholding Money from the Small Israelite Bankers, the Giant Edomite Bankers CAUSED the Great Depression: beCause there was NO MONEY TO LOAN, in spite of lots of Things that Needed Doing. Therefore, Adolf Hitler just Bypassed those Edomite Bankers, and Printed up his own New Money, and used it for Hiring the Germans to go to WORK, and called it the *National Socialist German Workers' Party,* which became known as the NAZI Party, which the Edomites Branded as the single most VILE Institution ever Invented by Mankind: beCause they were Envious of the Prosperous Germans, who got Out of the Great Depression within 6 Months of the Democratic Election of Adolf Hitler! Yes, they soon became the Financial Powerhouse of the World, which Required the entire Capitalist and Communist Worlds to Defeat them: beCause those Germans were Well Organized, and Knew HOW to make WAR, even as Robert E. Lee Knew HOW, and thus Lost about half as many Men during the Uncivilized War of the 1860's: beCause he was not Willing to Sacrifice his Men on the Altar of Capitalist GREED, as the Americans, Canadians, and Brits did during the Invasion of Normandy, which was a Military SUICIDE Mission, whereby they Lost more than 1,000+ Men for every German that they Killed! Yes, you might Imagine that it was well Worth it: because of not now Living under the Nazi Flag: beCause you have your FREEDOMS! Yes, that is what made it Well Worth the Sacrifices, you might say; but, no one ever Explained to you in **"The Public School of IGNERUNT FQLZ"** just WHY we were Fighting those Germans, who had **"The Swanky Sword of Divine Truths"** on their Side of many Important Issues, including the ECONOMY, which was the Best in the World in GERMANY! Indeed, there was ZERO Unemployment! But, that was never Mentioned in **"The Divided States of United Lies"**: beCause it was not in the Interest of those Edomites, who LOVE Unemployment, Under-employment, Low Wages, and Oppressions of all Kinds, whereby they can make more and more SLAVES to Serve themselves! Yes, the Overall GOAL is to Produce X-amount of SLAVES, which was Understood by General Robert E. Lee and Adolf Hitler, as well as the Inspired Author of this Extremely GOOD Book, which may not be Perfect, as I already stated; but, it can be FIXED, whereby it is made Absolutely PERFECT, if anyone is Interested in that. Moreover, there is only ONE Way to Do that, which is to DEMAND **"The Great Worldwide TELEVISED Court HEARING!" (That Great Meeting of the Most Intelligent and Wel-Ejukaatid Miindz!) By The Worldwide People's Revolution!®** Book 041. Yes, the Edomites would Like to Dominate that Meeting, and be in Total Control of the News Media at that Time: beCause they are Manipulators of the Worst Breed, who have Zero Interest in Discovering the Whole Truth about any Subject: beCause they are the SLAVE MASTERS! Yes, it is in their Greater Interest to MAINTAIN all such Slavery Systems, and at all Costs, including a Great Atomic Nightmare: beCause they do not Care how many Lives that they Lose: beCause they are Cold-hearted Cold-blooded MURDERERS, which they Proved when they Bombed the Railway Tracks and Bridges that went to the Nazi Concentration Camps in Germany and Poland, whereby they Starved their own fellow JEWS, and then Blamed it onto the Nazis! However, now that you have Learned the Truth about that, you will have to Rethink what you have been Brainwashed to Believe about the BADNESS and MADNESS of Adolf Hitler, who was Actually the GOOD Guy, who Tried his Damnedest to get RID of Communism and Capitalism, which he Judged to be the WORST of Economic Systems, which has now been Proven to be True: beCause Capitalism has Produced TRILLIONS of TONS of UNWANTED and UNNEEDED TRASH, Junkyard

168

Cars, and PILES of RUBBISH, like New Yuck City will be when the Master Farmer Arises to SHAKE TERRIBLY THE WHOLE EARTH! Indeed, when you are Living in one of those **"Beautiful Swanky PALACES,"** of what Need is there for any such TRASH? Answer: NONE! §§‡

34-08 [_] Well, my Friend, one could call that a Summarized History of what Actually Happened, except that most Americans do not Remember the Great Depression Days: beCause they never had to Suffer through it. Nevertheless, when it Happens AGAIN, they will Discover themselves in a Worse Situation than the People in Venezuela: beCause 95% or more of Americans Live in Cities of Confusion, who have no Gardens for Feeding themselves, nor any Way to even Survive such a Disaster when the RAIN STOPS, according to *Revelation 11,* which makes it Clear that one-third of all of the Trees in the World will BURN UP, and ALL of the Grasses will BURN UP, and almost all of those Wooden / Plastic Firetrap American Houses will BURN UP, whereby Great TOXIC Clouds of PURE Unadulterated Capitalist SMOKE will Ascend into the Skies, whereby the Whole World will be Contaminated with those ABOMINATIONS, which should have never been Built! However, it was in the Interest of the Edomite Insurance Companies to make those Houses as they are: beCause those Edomites have Collected no less than 10 Trillion Dollars from it! Moreover, they have a so-called "Healthcare" Scam going, whereby they have also Collected tens of Trillions of Dollars, and Plan on Collecting HUNDREDS of Trillions of Dollars during the next 1,000 Years: beCause they take Good Care of their Financial Interests, you might say. But, not to Worry: beCause **The Worldwide People's Revolution!®** has Plans for DETHRONING them! ‡

34-09 [_] O Elected King, I Judge that you have already Dethroned them within this one Chapter, which all Black, Brown, Yellow, Red, Blue, Green, Gray, and White Americans around the World should LOVE, and will Love, IF they get to Learn all about it; but, WHY would the Edomites be Interested in Advertising this Message every 10 Minutes on Televisions and Radios? Truly, Truly, I say to you, it would be of NO Interest to them. In Fact, they will likely do their Best to Slander you, O Righteous Man, and make you out to be WORSE than the Worst of the Neo-Nazis, Klqlus Kluks Klamz, and White Supremacists — all of whom are now on YOUR SIDE, O Colorful Peacock from Angel Ridge! Yes, even the Honest Black People are on your Side, as well as all Honest White People: beCause you are a UNITER, and NOT a Divider! Yes, Americans have been Looking for some Leader who might UNITE them, rather than Divide them, which is WHY they will Support you 100% on ALL SIDES, among all Colors and Races of People, Worldwide: beCause you Seek to make the Whole World GREAT AGAIN — not that it ever was very Great, except during the Time of Adam and Eve; but, that you will make it so, if you get your Way, which will even make it a Great Place for the Jews to Live: beCause they will be Invited to Build their own **"Beautiful Swanky PALACES!" (A New Concept in Living Habits — Swanky Palaces for Poor People!) By The Worldwide People's Revolution!®** Book 066. Yes, all Honest White Jews will AGREE with you, and will Check this Box [_] with an X, just to Indicate it. Moreover, all of those Phony Statues, Rebel Flags, and Worthless Monuments will come DOWN, while the Name of the Washington Monument will be called [_] "The Pentacle of Progress," or [_] "The Monument of Momentum," or [_] "The Phallus of American Inspiration," or [_] "The Erection of George Washington's Favorite Slave," or [_] "The Burial Tomb of George Washington," whose Bones will have to be Moved over there; while the Thomas Jefferson Memorial will have to be Renamed as [_] "The Beginning of American Propagandist Lies," or [_] "The Thomas Jefferson Tomb," or [_] "The Thomas Jefferson Deception," or [_] "The Last of the Supremacists," or [_] "The American Shame in Stone," or [_] you Name it:

34-10 [_] Well, my Friend, I am Glad that you can See the Beauty of Unity, which comes by SEPARATING the People who are Like Lions and Wolves from the People who are Like Sheeps and Goats; but, only IF they Want to be Separated in their own Beautiful Planned City States: beCause some People might Choose to Mix themselves with all Colors and Races and Kinds of Peoples: because they LOVE MONGRELIZATIONS, which is Okay with me: beCause I will get to Live with the Kind of People whom I Love, who are called the HOLY ONES, who can be of any Color or Kind; but, Like-minded People will just Naturally be of ONE Color or Kind: beCause those People who Like the Sound of the Violins Playing, will hardly Like the Sounds of Drums being Played by People who Like Noises Beating in their Ears, which is what Africans Like the most, which is also Okay with me: beCause I will not have to Listen to any such Noises, much less put up with any Highly Stinking Perfumes that all such People seem to Love: beCause of being Sold some Edomite Addictions. Moreover, if "Heaven" has any such Stinking Skunks in it, I have no Interest in going there — not that anyone is Actually going to Heaven with any Stinking Perfumes, which would be an Impossibility. Therefore, if anyone Agrees with me, they should Fill Out and File **"The Complete SURVEYS of our VALUES!"** **(SURVEYS of Religious Spiritual Political Governmental Sexual Social Moral Economic Business Labor Habitual and Miscellaneous VALUES!) By The Worldwide People's Revolution!®**, Book 059, on the Internet, for everyone to Study, if they Want to, whereby they might Discover other People of Like-mindedness by SEARCHING for them, which can easily be Done by the Computers, which can Sort Out the Like-minded People. For Example, which ones of the following Statements best Fit in with your Beliefs and Desires?

A-[_] I Agree that most People should be Living within Beautiful Planned City States with other People of Like-mindedness, whereby they can all Live in Peace: beCause of having most Things in Common among them — such as a Common Religion.

B-[_] I Believe that all Black People should Voluntarily Move Back to Africa, whereby they can Live in Peace with other Black People, and Help them to Build their own **"GLORIOUS Swanky Hotels Castles and Fortresses"**: beCause those Poor Ignorant People over there will not have any Idea HOW to Do that, who can be Assisted by Intelligent Well-Educated Black Americans, which will make all of them very Happy: beCause they will be Assisted by **"The New RIGHTEOUS One-World Government"** to Do that. After all, those Black People are more Tolerant of the Horrible HEAT in much of Africa, which will be Moderated by the High Elevations of the Upper Terraces within Swanky Fortresses, which may even Produce ICE: beCause of being so TALL, which can be Transported in Elevators to Lower Terraces, for their Ice Houses, whereby they can all be Comfortable. Moreover, they can Work in their Organic Gardens during the Cool Hours of the Mornings, and Rest in the Comfort of their Beautiful Stone Dome Homes during the Heat of the Day, where they can go Swimming in their Indoors Swimming Pools, and Play Tennis in their Tennis Courts, and Shoot Pool in their Game Rooms, and otherwise have a LOT of Fun in their own **"Beautiful Swanky PALACES!"** Book 066.

C-[_] I Confess that all of these Thoughts are very Strange to me: beCause no one ever Mentioned them before now. However, just to make Sure that other People Learn about all of these Wonderful Things, I am going to Do my Best to Help Publish the Inspired Books of **The Worldwide People's Revolution!®** Yes, I am going to Dress in my White Robe with Blue Trimmings and with a Red Belt with a Pocket, and put on a Black Mennonite Hat with a Wide Brim, and go about Passing Out Free Copies of Chapter 04 of: **"GOOD NEWS for REBEL WOMEN!"** **(HOW almost all Wives can become Moderately RICH without Leaving their Homes! Guaranteed!) By The Worldwide People's Revolution!®** Book 010, followed a Week later by standing on the same Street Corner with a Stack of those Inspired Books for Sale! Yes, that is HOW I can Earn some Honest Money, by Selling a single Copy for 10$, whereby I can Earn a Dollar per Copy, and also Send a Tithe of one Dollar to **The Worldwide People's**

Revolution!®, whereby, if enough People Do that, they will Furnish me and them with a Complete Set of their Books for Sale, which can be Displayed in Bookstores around the World!

D-[_] Damned if I am going to make a FOOL of myself by Dressing in any White Robe with Blue Trimmings and a Red Belt, whereby Ignorant People might Mock at me for Looking like Saint Peter, who had a Teeny Tiny Tally Whacker and no Chime Bells at all: beCause the Edomites Castrated him! Yes, at last they Crucified him Upside Down: beCause of his Faith in Jesus Christ, which is not something that I Want to Suffer with: beCause I like to EAT at those Royal Swanky Buffets, and for at least another thousand Years! §§

E-[_] Educated People already Know that **"The Swanky Sword of Divine Truths"** cannot be Defeated by any Means; and therefore, no one should Fear to Dress in a White Robe with Blue Trimmings and with a Red Belt on, in **"The Divided States of United Lies"**: beCause no one will Mock them, Spit on them, nor even Despise them: beCause, WHO could Despise the Oldest Order of Mennonites, who have a Good Reputation for being Peaceable Lovable People? However, if someone is Persecuted for doing that, or for Selling all such Books, that someone should Thank God that he or she is Accounted among the Holy Ones, who also Suffered for the Sake of Righteousness. Moreover, if 10,000 such Voluntary Working Soldiers were so well Dressed, and Marching down the Streets of Sin City, passing out Chapter 04 of **"GOOD NEWS for REBEL WOMEN,"** I dare say that they would be Selling no less than 10 Copies of that Book to everyone who had the Money to Buy it: beCause they would be Wanting to Send Copies to their Friends and Relatives, along with: **"Does a Good Soldier have to be a MURDERER?" (Seven Great Swanky Armies of Voluntary Working Soldiers!) By The Worldwide People's Revolution!®** Book 027.

F-[_] I Fail to Understand what the Contention is? Are you People Trying to Stir Up another World War, or what? Do you not Know that those Edomites will not Appreciate you putting them OUT of Business, which is the Business of Making more and more SLAVES?

G-[_] God Knows that they have Ruled Over us Slaves Long Enough, and are now Lined Up for the New NAZI Concentration Camps, if they do not Quickly Agree to DEMAND: **"The Great Worldwide TELEVISED Court HEARING,"** whereby we Tax Slaves might Discover whether or not Banks and Bankers are Necessary for True Prosperity!

H-[_] I Love the Honesty of this Inspired Book, which is NOT a Racist Bigoted Book, at all, nor is it Promoting any Violence, Race Riots, Civil Wars, nor any Evil Things.

I-[_] I am an Innocent Child, who cannot Understand all of the Thoughts within this Inspired Book; but, I Promise to Read it again, and again, until at last I do Understand it: beCause, if there is a Chance — yes, even a Slight Chance that I might get to Live for the Remainder of my Life in one of those **"Beautiful Swanky PALACES,"** it is in my Greater Interest to Help make that Possible, and not only for myself; but, also for all of the Healthy Happy Children in the Whole World, who will REJOICE with me, and Thank God that our Savior has Returned!

J-[_] Jesus Christ has NOT Returned, nor should you Believe that he has: beCause he will not Return for an Unholy Bride. Guaranteed. Moreover, when he does Return, it will be with Great Glory in the Awesome Dark Rolling Clouds of a FEARSOME Sky, along with tens of thousands of his Holy Ones in Flying Saucers! § {See: **"HOW to Become a HOLY Man!" (40 Good Reasons WHY People Should FAST and PRAY!) By The Worldwide People's**

Revolution!® Book 045, which is a Companion Book of: **"The Proper RULES for FASTING!" (The Complete Instruction Manual for True Repentance!)** Book 046.

K-[ ] King Jesus will be very Happy with this Inspired Book, except that he would likely make it much Longer: beCause there are so many Unanswered Questions, which are likely Answered within other Inspired Books by **The Worldwide People's Revolution!®**

L-[ ] Lots of Laughs! There is no Guaranteed Solution for Ships that are Sinking in the Oceans; and this Book is Like the TITANIC, which People Imagined was Unsinkable. Yes, this Book seems to be Foolproof to a Person who cannot Think; but, I am telling you that it is the Beginning of the END of Civilization as we know it: beCause there is no Way that Americans will GIVE UP their Stinking Noisy Polluting DANGEROUS Vehicles, and Move into any UGLY Swankless Fortresses, which would Require no less than 40 Years to Finish them, even if **"The New RIGHTEOUS One-World Government"** should HIRE **"Seven Great Armies of Working Soldiers"** to Build them, according to **"A List of FAIR Swanky Wages"**: beCause none of the Young People have any Interest in Eating at any Royal Swanky Buffets, where they Serve Fresh Fruit Juices by the Trainloads, and have Royal Dances at the Gold-ornamented Gymnasiums, after Watching *the Sound of Music,* staring Julius Caesar and Cleopatra, who were Reincarnated into Jewish Myths like this one. §§

M-[ ] My Heart is with the Man of Miracles from Galilee, who did not Mention anything about Swanky Fortresses; nor would he Recommend the Construction of any of them: beCause we are all going to Heaven when we Die, and leave this World for Satan to Govern: beCause it is the Home of the Edomites, who Deserve all of their Torments and Troubles: beCause of Rejecting Truths without any Justifiable Causes — such as the Great Truth about Swanky Fortresses having no less than 5,000 Good Reasons and Great Advantages for Building them and Living within the Borders of them! Indeed, I Challenge you to Think of anything else on this entire Earth, which has so MANY Good Reasons and Great Advantages for Doing it! Nevertheless, Jesus would Reject the Idea: beCause our Problems might be Solved, which he does not Want to be Solved: beCause he Loves our Sufferings, and also Hopes to God that we all have to be Crucified on the Road to Rome, rather than Preach a Good Sermon, like you might Discover in: **"The Gospel According to our Elected King!" (The Good News from the Most Modern Perspective!) By The Worldwide People's Revolution!®** Book 077. Yes, what an Amazing Book! But, do you Think that the Irreverent LOUDMOUTH Slothgut Windbag Hole-in-thy-Head has Read it with a Capital R? Absolutely NOT! And why is that? Well, he is Afraid that he might Learn that his Traditional Beliefs are WRong, whereby he might have to Change his Mind, which is far too Painful for him to Do: beCause he is Addicted to his Traditional LIES! Yes, he is a Proponent of Capitalism, which is the Love of Money in Action: beCause most People are POSSESSION Worshipers, who Want to OWN Things, whereby they are Willing to make SLAVES of themselves for that Purpose, rather than GIVE UP that Ownership Nonsense, and have all Material Possessions in Common among them, whereby no one Owns anything except his Toothbrush, Comb, Fingernail Trimmers, Books, Computers, Telephones, Clothing, and other easily Transported Things. Yes, why Burden yourself with Houses and Lands, which you cannot take with you when you Die? Therefore, Accept the Good Advice of the Apostle Paul, and be Contented with Foods and Clothing. However, that is not saying that you should be a Lazy SLOTH of some Color nor Kind, who is Afraid to Help other Voluntary Working Soldiers to Build **"Beautiful Swanky PALACES"** for yourselves to Live in: beCause God would Love you for it! Indeed, the Great Monasteries of the World were all Built by such Voluntary Workers, including Saint Peter's Basilica in Rome, which is considered to be the single most Beautiful Building in the Whole World, which was Designed by Michelangelo, himself, who is Honored as the Greatest Artist and Sculptor who ever Lived, who would be the First to Endorse those **"GLORIOUS Swanky Hotels Castles and Fortresses!"** (**Beautiful Planned City States for WISE Intelligent Well-Educated People with Common Sense and Good Understanding!**) **By The Worldwide People's Revolution!®** Book 019.

N-[_] Not everyone is a Radical Fanatical Nitwit like you, O Unelected King: beCause most People know that we cannot just ABANDON our Beautiful Cities of Confusion, and leave them for the Mice, Rats, Snakes, Skunks nor Owls to Inherit! Indeed, at all Costs, we MUST Maintain all of our Cities of Confusion, even if they will Cost HUNDREDS of Trillions of Dollars to Do so: beCause there is no Way that we can Adopt the Swanky Fortress Plan, seeing that we are Addicted to all such Nonsense as Driving Cars to Work, which none of the Spoiled Babies will Want to GIVE UP! Indeed, can you Imagine President Donald Trumpeter GIVING UP his Helicopter and Limousines? NEVER! NO WAY! §§

O-[_] Are there no Better Options to Choose from? Can we not just Build LITTLE Ugly Stone Dome Homes without any Expensive Polished Marble Tiles on the Walls, nor Polished Granite Tiles on the Floors? After all, I would be Contented to Live in a Stone Dome Home Complex that covers no more than 2,000 square feet of Floor Space: beCause I do not Need a Spacious Living Room Dome that is 24 feet in diameter and 20 feet Tall, having Polished Marble Walls that are 8 feet Tall around the Bottom of the Dome: beCause I am a Hermit by Nature. Therefore, I will Check the above Box with an X: beCause I Believe that there are many People who Agree with me — that a one-acre Garden on the Roof of a Spacious Stone Dome Home Complex is NOT Necessary for Feeding a Family of Idiots like me, who Live mostly on Granola and Bread, who have Stuffed Up Sinuses, who can hardly Sleep at Night: beCause of not being able to Breathe through our Noses. Yes, that Home-made Whole Wheat Bread might be Cheap to make, if you have lots of Wheat to Eat; but, the Results of such a BAD Diet could be the Ruination of one's Faith in God, after reading that Edomite Bible, which Promotes Bread and Meats, as if they were GOOD for us to Eat, when God knows that they are BAD, which can easily be Proven in a Courtroom: beCause the Meat and Bread Eaters Suffer with all Kinds of Sicknesses and Diseases, which Fruitarians do not Suffer with, even if they do Suffer with Deficiency Diseases: beCause of not Eating enough GREEN Leaves, which any Ape would know to Do, who is far Stronger than any Weak Lion, Tiger, or other Carnivore: beCause Apes are about 8 Times as Strong! And yes, they might Eat a small amount of Flesh, now and then; but, it is not their Habit to do so. §§ {See: **"DIETS!"** (**A Reasonable Solution for the "Eternal Controversy"!**) **By The Worldwide People's Revolution!®** Book 037.}

P-[_] People of all Nations have been Eating Traditional Foods for thousands of Years, and some Live to be Old, and some do not; but, the most Healthy ones Eat with Great Moderation, who might make a Meal on just a Banana or 2, if they are not doing Difficult Work — such as Building a Stone Wall 100 feet Tall, which must have a GOOD Solid Foundation to Build on, which might make the Base of that Wall no less than 50 feet WIDE! Therefore, that is a Job for Mechanical Slaves, and not for People, who can Operate those Mechanical Beasts, which is WHY God Provided us with those so-called "Fossil Fuels." Yes, he Gathered Up Great Herds of Dinosaurs, even BILLIONS of them, and Buried them under Solid Rocks, as much as 20,000 feet under the Ocean Floors, whereby their Bodies Decomposed into what we call Fossil Fuels, which are Full of Mercury, Arsenic, Cadmium, Lead, and other Heavy Metals, which is HOW those Oils and Gases stayed down there in the Ground: beCause of being Weighted Down by those Precious Metals; but, not with any Silver nor Gold, as they should have been. Yes, if a

Gallon of Crude Oil had a Cup of Gold in it, it would be Worth the Effort to Drill for it; but, sad to say, God Goofed Up, and put Silver and Gold within our Reach, whereby we can Mine it Out of the Rocks, and perhaps get one whole Ounce of Gold from a Ton of Rocks! Therefore, as long as the Price of Gold is 2,000$ per Ounce, it is Profitable to go after it, even if we have to Wreck the entire World to get it: beCause those Edomite Bank Vaults are Extremely Lonely without New Gold Bars to Cheer them Up! Yes, you should Hear those Gold Bars Rejoicing, and then you would Know that it is Well Worth any Expenses to get more Gold Bars down there in those Edomite Bank Vaults. §§

Q-[_] The Great Question is this: **"When will you Capitalist Babies GROW UP?"** Why not Hold an Election for Deciding what to Do with the 20 Trillion Tons of Pure Gold and Silver that is already Stored in Bank Vaults? §§

R-[_] If I Rightly Recall, there is less than one Gold Brick for every Finger and Toe in the World, which Means that we will not have Enough Gold for Decorating any New Cathedrals in Swanky Fortress Castles. But, I have also been Rightly called a Capitalist Liar, which is more in Line with the Truth. §§‡

S-[_] Satan has all of you Ignorant People Totally Deceived: beCause no Swanky Fortresses can be Built: beCause there is not enough Solid Bedrocks in the World to Build them on, which can be Proven at: **"The Great Worldwide TELEVISED Court HEARING!" (That Great Meeting of the Least Intelligent and Miseducated Minds!) By the Worldwide People's Puke!** Book 0000009999! Yes, I think that I will write my own Uninspired book about it. §§

T-[_] You are Totally Deceived: beCause we can make our own Bedrocks to Build on, even as was done for Saint Paul's Cathedral in London, English, which is not showing any Signs of Sinking in the Mud with Stupidity.

U-[_] I Understand that this Survey is Designed to SIFT OUT all of the Ignorant Idiots, who will be Afraid to Check any of the Boxes with X's.

V-[_] Queen Victoria would not Object to Checking the Boxes with Statements that she might Agree with. Indeed, she was no Spiritual Coward.

W-[_] I would rather Fight in World War 3, than to Check any of the Boxes with X's, much less to stand on any Street Corners with Stacks of Insane Books like this to SELL to Ignorant Idiots, who would Prefer to Live in their Wooden / Plastic Firetrap Mouse-infested Cockroach Dens, and Slave Away their entire Lives for the Edomites. §§

X-[_] X-amount of Ignorant People will Agree with you: because they cannot Understand Double Sarcasms, which is Good: beCause there is no Place Reserved for any of them in the Holy Kingdom of All that is GOOD.

Y-[_] There is nothing Good about a Double Sarcasm: beCause all Sarcasms are Forbidden in Courtrooms: beCause all such Statements might be making Things to Easy to Understand, and thus the Judge might be Sentenced to Life in Uganda or Uruguay: beCause of getting Red Ears, whereby the Unbiased Jury might Sentence him, each Year, to 20 Years of Hard Labor at a Rock Quarry! Yes, it would be like a Prison Sentence of 40 Lifetimes, whereby the Convicted Criminals would be Eligible for Parole after only 6 Months of Good Behavior, if that makes any Sense at all? §§

Z-[_] Zebras do not like to be Confused by so many Black and White Stripes Flashing all about. Can you not at least Try to make some SENSE? §§

— Chapter 35 —

A List of other Fascinating Literature by the same Inspired Author, which all Seekers of Truths will Love!

{HEADNOTE: The Missing Books in the following List are Mentioned within the Volume of the Book by Name and Number, whereby you can easily Discover them within a Swanky Truth-brary. However, if any of those Inspired Books are not Mentioned in the Volume of the Book, they can be Added, later on, by whomever is Willing to take the Time to do it: beCause it is Doubtful that any such Editors will Edit Out any Important Information within any of our Books, knowing that all of the Books will be Opened Up during the Day of God's Judgment, whereby they might be Judged. Indeed, the People who will be in the Worst Condition at that Time will be those People who Edit Out any Provable Truths, whereby they will Cause other People to Stumble and Fall, which is a Major SIN, which can easily be Prevented by leaving the Inspired Words of Provable Truths just as they are.}

35-01 [_] "LIGHTNING Versus the Lightning Bug!" (HOW almost Everyone can become Moderately RICH, without Telling Any Lies nor Selling Any Trash!) By The Worldwide People's Revolution!® Book 001. {See www.Amazon.com for all Related Books by The Worldwide People's Revolution!®, which amount to about 80 of them. Just Click your Mouse on the Author's Name, after Opening one of the Links to a Book.}

35-02 [_] "For the Love of Money!" (The Strange Things that People Say and Do to Get more Money!) By The Worldwide People's Revolution!®, Book 003, which is a Companion Book of: "The Root Cause for almost all Evils!" Book 078.

35-03 [_] "HOW to Prepare for CLIMATE CHANGES!" (The Wisest Plan for Mankind to Follow!) By The Worldwide People's Revolution!® Book 004, which is a Companion Book of: "UNLIMITED ENERJEE 99 Percent Pollutions Free!" (HOW to Obtain FREE ElecTrickery, Worldwide!) Book 029.

35-04 [_] "Why do I have to be Surrounded by CRAZY PEOPLE?" (Do almost all People Feel like they are Surrounded by Crazy People?) Book 005.

35-05 [_] "The PRAYERS of PUMPKINHEADS!" (Even God Needs a Little Humor to Cheer himself Up!) By The Worldwide People's Revolution!® Book 007.

35-06 [_] "WHY are some Preachers so POOR?" (HOW almost all Preachers can Get Moderately RICH, without Preaching any Outlandish LIES!) Book 009.

35-07 [_] "The CONSTITUTION for the New RIGHTEOUS One-World Government!" (HOW all Peoples can get True Justice, and Celebrate the Great Year of JUBILEE!) Book 016.

35-08 [_] "In thu Beeginingz uv Thingz!" (Thu Kreeaashun Stooree frum thu Beegining!) B-025.

35-09 [_] "God Speaks and the Whole World Listens!" (Fire on the Mountain from the Burning Bush by the Spirit of Truth!) Book 026.

35-10 [_] "A Sure Cure for GUN VIOLENCE!" (HOW TO STOP GANG WARS and CRIMINAL SHOOTINGS!) By The Worldwide People's Revolution!® Book 031.

35-11 [_] "The Nature of CAPITALISM!" (A List of the EVILS of CAPITALISM!) Book 038.

35-12 [_] "SWANGKEENOMIKS Rules the Roost!" (HOW all People can Prosper in a RIIT WAA, and STOP Polluting the Earth with Capitalist TRASH!) Book 039.

35-13 [_] "The Loathsome Burdens of the Independent Jackasses!" (A New Approach for Solving our Massive Problems!) By The Worldwide People's Revolution!® Book 051.

35-14 [_] "Are we Tax Slaves of a Lower Order than the Edomites?" (HOW to be Liberated from all Slavery, Worldwide!) By The Worldwide People's Revolution!® Book 052.

35-15 [_] "The Great False Economy is now DEBUNKED!" (Adolf Hitler had a much Better Economic System!) Book 053.

35-16 [_] "Those Ridiculous Contradictions within the Holy Bible!" (HOW to Read the Bible with an Open Mind!) By The Worldwide People's Revolution!® Book 057.

35-17 [_] "HOW to Get our PRIORITIES in ORDER!" (The Glories of Democracy; and, Does DEMON-ocracy have its Priorities in Order?) By The Worldwide People's Revolution!® B-060.

35-18 [_] "The New MAGNIFIED Version of the PSALMS of King David!" (The Understandable Version of the Famous Psalms in Plain English!) Book 064.

35-19 [_] "Has your Life become Extremely Complicated?" (HOW to Live a SIMPLE Life!) By The Worldwide People's Revolution!® Book 068.

35-20 [_] "The IDEAL Place to Live!" (HOW to Discover the Ideal Place to Live!) Book 069.

35-21 [_] "Our Elected King Who Speaks Out!" (It is High Time for some Sane Person to Get Control of this Insane World!) By The Worldwide People's Revolution!® Book 070.

35-22 [_] "LIGHTNING STRIKES Versus Lightning Bugs and Impotent Fireflies!" (A Memorial Photo Album of some Real American Heroes!) Book 072, which is a Companion Book of: "The BEST of CAPITALISM!" (Corrections for "LIGHTNING STRIKES Versus Lightning Bugs and Impotent Fireflies!) By The Worldwide People's Revolution!® Book 073.

35-23 [_] "What are the PUNISHMENTS for Dietary Sins?" (Have we Served ourselves Well at the Tables of Lusts?) Book 075.

35-24 [_] **"What is WRong with those CRAZY Christians?" (A Self-Examination of the Heart of the Body of Good Government!) By The Worldwide People's Revolution!® Book 076.**

www.ingramcontent.com/pod-product-compliance
Lightning Source LLC
Chambersburg PA
CBHW081724220526
45468CB00008B/1960